The Design of the Present

John F. Lynen

The Design of the Present

Essays on Time and Form
in American Literature

New Haven and London   Yale University Press   1969

Copyright © 1969 by Yale University.
All rights reserved. This book may not be
reproduced, in whole or in part, in any form
(except by reviewers for the public press),
without written permission from the publishers.
Library of Congress catalog card number: 69-15451
Designed by Helen Frisk Buzyna,
set in Caledonia type,
and printed in the United States of America by
The Vail-Ballou Press, Inc., Binghamton, N. Y.
Distributed in Great Britain, Europe, Asia, and
Africa by Yale University Press Ltd., London; in
Canada by McGill University Press, Montreal; and
in Latin America by Centro Interamericano de Libros
Académicos, Mexico City.

Excerpts from the poetry and prose of T. S. Eliot are
reprinted by permission of Harcourt, Brace and
World, Inc., and Faber and Faber, Ltd., from his
volumes *Collected Poems 1909–1962* and *Selected
Essays,* copyright 1932, 1936, 1950 by Harcourt,
Brace and World, Inc.; copyright 1960, 1963, 1964 by
T. S. Eliot.

To my mother,
Eleanor W. Lynen,
this book is affectionately dedicated.

Preface

The ideas in the present book concerning temporal form originated in Lessing's *Laocoön,* from which my work most directly derives. Among more recent studies of literary time, I am indebted to Adam A. Mendilow's *Time and the Novel* (London, P. Nevill, 1952), Hans Meyerhoff's *Time in Literature* (Berkeley, University of California Press, 1955), and Georges Poulet's *Studies in Human Time* (Baltimore, Johns Hopkins Press, 1956). I have inadvertently repeated certain points already very well expressed in Hilles Miller's excellent study of Eliot in his *Poets of Reality* (Cambridge, Belknap Press of Harvard University Press, 1965), which appeared after my own essay was completed, and by way of apology can only express the hope that readers will find my treatment of Eliot different enough to place these ideas in a new perspective. Of works on American literature, those which have had the greatest importance for me are Charles Feidelson's *Symbolism and American Literature* (Chicago, University of Chicago Press, 1953) and the late Perry Miller's two-volume work, *The New England Mind* (New York, Macmillan, 1939; Cambridge, Harvard University Press, 1953).

The essay on Whitman was written first, the Introduction last, and the other chapters in the order in which they appear. Though the essays are intended as parts of a single work which traces continuities of form and idea through successive phases of American literature, I have endeavoured to give each sufficient completeness so that it may be read separately by those whose interest is limited to the subject it treats. The Introduction may assist such readers with a general account of the book's thesis, though considered by itself it must, perforce, seem all too general.

My sincere thanks are also due to the John Simon Guggenheim Foundation for a fellowship for the academic year 1962–63; to the University of Illinois Library; and to Miss Eva Faye Benton, English Librarian, for whose frequent and kindly assistance I am much indebted.

Grateful acknowledgment is hereby given to the following publishers: Harcourt, Brace and World, and Faber and Faber, Ltd., for permission to quote from the poetry and criticism of T. S. Eliot; Farrar, Straus and Giroux, and Faber and Faber, Ltd., for permission to quote from T. S. Eliot's *Knowledge and Experience in the Philosophy of F. H. Bradley,* copyright © 1964 by T. S. Eliot, and from his *On Poetry and Poets,* copyright 1954 by T. S. Eliot; Holt, Rinehart and Winston, Inc., Holt, Rinehart and Winston of Canada, Ltd., Laurence Pollinger, Ltd., and Jonathan Cape, Ltd., for permission to quote from "A Servant to Servants" and "The Lesson for Today," from *Complete Poems of Robert Frost,* copyright 1930, by Holt, Rinehart and Winston, Inc., copyright 1942, © 1958 by Robert Frost, copyright © 1967 by Lesley Frost Ballantine; Alfred A. Knopf, Inc., Faber and Faber, Ltd., and McClelland and Stewart, for permission to quote from *The Collected Poems of Wallace Stevens,* 1955, copyright 1923, 1931, 1935, 1936, 1937, 1942, 1943, 1944, 1946, 1947, 1948, 1949, 1950, 1951, 1952, 1954 by Wallace Stevens; New Directions Publishing Corp. and MacGibbon and Kee, Ltd., for permission to quote from *Collected Earlier Poems of William Carlos Williams,* copyright 1938 by William Carlos Williams; The Belknap Press of Harvard University Press, Geoffrey Cumberlege, Oxford University Press, and the Trustees of Amherst College, for permission to quote from *The Poems of Emily Dickinson,* 3 vols., ed. Thomas H. Johnson, 1958, copyright © 1951, 1955, by the President and Fellows of Harvard College; Harvard University Press, for permission to quote from T. S. Eliot's *Poetry and Drama,* copyright 1951 by the President and Fellows of Harvard College, from Perry Miller's *The New England Mind: From Colony to Province,* copyright 1953 by the President and Fellows of Harvard College, and from *Handkerchiefs from Paul,* ed. Kenneth Murdock, copyright 1927 by the President and Fellows of Harvard College.

Contents

Introduction

Forever—is composed of Nows—
'Tis not a different time—
Except for Infiniteness—
And Latitude of Home—

Emily Dickinson

THERE is in American literature a curious duality which its fictional characters often illustrate. One sees it in Dimmesdale's capacity to believe his rationalizations while remaining aware of their falsehood, in Ishmael's admiration of the lovely coloration of the shark, in Gatsby's patience—the patience of a "Son of God"— as he awaits the telephone call he knows will never come. Writers of almost every age and country have portrayed the difference between experience and reality, a contrast commonly expressed in a formal way by granting the reader a wider understanding than the characters, if not the privilege of being more or less "right." Such contrasts are no less important in American work, but the kind of doubleness I would describe is of a different kind. It exists within the character himself; he either knows all along the truths he must discover, or at least, as is more nearly the case with Gatsby, we see him at certain critical moments when he is already aware of the fact that he is then engaged in learning. At their most interesting, the states of consciousness in American fiction and poetry exist doubly with respect to two kinds of truth:

1

what the self really perceives and what is really true. There is within the character's consciousness, but outside of his experience, a point of view from which the objective truth can be seen, for the self is itself divided, existing doubly as the person in experience and also as the spectator who stands outside his experience to judge it with reference to reality as a whole. Yet the truths of experience are not to be gainsaid; they are just as true to the character as that which his transcendent self perceives, and not to be replaced by any more objective facts. There is a sense in which Dimmesdale should not confess, in which Ishmael's shark is a horror, in which Daisy will surely phone. To be Dimmesdale is to be a minister and man of faith; to be Ishmael is to be a mortal man to whom sharks are fearsome for all their theoretically objective beauty; to be Gatsby is to possess the ideal and therefore perfectly faithful woman. They are mistaken—even Ishmael's transcendent appreciation of the shark is just an experience he must transcend by recognizing his finite human nature—but the lesson they learn from reality is more than stern correction. It involves their death—literally, in the case of Dimmesdale and Gatsby, and only in part figuratively, in the case of Ishmael, who survives as an "orphan" still isolated in the universe where he had sought to find himself at home. The experienced truth cannot be replaced, since it is a necessary condition of the character's life. Yet neither can he dispense with his role as spectator, since to have experience he must live by his faith that his experience reveals a reality beyond itself, even though the latter always threatens to cancel his personal response. The character, then, must exist doubly, for the man in experience and the transcendent self are irreconcilable aspects of consciousness, whose opposition can only be resolved at the cost of his identity.

That this duality has its source in the American author's view of time is most apparent in the transcendentalists, who find it within themselves and formulate it as the contrast between the finite individual and the universal spirit. In *Walden*, for example, Thoreau describes "a certain doubleness by which I can stand remote from myself as from another. However intense my experience, I am conscious of the presence and criticism of a part of me, which, as it were, is not a part of me, but spectator, sharing no experience, but taking note of it; and that is no more I than it is you." [1] Walt Whitman expresses the same idea with more humor, if less precision: "Apart from the pulling and hauling stands what I am . . . . Both in and out of the game and watching and wondering at it." [2] In theory, the transcendentalists seek to unite the two selves by asserting that the "I" and the Oversoul are in fact one, and in portraying their own experience, they are most interested to show it developing toward this self-realization. In practice, however, the union is never achieved, except faintly, as an intuition glimpsed, a momentary insight. That is why the transcendentalists are not much troubled by the thought that the true self "is no more I than it is you." There is no more danger of losing one's personal identity than of achieving perfect consciousness. Indeed, the very emphasis upon unity and the unremitting effort to realize it manifest the estrangement it is meant to overcome. The meaning of the transcendentalists' answer must be found in the question it resolves—in the felt disunity which even in moments of highest consciousness is only partially dispelled.

Because the finite self cannot really be left behind, the transcendentalists' resolutions are but momentary, and living is regarded as a continual repetition of the effort to discover one's transcendent identity. At each fresh moment it must be discovered anew in that moment's particular circumstances, in its unique terms. Yet the answer is there, in the moment, awaiting the recognition of the mind which is fully alive. For to the transcendentalists the present is the epitome of all reality, and it contains all things because it contains all times. It is just this one moment in which the self is conscious, but to the extent that one

1. *Walden*, Riverside ed., Sherman Paul, ed. (Boston, Houghton, Mifflin, 1957), chap. 5, p. 93.
2. "Song of Myself," sec. 4, in *Complete Poetry and Selected Prose*, ed. James E. Miller, Jr. (Boston, Houghton, Mifflin, 1959), p. 27.

realizes its total content, the whole of reality is revealed. To quote a characteristic passage from Emerson: "It must be that when God speaketh he should communicate, not one thing, but all things; should scatter forth light, nature, time, souls from the center of the present hour." [3] Though this is post-Kantian idealism and not uniquely American, Emerson's emphasis on the argument's temporal aspect is distinctive. One might say that he seems much more impressed that the God who created all in the beginning is putting forth the world at this very instant than that the Creation is God's work. Thus, in his attempt to express the idea of continuous creation, he converts it into a theory of duration. In Emerson's view of experience, its status as a present event seems the ultimate fact. As he continues in the passage quoted above: "Whenever a mind is simple and receives a divine wisdom, old things pass away,—means, teachers, texts, temples fall; it lives now, and absorbs past and future into the present hour." [4]

The transcendentalists habitually describe enlightenment in temporal terms as the process of discovering that all times exist within the present. And their reason for doing so is the belief that God's view, the total consciousness toward which experience develops, is a conspectus in which all things exist simultaneously as elements of a single landscape.

To define experience in this way—to conceive it as an exclusively present event whose content and meaning is a timeless and all-inclusive reality—is, in effect, to make all varieties of time reducible to the present and eternity. Not that other forms of time are rendered illusory, or that the now is regarded as the only credible time unit. The past, the future, and the sequences of moments one could define within them are entirely real. The point is that, ultimately, they exist as aspects of the present and eternity. The time is always now, and while time itself is as real as any other thing, it is real because the difference between man's limited consciousness and God's view is real.

3. "Self-Reliance," in *The Complete Works of Ralph Waldo Emerson*, 2, ed. Edward Waldo Emerson (12 vols. Boston, Houghton, Mifflin, 1903), 65–66.
4. Ibid., p. 66.

The doubleness which we have observed in such characters as Dimmesdale reflects the same assumptions concerning time which transcendentalist theory makes explicit. To be sure, the novelists do not portray time exactly as it is portrayed in Thoreau or Whitman and do not derive from the shared premises the same conclusions. Hawthorne and Melville expose transcendentalist belief to an often withering skepticism, and to Fitzgerald, writing many decades later, the opinions they question seem scarcely relevant enough to be entertained. But beneath the obvious differences—those between the novelists no less than those which set them apart from an Emerson—there is a family resemblance. For example, one might note the common tendency to explore the meaning of a symbol in terms of the contrast between its materiality, as an object of immediate perception, and its universality, as a point of focus for timeless truths.

The essential literary program of revealing universals through particulars takes a special form in American writing, because there the contrast between them seems simpler, harsher, more nearly absolute. And the same may be said of the difference between the two sides of selfhood; in American writing the transcendent aspect of consciousness is so distinct and, as it were, divorced from the self living within its place and time that the author finds it natural to assume that a union of the two would cancel the necessary conditions of human life. Such diverse European characters as Macbeth, Madame Bovary, and Raskolnikov live in a middle region where experience is neither so exclusively immediate nor the understanding which is possible at their finest moments so nearly all-inclusive as in the world the American character inhabits, for neither they nor their creators would define experience so narrowly as this presently transpiring perception or suppose that its potential meaning is the whole truth. Yet these seem to be the tacitly assumed premises underlying Hawthorne's account of finding that the letter, when held to his breast, generates an almost physical heat, and of Fitzgerald's description of the pile of gaudily expensive shirts with which Gatsby hopes to impress Daisy. Though Macbeth's dagger may

5

well be a more meaningful symbol than the scarlet letter, its claims, as a symbol, are more modest; its area of significance shades off imperceptibly toward ranges of meaning beyond its own, while the horizon of the letter's meaning cannot be less than reality as a whole: it means "meaning," and meaning is inseparable from being. Similarly, the cigar case which Madame Bovary finds, though indicative of her nebulous and impossible aspirations, is a symbol less inclusive with respect to the novel's total meaning than Gatsby's shirts, in which Gatsby's self-image as the "Son of God," incarnating his dream, and the historical limitations of the man are brought to ironic unity. The American novelists, though they do not usually render so pure an immediacy or indulge in so large a manner of generalization as the transcendentalists favor, share the assumption that experience is to be considered in a manner which makes the present and eternity the only ultimately valid points of view.

To illustrate the way this view of time influences American writing, I would like to compare Stevens' "Peter Quince at the Clavier" and Bryant's "To a Waterfowl." That they differ in so many obvious respects and belong to such widely separate periods will serve to emphasize the similarity of form they reveal. My purpose will be to describe a resemblance indicative of the American literary tradition, while at the same time illustrating the approach employed in the following chapters and some of my main assumptions.

By the title he affixes to his poem, Stevens dissociates himself from the man conversing with the lady in "blue-shadowed" silk; he names him Peter Quince, views him from afar as someone else, and a "character" at that. But Peter Quince is also an artist, who in his turn must stand off from his own present moment in the drawing room. He deserves his name because, like Shakespeare's character, he is committed to the ignoble shifts which the detachment of the artist requires—to representing the moon by a man with a bush and lantern, for example. The humor of the title is, then, directed at Stevens as well. His poem—any poem—shares the essential absurdity of "Pyramis and Thisbe"; for "Music is feeling . . . not sound"; art is true, not as art, but as experience.[5] And yet the immediacy of experience grows out of the artist's contrivance as a detached and coolly calculating technician, who stands in the studio, not in the picture.

This peculiar contradiction is the very life of Stevens' poem. In his portrait of Susanna he celebrates an experience of perfect immediacy—an experience which cannot properly be called experience, for Susanna is too nearly identical with her perceptions. Her beauty is her response to the beauty about her, and she is seen only as her response:

> She searched
> The touch of springs,
> And found
> Concealed imaginings.
> She sighed,
> For so much melody.[6]

This is not pure sensation. In her acceptance of the flesh Susanna passes beyond sense, purifying the sensuality of the elders by exceeding it and, as if by angelic intuition, possessing beauty itself, the eternal reality. Her beauty is also the virtue claimed for her in the Apocryphal story, since the intuitive witnessing answers all questions of right and wrong by the meaning it reveals in a world brought to the perfect order of music. Thus her every perception is melody, a part in the concert of immediately felt being.

But this vision of experience realized and made whole is the vision of the artist, and that Peter Quince can appreciate her feelings, appreciate them so perfectly that his consciousness is merged, for a time, with hers is the result of his power to stand outside of experience, hers or any other's. The elders hidden behind trelliswork are reproached for being both too detached and

5. *The Collected Poems of Wallace Stevens* (New York, Knopf, 1954), p. 90.
6. Ibid.

not detached enough. Peter Quince can respond to Susanna's beauty far more sensitively than they can through that transcendence which enables him to achieve a perfect reserve. Susanna's experience is his also, hers because it is his, a vision brought into being wholly by the artist's imagination. In other words, the ultimate immediacy is achieved by the ultimate detachment: the self in experience and the self which stands apart as transcendent spectator are functions of each other.

Thus it is that the most vividly felt sensation leads directly to an unqualified generality:

> Beauty is momentary in the mind—
> The fitful tracing of a portal;
> But in the flesh it is immortal.[7]

The contrast of spectator and participant is here brought to sharp focus by the way tenor is opposed to style. The poet stands off to generalize, in order to assert that reality is the immediate sensing which is the opposite of generalization. When the passage is considered not simply as an idea but as a gesture on the part of Peter Quince, the apparent contretemps dramatizes the principle by which the poem develops. Since the participant (or sensation) and spectator (or idea) are contrary sides of a single event, Stevens can reconcile them by forcing them further apart. Their separation demonstrates their interdependence by rendering more obvious the way each evokes the other.

The abruptness with which Peter Quince moves away from his own moment to a moment in a remote and mythic past emphasizes the disorder of the present. Considered by itself, the present lacks clarity and meaning. Its confusions are manifested in the emotional impropriety of the opening cadence, which is rather too majestic for the intimacies of a tête-à-tête, and in the visual scene, which, in its suggestion of potted palms and peacocks on the terrace, is too dangerously close to the elegance of perfume advertisements. Image and rhythm alike signify an oppressive

7. Ibid., p. 91.

8

luxury of sentiment. Not that the lady in blue is not beautiful enough to warrant the feelings she awakens in the poet, but that as mere feelings they threaten to blind him to the beauty which is their source and meaning. Feeling is music, yet if his music is to be more than "Death's ironic scraping"—the lust of the elders—the poet must find in it a permanent and therefore a general meaning, a meaning which can only be discerned by the spectator who stands aside to view the norms which prevail in all imaginable moments.[8]

The memory of Susanna is therefore but a phase in the process of transcendence by which Quince finds the meaning of the present. Stevens does not return, at the end, to the little situation in the drawing room, but moves to a level of abstraction from which the mind can formulate, in generalizations applicable to all times, the eternal reality which the memory of her has revealed. Susanna is reduced to an instance or example, as ultimately Peter Quince's remembering is also. And yet abstraction evokes sensations even more immediate and vivid than memory wakens. Idea demands metaphor and yields images which are the more poignantly sensuous in that they are highly generalized. "So evenings die, in their green going." [9] Susanna is seen at last, not as the phantom of fleshly splendor created by the imagination's make-believe, but as a memory. The poem ends with what is for us the most immediate reality, the remembering itself, which, like the evocation, not the sound, of the cello's note, becomes itself an object of sense.

The form of the poem illustrates well the consequences of assuming that with respect to time, the present and eternity exhaust the field of discourse. Stevens divides the self into spectator and participant, as separate functions of consciousness, because he feels that reality must be regarded from the now and always, as totally distinct and opposed points of view. One can object with reason that generalizing does not necessarily presuppose

8. Ibid., p. 92.
9. Ibid.

adopting the eternal point of view, but in Stevens this proves to be the case. By way of contrast, in Wordsworth's "Lines Written in Early Spring" the poet's summary refrain about "What man has made of man" seems to involve no perceptible wrenching of the mind from the scene of experience.[10] One senses that Wordsworth's generalizing differs from his perceiving and that here or in any poem the contrast is significant in that it manifests the distinction between universals and particulars. But in Wordsworth, and generally in English literature, the present moment extends smoothly outward to blend with a larger temporal landscape, while the area to which abstract terms refer seldom appears to be so distinct from the experiential moment or so categorically defined as the context of all times. Stevens is typically American in giving the present-eternity contrast an ultimate importance, so that the general and the immediate are made to correspond to these opposites. Although it is his intention to reconcile them by demonstrating the immanence of the permanently real, their assumed separation makes doing so a problem—the problem—the source of the poem's theme and form alike.

This contrast is revealed formally by the arrangement of elements on the page. After a brief portrayal of the speaker's present, the poem suddenly shifts perspective to depict a distant historical period and then concludes with another abrupt change of viewpoint, as the speaker returns to the present, which he can now understand in more inclusive, because more generalized, terms. It is a form which, as I shall later have occasion to show, is very characteristic of American poetry, though often the middle section portrays looking forward to a distant futurity rather than the remembering of a distant past. Stevens has underlined this pattern by marking the shifts in perspective through changes in the metrical form. The initial iambic rhythm gives way to the shorter lyric measures of the central section, which then become increasingly swift and tripping, until the conclusion effects a shift

10. *The Poetical Works of Wordsworth*, ed. Thomas Hutchinson, rev. Ernest de Selincourt (London, Oxford University Press, 1942), p. 482.

10

to a slower pace and more serene tonality. The metrical changes not only serve to express Stevens' governing musical metaphor, but illustrate the way poetic meter reflects, on the level of sound, the broader temporal scheme of a poem's development.

Arrangement on the page, however, is just one aspect of form and cannot be separated from a poem's conceptual content. Without making reference to the level of idea, one could not recognize that an earlier event—Susanna's experience, for example—is placed after a later one in the sequence of sentences and paragraphs. That B follows A is a story soon told. The problem for criticism is to discover the significance of the imaginative pattern which this arrangement helps to express and partially reflects. Thus, although brief references to this mechanical patterning are usually sufficient, it is an essential aspect of literary form, and in discussing literary time, though I must necessarily range freely through various aspects of form, I am always implicitly concerned with this as something at the center of my subject. For it is the sequence of words and events, through which one progresses as one reads a work, that time is operative as a formal principle.

William Cullen Bryant may be taken as representative of the early nineteenth century, a phase in American culture much closer to the world of the early Puritans than our own, and it is therefore significant that in such a poem as "To a Waterfowl" one can recognize the same contrasts operative in "Peter Quince" and a formal pattern which is strikingly similar. Bryant's poem seems very unlike Stevens' because it ends with what we nowadays are pleased to call a moral. A moral, however, is merely a concluding generalization, and Bryant's differs from Stevens' ending only in that it expresses a Christian idea or, more properly, an idea of the sort which flourishes in the atmosphere of Protestant piety. Stevens offers a lesson no less instructive, and as one can recognize by the crucial role of such a word as "sacrament," he finds it no less needful to invoke the language of religion. When the ending is considered as a statement made from a point of view, an

11

utterance whose meaning is created by the position from which the poet views reality, both poems may be seen to enact the same drama.

The most important point about the moral is that it comes at the end—is not merely general but conclusive. Its success depends, then, upon the poet's skill in managing his transition to it. The approach is all, and it is Bryant's failure in this respect that renders his ending extraneous and preachy. He begins, as Stevens does, with a direct perception which puzzles and confuses. As the sound of music leads Peter Quince to wonder how sound turns into feeling, seeing a waterfowl as it flies across the twilight sky leads Bryant to wonder how birds find their way through limitless space. In other words, the object directly perceived is problematical, because to know what it is involves knowing more than is immediately presented. How do the sense data—the sound or motion—disclose themselves as music or flight? With such questioning, the process of transcendence commences. The poet gradually finds that he does indeed know where the bird is going, and his power to project his mind toward that distant goal is anticipated by a movement of thought from the immediate to the hypothetical: "Vainly the fowler's eye/ Might mark thy distant flight to do thee wrong." [11] Having indicated the mind's freedom in this way, the poet then shows how it moves off toward a remote location, which, though hypothetical, is vividly particularized:

> Seek'st thou the plashy brink
> Of weedy lake, or marge of river wide,
> Or where the rocking billows rise and sink
> On the chafed ocean-side? [12]

The imaginary supposing at last reaches fulfillment in a vision of the journey's end:

11. *William Cullen Bryant: Representative Selections,* ed. Tremaine McDowell (New York, American Book Co., 1935), p. 9.
12. Ibid.

> And soon that toil shall end;
> Soon shalt thou find a summer home, and rest,
> And scream among thy fellows . . .[13]

The mystery of the bird's sure flight through the uncharted sky is portrayed in terms of the even greater mystery of the mind's power to travel in thought to a distant place and future time. Whereas in "Peter Quince" transcendence carries the mind backward to a remote past, here it brings a distant place into view at a moment fairly close in time. These differences, however, only serve to underline the sameness of the process by which the mind moves from the immediate object of experience to those realities beyond the visible horizon in terms of which current sense data are interpreted. And both poets use the transcendental process in the same way, implying that the limitless scope of man's thought betokens his power to discern a truth that is timeless. Though in "To a Waterfowl" the act of transcending is marked by a less abrupt and striking change of perspective, Bryant, like Stevens, moves toward the eternal point of view. He may speak of his own case, in the last stanza, and in fact the poem records a particular experience, but his concluding statement is to be understood as a formula for human life in general:

> He who, from zone to zone,
> Guides through the boundless sky thy certain flight,
> In the long way that I must tread alone,
> Will lead my steps aright.[14]

Again like Stevens, Bryant ends by converting percept into illustration: the bird becomes the exemplum for a lesson, which, though it is more crudely expressed, displays the same paradoxical contrast of style and tenor—the generalizing which asserts the antithetical immediacy.

It is Bryant's point that the "Power" seen directly in the bird as

13. Ibid., p. 10.
14. Ibid.

it crosses the darkening sky is the same mysterious force that guides him and all men. But to realize this—and express it—he must stand aside and analogize. The moral ending can only succeed if it contains all the other viewpoints within a more inclusive view; it must be a generalization broad enough to take all the poem's implications into account, and Bryant's ending fails because it deals with only one side of the paradox his experience presents. What he sees is a reality both immanent and transcendent, but the immanence is annulled at the end by reducing the ambiguous "Power" of stanza three to the exclusively transcendent God who reaches down from his throne to send bird and man alike along their proper paths. "Power" is surely the more appropriate term than the "He" of the last stanza, even though Bryant, if pressed, might have admitted that what he saw was Jehovah. Prematurely introducing the most inclusive term interrupts rather than forwards the movement toward ultimate generalization. Like Stevens' "memory," "Power" has just the right doubleness, suggesting, on the one hand, a purely natural force (instinct, for example), and on the other, fixed law, universally operative force, and hence eternal being. In "To a Waterfowl," as in "Peter Quince at the Clavier," the mind's objective, and so the proper ending, is a reconciliation of the present and eternity which relates the two as aspects of one experience. This is done by finding such a term as "Power," which, by looking both ways, brings the most general and most immediate to unity.

Probably Bryant let his true conclusion slip too soon because his allegiance to orthodoxy was just strong enough to prevent him from recognizing it. His mere ideas willfully forced his thought toward a conventional lesson. Yet theological doctrine is of slight importance in his poetry, except as a means of annotating points of view, and he uses it with shocking opportunism. In "A Forest Hymn," for instance, God as immanent spirit—"thou art here— thou fill'st/ The solitude. Thou art in the soft winds"—is simply set down side by side with God the transcendent ruler, whose creation is to be viewed as a message—"Written on thy works I read/ The lesson of thy own eternity." [15]

Bryant is a revealing example of the transition from the waning Puritan age to the mid-nineteenth century, because his confusions reveal the pervasive though shadowy influence of Puritanism in a mind apparently liberated from its system of beliefs. That Bryant, though the grandson of a dogmatic Calvinist, should find satisfaction in a vaguely naturalistic theism shows us how much the Puritan river thinned as it broadened, and serves as a warning not to suppose that Puritan influence can be traced in a strictly logical progression of ideas or causes and effects. Even so, the very vagueness of his faith—his mere sentiment, one is tempted to say—points toward its origin in Puritan theology. The reason for Stevens' tacit assumption that the ultimate points of view are the present and eternity becomes clear in the context of Bryant's piety, because there the modern poet's problem is still formulated in religious terms as the mysterious nature of a God who is totally distinct from the world—its Absolute Sovereign—and yet so intimately present that through his immanence as Spirit he constitutes the whole meaning of the moment of experience. Stevens' emphatic hedonism, his dismissal of religious faith as otherworldly, his insistence that life now is all and quite enough make him in a sense far more orthodox than Bryant. He celebrates the Eternal Incarnate as revealed not, to be sure, in a historic personage but at least in a beautiful woman, rather than merely a natural creature. Yet the very qualified sense in which Stevens finds it revealed and the transitory nature of the revelation indicate that his primary assumptions make incarnation both emotionally necessary and logically absurd.

Stevens is no Puritan, yet he shares with Bryant certain imaginative premises which Puritanism fostered, and which give to such a poem as "Peter Quince" characteristic traits of form. It may be asked to what extent Puritanism may be regarded as a

15. Ibid., pp. 50–51.

15

historical cause of Stevens' way of thinking and hence of writing. In the first of the following chapters I discuss some traits of Puritan literature which, as it seems to me, suggest a striking similarity to later American work. It is tempting to convert resemblance into cause, and in some measure I have yielded to this temptation and argued that Puritan thought helped to determine the forms which would become typical, even in such recent authors as Stevens. With respect to writers of clearly New England descent —Hawthorne or Robert Frost, for example—this line of reasoning will seem valid enough to most readers, but how far beyond New England the Puritan influence extends is a question so difficult because so little susceptible to clear historical answers that it would be unwise to speak of Puritanism simply "causing" a Stevens, or even a Melville, to favor certain literary techniques. Of the writers I treat, Franklin turned his back on the sectarian allegiances by which we usually identify Puritanism, both Cooper and Poe entertained a deep-seated distrust of the New England sensibility, while Whitman's social milieu makes Puritan thought nearly as irrelevant to his poetry as it is rendered by his distaste for the terms of theological discussion. Yet a good deal should and commonly is granted to the indirect influence of Puritanism, the effects of which have been so pervasive that one often finds critics commenting on the distinctively Puritan tone of our culture. The critical popularity of such themes as the Adamic myth and the Manichaean tendency illustrates a willingness to suppose that Puritanism has had a very wide reach. It will not, then, seem a rash surmise to imagine that when a work from a later period displays characteristics very similar to those of Puritan literature, the resemblance reveals a degree of influence. And just what degree need not be decided exactly, in view of the many other cultural influences, not the least among them that of southern Calvinism, and of the complex ways in which Puritan tendencies blended with those of very different origin. I may grant a somewhat more essential place to Puritanism in the American literary tradition than the reader is used to supposing, but it is not the thesis of this book to trace the historical effects of Puritanism or to picture it as the sole or even primary source of the imaginative premises I discuss. To state a point more fully treated in the first chapter, it seems to me as necessary to regard Puritanism as an effect as as a cause—to consider it the first manifestation of a set of constants in American experience more fundamental than its dogmas and capable of surviving when they have lost their credibility.

My purpose is to point out resemblances rather than causes, and if those described seem valid, it will be natural to see them as signs of historical continuity. They will agree with the reader's sense of history and find some confirmation there, or else, perhaps, alter somewhat his view of the past. Criticism cannot avoid implying a historical view, even if only because its statements about a work are convertible into statements about the way the author wrote it. Thus a story waits in the wings, and while the present book is not intended to offer a historical account, its implied version of literary history may seem to some readers the main standard for judging what I have to say. To anticipate some objections, I would suggest that in tracing the course of American literature, there is a danger of conceiving history itself both too narrowly and too broadly—of thinking of causation in too minutely atomistic a way, as is apt to happen, for example, in the sort of source study that reasons according to the formula, "because he read that he wrote this," and of supposing, on the other hand, that the experience an author's works record manifests the consciousness of the nation as a whole, a tendency illustrated by those facile equivalences between Emerson's bracing individualism and the mentality of the pioneer, or between Twain's cynicism and the bitter fruits of capitalist enterprise. Of course, literary history cannot be separated from the historian's view of the whole national experience, and it is also true that in explaining events, he must get down to particular cases, but even so, a credible account of the American literary tradition would define continuities which, though broadly inclusive, do not dissolve into grandiose myth, yet which at the same time are applicable to the particular details of a poem or novel.

The American author's sense of time is one such element of continuity, one aspect of thought general enough to illuminate the relationship between a great diversity of works, authors, and periods, but also having a precise relevance to the form and thought of an individual work. Whether one thinks of the content of a work as a set of ideas expressed and things portrayed or as an experience of which these thoughts and objects are elements, most readers will agree that the subject matter is determined by the world view within which these elements exist. Whitman's world may be a set of actual circumstances, but it is somewhat distinct from, say, Thoreau's world, for it not only has different contents, but constitutes the world as Whitman sees it, and its facts, though objectively true, have been organized in a unique way. To understand Whitman's meaning is to enter his world and see what the things he asserts or pictures mean there.

Now the structure of this world is very radically affected by his assumptions concerning time. And though time is only one such principle of organization, no other principle is more interesting, for since literature exists in the medium of language and therefore arranges its elements temporally, time manifests the unity of content and form. There is a common ground joining the time system of the author's world and the time created by the way the work itself develops.

To appreciate this, one should notice that action is an inevitable constituent of literary subject matter, not only in histories and narratives, and in the brief moment a lyric records (for this implies other times), but even in the work which pretends to depict an unchanging situation, since persisting without change is also an action. And when we turn our attention from the happenings a work portrays to the things it pictures—its people and physical objects—the influence of ideas concerning time proves scarcely less important. Since the nature of any individual thing depends upon what the author assumes concerning its origin, destiny, and purpose, its nature makes reference to the temporal structure of its world. If an author's sense of time were different, his characters would be of another kind, just as his events would happen in a different way. But the same view of time which leads the author to see his characters and events as he does will influence the way the work itself develops. For to succeed, its mode of happening must be consistent with the process it depicts. Otherwise the very existence of the poem or novel would demonstrate the falseness of its fiction, as I think is very often the case in bad art.

A work's own development and the action it depicts are distinguishable yet continuous. The difference is that between what is assumed and what exists as the object of thought. I would suggest that characters, events, and other such subject matter become credible and engage our feelings persuasively only to the extent that the author can induce us to share the assumptions which define his world. And his handling of time is perhaps his most powerful means of persuasion. For in organizing time, he works with an element that is utterly real to the reader—those moments and hours devoted to reading his work. It is our time that he reconstructs, and the new pattern he gives to this time leads us to engage in a particular process of perceiving and thus to share the premises of his experience. We enter into the author's world by existing within the time relations which largely define it. The remarkable power of this influence is shown by the fact that even thinking about the temporal arrangement as we read (or reread) does not free us from its tutelage, since in following the sequential pattern, as we must in order to read, we are engaged in the process it defines.

In practice, the author's handling of time is often no more conscious than the reader's response to it, and if a Cooper calculated his temporal arrangements far less than a Faulkner, this does not mean that their effect on his art is less real or relevant. But I believe that, on the whole, American authors have tended to be more conscious of literary time and the techniques it made possible than their European contemporaries, and that in America many techniques we regard as recent innovations were quite consciously employed in the colonial period.

The reader may feel that although language arranges words one after the other, like beads on a string, this fact does not tell us very much, since literature always seems intent on a vision of the world which would free the mind from any such narrow and mechanical scheme. It may even be said that literature tends to destroy or neutralize time by "spatializing" as simultaneous elements the things which words name one by one.[16] Hence the usefulness of many critical terms—form, image, structure, setting, focus, point of view—all of which seem convenient because they recognize spatial effects. Since modern physics has fostered distrust of axiomatic distinctions between space and time, one may also ask whether the idea of temporal form can have a valid theoretical foundation. Postponing comment on the last point, I would say that the first two objections are weak because they confuse structure with the imaginative effects it creates. It is true that literature *seems* to break free of chronological arrangement, and that writers can use language to conceal the movement of time, suggesting simultaneity and thus, often, an effect of spatialization. But this does not mean that a writer can in fact efface the sequential nature of literature. Words, paragraphs, events, facts do follow in sequence, and whatever fiction leads us to imagine, we encounter them in sequence as we read. However problematical the relation of time to space may be, the time spent in reading is not any the less time or the less influenced by the sequence of words we follow during that period. The point such objections are meant to make is really that the mere arrangement of things on the page is an ordering much too mechanical to be considered as the essential pattern of a literary work. This is

16. See Joseph Frank's well-known essay, "Spatial Form in Modern Literature," *Sewanee Review*, 55 (Spring, Summer, Autumn, 1945), reprinted in revised form in his *The Widening Gyre* (New Brunswick, N.J., Rutgers University Press, 1963), pp. 3–60.

surely true; as I have said before, such arrangement is but the outward, physical manifestation of a form which is largely conceptual and imaginative. Yet because language is the medium of literature, the sequence in which the elements are presented is a necessary means of creating form. To appreciate the truth of this, one need only consider the crucial effect of proportioning which results from brief or lengthy treatment of an episode, or how the placement of a sentence or image gives it an interpretive emphasis. Of course, a work's form is not the sum of such facts of arrangement, but they do provide useful "leads" into the structure of a poem or novel and help to confirm what we find there.

The comparison of "Peter Quince" and "To a Waterfowl" illustrates what seems to me the most crucial effect of time on form—the way it defines points of view. The kind of time one assumes determines the kind of experience one will have, because it establishes the horizon of consciousness and therefore locates the positions from which the mind perceives. Within any particular version of time only certain points of view are possible. Thus, in a very basic sense, kinds of time are points of view. The occasion of experience simultaneously defines a total history and the self's immediate situation. And all the possible points of view within the world thus revealed are one in that a person sees reality from all these positions at once and the sum of what they reveal is his consciousness. Yet they are distinct points of view even so, because a person's attention is much less inclusive than his consciousness. What he "thinks about" gives the main emphasis to what is revealed from one viewpoint, the other viewpoints then subsisting as merely potential ones, just as what they reveal subsists as that which is assumed—the background of tacit information against which the things he attends to are seen.

The reader may feel that what I call a system of viewpoints is merely a means of naming the multiple qualities of experience. And he may ask whether the points of view are not so different in kind that there is little to be gained by marshaling them under the same term. For example, in speaking of the eternal point of view, I must refer to a purely hypothetical position, since no human mind is omniscient. It is only by intending reality as a whole that one can imagine looking at it from the outside. The whole does not actually present itself to one's vision. Yet to speak of the present as a point of view is to name a real location: the thinker actually stands there. It would seem, then, that these viewpoints are incommensurate, the one physical, the other merely hypothetical. I would answer that both are equally hypothetical, as indeed all viewpoints are. It is in terms of our own world view that we judge other viewpoints, and though reality is more than our suppositions, it is inseparable from them, and our judgments are therefore dependent upon the points of view which we hypothesize as valid. With this in mind, one can see that the first objection—that points of view are just names for qualities of experience—is lacking in relevance. Since the qualities are qualities *of experience,* they exist with respect to viewpoints, and one must recognize the latter to understand what the qualities are.

Another possible objection is that "point of view" is merely a metaphor, and it may best be answered by studying what "merely" implies. A metaphor intends to be true in some degree; it asserts some measure of identity between the things compared. "Point of view" is indeed a metaphor; it expresses the relationship of the mind to its objects through that of the physical eye to objects in space, but this figure is a very convenient one, since physical sight is a true instance of the relations it symbolizes, even though it does not illustrate all aspects of the experiential process. A critical metaphor must be judged by its usefulness, and the fact that vision has always been an indispensable image for understanding is a good warrant for using it.

Behind these problems concerning temporal form and the concept of point of view lies a more basic, though simpler, question: whether in a critical study of this kind one can reason from any certainties concerning the real nature of time. My answer must be that there are no such certainties, because the kinds of time we can think of and discuss are those which we have in mind and which therefore cannot be freed from subjectivity. This is not to deny that objective time exists, but simply to assert that in practice, any epoch is an occasion of experience, if only a potential occasion; and any time system is projected by a state of mind (which in turn it helps to define). Literature presents many versions of time, and perhaps the study of them may allow for some true inferences concerning time as a thing in itself. However, quite aside from the fact that such inferences lie beyond the scope of literary criticism, it would appear that there is no way of confirming their validity. To know the true nature of time would require a final metaphysics, and the phenomenological approach can promise no more than a degree of objectivity. For although the critic may propose to do no more than observe the various kinds of time his authors depict, he brings to this study his own assumptions and, most particularly, his own sense of time.

It should then be clear that in a critical work concerned not with time itself but with versions of time, and even more narrowly, with a few of those versions which seem characteristic of American literature, the approach will have to be empirical—an exploration along specific lines of evidence toward conclusions that will seem true only to the extent that they cast some light on the works treated. The "present" and "eternity" have seemed to me pertinent terms because in most of the authors I discuss they are crucial terms, while in others—Cooper and Whitman, for example—I think it can be shown that they have the same importance, since approximately the same premises concerning time prevail. The same may be said for "duration": instead of reasoning from a preestablished definition of the term, I have tried to give an account of the kinds of duration the works actually portray. It should be clear that such terms as "finite time," "subjective time," and "human time" could have no practical meaning, since we cannot form a thought of the objective time with which they are supposed to be contrasted.

One of the main advantages of the study of literary time is that it helps one to understand the relationship between the work and the reading experience, thus providing a credible basis for judgments of value. Since the merits of a work can only be known as values encountered in one's experience as a reader, the problem of critical evaluation is essentially that of finding ways to discuss the work in such a manner that what can be called elements of the work as an object are convertible into elements of the work as an experience. Time, as I have tried to show, is one of the continuities which unites the work and the reading. By the way the reader's real time is reorganized, he is induced to participate in a mode of experience which is also a process of evaluating. The ethical standard the work assumes is not merely something he thinks "about"—and is certainly not reducible to the author's moral declarations; it is a system of judgments the reader himself makes.

But, of course, a reading is only an experience within an experience. The reader is never so completely deluded by fiction that he abandons his actual situation, and even as an inhabitant of the imaginary world, he remains an outsider, for he cannot share the circumstances of the characters or narrator. Attempts to destroy this isolation by involving him in the character's activity of organizing percepts into experience have the odd effect of augmenting his detachment: the more he is immersed in the data to be interpreted, the more he becomes aware of making his own interpretation. The outside view is a function of the inside view; and even the most vivid empathy involves seeing the fictive against the background of one's total consciousness, for credibility has its ground in the reader's own world. The affective fallacy is the mistake of supposing that the reading is the whole of the reader's experience, so that the work can be defined by what it "does to" the mind. But the work is the formal rather than the efficient cause of the reading. It is a system of statements which is identical with a system of intentions, and it "causes" the reading experience in somewhat the same sense that the score "causes" the performance of a piano sonata. It is not so much a question of what the work "does to" the mind, as of what one's mind does in approximating the work's intention as one reads or recollects one's reading. Thus the truth of the work is revealed not according to one's ordinary view of the world but by the way of experience in which one, as a reader, participates. Critical judgments are most persuasive when they describe what is implicit or potential in our own reading and thus name the experience in which the work's value is encountered rather than merely applying terms of censure or praise. This is the main purpose of studying literary time: to clarify for the reader the way he enters into the work's imaginative world, so that he can see for himself the values which life reveals when viewed from within this scheme of consciousness.

The world view a poem or novel projects is also distinct from the author's vision, since by setting down his experience in words he must necessarily interpret and transform it. Thus for him, as for the reader, the work is an experience within an experience, and to study the respects in which it reveals his mind, one must seek those elements of continuity which join the two. Again, time seems to be one of the most crucial elements, for while, on the one hand, the author's sense of time reflects the influences which have shaped his mind, it is, on the other hand, a governing idea, or premise, which gives to his experience a form that can actually be reproduced in language. In other words, the time he assumes constitutes a way of organizing the elements of his consciousness, which is also a way of organizing a poem or novel.

This time will always differ somewhat from that which his conscious reasoning pictures, because it is not an opinion but a premise of experience itself and prior to any thought he entertains. The study of literary time is therefore one means of looking beyond a writer's stated ideas to those habitual beliefs which form the most vital ties between any individual and his culture. I feel that it is in terms of such beliefs that the relations between American writers can be most accurately described.

The very idea of American literature commits one to believe that such disparate figures as Emily Dickinson and Mark Twain, or Henry James and Theodore Dreiser, share a common ground and must therefore resemble one another not just as Americans but as American writers. With respect to the content of their thoughts and experiences, however, the connections are so tenuous as to seem illusory. Their circumstances are too various and uniquely personal, and if one tries to connect them through their common interest in certain intellectual problems—that of freedom and necessity, for example—one loses sight of the element of nationality, since such concerns are surely as European as they are American. It must be in the *terms* in which these problems are formulated that a valid similarity is to be found. But to speak of habitual terms is to recognize even more habitual assumptions and perceive that the common ground is a set of premises and the varieties of experience they make possible. Moreover, since our concern is a literary tradition, the common premises which relate the authors most effectively must be those which are convertible into principles of form. The versions of time studied in this work differ significantly, and it has not been my intention to assert that the authors I discuss envision time in the same way. Rather, I would say that their versions of time illustrate some of the typical variations which grow from the same assumptions.

Such a view premises the American mind, but only in a sense so limited that the usual objections against the idea of national character do not apply. Of course, the American mind is not to be considered as exactly like an individual mind, nor, on the other hand, as a mere average or gross total, and the meaning of the term need not include the idea of a collective unconscious, national soul, or group personality. Rather, the term signifies a system of modes of experience which, though differing greatly, are yet related as alternatives within a single range of possibilities.

The student of American literature is more than slightly handicapped by his commitment to give greater emphasis to matters of nationality than they probably deserve, for he must somehow distinguish American writing from the English tradition as it concurrently develops. The great danger is that in seeking what is American, one may lose sight of what is simply human. It is true that one ought to keep in mind the flesh-and-blood author and the actual people who composed the America from which he wrote, yet there is a difference between seeing the author in his milieu and defining the milieu primarily in terms of its special American features. By regarding his human situation as a moment in the developing consciousness of the whole nation, one may sometimes, with certain writers, give a happy emphasis to the democratic values of literature as an expression of communal ideals and a more or less naturalistic record of the social landscape. But when seen in this perspective, such important writers as Edwards, Poe, Emily Dickinson, Henry James, and T. S. Eliot tend to seem irrelevant or out of step, while authors like Franklin and Hawthorne are given a distorted significance.

A literary tradition is always a highly selective expression of a people's whole experience, and to claim more for it as a mirror of the national past is to misrepresent the very values one seeks to enhance. In America the social import of literature has been more than normally oblique, because ethnic and regional differences have rendered the writer less representative of the population as a whole. Thus, for example, the democratic principles which have given the public its political unity as a nation have usually received more thoughtful treatment in American literature when the author questions them than when he affirms them. Quite significantly, the most widely popular authors have been conservatives, like Cooper and Frost, or uneasy ironists, like Twain and Fitzgerald, rather than men of Emersonian trust.

Unless it is balanced by a formal criticism which values the uniqueness of the experience a work records, the attempt to interpret American literature as a communal dialogue, and more especially a sociological and political dialogue, will tend to make literature itself a secondary concern. The practical result is well illustrated by the preeminence accorded to Emerson, who as a writer is hardly as important as Hawthorne or Melville. The insensitivity of such criticism to the aesthetic values of art cannot be excused on the ground that the interests of history are served, for in its tendency to reduce the works from complex records of experience to mere statements of opinion, it misrepresents their historical significance. This is not to say that the distinctively American qualities of our literature are unimportant; rather, I would suggest that, by the very nature of things, their value must be based upon the more broadly human values the literature expresses. For values can only be known in experience, and in living their experience, Americans are not only citizens and nationals but human beings.

The approach these introductory pages describe is intended, above all, to provide a theory of literary value which may serve to illuminate the distinctive merits of American literature. It should be clear that critical discourse can do no more than bring the reader to a point where he can see the special excellence of a work for himself. In other words, it cannot demonstrate the value of value any more than logic can demonstrate the harmony or consistency by which a statement is seen to be true within its assumed system of ideas. But it can describe value as a pattern in the reader's experience which also exists objectively as a pattern in the work. The question concerns not the names by which we should denote the values of the literary work, but the means by which the work leads the reader to participate in an experience that makes its values actual to him. This approach makes irrelevant the objection that the study of form fosters a sterile aestheticism, for it assumes from the outset that aesthetic and moral values cannot be separated. The value of a work as art is precisely its power to reveal values far more important to our lives than its own artistry, yet values which can only be known through this aesthetic form—by this way of experience—in this work of art. In discussing some representative figures in the American literary tradition, I have proceeded on the premise that their uniquely American traits are to be valued in that they not only illustrate our nationality but engage our humanity.

1
Literary Form and the Design of Puritan Experience

Thus there may exist provisional origins,
which practically and in fact form the first
beginnings of the particular tradition held
by a given community, folk or communion
of faith; and memory, though sufficiently
instructed that the depths have not actually
been plumbed, yet nationally may find
reassurance in some primitive point of time
and, personally and historically speaking,
come to rest there.

Thomas Mann

THE Puritan quality that has persisted in American literature, even to our own time, is not a creed or set of general propositions. And it is not something "handed down" from father to son. Its mode of transmission has been subtler and less conscious. Perhaps it had best be called a habit of mind, in that habit suggests learning of the most direct kind, the way in which the child is conditioned not just by what those around him say and do but by their manner—the style of their statements and the world their most casual gestures imply. Ideas inculcated and those later acquired from books can mean, after all, only what the point of view the child learned at a much more primitive stage will allow. So conceived, the habit of mind is not the content of experience but its form and condition. It exists in the child before he has sufficiently mastered language to understand ideas, and it is doubtless intimately connected with the possibilities his language system offers. It is a set of assumptions which are for the most part tacit and unrecognized, just because they are the most fundamental ones and are accepted without reserve or the criticism which would bring them into view—accepted as the terms of experiencing, without which experience would not be possible.

If the Puritan influence is found at this most basic and intimate level of mind, one can see not only why it persists but why, with respect to American literature, it is something less, as well as more, than a cause. The convenience of arranging our thoughts historically in a cause-and-effect sequence makes it very tempting to assume that Puritan theology came first and a certain sensibility was then created by the way dogma affected the mind. But when one asks whether the sequence couldn't be reversed— whether the habit of mind expressed itself by creating Puritan theology, rather than the theology producing the sensibility, as if from whole cloth—it becomes clear that priority in time is not so relevant as logical priority. No doubt the habit of mind and the theology grew up together, each fostering the other, but it is the habit of mind that has proved more fundamental, since it has persisted long after the doctrines of Puritanism have lost their authority. Because it is less than a religion, is merely a *form* of consciousness, it has been able to accommodate itself to altered subject matter. But while it is less than a religion, it is surely more than a theology; it is a way of thinking rather than just a particular system of thoughts.

By viewing the Puritan influence in this way, one can free oneself from the inconvenience of regarding it as strictly a matter of causation. That is, one does not have to assume that Puritan traits in later American writing are always or primarily the effect of causes originating in early New England. Of course, such causation is operative, particularly in writers as conscious of their place in the Puritan tradition as Emerson and Emily Dickinson, and thus the intricacies of Puritan theology continue to be significant even up to the close of the nineteenth century. But more often one feels that the Puritan quality of a novel or poem is a matter of relevance rather than causation—that James' *The American,* for example, illustrates the fact that James found Puritan assumptions natural rather than that he was historically conditioned to accept

30

them. While traditions surviving from the Puritan past may indeed cause certain modes of perception to persist, such influence is dependent upon the continuing relevance of Puritan assumptions; and this relevance is exemplified by the predominant role of New England in American cultural history, when compared to other colonial subcultures which enjoyed stronger political backing and were, in the short run, more viable economically. Puritanism and its close ally, the Scotch-Irish Calvinism of the South, exerted the most lasting influence because its theology expressed the most relevant definition of the American experience. Whether the situation is that of the early settler alone in the wilderness or that of a man alone in an urbanized world, where the continuities of his culture, if not already destroyed by immigration, are in any case concealed by the shifting phantasmagoria of technological change, it is, in its essential outlines, the human situation as Puritanism pictured it—that of the individual in his isolated present moment trying to interpret the immediate by a direct reference to the eternal.

Before considering the effect of such a view of experience in Puritan literature, I wish to glance briefly at a few errors that are apt to lead such explorations astray. One concerns cultural influences from abroad, another the influence of native geography, and a third, the relation between the Puritans' theology and their literature. The first two topics may be treated together by setting two typical commentaries side by side:

> The American space existed as an extension of European space but obviously free of its cultural accumulations and its congestions. . . . The experience of the new continent is a challenge to the self as venturesome and reliant spirit.[1]

> By emigrating before 1640, these Englishmen missed a vital chapter in English history. The ideals they had come to vindi-

1. Frederick J. Hoffman, *The Mortal No: Death and the Modern Imagination* (Princeton, Princeton University Press, 1964), p. 326.

cate in America—which they did vindicate—underwent a drastic overhauling at home. . . . New Englanders won the case for the Independent theory of 1630; they reported their result at the moment their former colleagues repudiated its fundamental tenet. . . . By 1648 English Independents had become greater strangers to *The Cambridge Platform* than were all those enemies against whom New Englanders believed they both waged common war.[2]

The common element in both statements is the assumption that the colonial mind can be regarded as a Lockean tabula rasa, a mind which passively accepts the imprint of external reality or, when it has once been impressed with an ideology, retains it until this inscription is altered by a foreign hand. In the first quotation, which is by Frederick J. Hoffman, space is metaphorically converted into mind, a mind as free of beliefs, allegiances, and communal forms as the wilderness landscape is free of walls and buildings. For the "cultural accumulations" of which he speaks are not, after all, mere objects in space but just such mental furniture as Puritanism itself. To describe the influence of geography in this way is to overlook the fact that the land which exerted this influence was the land as it appeared to that mind—according to its already established modes of perception. The second passage, which is taken from Perry Miller, may seem to differ greatly because it is concerned with what happened to the European ideas the settlers brought with them to the New World, but Miller's line of reasoning makes the colonial mind almost as passive as Hoffman implies. In "vindicating" the "Independent theory of 1630," the Puritans do no more than act out a preestablished European program. Having missed the next chapter in the history of English Puritanism, New England is soon arrested by its fixation on outmoded theory, and provides an example of how "America is repeatedly left with an institution on its hands."[3] Despite

2. Perry Miller, *The New England Mind: From Colony to Province* (Cambridge, Mass., Harvard University Press, 1953), pp. 119–20.
3. Ibid., p. 119.

the undoubted value of Miller's history, one is disturbed by the fact that at nearly every point in the story he chronicles, change is imputed to external influences—the exigencies of frontier life, the alterations in imperial policy, the rivalries between colonial families, the pressures exerted by alien sects, economic developments, and the ideas of the dawning enlightenment. The story of Puritanism is thus seen as the story of a decaying institution, whose internal developments are to be viewed merely as attempts to shore up its crumbling doctrinal foundations. But Puritanism was a world view rather than merely the dogma which articulated it, and the influences from outside, though surely important, must be seen in relation to a mind which was active in the process of being influenced.

By viewing influence in this way, one can look beyond those frequently described developments which show why Puritanism passed away, to those which explain the sense in which it has persisted. That New England clung tenaciously to beliefs which English Puritanism soon abandoned may underline the provincialism that would naturally have characterized America for generations in any case, but far from fiddling away the decades in the discussion of dead issues, New England was in fact developing along its own line toward Edwards' prophetic psychologizing of theology, Franklin's scientific pragmatism, and a more radical social experiment than Europe had yet thought to undertake. The prophetic nature of what may have seemed backwardness to the Englishman of 1750 or 1850 is especially important in literature. Though it is natural to suppose that the characteristics of twentieth-century literature reflect a broadly cosmopolitan sensibility, one purpose of this chapter is to point out that the techniques which seem to relate Eliot to Yeats and Faulkner to Proust have a very long history in America, and can be seen emerging in the early Puritan writers.

If one should regard the influences acting upon Puritanism from the outside as having been adapted and modified by the sensibility they influenced, it is even more important to free one's thinking from the idea that the characteristics of Puritan writing are simply the effect of specific theological ideas. Yet prevailing critical theories tend to treat the literature as if doctrinal requirements were the direct cause of all that makes it distinctive. Samuel Eliot Morison, Kenneth Murdock, and Perry Miller imply, as their working hypothesis, that since Puritanism stressed the instructive function of literature, the early New Englanders regarded writing as a worthy pursuit only to the extent that it might serve as the means of teaching wholesome doctrine and inculcating morality.[4] The assumption is that from this very practical aesthetic the pronounced didacticism of American literature and its focus upon ethical concerns are derived. Yvor Winters and, more recently, Richard Chase have cast this argument in a somewhat different form, suggesting that because Puritanism fostered a severe simplification of ethics, American literature is Manichaean in tendency, having as its central myth the conflict between good and evil.[5] Roy Harvey Pearce advances yet a third hypothesis, which amounts to an inversion of the didactic theory: he suggests that since Puritanism restricted art to the humble function of teaching orthodox lessons, the artist was forced into Antinomianism, with the result that the best American literature is characterized by the celebration of spontaneity, intuition, and the divinity within the self.[6]

These theories complement each other: no doubt the Puritans' attempt to marshal all human activities to the service of faith led

4. Samuel Eliot Morison, *The Puritan Pronaos: Studies in the Intellectual Life of New England in the Seventeenth Century* (London, Oxford University Press, 1936); Kenneth Murdock, *Literature and Theology in Colonial New England* (Cambridge, Mass., Harvard University Press, 1949); Perry Miller, *The New England Mind: The Seventeenth Century* (New York, Macmillan, 1939); *The Puritans*, ed. Perry Miller and Thomas H. Johnson (New York, American Book Co., 1938). See, for example, p. 64 in Miller and Johnson.

5. Yvor Winters, *Maule's Curse* (Norfolk, Conn., New Directions, 1938), p. 8; Richard Chase, *The American Novel and Its Tradition* (Garden City, N.Y., Doubleday Anchor Books, 1957), p. 11.

6. *The Continuity of American Poetry* (Princeton, Princeton University Press, 1961), pp. 41–42.

naturally to didactic writing, one consequence of which is a Manichaean habit of mind and another the Antinomianism that is bound to develop whenever the artist finds that received opinion and personal experience are at odds. But however such formulas are developed or related to each other, the result is not entirely satisfactory because, as in the usual analyses of influence, the Puritan sensibility is seen merely as the effect of causes it was powerless to modify or interpret. Everyone will grant that the Puritan writer's creed delimited his subject matter and discouraged the use of certain kinds of rhetorical ornament, and my quarrel is not with these familiar truths. Rather, I would suggest that the study of Puritan literature and its influence on later writing must concern not only the ideas the Puritan writer expresses, but the mode of experience in terms of which they are meant to seem true. Ultimately the two are inseparable, for the content of an idea cannot be sundered from the meaning it has for the person who considers it, and while it is true that the Puritan writer was brought up to believe in certain doctrines, yet to understand what in his own experience these doctrines meant, one must understand his vision of the world rather than merely his published articles of faith. My objective, therefore, will be to discuss those aspects of theology which seem to have the most direct bearing upon the Puritan writer's vision—to locate those assumptions which exist doubly, as doctrinal premises and as principles of experience. For it is not as a set of ideas accepted or reacted against, but as a mode of experience, that Puritanism, or any other system, is important in literature. If the literature of Colonial New England is Puritan, it must be Puritan in its point of view rather than merely in the ideas it expresses and the enforceable rules to which it conforms.

The most profound and lasting influence of Puritanism upon the American mind has been its effect upon the sense of time. By the sharp contrast between the present and eternity which its doctrine of grace fostered, it accustomed the imagination to conceive experience in terms of the purely present in relation to a total history or conspectus of all times. In establishing this habitual view of time, Puritanism affected the very nature of the artist's medium, for since language itself is sequential, the present-eternity contrast defines experience in a manner which bears directly on the writer's problem as to how perceptions, events, and ideas are to be arranged on the page. It is this relevance of doctrine to literary form that perhaps explains why America has excelled in literature, from an earlier date and more markedly, than in any of the other arts. By shaping a particular attitude toward time, Puritanism largely determined the ways a poem or novel would be organized and so founded the drama which in one or another of certain possible ways the American author has henceforth been destined to enact.

Two aspects of New England Puritanism must be kept in mind —the relative isolation which allowed it to develop freely according to its own nature, and its special place in the evolution of Protestant theology. While, in England, Puritanism was but one among many sects and was soon forced to accommodate itself to traditions and institutions which modified it at least as much as it altered them, in New England it was the dominant sect, with the result that the challenge of alien ideologies no less than the practical problems of colonization could be dealt with within the system of strictly Puritan assumptions. That is why New England's severest problems proved to be not those created by Indian wars, British interference, or subversive foreign ideas, but the heresies and irresolvable dilemmas which the contradictions within Puritanism itself brought to light.

The sharp contrast between the present and eternity is the result of the particular phase of Protestant thought which Puritanism represents. It is the phase in which God's immanence is conceived as a presence so absolutely immediate (within the moment of regenerative experience), while God's transcendence has been given so categorical a definition (as Absolute Sovereignty), that although the two aspects of deity can still be held together in thought, the mind is forever engaged in the violent shifting of perspective between the present and eternal points of view. Looking back to the earlier phases of the Reformation, one can see that the main tendency had been toward increased abstraction: God's freedom from obligation to fallen man, and man's consequent need to rely on "justification by faith" alone, lead naturally to predestination, but in Calvin predestination is more abstractly defined to give a bolder, more severely logical statement of God's perfect foreknowledge and foreordination of all things. Thus God is defined as ever more remotely transcendent by an increased emphasis upon Absolute Sovereignty, while, conversely, God becomes more immediately present as salvation is made a question of the self's own state of mind. For to the believer the question of his election must be studied within his own experience, and since experience is always a present event, the more conscientiously he searches his experience, the more purely immediate his idea of the present becomes.

Thus, as the first and third Persons of the Trinity come to seem increasingly divergent as eternal being and immediate perception, it becomes natural to assume that the present and eternity are ultimately the only relevant points of view. But although for convenience I have spoken as if theology caused the Puritan mind to think in this way, in another sense the mentality of Protestantism caused the doctrinal development, and this is nowhere more apparent than in the way the taste for rationalistic abstractions, particularly in the use of such terms as "all," "always," and "infinite," necessitated the widening contrast between immanence and transcendence. When this contrast is pushed a little further than the Puritans or their Calvinist brethren would attempt, Trinitarian Christianity collapses into the inspirational pietism of Antinomian and Quaker, or, if the emphasis falls on clear reason rather than ardent feeling, the rationalism of the Deist and Unitarian.

In Puritanism, however, the balance is perilously maintained —a fact which I think can be recognized in the tension between its Calvinist theology and its Congregationalist polity. It is the latter which most clearly distinguishes the Puritans from the Presbyterians. In espousing a theory of church government founded upon the belief in a corporate spiritual life, the Puritans contravened the logic of predestination, for if works are of no account and salvation is through God's foreordained grace alone, church membership and obedience to the moral law can have no effect upon the life of the soul. One logical conclusion to Calvin's doctrine is thus the Antinomianism for which Anne Hutchinson was banished, and the other great controversies, those concerning "preparation," the "half-way covenant," and admission to the sacrament, also appear to have resulted from the incompatibility of predestinarian and Congregational premises. The covenant theology emphasizes a communal rather than a personal relation between man and God. It was as a people—a church and, somewhat less importantly, a nation—that the Puritans enjoyed their privileged contractual arrangements with God, while predestinarianism gives a larger emphasis to God's presence in the regenerate individual than in the community. On the surface the two views may seem to fit together, since the Church was defined as the core of believers who could attest to some personal assurance of regeneration, and there were many arguments fashioned to reconcile the two—as, for example, that good works are a sign, though not a means, of grace. But since the intricacies of such reasoning give it the air of rationalization, one should look beyond it to the basic impulse that the covenant theology manifests. This is, above all, the desire to see God as present in the everyday life of the community, a desire the more urgent in Puritanism than in the less radical forms of Protestant faith (the Lutheran and Anglican, for instance), in that Calvinist theology had more completely estranged it from the medieval Catholic view of the Church. It was, I would suggest, the remoteness which Calvinism attributed to God as transcendent ruler which explains the Puritans' desire to conceive God's presence in an area more easily perceived than the obscure interior of the individual's heart—in a community, in a church. Perhaps a Scotch Presbyterian colony in

America would not have differed greatly from New England, but, even so, the Puritan allegiance to a Congregational form of church government gives added emphasis to the tension which the transcendence-immanence contrast created in the New England mind.

One clear sign of the way this duality influenced the form of Puritan literature is the didacticism so pronounced in the work of early New England authors. Not only their sermons, controversial writings, and works of mere propaganda but their lyric poems and diaries formulate meaning as a lesson and make its status as a lesson abnormally explicit. No doubt it is partly from Puritanism that later American literature derived its characteristic interest in ethical problems and the habit of formulating the answers to them in an abstract and often preachy manner; but in recognizing this connection, one is forced to ask if either a Puritan writer or an American novelist of the twentieth century is really more concerned with ethics than his European counterpart. For to say that the literary tradition which produced a *Phèdre* or a *Crime and Punishment* is less ethical would seem an absurd conclusion. My point is that Puritan literature and later American writing reflect a different, rather than a greater ethical, interest. Instead of appealing to Puritan statements about the instructive function of literature in their literary theory (the texts of which are, indeed, so scant that with respect to the purpose of art they may be thought to do no more than reflect the most commonplace of European aesthetic ideas), it would be wiser to suppose that the Puritans' didactic tendency is the result of their way of relating general ideas to the fictionally realized experience. Ethical truths become lessons delivered with didactic emphasis, not because the American writer is more earnestly concerned with morality, but because for him a generalization is an eternal truth which can only be seen by standing outside the moment of immediate experience. Moral maxims and proverbs spoken "in character" are common throughout literature; so, too, are auctorial pronouncements. But what seems distinctively American is the separateness of the lesson from either the characters' world or the author's. The American writer cannot remain "in character," even in his own, if he is to deliver the truth—a fact well exemplified by Hawthorne, as compared with Dickens. The author must stand at a distance to generalize, and having left his own present, he adopts eternity as the only other possible point of view. This is not done merely to make the lesson more explicit or to show that it is universally true, but to see it at all. There are, in the last analysis, no middle grounds between the eternity of instructive ideas and the moment of present perception. Thus fable suddenly turns into lesson, pure sensation becomes pure concept, and, conversely, the abstraction brought into experience becomes a question of conduct or technology, as one frequently observes in a Franklin, a Melville, or a Hemingway. What lies behind the Puritans' conscious belief that literature should teach lessons is the harsh simplification of time which makes truth take the form of timeless generalizations and renders experience a purely present event.

To the mind for which eternity and the present are the only relevant points of view, the most natural form of thought is analogy, and it is therefore not surprising that analogy is the dominant characteristic of Puritan literature. No other trait is so important, no other literary method so all-pervasive, for analogy is not merely a stylistic device but the very method and design of Puritan thought—a mode not only of interpretation but of having the experience to be interpreted. One can appreciate this by recollecting that New England itself was viewed as one vast analogy in which the settlers correspond to the Israelites, the wilderness to the Promised Land, and the theocratic community to the New Jerusalem.

The same thought process which created New England's essential myth and determined the broad outlines of the Puritans' image of themselves can also be seen in their abnormally great interest in providential interpretations. As the whole life of New England is viewed and, indeed, created by the analogy to ancient

Israel, so every detail of public experience is to be regarded as a possible sign of God's dealings with his people. One example will suffice to illustrate this very familiar method, and I will quote from Governor Bradford as a representative of the earliest immigrants, whose mental set was established before the American land could exert the mystical influence which has so often been imputed to our geography. In recording an earthquake, Bradford writes:

> It was not only on the seacoast, but the Indians felt it within land, and some ships that were upon the coast were shaken by it. So powerful is the mighty hand of the Lord, as to make both the earth and sea to shake, and the mountains to tremble before Him, when He pleases. And who can stay His hand?
>
> It so fell out that at the same time divers of the chief of this town were met together at one house, conferring with some of their friends that were upon their removal from the place, as if the Lord would hereby show the signs of His displeasure, in their shaking a-pieces and removals from one another.[7]

Providential interpretation served as the key to personal experience as well as the concerns of the community. In fact, its public uses were probably but a consequence of the angle of vision from which the individual looked at his world. Thomas Shepard's account of a calamity which occurred when he was on the point of setting out for America shows how naturally the life of faith fostered the habit of analogizing.

> So upon the sabbeth day morning boats came to our vessel from the town; and so my dear wife and child went in the first boat; but here the Lord saw that these waters were not sufficient to wash away my filth and sinfulness and therefore he cast me into the fire as soon as ever I was upon the sea in the boat, for there my first born child very precious to my soul and

7. *Of Plymouth Plantation: 1620–1647*, ed. Samuel Eliot Morison (New York, Knopf, 1952), p. 302.

dearly beloved of me was smitten with sickness; the Lord sent a vomiting upon it whereby it grew faint, and nothing that we could use could stop its vomiting although we had many helps at Yarmouth and this was a very bitter affliction to me, and the Lord now showed me my weak faith, want of fear, pride, carnal content, immoderate love of creatures, and of my child especially, and begot in me some desires and purposes to fear his name; but yet the Lord would not be intreated for the life of it, and after a fortnight's sickness at last it gave up the ghost when its mother had given it up to the Lord.[8]

That analogy could bring solace even in such heart-rending moments shows much more effectively than its application to theological controversies and political questions how directly it manifests the essence of the Puritan mentality.

But it may be asked whether providential interpretations are really analogies, for Bradford's earthquake and the death of Shepard's child are not mere parallels to God's will but enactments of it—revelations of divine purpose within the visible event. If that is so, "Providences" are metaphors, the two things compared becoming one in experience, whereas analogy is the drawing of parallels between things, or contexts, which remain distinct. And since the Puritan's whole purpose in seeking "Providences" is to see God in human events, it would therefore seem that he aims at metaphor or symbol rather than analogy. This is true in one sense, but false in another, for as I shall later explain, it is a matter of point of view whether an event is an analogy or a symbol. One must approach this difficulty by observing first that although providential interpretation is common throughout Protestant culture, it is of exaggerated importance in Puritanism, because the more predestination is emphasized, the more every event comes to seem a sign of God's will. If all that comes to pass is part of a fixed plan determined before the world was created,

8. *The Autobiography of Thomas Shepard*, Publication of the Colonial Society of Massachusetts, 27 (Boston, 1932), 381.

then each happening is an indication, because a necessary element, of the total design. Thomas Shepard can make sense of his terrible misfortune by reasoning that the child's death, like every other event in his experience, is the inevitable means to the end which God has determined for him.

Thus, though analogy and symbol seem opposites, Puritan analogizing leads to symbolism. It is symbolism of a special and limited kind, however, a symbolism deriving from the fact that to the Puritan mind the process of drawing analogies is itself symbolic. The analogy turns into a symbol when one shifts attention from the parallel between image and meaning to the mind which discerns this relation. Conversely, because one regards the things of experience as potential analogies, they are already symbols, they already have an inherent significance rather than functioning as mere signs which point toward meanings outside themselves. To have faith is a sign of regenerative grace; to draw analogies consistent with orthodox belief is evidence that one does have faith in the perfect wisdom and power which make all things expressions of the divine will.

Charles Feidelson has demonstrated that the main literary tradition in America has been a symbolist tradition because symbolism as a way of writing grows naturally from the way the American author's mind confronts his world. Yet Feidelson's analysis tends to limit the Puritan influence upon the later development of symbolist literature and, indeed, pictures Puritanism as more nearly an obstruction than a source. While granting that "Puritan rationalism . . . predicated an indivisible unity of thought, word, and thing," a view which would seem to have fostered the symbolist method, he emphasizes the Puritan allegiance to a discursive reasoning in which words are viewed as having as their meanings discrete objects in an "atomistic" universe, and reasons that this rationalistic bent at first restrained and finally canceled the symbolist tendency.[9] Thus the emergent

9. *Symbolism and American Literature* (Chicago, University of Chicago Press, Phoenix Books, 1953), p. 92.

symbolism of the American Renaissance is primarily a reaction to rather than a development out of Puritanism. Emerson meant "to rescue the intellect by showing that the [theological] controversies grew out of the nature of logical language." [10] For present purposes a distinction must be made between two senses in which the Puritan influence is considered—the theoretical and the psychological. Feidelson's main concern is with specific theories of language, reason, and symbol, and, with respect to these, Puritanism does seem to have developed toward a rationalistic formulation which allowed no scope to the symbolic imagination. But considered within the Puritan world view and the kind of belief which the salvatory doctrines define, Puritanism seems to have favored symbolist thinking much more strongly than its conscious reasoning on this subject allowed. When one considers the self's situation as it is understood in the Puritan scheme, one can see that Puritan experience rendered the symbolist mode natural— indeed, inevitable. Granted, the Puritan writer prefers the image that is merely typical to the symbol, and his statements tend to be propositional in form. Yet the perspective from which the typical image and theological idea are to be viewed has the effect of converting them into symbols. In the way they come to mind, in their happening as events in experience, they are regarded as potential symbols of the effects of grace, even though in content they remain analogues or abstract ideas. While in formal theory Puritanism developed in the manner Feidelson describes, and while it is not possible to trace a line of strictly literary influence in which Puritan poets may be seen providing an example that later poets recognized and imitated, it is safe to assume that the effects of Puritan beliefs upon the American mind habituated it to the symbolic mode of vision, with the result that eventually, in Emerson and other men of his time, the revolt against the jejune rationalism into which the formal theology had developed expressed a sensibility more fundamentally Puritan than the theoretical positions it rejects.

Admittedly, Puritan symbolism is different from that of the

10. Ibid., p. 97.

American Renaissance, more qualified and tentative, allowing for only momentary resolutions of the habitual analogizing. Yet American symbolism is symbolism of a particular kind, and what distinguishes it is the peculiar self-consciousness which is characteristic of Puritan experience, and which makes the symbolic process itself the center of attention. This is manifest by the very prominence—the obviousness—of the symbol in an American poem or novel. Whitman's thrush and Fitzgerald's green light, like Wallace Stevens' Susanna and Bryant's waterfowl, are more than images charged with symbolic import: their status *as* symbols is the essence of their meaning. *The Scarlet Letter* and *Moby-Dick* are two of the most characteristic as well as two of the greatest American novels because they present the most thoughtful explorations of the odd self-consciousness which makes the American abnormally aware of his symbolizing. They are also representative novels in the preference they manifest for symbols of either the most conventional or the most primitive kind. By greatly exaggerating a symbol's publicly acknowledged and traditional quality—which often produces the "gothic" effect of stylization—or by underlining the primitive aspects of symbols drawn from nature, the writer stresses the fact that his symbols are symbols indeed, and so is able to place the symbolizing process at the center of attention. A sharp contrast is usually developed between the traditional and natural symbols, so that, for example, Leatherstocking's marksmanship seems the more natural as the opposite of Judge Temple's laws and title deeds. There is often still a third sort of contrast designed for the same end: that between the dignity of conventional symbols and the humble commonplace of those derived from everyday experience. It must be stars or bowling balls, diadems or cookery, the grail or a cracked cup.

These ways of calling attention to the symbol as symbol illustrate the fact that in American literature the symbolizing can only be carried out within the larger process of studying one's own interpretation. The author's self-consciousness is but an aspect of the double view Puritanism fostered. Since he lives in a world where the level of meaning and the level of perceptions are antithetical, he is abnormally anxious to unite them in the symbol and yet painfully aware of the difficulties of doing so. Thus to symbolize and to study the symbolic process are for him the same thing. *What* the symbol means is really *how* it means, for that it has any given meaning at all is true only to the extent that the author can demonstrate how it acquires and expresses that meaning.

That a symbolism of this sort derives from the Puritans' rather simplistic contrast between the present and eternity becomes evident when one notices that, on the one hand, the meaning of such symbolism is always there—just as God's eternally preordained plan is implicit in all events—while, on the other hand, the meaning is always in the process of developing, a process which cannot end—just as for the Puritan, who could never have perfect assurance of election, each new moment initiates a fresh search for the signs of grace. The same attitude is revealed in the American writer's double view of the literary work, which he sees, on the one hand, as the touch-and-go affair of achieving "a momentary stay against confusion," and on the other, as a finite or imperfect version of the eternal poem—Poe's "plot of God." Depending on the author, the main emphasis will fall upon one or the other formula, but the two are opposite sides of the same coin. In the world of analogy the symbol's meaning is the universal order: "A leaf, a drop, a crystal, a moment of time, is related to the whole, and partakes of the perfection of the whole. Each particle is a microcosm, and faithfully renders the likeness of the world." [11] Yet because "always" and "now" are permanently separate, for there must ever be a contrast between the divine will, which is eternal, and human experience, which can only be immediately seen in a narrowly defined present, the symbol can effect but a brief and transitory reconciliation. Hence the symbolizing is an unending process. It is therefore the process of thought itself and the essential action of the poem or narrative.

Since American symbolism is so largely indebted to the design

11. Emerson, *Nature*, in *The Complete Works, 1,* 43.

of Puritan experience and its analogizing tendency, one should not be too contemptuous of early New England verse. It is not good poetry for the most part, and the usual ways of explaining its manifest failures are reasonable enough. To be sure, the Puritan colonists were too few, too poor, and too busy to produce a mature literature, but such patronizing arguments have the unhappy effect of glossing over the essential difference between American Puritanism and English culture. To immigrate to Massachusetts Bay was to see Puritan principles in a way different from that of a Milton or a Marvell, and if the poetry of the immigrant is pathetically crude compared to the best English verse of its time, that should not obscure the fact that it was different in intent, that the whole conception of poetry was of another kind.

One cannot say that in New England poetry mattered less and at the same time assert that the Puritans conceived it as the handmaiden of religion. Rather, the very crudeness of Puritan poems manifests the commitment to a new view of poetry, one in which analogy is the dominant mode. These lines from an elegy of Benjamin Tompson may be taken as representative of the norm:

> A lovely Cluster on a vine i saw,
> So faire it did my admiration draw,
> Climbing the sun side of an house of prayer
> & solacing it selfe in heavenly aire;
> Yet sudenly upon an eastward blast,
> The beuty of his boughs was over cast,
> The fairest grapes were pickt of one by one,
> (The) Dresser loocking like one half undone.
> Thers no undoing while a sauviour lives,
> Who takes no more than what he lends or gives.
> Three manly sons, grown up to Comly size,
> Two Daughters, apples in their parents eyes,
> Pickt out by envious Death; with us remains
> Their precious Dust abhorring sin or staine.[12]

12. "The Amiable Virgin Memorialized . . . ," in *Handkerchiefs from Paul: Being Pious and Consolatory Verses of Puritan Massachusetts*, ed. Kenneth Murdock (Cambridge, Mass., Harvard University Press, 1927), p. 10.

John Wilson's preface to Thomas Shepard's *The Church-Membership of Children* is a more amateurish example of the inevitable manner:

> Loe Her's a map, where we may see
> Well thresh'd an heap of corn to be
> By Thomas Shepard's happy hand
> Which from the chaffe pure wheat hath fan'd;
> The wheat in the Church-members right
> (Both great and little ones) to witt
> Unto the seal of Baptisme, all
> That are within the Gospel call.[13]

Urian Oakes' elegy for Thomas Shepard is of particular interest because it shows how the analogical habit persists, even in a poet who has gone beyond rugged popular versifying to the smoothness of a more cultivated poetic style:

> What! must we with our God, and Glory part?
> Lord! is thy Treaty with New-England come
> Thus to an end; And is War in thy Heart?
> That this Ambassadour is called hom.
> So Earthly Gods (Kings) when they War intend,
> Call home their Ministers, and Treaties end.[14]

That analogy was often developed at great length is well illustrated in Anne Bradstreet's charming comparison of her book to a feckless son. In "An Almanack for the Year of Our Lord 1648" Samuel Danforth belabors the analogy between the church and a tree through 12 stanzas or 72 lines.[15] But the brief analogy was also favored—by Cotton Mather, for instance, in his elegy for Urian Oakes:

---

13. Ibid., p. 85.
14. "An Elegie upon the Death of Mr. Thomas Shepard," in *Early American Poetry*, 4 (Boston, The Club of Odd Volumes, 1896), 7.
15. *Handerkerchiefs from Paul*, pp. 104–07.

> Ah! like a Silk-worm, his own bowels went
> To serve his Hearers, while he soundly spent
> His Spirits in his Labours.[16]

Inept as it is, Mather's comparison indicates how much the Puritan analogy resembles the metaphysical conceit. That the greatest of the colonial poets, Edward Taylor, belongs to the school of John Donne and George Herbert is thus a natural inference. But when one considers why Taylor, for all his merits, is not so good a poet, one finds the cause in a difference of attitude rather than skill. Something in Taylor's mind acts as an impediment to metaphysical poetry, forcing him to hold back, as it were. He cannot fully exploit the conceit, because however elaborately developed, it remains for him an analogy. In the well-known "Huswifery," for instance, he begins much as Herbert does with a homely comparison, praying that he may serve as the spinning wheel and loom upon which God will fabricate his salvation, but as the poem continues, one begins to miss the requisite opportunism of metaphysical poetry. Instead of developing the conceit toward a conclusive image or shifting through a series of conceits until such an image is found, he proceeds by a doggedly systematic spelling out of his comparison:

> Then cloath therewith mine Understanding, Will,
>   Affections, Judgment, Conscience, Memory
> My Words, and Actions, that their shine may fill
> My wayes with glory and thee glorify.
> Then mine apparell shall display before yee
> That I am Cloathed in Holy robes for glory.[17]

Thus the poem, which began with a daring conceit, ends in religious commonplace. The failure is significant: Taylor cannot

16. "A Poem Dedicated to the Memory of the Reverend and Excellent Urian Oakes," in *Early American Poetry*, 3, 6.

17. All quotations from Taylor are given according to the text of *The Poems of Edward Taylor*, ed. Donald E. Stanford (New Haven, Yale University Press, 1960), p. 467.

unite the sensible object and the universal meaning, because his way of seeing precludes his doing so.

The metaphysical poem develops toward a perfect fusion of vehicle and tenor. In the celebrated concluding line, "Therefore that he may raise the Lord throws down," Donne does not mean that his sickness is a sign or parallel of the afflictions by which God effects his salvation.[18] His being thrown down—his physical demise—is literally the divine means of raising him up to immortal life. But Taylor's holy robes are a mere sign and cannot be visualized as real clothing. Puritanism commits him to sustaining the contrast between the present and eternal aspects of reality. To end the poem by asserting their unity is the metaphysical poet's intent, but the Puritan can hardly believe that it is possible to reach such a point of rest. To do so, he would have to alter his whole view of experience.

Excepting images derived from God's revealed word, the Puritan views his symbols as but temporary points of resolution in the unending commerce between the mind's present moment and God's eternal will. If this perspective explains the failure of "Huswifery," it is also the source of Taylor's most typical successes. In the magnificent "Preface" to "God's Determinations," for example, the need to keep the temporal and eternal apart works in his favor. God's power is the theme, and in that it is an infinite and unimaginable power, the more Taylor can insist upon the disparity of vehicle and tenor the better. In that God is almighty, his power nullifies all distinctions between the greatest and the least, the precious and the base, the exalted and the trivial, so that the creation of the world can be imaged through the inventory of a dressing table:

> Who Lac'de and Filletted the earth so fine,
> With Rivers like green Ribbons Smaragdine:

18. "Hymn to God My God, in My Sicknesse," in *The Poems of John Donne,* ed. Sir Herbert Grierson (London, Oxford University Press, 1933), p. 337.

50

> Who made the Sea's its Selvedge, and it locks
> Like a Quilt Ball within a Silver Box? [19]

It is Taylor's point that these fantastic comparisons cannot be explained—that they in no way effect a reconciliation between the world known to man's experience and its infinitely powerful creator but point, rather, to the mystery of a God "Whose Little finger at his pleasure Can/ Out mete ten thousand worlds with halfe a Span." It is significant that in treating the Incarnation, Taylor is far more impressed by the mystery of God's becoming man than by the reconciliation it effects:

> Things styld transcendent, do transcende the Stile
> Of Reason, reason's stares neere reach so high.
> But Jacob's golden Ladder rounds do foile
> All Reasons Strides, wrought of Theanthropie.
> Two Natures distance-standing, infinite,
> Are Onified, in person, and Unite.
> In Essence two, in Properties each are
> Unlike, as unlike can be. One All-Might
> A Mite the other; One Immortall fair.
> One mortall, this all Glory, that all night.
> One Infinite, One finite. So for ever:
> Yet ONED are in Person, part'd never.[20]

The passage is not a distinguished one, but it shows that the wonder which gives Taylor's devotional poems their peculiarly charming excitement has its source in a mode of experience quite different from that of the metaphysical poet.

Even more than their lyric poetry, the Puritans' narrative writings reflect the dualism of the Puritan world view, for narrative action is a series of events developing sequentially through time,

19. *The Poems of Edward Taylor*, p. 387.
20. Ibid., p. 161.

yet such movement cannot easily be accommodated to either the divine or human viewpoints. To God all events are simultaneously present, so that from the point of view of eternity an action is really a static pattern; and eternity is, as it were, the "whole truth"—that which the human mind approximates to the extent that it sees rightly. On the other hand, when an action is regarded from the human point of view, from the present in which a man finds himself, its narrative movement also tends to be negated. Though the present is, in one sense, the opposite of eternity—time itself, the only time which really exists—it is also a duration within which no time passes; it exists only to the extent that time has been arrested.[21] To be sure, man sees events happen and time pass, but what is real and true in a story is to be found in the experiential now, where things simply *are*. Thus, whether consciously or not, the Puritan writer of narrative finds himself obliged to depict action through stasis. His developing story is perforce something in the past, whether or not he chooses to recount it in present-tense narration. But what is real to him is what now is or what always is. The story must therefore be brought into one or both of these areas of credible fact, and in the process it will, of course, cease to be a story—will no longer develop as a sequence of events moving forward through time.

Puritan histories are, in fact, notably static. In Bradford's *Of Plimouth Plantation,* for example, the story of cause and effect relations is much less important than the isolated episode. That it is through episodes that Bradford works is shown by the virtual disappearance of the narrative line after the arrival at Plymouth, by Bradford's admission that his data are arranged as annals, and by the difficulty the reader has in trying to place later events chronologically, with respect to each other. For example, at just which point does the story of Merrymount occur? One would have to look the matter up to answer, because, memorable and

21. What I have referred to as a present duration is sometimes termed the "specious present," presumably on the ground that it is subjective, whereas it is supposed that the time in terms of which every moment is divisible is not.

interesting as this episode is, its significance has little to do with its place in a sequence of other happenings. The causal relations are there, of course: Bradford explains how Wollaston established his trading post, how the group there fell into evil ways, how the Puritans came to take action. The meaning of the episode, however, is much less concerned with what preceded and followed it than with the reference it individually makes to transcendent truths. This is apparent in Bradford's analogy comparing the maypole to the Philistines' deity, Dagon, whose image fell to the ground in the presence of the Ark of the Covenant. Though the Puritan triumph over the revelers is a justification of the Puritan point of view and thus, it could be concluded, an explanation of what caused the successful establishment of the colony, still it should be noticed how very directly the line of causation runs back to God's will. What happened at Merrymount seems to be much less dependent upon such necessary preconditions as the arrival of the *Mayflower* than upon the immediate influence of the divine will. Bradford implies that the nature of things in the world God has created is such that behavior so offensive to the moral law and so contrary to the interests of God's people cannot for long go unpunished. One feels that the fate of Morton and his followers would be much the same at almost any time and place. Instead of tracing out causation through a sequence of events, Bradford illustrates causation by example. This is the natural procedure for a Puritan historian, for granting the assumption that to the predestinarian God all events coexist as elements of a timeless pattern, then it follows that each happening has this plan as its total meaning, and instead of sequences progressively developed in time, the historian considers each event as a unique point of view, a juncture at which the divine plan can be seen from a new angle.

It is this rationale that explains the mysterious charm and effectiveness of Bradford's history. The reader accepts it as history without quite knowing why, so much closer is it to a chronicle or memoir. Bradford seems quite innocent of the historian's usual purposes. Far from formulating any definite theory of history, he does not even seem to try very hard to prove the relevance of his theological ideas, which seem simply to be taken for granted. Having as his subject the experience of a few hundred people, he cannot focus upon events of the magnitude of those which political history has traditionally treated. On the other hand, the materials for a modern social history are too scant and incidental to place the work in that genre. Bradford's whole conception of what constitutes a historical event is, in fact, peculiar. The modern reader would agree with Bradford that the decimation of the Massachusetts Indians by plague is a historical event, but he would be inclined to laugh off the idea that the death by sickness of a cruel and profane sailor aboard the *Mayflower* was too.

One must ask, then, what point of view would allow a historian to regard both happenings as historical in the same sense. It would be one affording a perspective in which progression and development are relatively less important than the analogy between isolated occasions and eternal principles. It is with respect to causation that the sailor's death and the plague are too different to seem relevant to each other. Commines could treat such moralistic episodes historically because the persons involved are the greatest political figures, but Bradford's sailor lacks social importance and one cannot imagine how his death could possibly have much effect on other happenings. However, if the reader forgets about causation and considers instead the emblematic possibilities of our two events, he will see that they are mutually relevant. As emblems, they make reference to the same meaning.

In a very general sense all of Bradford's episodes are intended to show God's dealings with his chosen people, but this formulation is imprecise because the local significance of passages is various and usually a matter of implication. Indeed, Bradford is far less didactic than the now prevailing notions of Puritan literary theory would lead one to suppose. Rather than teaching succinct lessons, his events present different points of view, so that while all ultimately refer to God's plan, each episode reveals a unique aspect. The unity of the work is the result of Bradford's remarkable ability to make all the episodes consistent in tone and harmonious in implication. Thus, though there is a diversity of religious meanings—though, for example, the Merrymount tale focuses attention upon the ethical aspect of God's will, while such matters as the accounts of fishing and farming illustrate the chastening influences of Providence—these more particular meanings are so well integrated that the reader can infer an all-inclusive plan which is at once beyond man's understanding yet the source of reasonable explanations.

Considered by itself, the form of Bradford's history might seem fortuitous and one might be tempted to conclude that the unity of a work whose organization has so casual a look is the result, not of art, but merely of a consistent point of view. Yet such unity is a literary achievement of some importance, however unconsciously the author may have worked. The value, as art, of Bradford's literary method becomes more apparent when it is compared with that of such a contemporary historian as Edward Johnson.

Johnson has epic intentions, and his *Wonderworking Providence* begins fortissimo with an explicit account of God's purposes:

> Christ Jesus intending to manifest his Kingly Office toward his Churches more fully than ever yet the Sons of men saw, even to the uniting of Jew and Gentile Churches in one Faith, begins with our English Nation (whose former reformation being vere imperfect) doth now resolve to cast down their false foundation of Prelacy, even in the hight of their domineering dignity. And therefore in the yeere 1628, he stirres up his servants as the Heralds of a King to make this proclamation for volunteers, as followeth.[22]

The Deity's instructions are then set forth in the manner of Deuteronomy. But whenever Johnson descends from the moun-

22. *Johnson's Wonderworking Providence*, Vol. 10 of *Narratives of Early American History*, ed. J. Franklin Jameson (New York, Scribners, 1910), p. 24.

tain of panoramic vision to the level of the modest facts he has to relate, the effect is bathetic and confusing. Not that his theme is a minor one or less than universal in meaning, but that it is of a nature unsuited to his narrative method. Portraying God acting in the manner of an epic character (consider the statement that Christ "doth now resolve" to overthrow Prelacy) is difficult to square with predestinarian theory, but even more troublesome is the general perspective such statements assume. History is not to be seen from either of the two credible Puritan viewpoints—that of omniscience or that of the ordinary individual. Rather, it is to be witnessed in the traditional European mode of heroic narrative, where the main actors are somewhat bigger than life and their deeds are ritual enactments of communal experience rather than types of the average person's behavior. Within such a context Johnson's kind of fact is absurdly out of place, as the chapter headings frequently illustrate. Chapter 37 of Book I is entitled "Of the gratious goodness of God, in hearing his peoples' prayers in times of need, and of the Ship-loades of goods the Lord sent them in." Whether or not Johnson himself wrote the headings, the failure of tone in this one illustrates the failure of perspective throughout his history. The fault is neither in the theory of providential interpretation per se nor in Johnson's quaint worldliness in using it. It is in the procedure of treating emblematic episodes as if they were events in a cause and effect sequence. Doubtless the coming of the supply ships was an important event and therefore to the Puritan mind a fitting emblem of the providential help they often received, but as an event in a narrative sequence it is inappropriate because there its cause and effect relations are too narrowly practical to tie it in on any other level than that of physical causation. Providence caused the ships' arrival directly by supernatural means, not indirectly through a set of earlier events extending backward in time toward the period when the ships' keels were laid. Johnson's episodes are symbolic as individual facts rather than as parts of a larger story, with the result that his efforts to see narratively are always defeated by his unconscious preference for seeing typically.

The characteristic effect is one of petering out as the attempted narrative bogs down in random detail. For instance, when he undertakes an account "Of the laborious worke Christ's people have in planting this wilderness," he decides to proceed by using the foundation of Concord as an example, since Concord was the first inland settlement.[23] Thus, at the outset, story is replaced by emblem, since Concord's story is to stand for the whole process of colonization. Actually even Concord's story does not get told, the chapter consisting instead of an assortment of details and anecdotes, as for instance that the forest underbrush soon wears out stockings, that a maid lost her way but returned after three days, that the settlers often had no meat except such venison and "rockoons" as they could buy from the savages. Similarly, chapter 23 of Book II discusses the union of the New England colonies by giving some reasons for it and pointing out that in the resultant undertaking Massachusetts bore the greatest burden without having commensurate representation. Then the remainder and greater part of the chapter tells of Miantomeno's plot to murder Uncas and his eventual execution for the crime. The only relation of this episode to the uniting of the colonies is the incidental fact that a joint commission investigated Miantomeno's case. How the union was brought about—the events, the story—Johnson does not recount, nor does he indicate how, in terms of causation, the story about Miantomeno is related to other public events. Here, as throughout the *Wonderworking Providence,* the historian's vision is such that the customary narrative connections are out of focus.

As the most ambitious of seventeenth-century historical works, Cotton Mather's *Magnalia* provides the clearest evidence that Bradford's episodic method marks the beginning of a traditional form which becomes increasingly conscious and elaborate. The *Magnalia* begins with an account of the early years of the colony,

23. Ibid., pp. 111–15.

and since this is brief, adding little to Bradford's history, from which Mather borrowed, it has the air of a story. But when this initial sketching out of events is completed, Mather abandons chronological narration in order to go back over the same period again and again as he recounts the lives of notable magistrates and divines. In effect, the historical period 1620–ca. 1670 is held up as a unified whole for the reader's examination, as the successive biographical chapters display it from a series of different points of view. This is not a denial of time's passing or of history as sequence so much as a reformulation of them. It is because Mather is intensely interested in history, because he regards it as the medium through which God deals with mankind, that he would break down the generalized outlines of the New England past into specific episodes. For, with respect to the nation's history, the individual "lives" are episodes, just as the remarkable Providences are. Of course there is progression of a sort in the *Magnalia:* the groups of lives tend to be arranged by generation, though not much attention is drawn to this; and while the last book and the appendix deal primarily with the Indian troubles from the seventies to the end of the century, the sketches of notable Harvard graduates mark a shift to later decades. But the chronological pattern is muted by Mather's topical and illustrative manner of dividing up his materials. It is highly significant that he prefers to treat theological matters in one book, to group all the magistrates into another, and to devote yet another to the sundry trials of New England. In a history of this scope it is something of a feat to have avoided sequential narration as effectively as Mather has. One need only compare the plan of the *Magnalia* with that of the greatest English historical work of the period, Clarendon's *True Historical Narrative of the Rebellion and Civil Wars,* to recognize how fundamental is the Puritan historian's divergence from the norm of narrative progression, which even today seems the most natural arrangement.

The objection that Mather's method may have been a merely slapdash procedure is of but slight relevance. If it were true that he simply put together a brief history, borrowing most of his materials, and then added to this a collection of "lives," sermons, and miscellaneous articles, most of which had been written at an earlier time, one would still have to conclude that the arrangement of the *Magnalia* seemed to him an entirely proper form of history. Nor does the *Magnalia's* didactic intent alter the case: that Mather thought a history so written would be effective as propaganda indicates all the more clearly that its form reflects the prevailing sense of time. Actually there is much evidence of conscious artistry in the design of the *Magnalia,* most especially in Mather's use of sermons to frame and underline his meaning.

Mather's meaning is somewhat more narrowly defined than Bradford's, since his account is specifically designed to prove that the Puritans are indeed God's chosen by recounting how in the past the Deity rewarded their righteousness and punished their backslidings. Even so, Mather's meaning is of the same sort, a meaning which is always wholly there and never changes. It is the kind of meaning which history must necessarily have to the minds of men who believe that all events issue from the will of a predestining God. It is history having a form which foreshadows many of the distinctive traits of later narrative art in America.

The first of these is the paradoxical technique of arresting time, yet making it seem to run on toward infinity. By emphasizing the isolated moment, the Puritan historian intensifies the sense of time's passing, for in stressing the sameness of all moments in their potential significance, he implies an endless succession as well as a static eternity. In American fiction this duality is manifest in the technique of containing all time within the present moment, while simultaneously extending time in such a way as to imply that what now is will always be. Thus in Faulkner's *Light in August* Lena Grove's journey traces the unending path between December and August, birth and death, while Joe Christmas' end is also a beginning—Christmas, a moment which embraces every temporal phase in a single duration.

The second of such traits—the Puritan historian's technique of presenting his whole story in small before working it out in detail —is reflected in the American novelist's tendency to begin with a symbolic episode which summarizes his action by posing the question to be explained: Isabel Archer entering the garden, Huck Finn squirming under Miss Watson's religious instruction, Jake Barnes being disconcerted by Cohn's complaint that he isn't living life to the hilt, Hester Prynne stepping onto the scaffold.

However, the most striking of the resemblances between Puritan historical writings and American novels is the convertibility of story into state of mind and vice versa. The events which occur in series as parts of a temporally unfolding action are also to be thought of as the content of an all-embracing consciousness. The journey of the *Pequod* extends temporally as a narrative what is, from another point of view, the dialectic of Ishmael's philosophizing, and the mood of Quentin Compson and his roommate, Shreve, as they converse one night in 1910 contains the whole history of the Sutpens. How a novelistic form of this kind develops from the early historians' way of treating events is most effectively suggested by a familiar poem of Emily Dickinson. When the lady in "Because I Could Not Stop for Death" discovers where her courtly escort, Death, is taking her, she sees the whole journey in an instant, and sees, too, that it is a journey without an end:

> Since then—'tis Centuries—and yet
> Feels shorter than the Day
> I first surmised the Horses Heads
> Were toward Eternity—[24]

Since poetry requires a patterning which is more than merely serviceable, the traits and tendencies of Puritan chronicles are even more apparent in efforts at verse narrative. Here the failures are instructive as demonstrations of what could not be accom-

24. *The Poems of Emily Dickinson,* ed. Thomas H. Johnson (3 vols. Cambridge, Mass., Harvard University Press, 1958), 2, 546.

plished and therefore of the limits within which a proper form would have to be found. "New England's Crisis" is an exaggerated example of the Puritan's inability to make a story "move." [25] Though Benjamin Tompson's subject is King Philip's War, which by nature would surely seem to invite a simple linear progression and make any other plan seem difficult, Tompson is so fixed in his interest in the isolated episode that the task of linking the events into a sequence proves quite beyond his capabilities. Hence his work is not a narrative poem but a series of tableaux, even though they do appear in chronological order. While Tompson is no artist, his way of failing is characteristic. The static view merely arrests action rather than explaining it.

Wigglesworth is of course a more skillful poet—or verse-maker, at least—but *The Day of Doom* illustrates the opposite side of the Puritan's difficulties. Here sequence is all; instead of halting, the poet "runs on." Wigglesworth conceives the Last Judgment as a debate in which one by one, the classes of sinners step before God's throne to plead for salvation and Christ explains the predestinarian logic as it applies in each case. By repeating the same pattern, Wigglesworth can review the various objections to his theology and through Christ's replies elucidate the Puritan system. That the monotony of this plan was not thought a fault—the poem was extremely popular—indicates that it reflects a view congenial to its audience. The preternatural smoothness of the poem as it spins on and on as equably as a cart on ball bearings must have impressed the Puritan reader with the sense of divine inevitability. Since God's will is timeless, the Last Judgment is not really an event or completed action but a continuous activity —hence the oppressive monotony of Wigglesworth's repetitions: his simple linear movement is quite unsuited to his static subject, and he can only proceed by adding more and more and more.

Edward Taylor seems to have understood, as Wigglesworth did not, that the predestinarian faith bore directly upon the nature of narrative. In "God's Determinations" he provides the first exam-

25. See *Early American Poetry, 1,* 5–29.

ple in poetry of the rather special ways of manipulating time which would become characteristic of American narrative literature. The beauty of this remarkable work is not at first apparent. Except for two of the poems—the "Preface" and "The Joy of Church Fellowship"—the cycle is little known, but to be appreciated it must be read as a whole, and read several times, so that the mind can learn to adjust to Taylor's particular perspective. The total design counts for a great deal, and unless one reads the poems with that whole plan in mind, most of them will seem dull or, at best, naïvely primitive. To say this is to acknowledge the poet's understanding of his theme, his sense that for him or any believing Puritan the story developing through time in a series of events must also appear, from another point of view, as a fixed pattern, God's plan. Though he clearly believes the latter to be the whole truth, his healthy respect for time gives "God's Determination," a validity lacking in *The Day of Doom*. And Taylor's purpose, unlike Wigglesworth's, is not simply that of versifying dogma; he regards doctrinal instruction as merely the means to a larger intent—to hearten and inspire the despairing soul. Thus retribution is not pictured, is scarcely mentioned in fact, and at the end he tolerantly concedes that many who never enter the chariot of the covenanted Church will get to heaven afoot. Taylor's charitable purpose commits him to viewing the things of religion from within time, as the ordinary mortal must, and here he recognizes a torturing dubiety for which faith, rather than Wigglesworth's detached logic, is the ultimate answer. Taylor was enough of a theorist to see that he could not surrender the narrow present of human understanding because he must also believe in the deity's eternal will; and he was enough of a poet to see that his dual allegiance called for narrative of a double kind.

Taylor's essential method is to construct his story in such a way that at each stage it provides both a movement and a panorama. Like the Puritan historians, he works through static episodes. The individual poem, or group of poems, constitutes an isolated moment within which nothing happens, since this moment depicts a state of mind, not an event. Seen in sequence, however, the moments represent phases in the story of the soul's development, and Taylor can therefore trace a narrative movement as he progresses through a series of contrasting states of consciousness, even though within each state time is arrested. The method would not seem very different from that which is common in the sonnet sequence were it not that Taylor has complicated it by another sort of doubleness: seen as an individual, the soul is a character developing as he moves forward through time, but since the soul is also a type—the Christian at any point in history—in the soul's story Taylor represents universal history as the static pattern of God's will.

This double view is manifest in the contrast between the poem as story and as exposition of doctrine. In one respect, "God's Determinations" is a universal history: the "Preface" treats the Creation, the first poem pictures the Fall of man, the next two recount God's judgment of Adam, and the rest of the poems survey the consequences of original sin for those whom God has elected, concluding with "The Joy of Church Fellowship," in which the saints' immortal happiness is foreseen. But this history is of a peculiar kind. After the "Preface" and the first three poems, Taylor's focus is narrowed to the small band of the elect, and thenceforth no biblical events are portrayed, not even those of Christ's earthly mission. Even in the opening poems, events are strangely nonhistorical. The "Preface," for example, does not recount Creation as a story but celebrates it lyrically as a symbol of God's infinite power; while the following poem, as its title—"The Effects of Man's Apostacy"—makes plain, defines the human situation rather than describing the effects in and through happenings. In fact, it will be seen that all the poems are to be viewed doubly as pictures of particular persons at certain moments and as allegories in which the moments are hypothetical and the ranks of the elect but images of the soul. This duality is clearly illus-

63

trated by a revealing error on Taylor's part in entitling one of the poems "The Soul's Address to Christ against These Assaults," even though it is "we" rather than "I" who speak.[26]

The broad scope of this work—it runs to almost 2,000 lines, or scarcely less than Shakespeare's sonnet sequence—enables Taylor to manage various kinds of development. There is, for instance, a skillful modification of focus much like that by which the movie camera narrows from a panoramic view to a close-up. Taylor begins by limning the broad outlines of doctrine; for example, in the third poem, "A Dialogue between Justice and Mercy," he presents what may be called the rationale of atonement. From this diagrammatic view the poem gradually narrows to a poignantly immediate rendering of the individual soul's dilemmas. Then in the last few poems Taylor deftly draws the reader back to the more detached position, the more nearly all-inclusive view:

> In Heaven soaring up, I dropt an Eare
> On Earth; and oh! sweet Melody:
> And listening, found it was the Saints who were
> Encoacht for Heaven that sang for Joy.[27]

So begins the concluding "Joy of Church Fellowship," which seems no more than a precursor of the four-square-gospel hymn if we fail to notice the change of perspective it effects. The return to the panoramic view unifies the work by bringing the reader back to the initial mode of vision and in an important way enacting the everlasting by making it seem that God's all-inclusive view persists through all others. More important still, the concluding panorama is needed as a parallel to the initial ones as a demonstration that now the theological doctrines, though no less broad or abstract, can be seen as truths personally felt.

This effect can easily be recognized by comparing the "Preface" with "Our Insufficiency to Praise God Suitably." Both poems praise the infinite nature of God, and both do so by developing a

26. *The Poems of Edward Taylor*, pp. 404–05.
27. Ibid., p. 458.

paradox which is rigidly abstract. In the "Preface" the feeling
thus expressed is an awe which is mainly rational—the wonder of
encountering a mystery of logic: "Its Onely Might Almighty this
did doe . . . Which all from Nothing fet, from Nothing all;/
Hath all on Nothing set, lets Nothing fall." [28] In "Our Insufficiency," however, the emotion is more keenly felt, even though
the All-Nothing paradox is now even more abstractly stated. By
the stark rationality of geometrical progression—if every atom
were a world as populous as ours, and every pious man in every
world had as many tongues to sing, and if every tongue could sing
as many songs—Taylor somehow manages to give his extravagant
mathematics the quality of personal feeling:

> Now should all these Conspire in us that we
>> Could breath such Praise to thee, Most High
>> Should we thy Sounding Organs be
>>> To ring such Melody?
> Our Musick would the World of Worlds out ring
> Yet be unfit within thine Eares to ting.
>
>>> . . .
>
> Though eer our Tongues thy Praises due can fan
>> A Weevle with the World may fly,
>> Yea fly away: and with a span
>>> We may out mete the Sky.
> Though what we can is but a Lisp, We pray
> Accept thereof. We have no better pay. [29]

Thus dogma reappears as personal conviction, and what at first
was asserted as principle is at last justified as the wisdom of the
heart.

The design which informs "Song of Myself" and *Four Quartets*
is already emergent in "God's Determinations." It is the pattern of
movement from problematical generalities—"every atom belong-

28. Ibid., pp. 387–88.
29. Ibid., pp. 452–53.

ing to me as good belongs to you"; "Only through time, time is conquered"—to a personal experience which elucidates by interpreting them, and then, at the end, to the initial beliefs, which now at last have the authority of truths the self has lived as well as considered. Taylor, no less than Whitman and Eliot, realizes that managing an action of this sort is the art of repeating the whole pattern in small in each phase of the poem's development. At every point the reader senses that to some extent the event is presently transpiring and to some extent merely typical, and as the perspective shifts more toward one or toward the other view, his mind passes through various related but delicately distinguished modes of experience.

"God's Determinations" also reveals another and complementary sort of action, one which can best be described by saying that the nature of time itself is continually altering. As the duration—the panorama of times simultaneously viewed—is enlarged or contracted, not only the pace but the very structure of time changes. The "Preface" presents the widest imaginable view, as indicated by the way it begins: "Infinity, when all things it beheld . . ." In the twenty-first poem—"The Souls Doubts Touching Its Sins Answerd"—the moment is of quite a different kind:

SOUL
This is my Sin, My Sin I love, but hate
God and his Grace. And who's in such a state?
My Love, and Hatred do according rise
Unto Sins height, and unto Grace's sise.

SAINT
I thought as you when first to make me see
God powred out his Spirit sweet on mee.
But oh stange Fetch! What Love, yet hate to have?
And hate in heart what heartily you Crave? [30]

30. Ibid., p. 435.

Repeated readings are required to become sensitive to this delicate modulation of time, but the reader's patience is well repaid. For it is the subtle ground rhythm of the whole poem as it pauses or speeds, overleaps vast temporal spaces or paces slowly along the ratiocinative path, which brings the lines of individual poems to life. The reader participates in the movement as a change in his own perspective, and for that reason the beauty of the work cannot be illustrated well by quotation.

Taylor has Hawthorne's gift for winding into the center of the self's perplexities, and his analysis of the stressful moment shows very considerable skill. Consider, for example, these lines from the poem in which SAINT advises SOUL concerning "Some of Satans Sophestry."

> With Wiles enough, he on his thoughts intrudes,
>   That God's a Heape of Contradictions high,
> But when these thoughts man from his thoughts excludes
>   Thou knowst not then (saith he) this Mystery.
>   And when the first String breaks, he strives to bring
>   Into sins brambles by the other string.
>
> When God Calls out a Soule, he subtilly
>   Said God is kinde: you need not yet forsake
> Your Sins: but if he doth, he doth reply,
>   Thou'st outstood. Justice will vengeance take,
>   You to despare, beholding Justice bright.
>
> Though just before mans mountain sins were mites,
>   His mites were nothing. Now the scales are turn'd.
> His mites are mountains now, of mighty height
>   And must with Vengeance-Lightening be burn'd.
>   Greate Sins are Small, till men repent of Sin:
>   Then Small are far too big to be forgi'n.[31]

Read by itself, this passage seems no more than an exercise of intelligence, impressively forceful perhaps but hardly dra-

31. Ibid., p. 445.

matic. If one is struck by the vigor of the lines, one is apt to conclude rather too simply that it results from the sincerity of a "primitive" poet or that the robust health of metaphysical style still survives in Taylor's imitation. But sincerity and vigor are, after all, poetic effects—they must be conveyed somehow—and a closer examination of the passage will show that Taylor's forceful manner depends very much upon his rather odd undertaking, an attempt to ravel out the subtlest psychological dubieties in the most general language. Hawthorne's shadowy misgivings are of just the kind that Taylor's SAINT describes:

> Except for that small expenditure in the decoration of her infant, Hester bestowed all her superfluous means in charity, on wretches less miserable than herself, and who not unfrequently insulted the hand that fed them. Much of the time, which she might readily have applied to the better efforts of her art, she employed in making coarse garments for the poor. It is probable that there was an idea of penance in this mode of occupation, in devoting so many hours to such rude handiwork. . . . Women derive a pleasure, incomprehensible to the other sex, from the delicate toil of the needle. . . . To Hester Prynne it might have been a mode of expressing, and therefore soothing, the passion of her life. Like all other joys, she rejected it as sin. This morbid meddling of conscience with an immaterial matter betokened, it is to be feared, no genuine and steadfast penitence, but something doubtful, something that might be deeply wrong, beneath.[32]

The difference—and one can grant that it is a difference which proves Hawthorne the greater artist—is that Hawthorne's doubts are focused upon a more fully realized character: SOUL is but a sketch, Hester a flesh-and-blood individual. But this particularity is achieved through an augmented detachment—the immediate and the general being forced even further apart than they were in

32. *The Scarlet Letter*, ed. William Charvat et al. (Columbus, Ohio State University Press, 1962), chap. 5, pp. 83–84.

Puritan experience—so that the elaborately detailed personality is seen through the eyes of a narrator so remote that he stands outside of any formulated system. Hawthorne's narrator is not even *not* a Puritan, whereas the doubts expressed in Taylor's poem are simply the character's. SAINT knows exactly what SOUL's scruples are and why they are wrong. By contrast, it is Hawthorne, not Hester, who entertains SOUL's sort of worry. Hester in her simple way has merely taken a stand against pleasure, and it is through the narrator's suspicion that the reader becomes aware of the subliminal uncertainty beneath her resolve. The subtle presence of feelings so deeply buried in consciousness contributes to the effect of complexity that makes Hester a convincing character.

In Hawthorne the Puritan's agonized questioning has been split in two. It appears as the kind of subconscious and merely felt tension revealed in the characters because the intelligence which analyzes it as a conscious doubt is committed to an idea of the truth so abstract that all principles are problematical. Thus the character who is a skillful analyst is tragically isolated. And thus Hawthorne, the descendant of a Puritan judge, is "a writer of story-books," for eternity has swallowed up every other Puritan tenet. All is hypothesis and hence a fertile ground for fictional supposing, except the certainty that the truth is immutable law. The existence of language, of the letter, is the only undoubted fact, and its true meaning is signified by its fixity. Through language's power to make interpretation a continuous and universal process, Hester's world and Hawthorne's are made one, and the sameness of the human situation manifests man's fate by revealing its permanent conditions. But Hawthorne's fiction also illustrates the fact that the more the eternal nature of a truth is emphasized, the vaguer it becomes; he is naturally a novelist because he is convinced that there is an eternal design, yet is so uncertain of its pattern that he must see it with respect to various views.

Taylor enjoys the assurance of faith. He knows the pattern, and if his certainty makes him less subtle as a psychologist, it makes him more precise:

> Faith is without Assurance shuffled out,
> And if Assurance be, that's still a Doubt.[33]

There is much feeling behind this cool reasonableness. Though the problem is schematic in that it applies to the merely typical soul, so firm and so explicit is Taylor's faith that what is generally true of Man seems just as true of the individual. Without ever leaving the abstract level of dogma, Taylor is able to show how the self can writhe. Thus soul, though lacking character, is intensely human. He is caught in the web of tangled generalities—tragically ensnared because his bonds are, on the one hand, eternally fixed rules and, on the other hand, not bonds at all but elements of a rational design which the self, from within its narrow mortal span, is unable to discern. The immediate doubt lives in the abstract certitude, and its life endows Taylor's poetry with drama of a vivid kind.

The mode of thought revealed in the typical features of Puritan narrative is no less apparent in the Puritan way of viewing nature. The common Christian tendency to read nature as God's second book is abnormally prominent in Puritan literature, demonstrating again the taste for analogy. But if the Puritan mind regards nature as a compendium of useful texts, it favors no less the contrary view of nature as a very direct sort of revelation. Nature is simply the creation of the transcendent deity and therefore a volume to be read as evidence of the author's intentions, but it is also a world in which God's will is continuously operative and through the presence of his will in events in nature, his immanence as the Holy Spirit is revealed. Symbolism follows from the second view as analogy does from the first. The natural event is both God acting and yet merely a sign of his purposes. Though logic may cast doubt upon this paradox, to the Puritan mind it was valid and important.

33. *The Poems of Edward Taylor*, pp. 466–67.

Granted that the design of nature is not to be separated from the Creator's will—that, in as much as the order God willed at the beginning still persists, the willing also continues— Christianity nevertheless assumes that there is an absolute difference between the natural and spiritual orders. In Puritan thought this distinction receives unusual emphasis, for when the question of election becomes the self's primary concern, the means of grace acquire a corresponding interest, and when at the same time the mediation of priest, church, and sacrament is denied, God's influence upon the individual can only be considered in terms of the narrow alternatives of natural or supernatural means. In effect, no other kind of means exists. Puritanism assumed that the redeemed man is dealt with through exceptional means, while the reprobate is allowed to live out his days in the world of unredeemed nature and with the aid of his merely natural faculties, which are corrupted as a consequence of original sin. Providences are exceptional events in which God's hand interposes to alter the ordinary course of nature. The Puritan therefore always confronted the question of whether a particular event should be accounted unusual or normal. Thus Governor Bradford, after interpreting the earthquake as a sign of God's displeasure, went on to say:

> It was observed that the summers for divers years together after this earthquake were not so hot and seasonable for the ripening of corn and other fruits as formerly, but more cold and moist, and subject to early and untimely frosts by which, many times, much Indian corn came not to maturity. But whether this was any cause I leave it to the naturalists to judge.[34]

The question Bradford so casually raised gives a glimpse of the problem which in Edwards was to become critical. Bradford could feel sure about the earthquake and leave the bad weather to the naturalists, but the more introspective Puritan would be forced to recognize the problem of distinguishing in his experience between those things which were in the course of nature and

34. *Of Plymouth Plantation*, p. 302.

those which manifested the workings of grace. Even if the latter were found and the longed-for assurance obtained, nature would still remain problematical. The Puritan would still have to maintain the balance between his sense of God as transcendent ruler and as immanent Spirit, avoiding a heretical pantheism, while insisting upon God's presence in the natural phenomenon.

Taylor's "Upon a Wasp Chilled with Cold" illustrates the form of Puritan nature experience and the odd use of language it fostered. Its moralizing pattern is typical in that, like Bryant's waterfowl, the wasp is first described in a way which draws analogies to the human condition—she lies "In Sol's warm breath and shine as saving"; she rubs her head "As if her velvet helmet high/ Did turret rationality"—so that when the picture is complete, the reader has been prepared for the lesson the poet extracts:

> Lord, clear my misted sight that I
> May hence view thy Divinity,
> Some sparks whereof thou up dost hasp
> Within this little downy wasp,
> In whose small corporation we
> A school and a schoolmaster see;
> Where we may learn, and easily find
> A nimble sprit, bravely mind
> Her work in ev'ry limb: and lace
> It up neat with a vital grace,
> Acting each part though ne'er so small,
> Here of this fustian animal.[35]

"Divinity" and "grace" play the same crucial role as "Power" in Bryant's poem, striking a balance, through double-entendre, between God's immanence and transcendence. Divinity is seen as Godhead but also as mere theology; grace is meant in the spiritual sense but then as simply an outward beauty. From one point of view the wasp manifests God as present in the operations of nature; from another, it is a "school" indicating God's will

35. *The Poems of Edward Taylor,* pp. 466–67.

through the instructive ideas it suggests. And while Taylor depends more upon such verbal wit than upon Bryant's shifting of perspective, at the end he too departs toward higher ground:

> Till I enravished climb into
> The Godhead on this ladder do:
> Where all my pipes inspired upraise
> An heavenly music, furr'd with praise.[36]

Two lines are so indicative of Puritan experience that they may fitly be quoted once again.

> Lord, clear my misted sight that I
> May hence view thy Divinity . . .

The request is a peculiar one: Taylor prays that God will empower him to find the meaning he already sees. The self-consciousness already noted—the sort of awareness which makes the American writer unusually attentive to his own symbolizing—has its source in the scruple apparent here. Knowing is not enough. The Puritan conscience demanded what Edwards would call "a sense of the divine excellency" of religious truths rather than a merely "notional" understanding.[37] Thus the experience of nature was a crucial test; the self's spiritual condition could be seen no more clearly than in its way of responding to the physical objects immediately before it. Being able to draw appropriate lessons from nature was not a sufficient sign of grace, since the unregenerate could be as well informed in matters of doctrine and morality as the saints. One had to find evidence of something more than natural understanding, to discover the feelings of a sanctified heart. And the determining of one's true feelings was really a matter of discerning how they arose and whither they tended. The Puritan studied his symbolizing because he thought

36. Ibid.
37. See Edwards' sermon, "A Divine and Supernatural Light," in *Puritan Sage: Collected Writings of Jonathan Edwards*, ed. Vergilius Ferm (New York, Library Publishers, 1953), pp. 160–62, for a characteristic statement on this subject.

the power to interpret was in itself as auspicious a sign of grace as the interpretation. The tedious piety of Cotton Mather's journal illustrates how much assurance could be gained from the mere activity of symbolizing: a more sensitive man than Mather would have been concerned to see how well he symbolized rather than how much, would have questioned whether his feelings were behind his interpretations, whether his heart assented to the lessons he knew he ought to find, whether the motives which led to understanding were worthy, and whether the whole process of coming to know the meaning of his perceptions signified a will in harmony with God's or going its natural way.

The urgency of this self-questioning becomes understandable when one considers the terrible pressure under which the Puritan lived. Nature provided but the simplest and the clearest of the objects of his experience, in a world where all things were potential signs. Because nothing can be without significance in the creation of a predestining God, the Puritan assumed that every moment might be a revelation and that in every item he perceived there might lie a spiritual message. Fearing damnation, he sought everywhere the signs of grace; yearning for salvation, he attended upon the slightest evidence of God's regenerative spirit within his heart. Doubtless few men could sustain the requisite alertness continually, and presumably most Puritans most of the time yielded somewhat to indifference or self-deception. But the Puritan anxiety is not to be refuted by quotations from such texts as Sewall's diary, which merely reveal the evasions to be expected of an ordinary mind. To students of literature Puritanism is important mainly in its highest states of consciousness, not in phases of hebetude or collapse. And when the Puritan mind is most aware, it is a mind in doubt, a mind in that peculiar sort of doubt which makes doubting an essential function of all consciousness.

To believe that the destiny of one's soul is inalterably determined is to commit oneself to a life of continual questioning. Since it follows from predestination that the man who will be consigned to flame or raised to immortal life is the very same man who is presently experiencing, the question of election is really the question of one's own state of mind.

Thus in America what Robert Langbaum has aptly termed "the poetry of experience" appears at an early date, and its Puritan origin gives it certain distinctive features which persist to our own time.[38] Such traits result from the essential purpose of the Puritan's self-examination: since his objective is to view experience as evidence of his spiritual condition, he is accustomed to studying it from the outside as a single unit or specimen; and since the truth he would find is fixed and unchanging, his attention is directed to the present as the most immediate evidence of things which always pertain as they pertain here. The person that the Puritan is in God's sight is the same person he is now. Quite naturally, then, he conceives his experience as a static present duration and isolates the moment in order to regard it as an epitome of all time.

This focusing upon the present signifies not an indifference to other times but, rather, a radically different way of getting at them. Past and future are regarded as present events of consciousness and are seen, always, in terms of how the mind is now remembering or foreseeing. It is an epitome, not a continuity, that the Puritan seeks. He is not interested in observing his present as a phase in a larger development; indeed, his religion makes such an undertaking both improper and impossible. If he writes his life story, he views the events episodically as a series of tableaux each of which contains the whole truth, rather than as happenings in a causative sequence. Because the meaning of experience is its direct reference to the eternal instead of its relation to other times, remembering, foreseeing, and generalizing are more significant in the way they happen than in what they reveal. Their content is only true and important with respect to the behavior of the mind which considers it. The past, for example, is the past as

38. See his *The Poetry of Experience: The Dramatic Monologue in Modern Literary Tradition* (New York, Norton, 1963).

it is now known and is true only to the extent that one remembers well.

Because so definite a line is drawn about the present, the Puritan is both more aware and more interested in the way the mind transcends it. Thus, in a poetry of this kind, the shifts of perspective are just as abrupt as those that later occur in Bryant and Stevens. For the mind's positioning *is* the poetic action, and its movement from one to another point of view is the key to the meaning of its experience. Since how one perceives determines what one perceives, the poem means what the poet's mind does. If what one really is is the truth to be found, the way one thinks is the surest evidence, and if one is always the same person, one's present thinking provides the whole answer.

Perhaps no other work reveals the Puritan mode of experience more clearly than Anne Bradstreet's "Contemplations." As a nature poem, it is of particular interest, for since landscape and the things within it are at once the most immediate and the least humanized objects of consciousness, they illustrate, in the simplest form, the poet's manner of perceiving and interpreting. Because Mistress Bradstreet is herself aware of this, "Contemplations" is no mere picturing of nature but a study of the experiential process.

As the first section opens, Mistress Bradstreet recalls a splendorous scene which delighted her "Some time now past in the autumnal tide," when the setting sun gilded the brilliant hues of fall.

> I wist not what to wish, yet sure, thought I,
> If so much excellence abide below
> How excellent is He that dwells on high,
> Whose power and beauty by his works we know.[39]

39. All quotations from Anne Bradstreet are given according to the text of *The Poems of Anne Bradstreet: Together with Her Prose Remains,* ed. Charles Eliot Norton (New York, The Duodecimos, 1897). These lines are from the second stanza of "Contemplations," p. 249.

Though she is able to "improve" the scene quickly enough, there is that significant hesitation—"I wist not what to wish"—as if the mind were not quite sure what its reaction *ought* to be. Or if these words are meant to say that her delight was so complete it left nothing to wish for, there is in that some indifference to God. The nervous slurring over—"yet sure, thought I"—suggests the hurried intervention of conscience; and as the poet proceeds, her interpretations come to seem increasingly headstrong.

> Then on a stately oak I cast mine eye,
>   Whose ruffling top the clouds seemed to aspire.
> How long since thou wast in thine infancy?
>   Thy strength and stature more thy years admire.
> Hath hundred winters passed since thou wast born,
> Or thousand since thou break'st thy shell of horn?
> If so, all these as naught eternity doth scorn.[40]

Well and good; it is time now to look at the sun, which after a somewhat longer description, provokes the inquiry:

> How full of glory then must thy Creator be
> Who gave this bright light luster unto thee? [41]

Puritan literature is full of such moralizing, and while it may not be appropriate for the modern reader to question whether it is sincere, it is significant that Mistress Bradstreet herself does. She soon realizes that finding the right lessons does not induce the anticipated rapture. The mind which truly understands ought to rejoice, but she cannot raise her voice in praise, though even the cricket and grasshopper hymn the Creator. The last lines delicately hint at what has gone wrong:

> Shall creatures abject thus their voices raise,
> And in their kind resound their maker's praise,
> Whilst I as mute can warble forth no higher lays? [42]

40. St. 3, ibid.
41. St. 7, ibid., p. 251.
42. St. 9, ibid.

At this point there occurs the first of those sudden breaks which have led some editors to divide the poem as if it were a series of fragments or separate pieces.[43] In the first edition there are no such divisions, however, and the breaks should properly be seen as shifts of perspective. The second part depicts the poet turning to the past, remembering a remote time as a way of understanding the present. For sound doctrinal reasons, Mistress Bradstreet remembers Adam; her emotional failure is to be explained through its cause in the damage done by the first sin. But it is memory itself that most interests her, and the section begins with a comment on this odd phenomenon.

> When present times look back to ages past,
>   And men in being fancy those are dead,
> It makes things gone perpetually to last,
>   And calls back months and years that long since fled;
> It makes a man more aged in conceit
> Than was Methuselah or his grandsire great
> While of their persons and their acts his mind doth treat.[44]

One can see the relevance of this comment clearly enough by recollecting that the first object she noticed in the autumn scene was the oak, which impressed her by its great age. The taint of envy began there in the sad comparison between nature's permanence and man's mortality. By pointing out now that memory deludes us with the dream of long life, the poet makes her error explicit. Even if memory tricks us, however, it is nevertheless the way to understanding, and the pictures which follow emphasize the thought that knowing depends upon taking times remote into account.

43. When first published in *Several Poems* (Boston, John Foster, 1678), the second edition of Anne Bradstreet's poems, "Contemplations" was not divided into sections, the stanzas being numbered consecutively 1–33.

44. St. 10, in *The Poems of Anne Bradstreet*, p. 252.

> Here sits our grandam in retired place,
> And in her lap her bloody Cain new born;
> The weeping imp oft looks her in the face,
> Bewails his unknown hap and fate forlorn.
> His mother sighs to think of paradise,
> And how she lost her bliss to be more wise.[45]

Adam is viewed in the same way:

> How Adam sighed to see his progeny
> Clothed all in his black sinful livery,
> Who neither guilt nor yet the punishment could fly.[46]

Adam and Eve cannot foresee the work of salvation: he mistakenly dreads the future, while she can only regret the past. The poet knows better, however, because she can see the characters within the whole story. Thus, by remembering, she advances, comes to see that understanding her own experience requires viewing it within the conspectus of all history or, in Puritan terms, as part of the whole pattern of God's will. Though this is not entirely clear at the end of the second part, which concludes by asserting only that man must learn to remember his mortal state, when she turns again to experience in nature, it becomes apparent that her remembering has prepared her to resolve the doubts which had troubled her:

> Shall I then praise the heavens, the trees, the earth,
> Because their beauty and their strength last longer?

The question that nature posed is now clear, and it reveals its own answer.

> Nay, they shall darken, perish, fade, and die,
> And when unmade so ever shall they lie;
> But man was made for endless immortality.[47]

45. St. 12, ibid.
46. St. 16, ibid., p. 253.
47. St. 20, ibid., pp. 254–55.

This is surely the truth she had failed to keep in mind, yet as a mere idea it is not much more satisfying than her earlier "improvements." For it is experience she wishes to understand, and what she knows as principle must be seen there as perception.

In the nature description which follows, the poet records a new and better state of consciousness. She is still interested in moral meanings. The stealing stream supplies yet another lesson:

> Thou emblem true of what I count the best,
> Oh, could I lead my rivulets to rest!
> So may we press to that vast mansion ever blest! [48]

The moralizing is now subtly different, however: it develops from observation—from a convincingly felt resemblance between the river's flow and the movement of the mind—so that even without accepting her analogy one can see how she arrived at it. That she has achieved a more complete awareness becomes apparent in the charming picture which follows:

> Ye fish which in this liquid region abide,
>   That for each season have your habitation,
> Now salt, now fresh, where you think best to glide,
>   To unknown coasts to give a visitation,
> In lakes and ponds you leave your numerous fry
> So nature taught, and yet you know not why,
> You watery folk that know not your felicity.[49]

Here the usually inept Spenserianizing catches just the right details in its careless cast; everything draws attention to the difference between instinct and consciousness. The fish know not their felicity—a point nicely enforced by the reference to their casual breeding—but the poet's consciousness is so inclusive that she even has in mind the "unknown coasts" they frequent, as Bryant is aware of the Louisiana bayou.

48. St. 23, ibid., p. 256.
49. St. 24, ibid.

It remains only to make the point explicit—to show that human consciousness is manifest in the power to remember and foresee.

> O merry bird, said I, that fears no snares
>   That neither toils nor hoards up in thy barn,
> Feels no sad thoughts, nor cruciating cares
>   To gain more good or shun what might thee harm,
> Thy clothes ne'er wear, thy meat is everywhere,
> Thy bed a bough, thy drink the water clear,
> Reminds not what is past, nor what's to come dost fear! [50]

For Mistress Bradstreet, as later for Whitman, the self's transcendence of its temporal place in nature is proof of its immortality. This proof may strike the modern reader as unconvincing in itself, but considered dramatically, it is valid as a thought the poet has and the point at which she arrives. What Mistress Bradstreet has done, and done very well, in this second passage on nature, is to depict the kind of experience in which the Puritan could find assurance that the soul, whether damned or saved, will never die. It is an experience of the mind's transcendence—of the way it overleaps every temporal limit that might be set to its existing.

The conclusion is managed with great tact. Its theme is the need to take the large view. Man's misery—"Each storm his state, his mind, his body, break"—should make the duty to see all things in the light of the soul's destiny a source of joy as well:

> And yet this sinful creature, frail and vain
>   This lump of wretchedness, of sin and sorrow,
> This weather-beaten vessel racked with pain,
>   Joys not in hope of an eternal morrow.[51]

Man is like the mariner who yearns for port only in bad weather; affliction alone can teach him that "Only above is found all with security." All else shall pass away:

50. St. 27, ibid., p. 257.
51. St. 30, ibid.

O time, the fatal wreck of mortal things,
That draws oblivion's curtains over kings!
Their sumptuous monuments men know them not,
Their names without a record are forgot,
Their parts, their ports, their pomps, all laid in the dust,
Nor wit, nor gold, nor buildings 'scape time's rust.
But he whose name is graved in the white stone
Shall last and shine when all of these are gone.[52]

Coming at the end of the poem, this conventional stanza on the ruins of time has a peculiar eloquence. It seems fitting just because it is conventional, because in a sense the whole purpose of the poem has been to arrive at this moment when orthodox opinion could be voiced appropriately. It seals the reader's conviction that the poet has at last come to feel the truth of her formal beliefs. The reference to Revelation 2:17—"To him who conquers I will give . . . a white stone, with a new name written on the stone which no one knows except him who receives it"—illustrates the fine restraint which Puritanism could foster.[53] The poet does not claim to be sure now that she has received such a token from God; she will stop with the assertion that some do and remain content with the hope, the bare possibility.

Her only real evidence of salvation is the moralizing itself, and the whole purpose of the ending will be missed if one fails to recognize this as a dramatic event. It is the way she comes to voice the commonplaces of piety, the way they emerge to consciousness in the process of her experience, that shows her her heart is right. The moralizing itself is the act of taking the large view, by means of which the poet shows that she comes to recognize her own error of forgetfulness by seeing it within the whole

52. St. 33, ibid., p. 258.

53. It is not necessary to suppose that Bradstreet uses the image of the white stone as scriptural proof of the predestinarian doctrine. According to *The Interpreter's Bible, 12*, ed. G. A. Buttrick et al. (12 vols. New York, Arlington Press, 1957), 387: "possibly the reference is to a kind of phylactery or amulet with the secret name of Jesus, which the martyr has not denied, engraved on it so as to protect him in this life and to insure a blessed immortality in the next."

scheme of God's plan for mankind. The ending, then, portrays in a dramatic way the last phase in the process by which the mind comes to terms with its experience.

"Contemplations" is not a great poem; like nearly all the writings of colonial New England, it will seem crude and trivial when compared with the best English work of the period. But it is evidence that we should credit Anne Bradstreet with a kind of thoughtfulness which in her place and time was perhaps more valuable than talent. She could not write smooth verses, she could not make her words behave, but she understood with remarkable prescience the kind of poetry American experience would require. "Contemplations" is the earliest example of the ways of manipulating time which become typical of the best American poetry. Here, as in "When Lilacs Last in the Dooryard Bloom'd," the arrangement of materials is such as to create a formal enactment of the process of interpreting the experiential moment by placing it with reference to past and future times. For Bradstreet as for Whitman, memory not only supplies enlightening facts but is important in itself as a dramatization of that transcendence which demonstrates the self's spiritual nature. And for both poets, memory is also prophecy. To recall the past is to bring to consciousness history as a whole and thus to define man's destiny. Nothing more clearly illustrates Mistress Bradstreet's achievement than the way in which her poem foreshadows Whitman's technique of concluding a poem by projecting the perceptual act he has depicted into the future so that it seems to continue to the end of history.

Since Marvell and Milton were also Puritans, the common theological ground Mistress Bradstreet shares with them makes the distinctively American form of her poem the more obvious. Marvell concludes "The Garden" by making the rather subtle point that the garden-time which the bees measure as they circle the clock of flowers is a time both the same as and distinctly different from our ordinary time. The garden's innocence defines an eternal present of timeless types: nature and its species abide just as the sunny stillness of the garden seems to cancel time's movement. Thus eternity and time are deftly reconciled by the implicit presence of each in the other. The garden is a retreat from a world where the effects of Adam's fall make the passing of time painfully real, but on the other hand, the garden exists within this world, whose essential realities are epitomized by its flowers and trees. Marvell's recollection of Eden, however, requires no abrupt shift of perspective, nor does the poet make the remembering itself a topic of discussion. Instead, Eden comes up quite casually, as if by an automatic association of ideas. The latent delights of "luscious clusters" and the latent dangers of being "ensnared by flowers" smooth the way for the somewhat whimsical comment that Eden is a bachelor state. In "The Garden" the process of transcending is treated as a natural development and refinement of ordinary experience. The "green thought in a green shade" blurs the subject-object contrast, so that when the reader comes to the picture of the soul as a bird preening itself in a treetop, this dream image seems the symbol of a mood rather than of a specific mental process. The key verbs, "sliding," "glide," and "run," manifest a poetic action which is progressive, a world view in which time smoothly advances, an experience which develops chronologically.

"L'Allegro" and "Il Penseroso" illustrate the same progressiveness in Milton's treatment of nature. Though there is a good deal of transcending, this is never set in contrast to the immediate perceiving of scenery and natural objects. Rather, it seems to be a primary intention of these poems to show that landscape and human culture are so perfectly synthesized in the beholder's mood that what is, in one sense, a visible prospect is, in another, a state of mind. Thus, though the mind of Milton's persona ranges through wide areas of historical and artistic association, these fields are made to seem continuous with the reaches of the "landskip" the physical eye "measures," and where the persona is geographically becomes a function of his place within culture and history. One does not find Milton pausing to consider how the evening of "Il Penseroso" brings Aeschylus to mind. It is a sufficient rationale that attending (or reading) an antique tragedy is one kind of evening entertainment, and after looking behind the mere logic of this, one is satisfied to conclude that the story of "Pelops line" suits the melancholy mood. Milton does not stand aside from the moment of experience to judge it critically with reference to some constellation of fixed truths. For one thing, Milton's moment keeps changing, and it is a continuum rather than a duration that he portrays. Then, too, the developing present is organically related to manifold past times whose currents flow into and interpret the things of present experience by infusing them with traditionary meanings which are to be intuited rather than analyzed, combined and integrated rather than sorted out and interpreted.

The different sensibility these poems illustrate shows the crucially different effect Puritan beliefs had within the more cosmopolitan and broadly humanistic culture of the English poets. But even in Bunyan, who seems much closer in point of view to Mistress Bradstreet's world, there is a marked preference for a kind of forward-moving narrative development, which makes it seem probable that recent critics are right in stressing the priority of the mere story of *Pilgrim's Progress,* with its fine dramatic moments and psychological acuity, over the allegorical meanings, however explicit and earnestly meant.

Mistress Bradstreet's historical importance is revealed by her lucid recognition of the question that has ever since confronted the American imagination. "How," she asked, "can eternal truth be found within the moment of my own present experiencing?" It is a question obvious enough—perhaps merely a rather specialized formulation of that with which Luther's and Descartes' reasoning began. Even so, the question was posed by her Puritan faith, and that faith also supplied a simple answer: "View the present as the emblem of all times." It is her understanding of this elementary formula that is distinctive, her clearness as to how narrow the present of Puritan experience had become, and how wide, in consequence, the gulf between now and always must be. More important, she seems to have been the first American writer to realize that the epistemological question was a literary one as well, and demanded, by way of answer, a new kind of poetic form. Her poetry would exert no significant influence upon later American poets, but her question abides, and it has had its consequences.

2

The Choice of a Single Point
of View: Edwards and Franklin

While the public funds are poured out for
festivals of brotherhood, up in the clouds a
bell of pink fire rings.

Arthur Rimbaud

As THE two most eminent writers of the American eighteenth century, Jonathan Edwards and Benjamin Franklin inevitably invite comparison. They seem to divide the century—Edwards, as the apologist of the declining New England theocracy, summarizing the Puritan past, and Franklin, the scientist and man of affairs, exemplifying the technology and tolerant pluralism of the coming democracy. We find ourselves looking backward from Edwards but forward from Franklin, impressed by contrasts which augment the distance between colonial New England and the America of today. In that Franklin is prophetic, Edwards appears reactionary, and our attention is arrested by differences alluringly vivid: between theology and science, predestination and self-improvement, grace and "doing good," mystical experience and business success.

The list of contrasts, which might easily be lengthened, is not the less useful for being familiar. One objects, however, to its implication that a line so sharp can be drawn. The influence of the new science upon Edwards is but the most obvious example of his tendency to drift over to Franklin's side of the antithesis. And it is not hard to imagine a man who could devote himself to Franklin's kind of good works without in any respect abandoning the belief that salvation comes from grace alone. Indeed, arguments for the difference between Edwards and Franklin are often drawn from Max Weber or R. H. Tawney, who are at pains to show that the bourgeois morality, which, in America, Franklin typifies, has its source in Protestant theology.[1]

Such strong contrasts seldom describe a real opposition, partly because the terms are not commensurate, as in the case of grace and "doing good," and partly because the beliefs attributed to the two men are not mutually exclusive, or because statements meant in quite different senses have been forced into a single context. That Franklin, for example, does not repudiate the doctrine of regeneration but simply has nothing to say on the subject suggests a difference, but not necessarily one between the old and the new.

The whole enterprise of setting Franklin, the new American, against Edwards, the last Puritan, seems dependent upon rather narrow suppositions as to which cultural tendencies would later prove the most significant. If Franklin anticipates Henry Ford, it is Edwards who more clearly foreshadows Emerson and Melville. The Great Awakening, that revolution in sentiment which Edwards instituted, is hardly less important to the development of the American mind than the revolution in outward political forms in which Franklin played a part. Franklin, to be sure, is the first prominent scientist which America produced, but Edwards, among American writers, is the first to attempt to trace out the full implications of Newton's physics. And if in Franklin the political understanding is more highly developed, Edwards is a far more astute student of psychology. The differences between them are real, important, unquestionable, but unless we are willing to

1. See Max Weber, *The Protestant Ethic and the Spirit of Capitalism,* trans. Talcott Parsons (New York, Scribners, 1958); R. H. Tawney, *Religion and the Rise of Capitalism* (London, John Murray, 1926). For an example of studies based upon Weber and Tawney, see A. Whitney Griswold, "Three Puritans on Prosperity," *The New England Quarterly,* 8 (Sept. 1934), 475–88.

reason from very arbitrary axioms, we had best abandon the effort to explain these differences as contrasts between an earlier and later phase of American culture.

More probably, Edwards and Franklin belong to one phase, represent two sides of a single state of mind, or, to put the matter more technically, manifest the two most thoughtful modes of experience possible to a person born in their age and culture. That both men were nurtured in the New England of the early eighteenth century is a fact which otherwise is not easily to be explained. In point of time they were almost exact contemporaries; and although the printer survived the theologian by some thirty-one years, the essential pattern of his thought was formed during the period when Edwards served as pastor at Northampton and suffered exile at Stockbridge. Chronology provides some instructive surprises. When Franklin began *Poor Richard*, only one treatise by Edwards was as yet in print; Franklin founded the American Philosophical Society three years before the first of Edwards' major works, that on the *Religious Affections*, appeared; the kite experiment preceded *Freedom of the Will* by two years; "The Way to Wealth" was published in 1757, *The Great Christian Doctrine of Original Sin Defended* not until 1758. Finally, Franklin's account of his life in the *Autobiography* takes us no further than 1757, so that while the book was written later, the man it depicts lives in the age, if not in the world, of Jonathan Edwards.

But one may question whether Edwards' world is really very different from Franklin's. The dissimilarities, however striking, may be but the consequence of a difference of point of view, and to see Franklin and Edwards differing in this sense clarifies the difficulty of formulating their beliefs in such a manner as to produce a true contradiction. It is not a matter of comparing what Edwards says with what Franklin says, for their statements belong to different modes of discourse, which are, in turn, created by their respective points of view. One cannot separate the sense of a statement from the situation of the speaker; the meaning is to be judged with reference to the kinds of knowledge and scope of vision possible from the position the speaker imagines himself occupying.

Edwards speaks from the eternal point of view—not through the unlikely pretense that he himself is perfect in knowledge, though the authority of revelation gives him considerable confidence, but in undertaking to describe reality as an eternal and all-inclusive design. To view matters in this panoramic way is to assume, at the least, that God's perfect vision would have the same form and be taken from the same point of view. Whether any theologian can ever quite dispense with this premise, it is surely an inherent temptation of theology.[2] The predication of God's omniscience makes statements true according to their concurrence with reality as God knows it, so that even an insistence upon mystery is often merely a way of saying that in God's sight man is ignorant of certain things. Edwards' greatness is largely due to his having understood the presumption of the theologian's point of view so well that he could make the adopting of it an enactment of worship and a literary mode.

Franklin, by contrast, always speaks from within the world he describes—from the position of the particular individual. His statements are to be judged with respect to the vision of the experiential moment, and instead of a universal panorama, they present a view qualified and limited to just that portion of reality which appears within the self's horizon. Franklin's scientific work, though seeming to present a contrary view, is in fact but a particular application of the individual viewpoint, since insofar as the validity of scientific formulas is to be judged by the experimental method, they are to be proved true in personal experience; repeating Franklin's experiments, any individual will arrive at the same result. The same may be said of Franklin's social and ethical doctrines: however broad his generalizations, they are framed with an eye to what may be discerned and reasonably

2. See Karl Barth's discussion of the meaning of the word "God" as the God revealed historically rather than defined from a point of view outside of revelation, in *Church Dogmatics: A Selection*, ed. G. W. Bromiley (New York, Harper Torchbooks, 1961), pp. 29–38.

asserted from the individual point of view. The appeal is to personal experience, and this, in the end, is an affair of the moment.

The essential difference between Edwards and Franklin is, then, that between the two sides of the Puritan consciousness. This is not to say that one speaks for God's eternal plan and the other for the self's momentary experience—as if either aspect of reality could be thought of without taking the other into account —but rather that Edwards and Franklin redefine both aspects as points of view and commit themselves to studying reality entirely from one or the other position. That this represents a new phase of consciousness is made manifest by the fact that they found it necessary to choose. Their writings present alternative responses to the problem of Puritan experience—indeed, the two most promising answers which that problem itself suggested—and their motive for seeking an answer is not obscure. The tension caused by the Puritan's allegiance to two standards of truth and two views of reality is resolved by making a choice between them. The reward for thus choosing is a harmony which pervades subject and form alike. Harmony is their common theme; they are dealers in consistencies and reconciliations. It is the object of each to depict a perfect adjustment of momentary experience and eternal being. Franklin's image of himself as a man who has learned to adjust with perfect prudence and efficiency to the world as it is is an inverted image of Edwards' God, who disposes all things according to his will.

The harmony is that of the European eighteenth century—a peace won by marshaling events into processes and equating process with eternal law. But Edwards and Franklin exploit this maneuver in a peculiarly American way. They stress the convertibility of law and process into points of view (process being law as seen from within time), and they have a Puritanical distaste for considering more than two viewpoints. Some experiences are better than others—more true—but a multiplicity of human viewpoints is not really granted. Each writer thinks in terms of a single normative human situation. For Edwards the saint occupies the same position as the natural man, though grace has radically altered his understanding of what can be seen from there. Franklin, for all his tolerance, will only concede that there are various *ways* of understanding, and in the end he proves as loyal as Edwards to the belief that the epistemological situation is the same for all men.

Furthermore, the Americans, unlike English and Continental thinkers of the period, are not interested in viewing knowledge as a communal enterprise. They may agree that the self learns largely from others, but they tend to regard what is thus acquired as mere information, which becomes knowledge only to the extent that the individual can make sense of it. Thus in Edwards the traditional Puritan distinction between ordinary and special grace is converted into a psychological contrast between a "notional" understanding of God's word and a heartfelt sense of its truth. And the same attitude toward knowledge derived from others explains the cynicism behind Franklin's tolerance—the hint that communal beliefs are important merely as facts for the self to manage and turn to account.

This unwillingness—even, perhaps, incapacity—to imagine any points of view except those of the isolated self and the omniscient diety explains the difficulty of placing the two Americans with reference to contemporary European culture. Though one recognizes that they represent two versions of the thought of the eighteenth century, one cannot quite overcome the feeling that in their work the familiar ideas of the period are seen from an angle which oddly distorts. The ideas do not have quite the same meaning as they do in European thought; Edwards and Franklin force them to play a somewhat different role by holding them strictly to the dramatic conventions of Puritan experience.

That Edwards and Franklin reveal the alternative sides of a common state of consciousness is exemplified by the contrast between their kinds of literary achievement. This may be seen as a difference between manner and matter—between Edwards as the first American prose stylist of importance and Franklin as the first American author to create a great fictional character—for each succeeds in a way which corresponds to his point of view. Edwards' style grows from his severe detachment; it is, as we shall see, a style whose main merit is its impersonality. In Franklin, however, it is the writer's self-image that is most important; his greatest work is the *Autobiography*, and one reads his other compositions with the object of understanding their author. To be sure, this is true because Franklin interests us much more than Edwards as a "historical" figure; but even that fact makes the same point in another way. Franklin holds our attention as a man acting in history, whereas we scarcely see Edwards at all. His "Personal Narrative" is a short and minor work, and if we study his writings to discover his personality, this in turn is but a means to understanding what he says. In reading Franklin, the author himself is the main question.

Edwards is a theologian, not a philosopher, and, as I shall undertake to show, his mere system cannot stand alone. It is incomplete; indeed, it does not make sense unless it is considered with reference to a vision or experience which transcends the rational scheme. The latter is, as it were, a kind of notation or way of speaking by which Edwards would indicate something beyond the reasonableness of his arguments.

Nevertheless, there is a system to be grasped, and for the study of this, Edwards' short essay on the Trinity provides a logical starting point. For since God is being itself, in Edwards' view of God's triune nature, the basis of his metaphysics is revealed. While this essay is neither one of his most celebrated works nor one of the most strikingly original, it illustrates particularly well the rationale underlying his synthesis of ideas derived from Locke and Newton. Like Berkeley, though apparently without studying that philosopher, Edwards reasoned that Locke's analysis of secondary qualities had the effect of destroying the independence of any object from thought and that in consequence all things have their being in consciousness. In Newton's conception of nature as a system of unchanging and universally operative laws he found not only warrant for the deterministic assumptions of predestination but, what is much more fundamental than this, a way of rendering nature's processes identical with God's thoughts. Since the Creation has its origin and ground in the Creator, Edwards' doctrines concerning the relation of the world, and particularly of mankind, to God are considerably clarified by his thought concerning God's own nature.

Readers familiar with the main Augustinian tradition concerning the doctrine of the Trinity will recognize the very close resemblance of Edwards' thought on this subject to Augustine's, but the similarity is far from complete; there are crucial differences, and these reveal the distinctive features of Edwards' theology.

Edwards describes the unity of the Trinity by identifying the three persons as three aspects of cognition: the thinker, the idea, and the thinking. God the Father exists through taking thought of himself, and the Son is the idea or "image" of himself in the Father's mind. The Father and Son are identical because, in his perfect wisdom, the Father perceives a perfect image of himself, exact in every respect. As the process of thought the Holy Spirit is at one with the Father and the Son, both of whom have their existence in the Father's thinking. But the identity of the three persons is in emotion as well as in thought. To Edwards as, later, to T. S. Eliot, thought and feeling are aspects of a single event; one might say that considering an idea is an act of willing, since it reflects a preference and a preference is a feeling. The Holy Spirit is not only the Father's thought but his love of his Son, the thought of his own perfect goodness which the Son with perfect love returns. God *is* love; love is not a deed or emanation of the deity but God himself existing as action: "So that the Godhead therein stands forth in yet another manner of subsistence, & there Proceeds the 3d Person in the Trinity, the holy spirit, viz. the Deity in act, for there is no other act but the will." [3] The Father and the Son live in this action and are identical with it. As Edwards concludes:

3. *An Unpublished Essay of Edwards on the Trinity*, ed. George P. Fisher (New York, Scribners, 1903), p. 94.

The Father is the Deity subsisting in the Prime, unorganized & most absolute manner, or the deity in its direct existence. The Son is the deity generated by God's understanding, or having an Idea of himself & subsisting in that Idea. The Holy Gh. is the Deity subsisting in act, or the divine essence flowing out and Breathed forth in Gods Infinite love to & delight in himself.[4]

In the "Personal Narrative" Edwards confesses that "Absolute Sovereignty is what I love to ascribe to God," and his Trinitarian theory reveals the metaphysical means to this end.[5] By equating being and cognition, he is able to make for Absolute Sovereignty the broadest imaginable claims. God's immanence is not only his presence in the world but his identity with the world; God is all things in the sense that they exist in his thinking. For every creature, and every event, is a direct consequence of his will as it now acts, and not merely a consequence of the original Creation. This leads us to a conclusion often noted before: that Edwards gives to predestination a larger statement than earlier Puritanism afforded. Quite clearly the object is to free Absolute Sovereignty from any limitation whatsoever. Yet such a maneuver would not have been possible within the Christian context of Puritanism were it not for the other side of Edwards' Trinitarian theory, the side indicated when he describes the Father as "the deity in its direct existence." Though in the cognitive event God's thought is the being of all things, still as the thinker God remains distinct. Indeed, his transcendence is more ambitiously asserted in exact ratio to the extent that his immanence is augmented. Thus the doctrine absolutely indispensable to Puritan theology, the belief that God exercises his will in perfect freedom, is not only preserved but given a more forceful expression.

Though Edwards' doctrine of the Trinity is derived from the Augustinian tradition, it is important to notice that Augustine's formulation—Memoria, Intelligensia, Amor—has been radically

---

4. Ibid., p. 110.

5. *Jonathan Edwards: Representative Selections*, ed. Clarence H. Faust and Thomas H. Johnson (rev. ed. New York, Hill and Wang, 1962), p. 59.

altered, in that Edwards' thinker does not correspond to Augustine's Memoria. Augustine's formulation is derived from human nature and therefore has a largely metaphorical application. Memoria, Intelligensia, and Amor are discerned to be the three necessary elements of human self-consciousness, and Augustine trusts that they may, to some degree, shadow forth God's nature, because man is made in the image of God. In spite of Edwards' disclaimer that the mystery of the Trinity can ever be explained, his doctrine is less figurative and more axiomatic. He is careful to assert, as Augustine had, that the three aspects of knowledge cannot be divided among the three persons, for each thinks, understands, and loves. But this does not dispel the logical (not temporal) priority of the Father to the second and third persons. Though the thinker exists in the event of his self-consciousness and therefore in the unity of the three persons, the thinker is not Memoria—not an aspect of this event. He is "the deity in its direct existence." To the extent that this expression is clear, it attributes to the Father a mode of being distinct from the event of self-consciousness, for it predicates a separateness from the triune relationship which is not granted to the second and third persons. Thus the second and third persons are less distinguishable from created beings than in the traditional view. For after granting that, to Edwards, Sonhood and Procession indicate an origin different in kind from Creation, it is nevertheless true that in Edwards' metaphysics the most important contrast is not that between God and the created world but between God as thinker and his thought.

The dualistic tendency of Edwards' conception of God's nature is the ultimate source of his subtle and often confusing ambiguity. Because the first and third persons of the Trinity are distinct as agent and act, though united as aspects of God's being, everything is to be viewed doubly with reference to essence ("the Deity in its direct existence"), on the one hand, and becoming ("the Deity in act"), on the other. As a consequence, Edwards' statements must be taken in two contrary senses, and that difficulty is compounded by yet another sort of double-entendre concerning the form of his statements. Just as the Son, as idea, is both distinct from and identical with the Father, concept and reality exist in the same double relation. For example, the word of God, in Edwards' thought, is in one sense literally meant and in another only figuratively.

Attempts to dispel Edwards' ambiguity misrepresent his thought, as Douglas J. Elwood does when, in his otherwise excellent book, he asserts that Edwards believes God transcendent as greater than but not separate from the world.[6] As Elwood astutely observes, a deity who is merely transcendent could soon dwindle to a detached and irrelevant being difficult to distinguish from the "First Cause" of deism. While it is true that Edwards understood that immanence must be insisted upon if one's reasoning is not to end in the sort of conclusions the term "world machine" suggests, he would not for that reason dispose of transcendence, which is really the effect of Elwood's "greater than." It is the essential feature of Edwards' theology to describe immanence in such a manner that transcendence is not only preserved but given a more ambitious formulation. His position reveals his loyalty to the Puritan past. Though time and eternity are no longer opposites, the old duality persists in a new form—as the contrast between the human and divine points of view.

Edwards' conception of God's nature provides the metaphysical basis for his most characteristic theological views, those concerning Absolute Sovereignty, divine intervention, sin, and regeneration. In describing Edwards' treatment of these subjects, my purpose will be to show that with respect to each, the complications of his theory arise from the transcendence-immanence duality. The topics to be considered were of such crucial interest to the theologian that the rather technical discussion required even in a brief account will, I trust, be excused. To study Edwards' rendering of experience, one must first bring the main

6. *The Philosophical Theology of Jonathan Edwards* (New York, Columbia University Press, 1960), pp. 21–23.

outlines of his world into view, and doctrines abstruse in themselves come to life again when considered as elements of a world view—which was, indeed, how Edwards himself intended them to be understood.

Edwards' theory of causation is crucial, for it is through this that he explains God's intervention in the world he has created and hence the way in which grace is made available to the sanctified self. Christ's miracles are a sufficient reminder of the Christian's obligation to distinguish between spiritual and merely natural events. In spiritual events God is more intimately and directly present than in happenings in the normal course of things. But nature is God's creation, and a universe established by a deity of perfect wisdom and power ought not to require any later adjustments. That God's work was marred by original sin does not fully explain matters, for in one way or another the implication persists that a perfect creation would have survived and compensated for any possible happening. Thus providential intervention seems to call the Creator into question, yet unless one believes that God does directly intervene in human affairs to alter the normal course of things, one has lost an indispensable means of asserting his overlordship, his presence, his character as a person dealing with individual men, and his freedom to act as he wills. Hence two contrary views of the way God causes events must be maintained. Events must be supposed to follow in sequence by causative necessity from the original act of creation, but at the same time it must be argued that throughout the causative sequence God intervenes to produce events which would not otherwise follow from his original act. Furthermore, if many events are merely natural, then much that comes to pass is of but slight spiritual significance, serving simply as God's means of setting the stage for the drama of spiritual life. Such a view of natural events was not congenial to Puritanism, since it could not easily be harmonized with the belief that even the most ordinary events in personal experience are potential emblems of God's will.

These problems arise from a false distinction between God's original and subsequent causing, and Edwards saw that the two could be proved one if considered with respect to points of view. In experience causes appear to precede effects, and common sense therefore concludes that a cause is efficient or has an inherent power to "produce" the later event as its effect. For Edwards, however, causation is not efficiency but, rather, a connection, "consent," or appropriateness such that the idea of one thing involves that of another.[7]

Whether he followed the path of reasoning traced in Hume's destructive analysis of causation, Edwards' language suggests that he arrived at much the same conclusion. In a helpful passage in "Notes on The Mind" he points out that one cannot properly say, "the material Universe exists no where but in the mind," if what is meant is "that all the world is contained in the narrow compass of a few inches of space, in little ideas in the place of the brain." For

> the human body, and the brain itself, exist only mentally, in the same sense that other things do and so that, which we call *place* is an idea too. . . . things are truly in those places; for what we mean when we say so, is only, that this mode of our idea of place appertains to such an idea [i.e. of a thing].[8]

The same argument must necessarily apply to time. If place is an idea and the location of a thing "a mode of our idea of place," then time too is an idea, and the period of time during which a thing exists is a mode of that idea also.

Thus to Edwards the only true distinction is between points of view. He can conceive the world as common sense does—see it as

7. See Paul Ramsey's Introduction to *Freedom of the Will*, in Paul Ramsey, ed., *The Works of Jonathan Edwards, 1* (2 vols. New Haven, Yale University Press, 1957–59), 34–37.

8. *'The Mind' of Jonathan Edwards: A Reconstructed Text*, ed. Leon Howard, University of California English Studies, No. 28 (Berkeley, University of California Press, 1963), pp. 91–92, Note 32.

a sequence of causes set going by the first act of creation—for that is how it appears when observed from within time. And he can conceive the world as a static pattern within which all events coexist as harmonies or consents, because that is how it appears when seen as a total conspectus. A cause is truly prior to its effect, but this priority is ideal, for time is generated by God's consciousness in the same way that space and objects are. Time is but a dimension of God's creative willing.

It follows, then, that there is no true inconsistency between the first Creation and God's later acts of interposing. In fact, the first Creation is first only when seen from within time. What I have inferred from Edwards' remarks on space is confirmed by his arguments for continuous creation. " 'Tis certain with me," he writes, "that the world exists anew every moment, that the existence of things every moment ceases and is every moment renewed. . . . Indeed, we every moment see the same proof of a God as we should have seen if we had seen [Him] create the world at first." For we can only explain the continuous existence of a creature by God's continuing consciousness of it:

> For instance, in the existence of bodies there has to be resistance or tendency to some place. 'Tis not numerically the same resistance that exists the next moment. 'Tis evident because these existences may be in different places, but yet its existence is continued so far that there is respect had to it in all the future existences. 'Tis evident in all things continually, how past existence can't be continued so that respect should be had to it otherwise than mentally.[9]

One should not conclude that for Edwards time is unreal or the distinctions commonly indicated by "before" and "after" mere illusions. The point is simply that they are not *temporal* distinctions in God's sight: "Nothing is new to God, in any respect, but

9. *The Philosophy of Jonathan Edwards: From His Private Notebooks*, ed. Harvey G. Townsend (Eugene, University of Oregon Press, 1955), p. 76, Item 125.

all things are perfectly and equally in his view from eternity." [10]

Edwards' theory of causation enables him to set forth God's Absolute Sovereignty in the most extravagant and unqualified manner. Thus his theology itself constitutes an act of worship. While he preserves the difference between natural and spiritual things, his idea of cause serves to demonstrate that natural events are of no less spiritual use and meaning than any others. Nature is not merely the stage upon which the drama is played; it is a medium through which God acts, even when effecting events out of the normal course of things.

One can readily see, then, that the most dramatic problem which predestination raises—that of God's apparent responsibility for sin—is made even more urgent in Edwards by his insistence that in no respect can any event occur excepting as a direct consequence of the divine will: "God permits sin; and at the same time, so orders things, in his providence, that it certainly and infallibly will come to pass, in consequence of his permission." But, as he continues:

> There is a great difference between God's being thus, by his permission, in an event and act, which in the inherent subject and agent of it is sin (though the event will certainly follow on his permission), and his being concerned in it by producing it and exerting the act of sin.[11]

It is the absence of God's saving guidance which makes sin possible—indeed, a certain consequence. Left to the processes of unredeemed nature and his own fallen state, the self must surely err. Yet God is not therefore responsible:

> It would be strange arguing indeed, because men never commit sin, but only when God leaves 'em *to themselves,* and necessarily sin, when he does so, that therefore their sin is not *from themselves,* but from God; and so that God must be a sinful

10. *Freedom of the Will,* in *Works, 1,* 434.
11. Ibid., pp. 403–04.

being: as strange as it would be to argue, because it is always dark when the sun is gone, and never dark when the sun is present, that therefore all darkness is from the sun, and that his disk and beams needs be black.[12]

Nevertheless, it is significant that Edwards rejects with scorn the liberal argument that God's permitting sin to occur is not the ultimate cause of sin, maintaining that he knowingly disposes things in such a way that it will occur.[13] It would have to follow, then, that God does will sin, were it not that Edwards' theory of causation enables him to place the event of sin in two distinct contexts. Man, within time, wills particular acts; God from eternity wills the whole of being of which these events are a necessary part: "God don't will sin as sin, or for the sake of anything evil; though it be his pleasure so to order things, that he permitting, sin will come to pass; for the sake of the great good that by his disposal shall be the consequence." [14] The point is clarified by a rather startling example. "Christ's crucifixion," Edwards writes, "though a most horrid fact in them that perpetrated it, was a most glorious tendency as permitted and ordered of God." [15]

Edwards' desire to define God as the ground of all being is revealed in clearest form here. While the God who disposes all things must necessarily be the cause of every event, even the wicked action, it does not follow that the evil thereof is God's responsibility. Willing, as we have noted, is not to be distinguished from feeling. Every act is also an emotion, and it is the choice of evil that constitutes sin, whereas in God's willing, the event is caused with the whole of reality in view and for the best purposes. God is present in the event without in any way sharing its sinful character.

This view of sin is of the greatest importance to the argument

12. Ibid., p. 404.
13. Ibid., pp. 399–403.
14. Ibid., p. 409.
15. Ibid., p. 412.

of *Freedom of the Will.* Contrary to the opinion of many readers, this work is not designed to disprove man's freedom. Edwards is committed to belief in the soul's liberty to choose, for this alone makes the self responsible and justifies the dispensation of eternal punishments and rewards, which would otherwise have no meaning. Edwards therefore insists that man's choices in every case come from his own willing. God determines whether the self shall be saved or damned only in the sense that he ordains the kind of person that self will be—hence the nature of individual preferences. If God forbears to transform a person, that man must sin in consequence of his fallen condition. But the wicked choices which convict him are the work of his own free willing. It is he who has chosen evil. The well-known analysis by which Edwards shows that there is no such thing as the human will, but only human willing, is indicative.[16]

God alone has what Edwards calls "direct existence." The human being, like all other creatures, is a phenomenon, existing in God's thought. Thus the supposition of a human will leads to the absurdity of an infinite regression: the will which determines willing an act must itself be determined by another will, and this by another, and so on without end. Only in God as first cause can the origin of the event be found. The ultimate cause cannot be confined within anything less than the whole of reality, which is God, and therefore will, as opposed to willing, can only be assigned to a being who transcends the world of process and exists in himself. Once again one finds that Edwards' final resort is the theory of point of view: to conceive a will is only possible if one imagines a thinker who surveys the whole panorama of the universe.

Readers unfamiliar with Edwards tend to imagine him as the gloomy proponent of Calvinistic terrors, a personage who seems all the more depressing in that he fought a bad cause well. What is new in his thought, they suppose, was merely stolen from Locke and Newton for the purposes of defending intellectual re-

16. Ibid., pp. 171–74.

action. But the greater part of Edwards' writings, and the whole of his career, reveal a man whose mind was focused upon God's saving, not man's perdition, and it may be said without mitigating the offensive aspects of Edwards' dark doctrines that they are but a consequence and secondary aspect of his interest in the workings of divine grace. "God Glorified in Man's Dependence," a sermon whose title makes the point well, demonstrates that Edwards places the main emphasis upon God's goodness, even when man's guilt is most uncompromisingly asserted. It is characteristic of Edwards to argue in this sermon that, with respect to salvation, the "grace in bestowing this gift is great in proportion to our unworthiness to whom it is given; instead of deserving such a gift, we merited infinitely ill of God's hands." [17] Edwards' gloom is created by the art of chiaroscuro. The whole purpose is to define the light. The reader ought to keep this in mind as he turns to consider Edwards' doctrine of election. It is not just another topic or side of the theological system; it is the main subject. The metaphysics which originates in epistemology has its center of focus in psychology. For Edwards, God's presence to the sanctified individual is the dénouement of the universal drama.

Essentially, Edwards' problem is to explain this presence in a way which will preserve God's independent identity and yet demonstrate that the deity lives within the redeemed heart. Developing again the paradox of identity but difference seen already in his view of the Trinity, Edwards is careful to deny that "the saints are made partakers of the essence of God, and so are 'godded' with God, and 'christed' with Christ." [18] Yet if God is present within the self, how is the difference between them to be maintained? The problem is aggravated by Edwards' desire to make the largest possible claim for God's presence, so that the psychic event will seem entirely caused by the deity. Apparently

17. *Sermons*, in *Select Works of Jonathan Edwards*, 2 (3 vols. London, The Banner of Truth Trust, 1959), 36.
18. John E. Smith, ed., *Religious Affections*, in *The Works of Jonathan Edwards*, 2, 203.

he seems to settle for the questionable argument that difference is a matter of degree:

> The grace which is in the hearts of the saints is of the same nature, with the divine holiness, as much as it is possible for that holiness to be which is infinitely less in degree; as the brightness that is in a diamond which the sun shines upon is of the same nature with the brightness of the sun, but only that it is as nothing as to degree.[19]

But the sun metaphor is significant, and when Edwards' use of it in the essay on the Trinity is considered, it becomes clear that something more than difference of degree is here proposed:

> The father is as the substance of the Sun. (By substance I dont mean in a philosophical sense, but the Sun as to its Internal Constitution.) The Son is as the Brightness & Glory of the disk of the Sun or that bright & glorious form under which it appears to our Eyes. The Holy Gh. is the action of the Sun which is within the Sun in its Intestine Heat, &, being diffusive, enlightens, warms, enlivens & comforts the world. The Sp., as it is Gods Infinite love to himself & happiness in himself, is as the internal heat of the Sun, but, as it is that by which G. communicates himself, it is as the Emanation of the suns action, or the Emitted Beams of the sun.[20]

God himself is truly present in the sanctified person, but only in his one aspect, as process, or "the Deity subsisting in act." The saints, then, are at one with God as participants in his love, but to share thus in the divine process is not to be God himself, any more than the diamond which contains the light of the sun is the sun itself.

The most interesting aspect of Edwards' analysis of regeneration is that which he worked out partly as an answer to the critics who deplored the excesses of the Great Awakening. During the

19. Ibid., p. 202.
20. *Essay on the Trinity*, pp. 124–25.

period of remarkable conversions over which Edwards and Whitefield presided, there were a number of deluded enthusiasts who claimed sanctity on absurd evidence—magical powers, fantastic visions, and the like—and *A Treatise concerning Religious Affections* is in large part Edwards' defense of the rationale of the Awakening against the follies which discredited it. The psychology Edwards there sets forth is prophetic of modern thought in its assertion that nature is the medium of all psychic phenomena, those involving God's direct intervention no less than merely natural ones. In the crucial experiences of regeneration, Edwards argues, man's natural faculties are the necessary means. And the psychology of the man reborn of the Spirit reveals no unusual powers but only natural faculties so perfected that the individual has a new sense of things. Instead of seeing wonders unknown to him before, the saint beholds the familiar objects of experience in a new way. Through regeneration God changes man's very nature rather than merely rearranging the scenery before an unregenerate mind. Thus Edwards anticipates Freudian psychology by grounding mental states in physical functions, and he anticipates theories of Gestalt by suggesting that physiological patterns and the ordering of perceptions in consciousness are aspects of a single design. The Gestalt or form of the regenerate man is God's will, and of this form human feeling is merely an aspect. Thus a state of grace is not to be thought of simply as an emotional condition, as enthusiasts too often assumed. On the other hand, it does not follow that emotion is unimportant in religious experience. Edwards scouts the folly of rejecting the heart's response: "This is the objection which is made: 'tis looked upon as a clear evidence that the apprehensions and affections that many persons have, are not really from such a cause [i.e. grace], because they seem to them to be from that cause." [21] But though emotion is crucial in Edwards' psychology, that is not sufficient reason for placing him among the pre-Romantics. He is interested in feelings as effects—"affections"—and instinctual and vitalistic creativity

21. *Religious Affections*, in *Works*, 2, 139.

of mind are left to the damned, whose experience Edwards but sketchily describes.

Nor is Edwards' theology to be explained by its European origins alone, as if it were just one more system growing out of Newton and Locke. Historical hindsight can lead to serious error: although we now know that science did in time call the authority of revelation into question, we must resist the tendency to suppose that for Edwards this seemed the probable outcome and that he set about constructing a system in which scientific ideas, like captured cannon, are turned about to defend the citadel of New England orthodoxy against a hostile modernism. While contemporary Christian apologists abroad undertook to refute the various sorts of deism and atheistic rationalism which science fostered, Edwards did not trouble to answer those who questioned revelation. He opposed the heresies of convinced Christians, for the most part Protestants in the Calvinist tradition, and far from imagining that the new thought was a natural ally of irreligion, he embraced it with at least as much enthusiasm as Bolingbroke or Montesquieu.

It would be difficult to find an instance in which Edwards views scientific fact as inconsistent with revealed truth. He seized upon the ideas of Newton and Locke because they seemed true, and he rejected or ignored other influences nearer at hand and, from our point of view, much less damaging to Christian belief. What he took indicates what, to begin with, he believed. That his theology differs radically from the systems characteristic of the European Enlightenment is evidence that in his work one observes an American mind choosing and exploiting ideas from abroad to its own particular ends. The new thought did not force new purposes upon Edwards, but confirmed the doctrines he already believed in. Even a casual reading should suffice to convince one that he conceived himself amplifying and gloriously extending the faith of his fathers, rather than contriving for it a plausible defense.

Edwards' special way of using Newton and Locke illustrates

the need to look beyond his arguments to the world view they help to express. Therefore I shall now consider the quality of Edwards' consciousness—the sensibility and the way of thought from which the theology developed, for only with respect to this can his shadowy and distorted mirroring of the Enlightenment become understandable and the motives behind his reasons be appreciated. My brief though perhaps inevitably tedious survey of his main theories is offered partly as proof, partly as illustration, of a central fact concerning Edwards: that in his thought there is manifested a new and markedly different version of the Puritan sense of time. I have already defined the basis of his system as a theory of point of view and have attempted to show that this theory provided a way of resolving problems which in Puritanism take on an aggravated form. But for Edwards this theory was a fact as well. It proved so convenient a means of solving abstract problems simply because it accorded with his way of seeing things.

The best record of Edwards' own experience is to be found in the "Personal Narrative." This work is not a success, and as Robert F. Sayre points out, its failure is primarily due to the unsuitableness of the traditional form of autobiography to Edwards' kind of self-analysis.[22] Edwards feels himself committed to telling a story, but his real purpose is to analyze moments, and since the form is at war with the matter, he usually fails to catch the experience he means to record. The language is too vaguely general:

> This I know not how to express otherwise, than by a calm, sweet abstraction of soul from all the concerns of this world; and sometimes a kind of vision, or fixed ideas and imaginations, of being alone in the mountains, or some solitary wilderness, far from all mankind, sweetly conversing with Christ, and wrapped and swallowed up in God.[23]

22. *The Examined Self: Benjamin Franklin, Henry Adams, Henry James* (Princeton, Princeton University Press, 1964), pp. 37–38.
23. *Jonathan Edwards: Representative Selections*, p. 60.

To say that this is mystical experience provides no clarification, for applying the term "mysticism" does not make it any easier to say what the experience itself was like. In only a few passages is the moment convincingly rendered:

> And scarce any thing, among all the works of nature, was so sweet to me as thunder and lightning; formerly, nothing had been so terrible to me. Before, I used to be uncommonly terrified with thunder, and to be struck with terror when I saw a thunder storm rising; but now, on the contrary, it rejoiced me. *I felt God, so to speak,* at the first appearance of a thunder storm; and used to take the opportunity, at such times, to fix myself in order to view the clouds, and see the lightnings play, and *hear the majestic and awful voice of God's thunder,* which oftentimes was exceedingly entertaining, leading me to sweet comtemplations of my great and glorious God. While thus engaged, it always seemed natural to me to sing, or chant for my meditations; or, to speak my thoughts in soliloquies with a singing voice.[24]

What sets this passage apart is the tension of the experience it records—not dramatic conflict, for there is no crisis, but, rather, a graceful equilibrium, as of a man standing on a rolling deck—a balancing easy but continuous between two sides of perception.

What Edwards sees is, in one sense, God himself present in the natural event and, in another sense, a mere sign or imprint of the transcendent Creator's hand: "I felt God, so to speak, at the first appearance of a thunder storm." God's presence is immediately perceived—"felt"—but the fall into pantheism is quickly averted by the saving qualification—"so to speak." The voice is the thunder's, not God's, so that on the surface an orthodox separation is maintained; yet, *as* a voice, a voice speaking God's glory, it is also the deity's own utterance. The equilibrium is pleasurable —in terms of language, a smooth and graceful shifting of emphasis through gradations of verbal meaning—and in the world view

24. Ibid., p. 61. Italics mine.

which this use of language manifests there is a felicitous reconciliation rather than a stressful contrast. For Edwards finds no real contradiction between witnessing God's presence in the landscape and recognizing his transcendent overlordship. Present experience and eternal reality merge in the self's response, which is both Edwards' own cheerful preference and an automatic consequence of God's will. "While thus engaged, it *always seemed natural* to sing or chant for my meditations."

One is reminded, by contrast, of Anne Bradstreet's dismay at her inability to sing. Though Edwards is saved, while the poet of "Contemplations" hopes only for a sign of grace, their situations are similar enough to demonstrate how much the Puritan sensibility gradually altered. Perception in itself does not reassure Mistress Bradstreet. For her the meaning of things directly beheld is to be explained by the mind's transcendence. She must move away from her sense data to possess them—must "realize" the universal scheme in terms of which sensation is meaningful. Edwards, however, is free from this need to change position. He does not have to journey toward times remote; there is no busy commutation between the now and eternity. He perceives a single reality which is interchangeably eternal being and temporal process: the spirit in the thunderhead and the great conductor directing the storm from on high are but alternative ways of speaking. Given Edwards' view of time as an emanation of the divine will, this resolution of the transcendence-immanence contrast must necessarily follow, for any moment in which God is immanent is a portion of time, and time itself issues from his creating will. And though at every moment God continually wills his own existence as well as that of all extant created things, the word "continually" in this statement refers to the time God creates, so that there is no difference between the God who now wills—within time—and the God who wills time. Nor is there any sense in which one is superior to or more real than the other. All that survives of the old contrast is the difference of points of view.

The passage on thunderstorms is of the greatest value in that it provides a rare personal record of the mood which pervades Edwards' theology. One supposes that as a theoretician he was content to convince by sharp argument, since it is difficult today, in an age which has little interest in theology, to remember how deeply felt the issues were and to imagine what it was like to believe that questions of doctrine were life-and-death matters. But if we recall the circumstances within which Edwards wrote —if we remember that his sermons were meant as exhortations for the good of his auditors' souls, and that his dissertations were controversial tracts in defense of the faith as he understood it— the cool rationality of his prose becomes significant. The serenity, the blandness, the preternatural calm, which on some occasions, as in "Sinners in the Hands of an Angry God," takes the form of a terrifying *sang-froid,* manifest an emotional appeal of great power.

To recognize this is to recognize the need to make Edwards the literary artist a central consideration in any study of Edwards the thinker. For the import of his arguments cannot be separated from their spiritual purpose as statements made to actual human beings. Edwards' philosophic or theological meaning must be understood within the world he defines poetically by using language to dominate and transform the audience's imagination rather than merely to convince their understanding. A theologian who believed that "notional" knowledge is of no value unless the feelings be engaged would hardly favor a mode of writing which is no more than lucid and serviceable. Edwards' style, though at first it may seem only the transparent medium of technical writing, manifests great artistry in the still and clear atmosphere it creates.

What Edwards aimed at was the feeling of impersonality—an effect not to be confused with indifference—the numbness induced by the financial page, the business letter, the official report. The impersonal effect is that of white on white. It is as if the speaker were so perfectly harmonized with the universe he describes that he is almost indistinguishable from his background. Concerning such "flat characters" as Mr. McCawber or Major

Pendennis, Edwin Muir observes that the art of creating them consists of making the one trait in view hint at the existence of others which have been suppressed.[25] Edwards' impersonality develops from a similar method. His style conveys a sense that someone is speaking but not as himself; the speaker seems depersonalized in that he is possessed and made the mouthpiece of an ineluctable logic. Edwards in this way records the same variety of emotion that Thoreau would describe through ironically humble illustration: "It was no longer beans that I hoed, nor I that hoed beans." [26] The reader senses the speaker by his absence, for it indicates a very precise and powerful feeling: that of submitting unreservedly to objective facts and, since it is to certainty that he surrenders, ceasing to be himself by becoming the truth.

Without pretending to offer any exact account of Edwards' style, I shall point to one major technique which illustrates the atmosphere of feeling that his language creates. This is the technique of exact repetition. By continually returning to a few key words and syntactical forms, Edwards casts over his arguments an appearance of the precise, the inevitable, and, in a sense, the automatic. The effect is to convert ratiocination into a state of feeling, a condition in which self and world are perfectly harmonized. A fairly long passage is required to illustrate this method, but the reader who follows the fortunes of such key words as "all," "spring," "world," "pursuit," or "busy" will not, I believe, find this example dull:

> Such is man's nature, that he is very inactive, any otherwise than he is influenced by some affection, either love or hatred, desire, hope, fear, or some other. These affections we see to be the springs that set men agoing, in all the affairs of life, and engage them in all their pursuits: these are the things that put men forward, and carry them along, in all their worldly business; and especially are men excited and animated by these, in

25. *The Structure of the Novel* (London, Hogarth Press, 1963), pp. 144–46.
26. *Walden*, chap. 7, p. 350.

all affairs wherein they are earnestly engaged, and which they pursue with vigor. We see the world of mankind to be exceeding busy and active; and the affections of men are the springs of the motion: take away all love and hatred, all hope and fear, all anger, zeal, and affectionate desire, and the world would be in a great measure motionless and dead; there would be no such thing as activity amongst mankind, or any earnest pursuit whatsoever. It is affection that engages the covetous man, and him that is greedy of worldly profits, in his pursuits; and it is by the affections that the ambitious man is put forward in his pursuit of worldly glory; and it is the affections also that actuate the voluptuous man, in his pursuit of pleasure and sensual delights: the world continues, from age to age, in a continual commotion and agitation, in a pursuit of these things; but take away all affection, and the spring of all this motion would be gone, and the motion itself would cease. And as in wordly things, worldy affects are very much the spring of men's motion and action; so in religious matters, the spring of their actions is very much religious affection: he that has doctrinal knowledge and speculation only, without affection, never is engaged in the business of religion.[27]

The chiming and revolving effects of such repetition produce a language so smooth in its movement that the argument glides forward as if it were developing itself—an impression that is exactly suited to Edwards' subject. The style enacts the inevitability of the divine will, so that the God who disposes all things according to his infinite wisdom and power is made to seem present in the theological demonstration of his Absolute Sovereignty.

Exact repetition implies a great deal. It suggests that there is a governing vocabulary—a few spare and essential words in which all meanings meet—and that the process of abstraction by which the mind marshals phenomena under these sovereign terms is the

27. *Religious Affections*, in *Works*, 2, 101.

penultimate phase of its journey toward the Word. Thus Edward's style dramatizes a simplification without itself becoming simple. As the same word, or a variant form of it, appears in changing contexts, its meaning undergoes delicate modifications. It shimmers, as if in a changeable light, revealing varied and unexpected hues. In the paragraph quoted, for example, "worldly business" and "extremely busy" sum up well Edwards' picture of the continual activity that man's affections stimulate, but when "the business of religion" appears at the paragraph's end, "business" has come to mean a purely purposeful process, and all its vain qualities—preoccupation, compulsive behavior, distraction —fall away.

The general tone of Edwards' style is encountered again in the poetry of Poe and Eliot. Though they achieve it in a different manner, those poets share with Edwards a quality of feeling at once somber and strangely joyous. They are poets who are naturally attracted by metaphysical formulations of selfhood and share Edwards' sense that in the vision of the Absolute the self is canceled. It is not surprising, then, that their poems make strikingly similar use of repetition—in *Ulalume,* for instance, and the passage on the Word in *Ash Wednesday.* And looking back to the seventeenth century, much the same manner and effect can be found in the jingling stanzas of *The Day of Doom.* Edwards' plangent certitude and Poe's and Eliot's incantatory mood point to the same end—an impersonality by which words are made to emerge as if dictated by the logic of the cosmos.[28]

Edwards' theory of language offers another way of defining the subtle vibrancy of his style. One side of his view is expressed in Emerson's simple formula:

> 1. Words are signs of natural facts. 2. Particular natural facts are symbols of particular spiritual facts. 3. Nature is the symbol of Spirit.[29]

28. See Perry Miller's sensitive commentary on the qualities of Edwards' style in Perry Miller et al., eds., *Major American Writers, 1* (2 vols. New York, Harcourt, Brace, and World, 1962), 91–92.

29. *Nature,* in *The Complete Works of Ralph Waldo Emerson, 1,* 25.

But there is for Edwards a sense in which language is quite separate from Spirit. "Words," he remarks, "were first formed to express external things," and from this he concludes that language is inadequate to express the things of religion.[30] Language belongs to the realm of created things; though it manifests Spirit, or God as act, as all created things do, it is utterly separated from the transcendent deity. Words tend toward the Word, and, in spite of the fact that they never quite reach that destination, by means of their very tendency they acquire the mysterious power to evoke or create meaning rather than just mechanically refer to their objects as things distinct from themselves. Since they only tend, however, they are simply words after all, and reality is more than mere talk.

This attitude toward language is reflected in the admirable discretion of Edwards' prose style. Though he deals in dogmatic certainties, he seems never to claim too much. His sense of the power of words saves him from a manner which is pat, mechanical, while, on the other hand, his respect for the mystery of things is such that he writes, always, as one who knows that at best statements merely approximate, suggest.

The calm and inevitability of Edwards' style are most impressively symbolized by the shrewdness of his logic. He is admired most commonly for the exacting precision of his thought, though in fact his arguments are often opportunistic and he favors the rather unfair tactic of shifting his grounds. "The question," he once remarked, "is not, whether what is said be metaphysics, physics, logic, or mathematics, Latin, French, English, or Mohawk but, whether the reasoning be good, and the arguments truly conclusive." [31] This is to be forthright in a tentative way: right reasoning can apparently play the field, moving about from one context to another at will, so long as its conduct is correct. But if the mode of discourse keeps changing, the standards of truth do also. How then can one know whether the reasoning is right? Edwards' answer is that the ultimate test of truth is feeling,

30. *Freedom of the Will*, in *Works, 1,* 376.
31. Ibid., p. 423.

and thus that reason appeals to the mind's sense of harmony, of the "sweet, mutual consents" between ideas.

This is not to say that for Edwards reason is a will-o'-the-wisp. Rather, he sees reason as an experience, which demonstrates by portraying. Arguments, in his view, do not of themselves form true connections; they fit together according to one's sense of what constitutes a valid relation. The authority of Edwards' ratiocination is derived, ultimately, from the consistency of an imaginative vision toward which his arguments point but which transcends them.

Were Edwards' theology no more than a system, it could be challenged by attacking its premises. But finding his premises is in practice not possible, for every assumption one isolates turns out to be not quite what Edwards really assumes; it is enmeshed in so many qualifications, defined in such various contexts, that one can only formulate it ad hoc according to the particular occasion and one's own purpose. For example, Edwards seems a fundamentalist in the literalism of his Gospel proofs, but at the same time, he maintains that the true meaning of Scripture can be discerned only by minds illuminated with the light of grace. Such apparently antithetical views are not real contradictions: the two ideas do fit together in a larger context, but one must be forever drawing a more ample boundary as new complications come into view. Thus the discursive expands toward and implies the visionary.

Edwards has created, in our modern term, a myth of reasonableness, and it is this that gives to his arguments the air of impeccable demonstration. Thus logic is poetry; it provides conclusive proofs, because it has also the power to suggest the world of which its proofs are true. Such an achievement is possible only to a writer of great genius. In reading Edwards we may disagree with his premises, we may protest against his conclusions, but we have to grant that that is the way he saw things. Even as we question the doctrine, we accept the vision.

It is as symbolist and student of symbolism that Edwards most clearly anticipates later American literature. He opens to the reader's mind the inspiriting possibility of an experience in which, as Emerson would write, "the world shall be to us an open book, and every form significant of its hidden life and final cause." [32] Edwards' thought manifests the Puritan source of transcendentalism, and the relation between them is nowhere more apparent than in their common tendency to describe human error as a failure of perception. To the transcendentalists sin is inattention, a state of dullness, sluggishness, sleep. It is the failure to be aware of the symbolic meaning of things, and it is wrong as a refusal of life because it is a turning away from the deity that experience reveals. It is, in short, the condition of unresponsiveness which Edwards attributes to the unregenerate man.

But while the transcendentalists assume that anyone can rub his eyes, in Edwards' view the light of understanding is not given to all. This difference points to a more fundamental one between Edwards' theology and transcendentalism. In Edwards monism is balanced by dualism, as two sides of a true account, but in transcendentalist thought dualism is the difficulty to be overcome, the false appearance which in the highest states of consciousness is resolved by a vision of absolute unity. Thus to Emerson symbol is revelation: we may see God in the object if we try hard enough; while to Edwards symbols are but "Images or Shadows of Divine Things," and our power to see them is mysteriously given by a transcendent God, if given at all. Unlike Emerson, Edwards balances two views of symbol. He regards the symbol as continuous with its meaning, as Emerson argues, but he also regards it as markedly distinct. Edwards' healthy respect for the common-sense view of symbols as mere signs pointing to objects other than themselves follows from the fact that in his view meanings refer to a God entirely separate from the universe as well as immanent.

"Christ," Edwards remarks, "often makes use of representations of spiritual things in the constitution of the [world] for argument,

32. *Nature*, in *Complete Works*, 1, 35.

as thus: the tree is known by its fruit. These things are not merely mentioned as illustrations of his meaning, but as illustrations and evidence of the truth of what he says." [33] Symbols, then, prove as well as express. That a tree is known by its fruit is not merely a figure or diagram of the idea that a man is known by his actions but also proves that idea true. Again Edwards appeals to a standard of harmony: the validity of the symbol is revealed by the "consents" between physical image and spiritual significance. The image is not simply an epitome or, on the other hand, a mere parallel. It is both at once, yet neither absolutely—an epitome in the sense that God's immanence makes the meaning inherent in the image (for its meaning is his thought, which is operative within the world as process), a parallel in that, with respect to God's transcendent being, the image is an analogue of his thought. As a result of the image's double nature, Edwards' symbolic interpretations are at once very pat yet mysteriously suggestive and poignant in effect. In *Images or Shadows*, for instance, the moralizing is of a kind quite different from Anne Bradstreet's or Cotton Mather's:

> He that is travelling up a very high mountain, if he goes on climbing, will at length get to that height and eminence as at last not only to have his prospect vastly large, but as he will get above the clouds and winds, and where he will enjoy a perpetual serenity and calm. This may encourage Christians constantly and steadfastly to climb the Christian hill. The perfect and uninterrupted serenity and calm there is on some very high mountains is also a type of the heavenly state. [34]

Here the facts are not simply "read"; they effuse the meaning as a sort of atmosphere, so that the lesson seems to be irradiated from sensation. This is manifest stylistically by the way "serenity" and

33. *Images or Shadows of Divine Things*, ed. Perry Miller (New Haven, Yale University Press, 1948), p. 49, Image 26.
34. Ibid., p. 68, Image 67.

"calm" change from physical to psychic qualities, and the visual "prospect vastly large" is transformed into the conceptual "heavenly state."

The passage, though a mere jotting, is quite typical of the tone and emotional ambiance of Edwards' work. He looks downward to experience from the level of dogmatic generalization, but he does so in a way which suggests the opposite view. His images have the radiant quality of objects reflected in water, spiritualized and somewhat diaphanous. But one feels, always, that they are the things of ordinary experience as these would appear in the light of grace. The effect is of a familiar landscape seen by midnight lightning, radiant with intimations of both beauty and inexpressible dread. This disquieting effect appears later in Hawthorne and Poe, and then again in Eliot. It is something much more unnerving than predestinarian ideas or Poe's melodramatic horrors. Its ominous quality is the shadow cast by reverence, and though in this emotion terror is an essential ingredient, we should recollect that awe is a good deal more than fright.

In turning to Benjamin Franklin, it will be advantageous to begin by considering him as the practical man of public projects and useful gadgets, the proponent of good works rather than grace—in short, the Franklin who least resembles Edwards. The purpose will be to find a similarity at the heart of the all too obvious difference and thus make credible the fact that Franklin and Edwards were both nurtured in the society over which Cotton Mather presided. In the *Autobiography* Franklin discusses at some length a plan which he formed, during one of his sojourns in London, for cleaning the city streets. Noticing an old woman sweeping the pavement before his house, he offered her a shilling to clean the entire street, and when the task was done, it occurred to him that "if that feeble woman could sweep such a street in three hours, a strong active man might have done it in half the time." The project this idea inspired takes account of the most minute details. Franklin proposes, for example:

That the Mud when rak'd up be not left in Heaps to be spread abroad again by the Wheels of Carriages and Trampling of Horses; but that Scavengers be provided with Bodies of Carts, not plac'd high upon Wheels, but low upon Sliders; with Lattice Bottoms, which, being cover'd with Straw, will retain the Mud thrown into them, and permit the Water to drain from it, whereby it will become much lighter, Water making the greatest Part of its Weight.[35]

Aware that his zest for the practical brings him to the edge of the absurd, Franklin flaunts good sense, like a clown his bandana, to call attention to a point rather more important than the idea that streets ought to be kept clean:

Some may think these trifling Matters not worth minding or relating. But when they consider, that tho Dust blown into the Eyes of a single Person or into a single Shop on a windy Day, is but of small Importance, yet the great Number of the Instances in a populous City, and its frequent Repetitions give it Weight and Consequence; perhaps they will not censure very severly those who bestow some Attention to Affairs of this seemingly low Nature. Human Felicity is produc'd not so much by great Pieces of good Fortune that seldom happen, as by little Advantages that occur every Day.[36]

"Little Advantages"—how well this despicable phrase sums up the monstrous "model American" against whom Lawrence railed.[37] Having assumed the role of Swiftian "Projector," Franklin asks us to forgive, to accept, even to applaud this personage on the grounds that he is really in the right, could we but see it. The offense is then compounded by an even more risible instance of "doing good."

35. *The Autobiography of Benjamin Franklin,* ed. Leonard W. Larabee et al. (New Haven, Yale University Press, 1964), p. 206.
36. Ibid., p. 207.
37. *Studies in Classic American Literature* (Garden City, N.Y., Doubleday Anchor Books, 1953), p. 20.

Thus if you teach a poor young Man to shave himself and keep his Razor in order, you may contribute more to the Happiness of his Life than in giving him a 1000 Guineas. The Money may be soon spent, the Regret only remaining of having foolishly consum'd it. But in the other Case he escapes the frequent Vexation of waiting for Barbers, and of their some times dirty Fingers, offensive Breaths and dull Razors. He shaves when most convenient to him, and enjoys daily the Pleasure of its being done with a good Instrument.[38]

It is hard to destroy such an argument by striking out in Lawrence's manner, for, like a wily pugilist, Franklin is always just out of reach. His satire on parsimonious philanthropy—good advice is more valuable than money—makes the example doubtful, but the reader cannot feel certain that it is not really meant. Franklin's humor is persuasive rather than shifty: he presents a theory by demonstrating its usefulness in the worst case. The most trivial instance of "doing good," for the least inspiring motives—even practicality for its own sake—makes a good deal of sense. Dust in the street is an undeniable evil, if a minor one, and it would be a prideful presumption to deny that in the long run it has "weight and consequence." And the same may be said of the inconveniences of being publicly barbered. No one can see far enough ahead to know where such little irritations will lead, but by minor advantages one will not be misled. They advance no false claims; they are benefits enjoyed now. If in the future they become disadvantageous, they can always be rejected—back to the barber. But it is probable that what works now will work again. If dusty streets lead off toward catastrophic possibilities, the little advantages to be derived from clean streets may inaugurate incalculable blessings. Because one's prospect is too limited to reveal the ultimate effects of action, the wisest course is to proceed by the "feel" of experience, trusting that a benefit, however slight, betokens a momentary adjustment of the mind to the real order of things.

38. *Autobiography,* p. 207.

The argument that the poor young man might only be harmed by the gift of a hundred guineas proceeds in the same way. The money, like other "great pieces of good fortune," is a merely theoretical good in a generalized scheme, not a known good in the world of actual experience. Though cash *can* procure advantages, there is no assurance that it will do so on particular occasions. To enjoy a fortune, the poor young man would have to know what was worth buying—where his real interests lay—which is to say that to be prudent, he would have to be virtuous. There is, then, no such thing as a merely practical good. It is a good as it is experienced; it exists in a moral as well as merely material situation.

That to Franklin prudence and virtue are continuous is a crucial point. Nearly all the complaints against him involve imputing to him precisely the dualism that he satirizes here, and which he continually rejects. It is objected that his sense of values amounts to little more than a passion for contriving worldly conveniences —money profits, physical comforts, good health, applause, security, and the like. If the sphere of practical concerns were distinct from that of men's more ennobling interests, then it would indeed follow that such matters as public sanitation should not much engage a healthy mind. But surely Franklin does not grant that premise. Often, as in the passage we have been considering, he pretends to adopt it in order to illustrate its absurdity, but the whole tenor of this passage, with its satiric glance at Lucretius and its humorous reduction of the clay of man's mortality to dust in the streets and motes in the eye, is to assert that even the most determined practicality must assume values beyond the practical.

Franklin would have the reader cultivate his sense of situation, see objects within the landscape of consciousness, conceive value as an experiential event rather than a lump sum—look to the human circumstances. And these circumstances, as Franklin conceives them, are those of an individual person—not necessarily Franklin himself, but someone in particular. Hence in Franklin's thought there is much philosophizing but no philosophy. His generalizations, since they are always framed with reference to what the individual can know, are too tentative to serve as arguments in support of a system.

Generalization—a great deal of it—can of course be found in Franklin's writings, but its value is of a peculiar kind. Since the meaning and truth of a statement are determined by personal experience, one's generalizations are continually subject to revision. The self learns much at second hand; otherwise, there would be no point to the notoriously instructive sayings of Poor Richard, who in the almanac for 1743 observes that "Experience keeps a dear school, yet fools will learn in no other." [39] But the lessons derived from general experience are valid only to the degree that they approximate personal experience. For the self the truth of a statement is its use: it means what it "does" and is true to the extent that it "works." For that reason Franklin avoids speaking of opinions as false, preferring, rather, to reject them as of little use or tending to undesirable effects.

This pragmatic conversion of truth into function follows from Franklin's appeal to the self's situation, the limits of which allow only a very partial view of things. While he sometimes notes the effects of social and geographical circumstances upon knowledge, he is far more impressed by the general circumstance of the self's place in time. His strongest emphasis is on man's ignorance of the future, with the consequence that knowledge of the past appears to him nearly as doubtful, since fresh experience must necessarily alter our interpretations of what has happened. As in Anne Bradstreet or, looking ahead, in T. S. Eliot, knowledge is a function of the power to remember and foresee.

Franklin's and Edwards' modes of vision can be seen as nearly exact inversions of one another. The certainty from which Franklin reasons is experience in time, whereas Edwards' point of departure is the universal scheme revealed by God's word. Yet from

39. *Poor Richard's Almanac: Selections from the Prefaces, Apothegms, and Rimes,* ed. Benjamin E. Smith (New York, Century Co., 1898), p. 116.

their contrasting positions, the two men look at the same world, and this agreement is to be understood not merely in the sense that they both see the world as it appeared to eighteenth-century Americans, nor in the sense that all theories are interpretations of the same reality, but in the stricter sense that Franklin and Edwards both envision a world in which thought must choose between the same set of alternative viewpoints. This common ground is most clearly shown by the tendency of each to make the other's point of view the center of attention. Edwards so organizes dogmatic generalizations as to focus his study of salvation within the momentary personal experience of regeneration, while Franklin interprets experiences as a means of inferring the all-inclusive design. That is why Franklin too often seems a merely typical person and his life full of lessons for everyone. Franklin's paradoxical relation to Edwards can best be understood by recognizing that, since a view—as this term is used in speaking of point of view—is always a view of something other than itself, in the concept of experience the idea of an order transcending experience is implicit. Franklin's great sensitivity to the limits of man's understanding would not be possible without an assumed world having the same orderliness, inclusiveness, and independence of human interests and thoughts as the world which Edwards portrays. The more one insists that an actual experience is always that of someone in particular, the more one becomes aware of the necessity to posit a world which transcends all views except the all-inclusive vision—God's consciousness.

Franklin's fundamental agreement with Edwards serves to explain why his empiricism is often concealed and even seemingly contradicted by his confident rationalism. Considering his moral maxims, his taste for making deistical deductions from the laws of nature, and his fiddling with codes, bylaws, and constitutions, it is hard to imagine that he had any very serious doubts about the scope of human understanding. So assured are his formulas that one can overlook the skepticism they are designed to accommodate. Since the tolerance Franklin recommends is dogma today, one can easily fail to notice that he justifies political and religious liberalism and a morality of rules of thumb on the ground that in human thought there is little certainty. Taking his doubts for granted, we doubt much less than he. But Franklin the rationalist is abetted by Franklin the empiricist; indeed the first could not exist without the second. In terms of motive alone, what stronger incitement can there be to the search for broad formulations and general rules than the belief that their usefulness alone is sufficient to justify them? Only, perhaps, Franklin's complementary premise that even the most ambitious generalization can be put to an immediate test. If for no other reason, the empiricist would be a rationalist, because a universe governed by fixed principles is a great convenience.

Franklin will, perhaps, always remain an enigma, for although his rationalism is a function of his empiricism, the two are in continual conflict. But an enigma is a paradox, not an absurdity, and the doubleness of Franklin's thought attests to the unity of his vision. So long as we relate his ideas only to one another, Franklin can be for us no more than a point of collision for contradictory beliefs. We cannot in any convincing way reconcile the gadgetry with the pure science, the faith in Providence with the argument that this belief ought to be maintained merely because the common people need to believe in it, the belief in progress and democratic principles with the skeptical view of human understanding, the financial shrewdness with the voluntary risking of life and fortune. So long as we attend only to relating Franklin's opinions to each other, we are faced with either-or choices and our view of Franklin himself must be arbitrary.

Neither Franklin the hero nor Franklin the humbug seems credible, for each is produced by suppressing a large part of the evidence; either we ignore the skepticism and prudential connivance in favor of the high principles (usually the political ones) or we take the high principles as a mere façade for cynicism and selfish interests. To avoid this false choice, one is tempted to settle for the "many-sided Franklin," who is not one person but several, and this typically modern preference has the advantage of flattering our taste for believing that selfhood is a closetful of masks.[40] But one need only ask what a mask may be to recognize the evasion. Franklin's roles are, we say, "Franklin's." They must form a system defining some true identity at the center, and that self can be described only as a state or mode of consciousness.

It is, then, only within Franklin's vision that his ideas can be brought into harmony, not in their relations to each other. Each contradiction must be referred to his imaginative view of the human situation; and when this is done, the conflict will then be seen not as an opposition of thought but as a contrast between the senses in which statements are meant. For example, when Franklin asserts the usefulness of belief in Providence as a prop to morality, he is not speaking in the same sense as when he asserts that Providence does in fact govern the affairs of men.[41] The first statement appeals to the limits of man's knowledge as an individual living in time, while the second appeals to the necessity of hypothesizing a universal order. Resting upon the belief that a true generalization can be made—that the real principles of the universe can be expressed in the same form—the second statement intends to assert a truth about the actual order of things, whereas the first asserts a truth only about data lying within the horizon of individual experience.

The paradoxes which make Franklin so difficult to understand have their source in his manner of imagining the thinker's circumstances with reference to two standards—the limits of the thinker's view, on the one hand, and the rational orderliness of the reality of which it is a view, on the other. One must confront this ultimate fiction—this picture of the self—and thus it is Franklin the artist who matters most to those who would understand

40. I have borrowed this phrase from the title of *The Many-Sided Franklin*, ed. Paul L. Ford (New York, Century Co., 1899).

41. "For, without the belief of a Providence that takes cognisance of, guards, and guides, and may favor particular persons, there is no motive to worship a Deity, to fear his displeasure, or to pray for his protection" (Letter to Thomas Paine, ibid., p. 166).

Franklin the historical personage. Before considering the art of the *Autobiography*, however, I shall briefly survey some particular examples of the mode of thought I have tried to define.

I will cite first that extraordinary work of Franklin's youth, the *Dissertation on Liberty and Necessity, Pleasure and Pain*, an astounding performance in which the nascent exponent of self-help develops a necessitarian thesis and the future moralist concludes that since the individual cannot be free, he is not morally responsible and "Virtue and Vice are but empty distinctions." [42] Yet the greatest surprise of the essay is the picture it gives us of a Franklin we do not see again—Franklin the metaphysician. Franklin, to be sure, soon rejected his shocking little pamphlet, and ever after professed a great distaste for speculations of this kind. The *Dissertation*, then, is the product of a formative phase, yet it is for that very reason of great importance, since it shows us what he believed at an early stage of his development, and, to the extent that it is not typical—that the arguments it contains were rejected—it shows us the reasoning he revolted against—the background of ideas with reference to which his later thoughts were framed.

Franklin's odd criticism of the *Dissertation* in the *Autobiography*—"I doubted whether some Error had not insinuated itself unperceiv'd into my Argument, so as to infect all that follow'd, as is common in metaphysical Reasonings" [43]—reveals a radical shift of ground: the mere suspicion that his reasoning was faulty is now sufficient to discredit it. Franklin will not even trouble to conjecture what his error might have been, for it is not, indeed, the reasoning of the *Dissertation* that he rejects, but the whole mode of reasoning in terms of which his argument could be judged true or false. Refusing to play the metaphysical game, he dismisses the work not for its questionable arguments but for its practical effects. It is the work of the youthful freethinker, whose arguments misled others, and who was soon to discover that the

42. *Autobiography*, p. 114.
43. Ibid.

deists among his friends had turned out to be scoundrels and sybarites.

This change of Franklin's entire perspective, this turning from the question of what in the abstract is true to the problem of what in experience will "work" is actually foreshadowed in the *Dissertation* itself. Its most crucial argument, that concerning freedom of the will, can only lead to empiricist conclusions. If, the reasoning runs, an individual were entirely free to choose according to his own will, then

> Among the many Things which lie before him to be done, he may, as he is at Liberty and his Choice influenc'd by nothing, (for so it must be, or he is not at Liberty) chuse any one and refuse the rest. Now there is every Moment something *best* to be done, which is alone then good, and with respect to which, every Thing else is at that Time *evil.* In order to know which is best to be done, and which is not, it is requisite that we should have at one View all the intricate Consequences of every Action with respect to the general Order and Scheme of the Universe, both present and future; but they are innumerable and incomprehensible by any Thing but Omniscience. As we cannot know these, we have but one Chance to ten Thousand, to hit the right Action; we should then be perpetually blundering about in the Dark, and putting the Scheme in disorder. . . . Is it not necessary, then, that our Actions should be governed and over-rul'd by an all-wise Providence? [44]

Franklin could call such a position deism, but it is more properly Puritanism in deistic trappings. The picture of the self's situation is almost exactly that which the Puritan faith assumes: again the individual is seen in his severely isolated present ("there is every Moment something *best* to be done, etc."); again the problem of knowledge is that of explaining how, from within this moment, the mind can discern how the present facts—its options—fit into

44. Leonard W. Larabee et al., eds., *The Papers of Benjamin Franklin,* 1 (11 vols. New Haven, Yale University Press, 1959), 62.

the eternal design; and again, to draw the last and most obvious parallel, the eternal design is equated with the consciousness of the omniscient God who foreknows and predestines all things.

For Franklin the "feel" of experience proves his necessitarian argument. He appeals to our sense that the self is not "perpetually blundering about in the Dark," but does make the right choices more often than by the laws of chance it could. Even so, the truth as mere feeling and the truth as rationally deduced from fixed principles coincide. Though the self cannot discern the consequences of its sundry options, they are assumed to exist within a pattern as fixed and immutable as the will of the Puritan deity. The whole case for Franklin's radical empiricism is here, and to grant the dissertation's main argument is to recognize, as Franklin quickly did, that in human understanding there is too little certainty to support metaphysical generalizations, since these must be judged, always, within an incomplete vision of reality.

It is of the greatest importance to notice that Franklin's revulsion against speculations of a philosophic kind is not a despairing surrender to ignorance. He does not dismiss the questions philosophy raises as unanswerable—does not, as it were, throw up his hands. Writing to Benjamin Vaughn in 1779, he explains that "The great uncertainty I found in metaphysical reasonings disgusted me, and I quitted that kind of reading and study for others more satisfactory." [45] Certainty, then, is the standard, such certainty as metaphysics promises but fails to deliver. As Poor Richard complains, "Philosophy as well as foppery often changes fashion," a comment which emphasizes the limits of the philosopher's point of view by asserting that his criteria are the changeable preferences of an epoch rather than the truth itself. [46] And theology, insofar as it aims at demonstrable truths, is dismissed as an even more hopeless game: "Many a long dispute among divines may be thus abridg'd, It is so: It is not so, It is so; It is not

45. *Benjamin Franklin: Representative Selections*, ed. Frank Luther Mott and Chester E. Jorgenson (New York, American Book Co., 1936), p. 411.
46. *Poor Richard's Almanac: Selections*, p. 142.

so." [47] Such comments reflect a distaste for the methods of the philosopher and the theologian, not a dismissal of the problems they consider. Franklin did not simply shuffle aside these problems or satisfy himself with half-hearted answers. Most especially, it is absurd to conclude that Franklin's frequent comments upon religion are only the gestures of a man trying to get a troublesome subject out of the way. Those who voice such a lazy answer, will very probably be asking, in the next breath, why Franklin is so remote from the Puritan world which nurtured him, and reminding us how, in their one encounter, Cotton Mather warned him to stoop lest he bump his head.

Franklin's comments on religion, though scattered and often casual or ad hoc, follow an implicit pattern which becomes clear when they are considered in the light of his idea of Providence. His faith in providential guidance is supported by so many examples that only one memorable instance need be cited: his brief speech recommending that prayers be offered at the Constitutional Convention. Addressing the delegates at a time when their debates had reached an impasse, he recalled the experience of the revolution.

> All of us, who were engag'd in that Struggle must have observ'd frequent Instances of a superintending Providence in our Favor. . . . I have lived, Sir, a long time; and the longer I live, the more convincing Proofs I see of this Truth, *That God governs in the Affairs of Men!* And if a Sparrow cannot fall to the Ground without his Notice, is it probable that an Empire can rise without his Aid?—We have been assured, Sir, in the Sacred Writings, that "except the Lord build the House, they labor in vain that build it." [48]

That this statement and others like it were offered with a practical end in view does not discredit Franklin's sincerity; the same conviction is often manifest in private jottings and records of

47. Ibid., p. 116.
48. Mott and Jorgenson, *Benjamin Franklin: Representative Selections*, p. 490.

conversations in which, were it not that he had it at heart, the subject need never have come up.

Franklin's trust in Providence will seem cynical or thoughtless only if we suppose that it requires crediting the notion of a hand reaching down from the sky—a notion which Edwards also found absurd. The commonly recognized problem in Puritan thought as to how providential intervention could be logically reconciled with the natural laws ordained at the Creation was quite obvious to Franklin. Sometimes, indeed, he thought the dilemma an apt subject for satire. In the Swiftian hoax perpetrated against a poor astrologer and almanac-maker—Titan Leeds—Franklin, having prophesied Leeds' death, as Swift had Partridge's, explained that if Leeds were still alive, the event foretold had been forestalled by providential intervention.

> For the Stars only show to the Skillful, what will happen in the natural and universal Chain of Causes and Effects; but 'tis well known, that the Events which would otherwise certainly happen, at certain Times, in the Course of Nature, are sometimes set aside or postpon'd for wise and good Reasons, by the immediate particular Dispositions of Providence; which particular Dispositions the Stars can by no Means discover or foreshow.[49]

The implications of this pleasantry make it clear that Franklin did not consider Providence as superceding natural law but, like Edwards, as effecting God's will through the medium of nature.

Several bits of evidence which on the surface seem no more than amateurish and fashionably deistical opinions are indications of how Franklin sought to bring nature and Providence into harmony. One example is to be found in the recollections of David Williams, an English thinker who collaborated with Franklin in the project of founding a sect based upon "a rational Faith in God." Williams remembered that the liturgy they drew up asserted:

49. *Papers of Benjamin Franklin*, 1, 350.

The God of Newton was probably the regulating Principle or Good of the Solar System. . . .

What Principles may govern or preserve other Systems we know not, and Therefore know not their Gods. It is probable that all the Systems of Nature are governed and preserved by a relative Principle or Law, and that governing Principle is the Universal God.[50]

Williams' report seems trustworthy, for it makes much sense of that peculiar document, the "Articles of Belief and Acts of Religion," in which Franklin argues for the existence of a multiplicity of gods: "There is one Supreme most perfect Being, Author and Father of the Gods themselves"; but since the Supreme Being is infinitely above man and can have no concern for him or satisfaction in his worship, there must be, according to the notion of plenitude, as many degrees of being superior to man as beneath him; therefore, "The INFINITE has created many Beings or Gods, vastly superior to Man, who can better conceive his Perfections than we, and return him a more rational and glorious Praise." Franklin concludes that the deity he worships is the "particular Wise and good God, who is the Author and Owner of our System [i.e. the solar system]." [51]

We cannot know how long Franklin adhered to polytheism, but two assumptions behind his theory are of great significance. First, polytheism is asserted on the grounds of a post-Lockean idealism. The existence of the Supreme Being depends upon his being known to intelligences able to "conceive his Perfections"; and, conversely, since men are of too little account for his notice, there must be lesser gods to take thought of them. Clearly, being, as in Edwards, is to be defined as appearing to consciousness. That Franklin ends in what to Edwards would be unspeakable heresy is the result of rather too inconsiderate definitions of great, lesser, and infinite.

50. David Williams, "More Light on Franklin's Religious Ideas," *American Historical Review*, 43 (July 1938), 812.
51. *Papers of Benjamin Franklin, 1*, 102–03.

Secondly, Franklin's gods are equivalent to "principles," and the Universal God is "a relative Principle or Law" which governs all the systems. This equivalence demonstrates well Franklin's way of bridging the gap between the eternal and present points of view. What in reality is principle in experience is process, and men's generalizations from observed phenomena in time—the laws they formulate—bear witness to God's immanence; for while our formulas only approximate the true principles of the universe, the latter are present to experience, though never fully seen. Thus the Puritan contrast between the immanent and transcendent aspects of God is resolved in a manner essentially like that of Edwards.

The system of many gods is not necessary to Franklin's basic design but serves as a means—though a rather awkward means—of accounting for the manifold modes of God's acting. By identifying natural law with God as immanent deity, and explaining the seeming difference between nature and the Eternal Father as a consequence of our inability to view reality in a total conspectus, Franklin at once makes God the cause and ground of all being and yet, quite in Edwards' way, preserves the separateness of the transcendent deity.

That this scheme is patly mechanistic should, I think, be disproved by Franklin's belief that principle is indistinguishable from value. As shown by Williams' phrase, "the regulating Principle or Good of the Solar System," it is assumed that being is goodness, and the gods are regarded as superior to men in ordering more extensive spheres. Their existence and their excellence are alike functions of their degree of consciousness. In beings, whether men or gods, the degree of value and the scope of awareness are identical.

This belief is, to be sure, susceptible to narrow interpretations and correspondingly ludicrous conclusions. It might easily be put to the service of uncritical materialism and used to show that good is no more than efficiency or orderliness, as if the value of these values did not need to be explained. And at first it may seem that that is just the error of which Franklin himself is guilty. Because he fails to define exactly his habitual value terms—"benefit," "success," "profit," "felicity," "convenience"—one might suppose that he thought their meaning self-evident. And, since they are all suggestive of either physical satisfactions or social advantages, one might conclude that such were the values Franklin had most at heart. But comfort or public esteem are not in themselves evil; they may be continuous with virtues, just as the "little Advantages" of clean streets are continuous with peace of mind and public order. Unless practical and moral value are harshly separated—in which case far the greater part of experience must be considered of no ethical importance—a scale or continuum of values must be assumed; and once the need for such a scale has been granted, the question becomes one of point of view—of where, along the continuum, the approach to an ultimate good begins.

With respect to action, this question concerns the first step, while with respect to thought, it concerns the first perception or most immediate datum. Both, Franklin assumes, are to be found in the area of personal experience, where the good most commonly appears in humble and practical forms. Furthermore, the individual's view is too limited to allow for the definition of absolutes; since he sees processes, not essences, goodness, as it is known to him, is a way of happening, not a timeless object. Franklin's use of value terms is, then, largely dramatic—a means of directing attention to the personal point of view and of defining the situation shared by him and his readers as one in which knowledge is so limited that the only names for values that can be generally agreed upon are those of a practical kind. Beyond this, such words as "profit" or "felicity" have only the general meaning "good."

Since Franklin is an instrumentalist, it is a vain objection to complain that he neglects ends in his obsession with means: ends, he would reply, are only known to us as means. One may legitimately disagree with this way of thinking, but there is gross illogic in the criticism that Franklin's values are degraded. He has no interest in defining values—does not believe it can be done. His concern, rather, is with the experience of value and the means by which it can be achieved.

This concern is most apparent in the notorious table of virtues which is so frequently decried on the ground that many of the thirteen virtues listed are not virtues at all, but merely traits of prudence. "Silence" or "Cleanliness," it is argued, cannot be placed in the same order of value as "Justice," since the former are but means to the good, whereas justice is a good in itself. Since among the traditional Judeo-Christian virtues, those which are not omitted are given a cynically reductive form—chastity, for example—Franklin seems to have been intent on subverting where he does not deny. But in view of his pragmatic purpose, Franklin's list is not so unorthodox as it appears, for his disconcerting shifts of emphasis are merely the consequence of transposings ends into means, rather than proposing new ends. In subsuming "Charity" under "Frugality," for example, he does not intend to exchange the one for the other, but merely to recommend frugality as the means to charity. Franklin's critics commonly imply that he has elevated behavioral modes into intrinsic merits when in fact it is the very purpose of his instrumentalism to preserve this distinction.

In any case, it is well to heed Robert Sayre's warning not to take the table of virtues *au grand sérieux*.[52] It is a part of the autobiographer's highly amused account of a brash enterprise, and the fair-minded reader will find the anecdote of the speckled axe a sufficient proof that in his maturer days Franklin doubted that morality could be learned so easily or so fully. Furthermore, in composing—or, later, editing—the list, Franklin indulged his taste for satiric exaggeration. The rubric on "Chastity," for example, is an extravagant overstatement of the principle that a virtue is what it does, and surely Franklin's admission that he could only

52. *The Examined Self*, pp. 27–31.

achieve the appearance of humility is meant to imply that human virtues are less merits possessed than modes of behavior which faintly approximate goodness. One hesitates to go quite so far as Mr. Sayre in judging the list a canard; no doubt Franklin believed in it, at least to the extent of thinking that a person who followed its precepts would become a better man. But Mr. Sayre is right in insisting on Franklin's irony; the list is not meant in the sense assumed in most of the earnest attacks upon his ethics.

Franklin's irony is not of a random kind but arises from the essentially comic nature of the self's situation, a situation within which reason and experience never quite match. A man must live by rules, general concepts, formulas, and the like, yet his understanding is so imperfect that he cannot get his principles straight or even understand what they mean. There is always some discrepancy between the universal truth and the human formula for it, and between what we think we mean by a given statement and the meaning our statement would have if we could see all its implications, yet man's rules would not be rules if they did not pretend to universal validity; they mean to be the actual principles of reality, though in fact they are but inferences from a partial view of things. The self is thus placed in the comic position of having to act upon its generalizations as if they were certain truths while, at the same time, remaining aware of their provisional character. To forget that the rules are but rough approximations is to take on their false pretentions, but the man who refuses to accept them as universally valid is hardly less absurd than the credulous believer, since he cannot act at all, except as he is willing to pretend. Sanity is a balancing between belief and doubt in which even the wisest man is forced to some laughable contortions.

Hence Franklin's role-playing is the result of his awareness that a man's self-image is but one more provisional opinion. The wise man must doubt that he is really the person he takes himself to be, and since that personage is, in some degree, an impostor, the self grows accustomed to watching its identity transmigrate through a sequence of roles. But such role-playing should not be regarded as a kind of deception engaged in at will for ulterior motives, whether cynical or playful. Nor are the roles delusions, on the one hand, or, on the other, rhetorical devices, though in writing Franklin does exploit them as such. Franklin's roles emerge from his need to act within particular circumstances, and he assumes new roles as his situation alters. This fact bears witness to the other side of the paradox: though the self's roles are, in one sense, fictions, the self must believe in them, for to act is to assume that the self one has in mind is identical with one's actual self. By this rational necessity, the roles indicate the actor and are far more real than disguises.

That this ambiguous way of viewing his own identity has its source in Franklin's peculiar blend of empiricism and rationalism is illustrated by a well-known letter to his parents.

> You both seem concern'd lest I have imbibed some erroneous Opinions. Doubtless I have my Share, and when the natural Weakness and Imperfection of Human Understanding is considered, with the unavoidable Influences of Education, Custom, Books, and Company, upon our Ways of thinking, I imagine a Man must have a good deal of Vanity who believes, and a good deal of Boldness who affirms, that all the Doctrines he holds, are true; and all he rejects, are false. . . .
>
> I think Opinions should be judg'd of by their Influences and Effects; and if a Man holds none that tend to make him less Virtuous or more vicious, it may be concluded he holds none that are dangerous; which I hope is the Case with me.[53]

This is very modest but very self-assured also. The empiricist stands to the fore, insisting upon the limits which environment places upon understanding; but the rationalist can easily be detected behind him, ready with the assurance that Franklin possesses ethical standards so certain that he can judge the moral effects of his opinions.

53. *Papers of Benjamin Franklin*, 3, 202–03.

In notes listing questions to be asked the Junto, the same paradox is applied to epistemology:

Q. What is Wisdom?
A. The Knowledge of what will be best for us on all Occasions and of the best Ways of attaining it. . . .
What is the [*written above:* "is there any"] Difference between Knowledge and Prudence?
If there is any, which of the two is most Eligible? [54]

Wisdom is apparently to be defined as the self's knowledge of its strictly personal interests, but this in turn depends upon knowledge of universal goodness for this is the only standard by which the self can judge the actual usefulness of its ideas. One should also notice that the empiricist bent of Franklin's questions is balanced by his faith that questions so broad are answerable. If knowing the answer to Franklin's last question were not an instance of wisdom, Franklin would not have asked it; but if this answer is an instance of wisdom, then wisdom involves more than "knowledge of what will be best for us on all Occasions." It would be knowledge of reality itself, as well as of man's interests. The same doubleness appears in the educational objective Franklin proposes in his plan for the Pennsylvania Academy.

The Idea of what is *true Merit,* should also be often presented to Youth, explain'd and impress'd on their Minds, as consisting in an *Inclination* join'd with an *Ability* to serve Mankind, one's Country, Friends and Family; which *Ability* is (with the Blessing of God) to be acquir'd or greatly encreas'd by *true Learning;* and should indeed be the great *Aim* and *End* of all Learning.[55]

"*True Merit*" is not an essence but a process—a way of feeling and of acting—but the latter is dependent upon "*true Learning,*" which is "true" by the standard of reality rather than of usefulness.

54. Ibid., *1*, 262–63.
55. Ibid., *3*, 419.

Franklin's way of thought is nowhere more clearly summarized than in the Dunker's speech in the *Autobiography*. When Franklin asked this personage why the members of his sect had not drawn up a written creed, he replied:

> When we were first drawn together as a Society . . . it had pleased God to inlighten our Minds so far, as to see that some Doctrines which we once esteemed Truths were Errors, and that others which we had esteemed Errors were real Truths. From time to time he has been pleased to afford us farther Light, and our Principles have been improving, and our Errors diminishing. Now we are not sure that we are arriv'd at the End of this Progression, and at the Perfection of Spiritual or Theological Knowledge; and we fear that if we should once print our Confession of Faith, we should feel ourselves as if bound and confin'd by it, and perhaps be unwilling to receive farther Improvement; and our Successors still more so, as conceiving what we their Elders and Founders had done, to be something sacred, never to be departed from.[56]

To conceive the human situation in this way is to see it dramatically, because within this scheme ideas appear always as events—as the actual thought of a person in his particular circumstances—and the world itself has the status of an interpretation, being, as it is known, inseparable from the self's act of interpreting. Thus in human thought there is no such thing as a purely objective truth: the truth appears only within a perspective, and man's thinking is right in degree according to the breadth of his vision. The consequent perspectivism explains why it is that of all eighteenth-century Americans Franklin is the most fully rounded historical figure. Modern readers respond to Franklin as a realized character in their myth of the eighteenth century because he so consistently viewed himself in the same way. Though the period did not appear to him as it now does to us, he himself thought of it *as* a period, and his sundry roles—as printer, gentleman of leisure, backwoods' moralist, or sage of the Enlightenment

56. *Autobiography*, p. 190.

—are the consequence of his world view and of the kind of self-interpretation it called for, rather than of his world as it actually was. Of course, the real conditions of his age caused him to see his situation as he did, and he may have been right in judging that these conditions forced the self to play diverse roles. But granting agreement upon this point, his view of eighteenth-century America is different from ours, and we should not bend his thought to our own conclusions. Since we look back to him from a culture disordered by excessive complexity, it is tempting to see his role-playing as a characteristically modern attempt to rescue identity by seeking a true self among the multiple selves which the conditions of today compel a person to be. But Franklin did not find his own diversity an obstacle, much less a misfortune, and the tone of good-humored confidence which pervades his writings indicates a man who never doubted he had a real identity.

There is an important difference between asking "What sort of person am I?", as Franklin did, and asking "Am I a person at all?" Franklin's question assumes that there is a self to be found, and thus his search for identity is a pleasant adventure, while in modern literature, identity itself is often at stake, and seeking it is a desperate struggle to survive. But agreeable as Franklin's quest is, the absence of pain from the record he has left does not lessen its dramatic quality. His drama is of a different kind—comedy, it could be called, since all turns out for the best. It is a drama created by perspectivism, which, instead of juxtaposing distinct characters, as in a play, develops its action through the contrast between the author and his earlier states of mind.

Franklin's reasoning inevitably led to the art of autobiography, for given his view of the self's situation, identity becomes problematical. The self is the center of its own experience, but it is constantly in motion—hovering, as it were, between two different modes of existence, the present event and the accumulated past. It is the person of this moment, but then, too, it is the person of all its moments at once, which is to say, that such a person never existed in any of them. Since both of these selves are equally real, yet each excludes the other, the true self can only be seen in their relation—in the constant interplay between the transcendent and immediate views of identity. The transcendent view is that of the whole lifetime considered at once, and this is such a view as theology would attribute to the deity, but in looking back upon one's own life, one has to give one's own view the same form. While realizing that he cannot see his entire lifetime perfectly, Franklin must assume that he is omniscient relative to all his earlier states of mind, since his present view of his lifetime is the truest of all those he has to choose from. Thus the author of the *Autobiography* plays God, and the paradox of one God who is both eternal being and immanent spirit is shifted to the self, who is at once a man living in a particular moment and a consciousness which transcends all its lived moments in the act of regarding them from the outside as elements of a single lifetime.

Autobiography is a more demanding form of retrospective literature than either history or biography in the sense that the present from which the past is viewed and judged is more precisely defined. The historian's or biographer's present subsists merely implicitly as a system of tacit assumptions, but when a man writes of his own life, the present is embodied in his personality at the time of writing, and every fact he reports about his past reveals the author by showing what he now thinks of himself. Thus even a dishonest autobiographer would fail far less through the objective falsehood of his facts than through the resultant contrast between what he alleges about his past and the authorial personality his claims imply. More commonly, the failure is unintentional and consists either in making the past self so like the author that there is no development—and hence no story to tell—or in making the past self so different from the author that it is someone else's story rather than his own that is told. An exact balancing of identity and difference is required. The author must show us—and Franklin's theory of experience was ideally suited to express—one self through two persons.

Franklin the author represents the transcendent side of consciousness, the spectator who surveys the whole of his life, and his transcendent view is symbolized by the book's didactic purposes. The lessons and generalizations he offers claim, or at least aim at, universal truth, and they are to be credited on the ground that they hold true for all the author's lifetime.

Whatever Franklin's practical or artistic intentions may have been, it is an essential part of the book's meaning that it was written to instruct. He offers general truths, which are "proved," as it were, by the success and felicity of his own life. In the opening address to his son, Franklin expresses the hope that "the conducing Means I made use of, which with the Blessing of God, so well succeeded" may serve his posterity "as they may find some of them suitable to their own Situations, and therefore fit to be imitated." [57] The didactic purpose is again emphasized at the beginning of the second part by the insertion of letters from Abel James and Benjamin Vaughn, urging Franklin to complete the work. "Your Biography," as Vaughn writes, "will not merely teach self-education, but the education of a *wise man;* and the wisest man will receive lights and improve his progress, by seeing detailed the conduct of another wise man." [58]

To be sure, the author changes character somewhat in the course of his narrative, and Sayre has suggested that the three main parts correspond to three distinct views of himself, each formed with an eye to Franklin's actual circumstances at the time of writing. But these changes are alterations not so much in the author's role as in that of the actor. It is the young and middle-aged man, not the child or youth, whose projects the elderly narrator criticizes; and Franklin the politician cannot properly emerge until the author reaches that portion of his life. The roles played by past selves must be distinguished from the authorial role, which, throughout, is that of the urbane but venerable sage, offering lessons, whether moral, political, or merely prudential,

57. Ibid., p. 43.
58. Ibid., p. 136.

for the reader's instruction. The fundamental contrast, so far as the book's form is concerned, is not that between the various past selves but that between the man who looks back on the past and the man who lived it. The act of generalizing defines the author as the total consciousness toward which the actor is at every point developing. The author's lessons, though they are not final truths, are the truest opinions he can find, because they are derived from the widest view—the most extensive experience. But since the actor is also engaged in formulating general truths, generalizing unites as well as separates the two. In that the author knows better, he is distinct from the actor; but in that both participate in the same process, they are as one person, the Franklin of the *Autobiography.*

It is significant that Franklin views his childhood as if from the outside. He does so because he supposes that the ability to generalize is not sufficiently developed in the child to permit him to depict the child's state of mind by contrasting its generalizations with the author's. This assumption is quite in line with the typically eighteenth-century view of the mind's development expressed in the *Dissertation:*

> All our Ideas are first admitted by the Senses and imprinted on the Brain, increasing in Number by Observation and Experience; there they become the Subjects of the Soul's Action. The Soul is a mere Power or Faculty of *contemplating* on, and comparing those Ideas when it has them; hence springs Reason: But as it can *think* on nothing but Ideas, it must have them before it can *think* at all.[59]

In the first pages, therefore, the child is seen indirectly through his family, and Franklin underlines facts which foreshadow his own maturer traits: his uncle Thomas' "public-spirited" undertakings," his grandfather Folger's poem in favor of religious toleration, his father's good sense and mechanical ingenuity, the tradi-

59. *Papers of Benjamin Franklin, 1,* 69.

tion of religious dissent which foreshadows Franklin's rebellion against the crown.

Franklin's handling of the first experience treated at length, and the only one from childhood—the account of how he and his playmates stole building stones to construct a wharf—exemplifies his perspectivism very well. The author explains that he was then already "a Leader among the Boys," who, when the theft had been discovered, "pleaded the usefulness of the work," and even more obviously turns the episode toward the future by concluding that it illustrates an "early projecting public Spirit, tho' not then justly conducted." By such touches the reader is made to feel the identity of the child with the good citizen of Philadelphia who founds a library, improves the streets, and organizes the first fire company. But the difference between child and author is also insisted upon, for Franklin is pictured at that embryonic phase of life when even he did not yet realize that "nothing was useful which was not honest." [60]

In the most memorable episode—Franklin's arrival at Philadelphia—the literary advantages of this perspectivism are apparent. Since the author points it out, every reader recognizes the contrast between the young man's humble beginnings and the venerable autobiographer's achievements. To be sure, this contrast emphasizes Franklin's success and makes the point that a poor youth can rise to greatness if he follows the precepts of Poor Richard. But these ideas would be far less forcefully expressed were it not for the vividness of the picture of the young man walking up the street with his rolls. It is the image which persuades, and, in the last analysis, the image is created by the contrast of perspectives. Young Franklin has the roundness and movement of a living person, because he is seen within his world —in terms of what he knows—and the youth's knowledge, in turn, is revealed by comparison with what the author knows: "Thus I went up Market Street as far as fourth Street, passing by the Door of Mr. Reed, my future Wife's Father, when she, stand-

60. *Autobiography*, p. 54.

ing at the Door saw me, and thought I made as I certainly did a most awkward ridiculous Appearance." [61] That young Franklin did not recognize the girl in the doorway is a nice instance of the way he is placed within his unique moment and circle of consciousness. But since he is shown to have seen himself more accurately than Miss Reed, who would have judged his appearance differently had she known the accidents of his journey or his quite natural mistake about the price of Philadelphia bread, young Franklin and the author become identical in the process of interpretation, for both are engaged in placing the moment within the life already lived.

Because this process is constant, Franklin can exploit it as the means of giving continuity to the events he chronicles. His essential method is to treat each phase of the actor's story as an approximation of the author's consciousness. In almost every episode his opinion at the time contains a truth he will later improve upon in the midst of errors he will come to reject. For example, when he learns the Socratic mode of argument from excerpts in a rhetoric book, young Franklin amuses himself with confounding others by this means, but in time he abandons the method, except for the deferential manner of speaking. Similarly, though his youthful habit of trusting others is soon shaken by the treatment he receives from such men as Governor Keith and James Ralph, later experience tends to confirm the general principle of acting upon good faith.

In the latter part of the *Autobiography* the contrast between actor and author is not so sharp simply because the time gap has narrowed and the two are more nearly of an age. Fortunately, the importance of Franklin's public career keeps the temporal contrasts crucial enough as the gulf between past and present narrows. There is great interest in the differences between Franklin's opinions of 1740–57 and those of 1784–88. The account of his public-spirited projects is written with an eye to their later success, while the more strictly political episodes—those concerning

61. Ibid., p. 76.

the French and Indian War and the Pennsylvania legislature's struggle with the proprietors—are clearly designed to anticipate the Revolution. Franklin the political leader is always seen to be right in principle though distanced from the author by errors of judgment which, for the most part, only hindsight can correct. During Braddock's disastrous campaign, for example, he is still bemused by the prestige of British power, and yet, even then, he has a shrewd grasp of the difficulties of wilderness fighting which would turn the scales at Saratoga. Similarly, he shows remarkable foresight in recognizing the need for a central government in America and legislative control of taxation, but he has yet to learn that these measures are not possible within the imperial system.

As he sees Franklin approaching, in his opinions, the statesman of 1784, the reader can observe, through beautifully managed gradations, how the coming crisis began to emerge. In a mere joke there is dark prophecy. When a friend of Governor Morris asks Franklin why he has sided with "these damned Quakers" in the assembly—"Had not you better sell them? the Proprietor would give you a good price"—Franklin laughingly replies that the Governor "has not yet black'd them enough." [62] Whether the colonists were "slaves" would be discussed in different tones a decade later, but it would be the same question.

The continuity achieved by this use of perspective has the effect of placing all the events within a firm pattern of causation. Though the *Autobiography* is as episodic as Puritan narrative, it moves forward smoothly as a developing action. Like the Puritan historians, Franklin thinks in terms of particular striking events, each of which stands as an epitome of his whole life and is symbolic very much in the Puritan way. As a result, the most memorable moments have the quality of snapshots—Franklin slipping the "Dogood Papers" under the door of his brother's printing house, Franklin entering Philadelphia, Franklin pushing his wheelbarrow to create the appearance of industriousness, and the like. Yet seen within the autobiographer's double perspective, all

62. Ibid., p. 214.

146

the happenings make reference to the beliefs of the author at the
end of his life. Thus the gaps between episodes are bridged, and
each event is given the status of a phase in the cause-and-effect
sequence by which the actor becomes the author. The elaborate
web of causation is illustrated by the account of the controversy
over the issuance of paper money. The bill enabling the Pennsylvania legislature to do so was opposed by powerful interests, and
Franklin wrote a pamphlet in favor of this measure:

> It was well receiv'd by the common People in general; but the
> Rich Men dislik'd it . . . and they happening to have no
> Writers among them that were able to answer it, their Opposi-
> tion slackn'd and the Point was carried by a Majority in the
> House. My Friends there, who conceiv'd I had been of some
> Service, thought fit to reward me, by employing me in printing
> the Money, a very profitable Jobb, and a great Help to me.[63]

Franklin had then just bought out his partner in the printing
business, and the success of the pamphlet was a crucial step on
the road to wealth, but it also served as the cause of future political achievements by enhancing his reputation in the legislature.
By writing the pamphlet, Franklin aligned himself with the common people in a progressive cause, and began to move toward the
liberal politics of the revolutionary period. Yet if the incident
opens upon the future, it also stands as an effect in which earlier
events are summarized. Franklin confines himself to saying that
the success of the pamphlet was "another Advantage gain'd by
my being able to write," [64] but much more lies behind this episode. Franklin's youthful reading, the founding of the Junto, in
which he began to educate himself in public affairs, his previous
publications, his experience in printing money for the New Jersey
colony, his earlier uses of credit, even the experiments in simplified diet by which he gained time for self-education contribute to
this event. Throughout the *Autobiography* each event emerges as

63. Ibid., p. 124.
64. Ibid.

an inevitable consequence of earlier ones and, in turn, prepares the way for those which follow.

Yet the effect is never mechanical. The episodes are not fitted together in a diagrammatic pattern but flow and merge naturally. Instead of tracing out the lines of causation, Franklin creates an atmosphere of relevance, so that one feels they *could* be traced. The action develops organically through manifold relations between happenings, relations so subtly reticulated that any given event seems to summarize and anticipate more than the reader can discern. Franklin's narrative is a unified action rather than a maze of potential patterns, because it implies at every point a governing logic whose presence is felt even though it is never made explicit.

In part, this is the consequence of Franklin's fine discretion, his unwillingness, though he is ready enough at proposing general rules of conduct, to explain the cause-and-effect relations in particular cases. On this subject he offers only brief comments here and there, but these suffice to imply much more than he pleases to specify and, indeed, can discern. Such reticence reflects, once again, Franklin's double perspective. As the author of the *Dissertation* argued, only omniscience can see "all the intricate Consequences of every Action with respect to the general Order and Scheme of the Universe." [65] But the fact that the author sees more clearly than the actor persuades the reader that there is a real order of which both are approximations. The book is only the author's view, as his tentative manner and skeptical comments constantly remind us. Thus Franklin's episodes stand free—invite other interpretations—exist as events in the real world, having definite meanings but implying also a total meaning which transcends all interpretations.

To see events in this way is to see them with the artist's eye, and it is perhaps the greatest paradox of a paradoxical life that Franklin succeeded so well in his art that he has commonly been judged as if he were no artist at all. His critics, with a few rare

65. *Papers of Benjamin Franklin, 1,* 62.

and recent exceptions, have proceeded as if they were dealing with the real man, the historical figure. But if it is asked how they know of this personage, the answer is through the imaginative self-image he presents in the *Autobiography*. Much additional evidence is to be found in his other writings, of course, but such is the power of this book that there is no way to avoid interpreting the rest in the light of it, and even its omissions are, by the motives they suggest, almost as influential as the facts it includes. That we cannot avoid taking the Franklin we see in the *Autobiography* as the actual man is the surest proof of his literary achievement. As process is principle seen from within time, the process of Franklin's self-interpretation points toward the principle of his identity. We know Franklin as a way of seeing, but so coherent is the vision and so convincing the drama of its development that we feel we know the man himself. And which of us would say this opinion is false?

It is generally thought that Franklin and Edwards should be placed in the American tradition at a point of transition between the Puritans and the transcendentalists. In considering Edwards' view of symbol, we have already noted that he does, in an important though limited way, anticipate Emerson. Similarly, Franklin looks forward to Thoreau, who in "Economy" seems to confirm Franklin's prudential philosophy through the very act of satirizing it. Franklin would surely have agreed with Thoreau's definition of the price of a thing as the amount of life required to procure it, and in Thoreau's humorous lists of expenses and earnings we recognize Franklin's kind of practicality. That Thoreau could not have read the *Autobiography* further strengthens the similarities by making them seem to come from instincts that both inherited rather than from imitation on Thoreau's part. But no one would venture to say that Thoreau is very much like Franklin. They differ most obviously in the relation they assume between the self and society, which for Franklin is nearly identical with the world itself, while for Thoreau it is an antagonist to

149

be circumvented by self-reliance and the formation of a society of one's own choosing. In this Thoreau reflects a common prejudice of his time, which Emerson makes plain in "Nature" when, after defining nature as all that is "NOT ME," he rather oddly comments that though philosophically speaking nature includes "art, all other men and my own body," men's creations amount to no more than "a little chipping, baking, patching, and washing." [66] By this questionable excuse, institutions, tradition, and the community itself are excluded from the nature with which the transcendentalist would bring himself into harmony.

Important as this difference is, it is but an outgrowth of a more fundamental disagreement concerning the nature of experience itself. For the transcendentalist, who is closer to the Puritan in this respect, experience is an event having two distinct aspects. It is the perception of the present moment and it is the revelation of eternal truth. Though the two are really one and can be recognized as one in moments of greatest insight, there are no middle grounds between them, no terms for describing experience which would make it something more than momentary as an event in time or less than eternal in the meaning it intends and thus epitomizes. But one primary objective of Franklin and Edwards was to provide a middle term. They undertook to resolve the dualistic tension of the Puritan mind by discovering the answer which that mind demanded, seeking to unite the self's experiential moment and the eternal will of God in an image of perfect harmony. They were able to find their answer within Puritan thought, with its insistence upon divine foreknowledge and habitual emphasis on the difference between God's consciousness and man's. By conceiving of knowledge with respect to where the knower stands, Edwards and Franklin could explain why experience falls short of the whole truth and yet is a potential summary of reality. Thus their answer to the need for a middle term is point-of-view itself. And the rewards this solution afforded can be seen by comparing

66. *Nature*, in *Complete Works*, 1, 5.

Franklin's kind of experience with that which Thoreau depicts: the former is harmonious, confident, serene; the latter stressful, excited, and enigmatic. For Franklin's essential subject is a process of smooth, progressive development within a temporal continuum which the juxtaposition of points of view creates, while Thoreau's subject is the isolated moment which, though all-inclusive in its import, is unique and autonomous as the only time in which one lives. Therefore, instead of supposing that Edwards and Franklin represent a logical step toward the development of transcendentalism, it would be wiser to see in them one response to the Puritan dilemma, a version of experience which is related to that of transcendentalism in that both grew out of the persistent assumptions of Puritanism.

If Franklin and Edwards foreshadow the transcendentalists, they more directly anticipate Hawthorne, Melville, and James, in whose novels the same double perspective causes the symbol to generate multiple interpretations. Whether the fiery "A" which Dimmesdale sees from the scaffold means "Adulterer," as he supposes, or "Angel," as the good townspeople interpret it, depends upon the observer's personality as the center of the facts he knows. This would not be the case were the symbol merely invented by the perceiving eye. Quite clearly, diverse meanings arise because the symbol exists in a real world which extends beyond those of the interpreters and has a true meaning which is more than what they can discern in it. Here then, already, is the novel of point of view, and we can recognize how natural it was for James to begin as a student of Hawthorne. The rationale of such fiction is summed up by Melville's Pip: "I look, you look, he looks; we look, ye look, they look." [67] But the novelists can only make their multiple views add up by adhering also to the other side of the paradox Edwards and Franklin explored. They must assume that there is a true meaning, though we only get views of

67. *Moby-Dick,* ed. Charles Feidelson, Jr. (New York, Bobbs-Merrill, 1964), chap. 99, p. 556.

it. This meaning is "there," in the symbol, and at one with it, rather than merely a meaning projected upon the symbol by the observer of the moment. The fragment of red cloth radiates its own mysterious heat. To those who deplore Franklin's materialism or Edward's otherworldliness, it is perhaps best to reply that the one loved things for their real meanings, and the other loved God for having created real things.

3
The Fiction in the Landscape: Irving and Cooper

There were many words that you could not
stand to hear and finally only the names of
places had dignity. Certain numbers were
the same way and certain dates and these
with the names of places were all you could
say and have them mean anything.

Ernest Hemingway

WOLF, unlike Argus, fails to recognize his long-absent master,
though Rip has been gone no longer than Odysseus. Perhaps the
dog is not Wolf, after all. Rip takes him for his own, but it is
typical of Washington Irving's art to allow us to remain in doubt.
The consequent stress upon our credulity serves to make us consider what the basis of belief should be. We cannot very well
appeal to the conventions of common sense in such matters and
judge, for example, according to our notion of the life expectancy
of hounds. If we decide the dog cannot *really* be Wolf, we find we
have been considering Irving's facts so trustingly that we have no
valid excuse for not taking seriously the question as to whether
Rip was *really* asleep for twenty years. That is, as Huckleberry
Finn would say, a "stretcher," and Irving refuses to allow us to
accept it as simply another fictional hypothesis. Rip's long sleep is
not to be believed in in the way we credit the statement that in a
village near the Kaatskills, "there lived, many years since, while
the country was yet a province of Great Britain, a simple, good-

natured fellow, of the name of Rip Van Winkle." [1] Instead, Irving teases us with doubts, most especially at the end, where we are told that the story we have just read is an exact record of Rip's own account, and that this, in turn, is a tale much improved in the telling:

> He used to tell his story to every stranger that arrived at Mr. Doolittle's hotel. He was observed, at first, to vary on some points every time he told it, which was, doubtless, owing to his having so recently awaked. It at last settled down precisely to the tale I have related, and not a man, woman, or child in the neighborhood but knew it by heart. [2]

The humor of this skeptical aside seems directed as much at Irving as at Rip, for it is scarcely less ridiculous that the author should insist on the falsehood of his tale than that Rip should have lied himself into belief. But the author here is only Irving as he pretends to be, and the narrator is so managed that his doubts generate conviction. The more unlikely Rip's story appears, the more sharply our attention is focused upon its truth. For the question we are to decide is not whether a man could enjoy a twenty-years' nap, but how it is that this patent lie appears interesting. Why do the simple Dutch farmers enjoy Rip's story? Why do we consider it a significant fiction?

To the usual remark that in Rip Van Winkle and Ichabod Crane Irving has created mythic figures should be added the observation that he was able to do so because he was interested in understanding myth as well as in creating it. The two operations are not to be separated. In the few brief masterpieces which make Irving important to American literature, he presents fables of fable-making, myths of how myths come into being. The essential action of "Rip Van Winkle" is not the hero's return but the birth of his story. And so, of course, it must be a story in the most obvious sense—a fantastic fiction, whose facts are so at odds with

1. *Washington Irving: Selected Prose,* ed. Stanley T. Williams (New York, Holt, Rinehart, and Winston, 1962), p. 92.
2. Ibid., p. 106.

what we take to be probable that we can consciously compare fiction to fact.

Such a view suggests that Irving ought to be placed at or very near the beginning of the tradition of symbolism in American fiction—not as the originator of what in Hawthorne and Melville becomes a conscious literary method, but as the best representative of the phase of the American sensibility which leads naturally to theirs. Though symbol is not yet the central concern in that phase, attention is directed to the way fiction itself should be taken and to its modes of reference to what we assume is fact.

The greatest work of imaginative literature in the American eighteenth century presents itself quite simply as Franklin's *Autobiography*. A "True History" it might have been entitled if it had been written by an English novelist, but Franklin, knowing though he was, had no idea of offering a fiction in the factual guise of novelistic confessions or memoirs. For him it was a true history according to its author's most searching view of what a fact can be. And as such it has, quite rightly, been accepted, which is why, when all has been said about American fiction before 1809, the development from Franklin to Irving seems startling and sudden. It also seems impenetrably mysterious unless one takes into account the very qualified way in which Irving believed that fiction could matter.

I have pointed to the cloud of humorous doubt hovering over Rip Van Winkle's story in order to suggest how strictly defined Irving's acceptance of make-believe is. The whole weight of his faith in fiction seems to rest on the pin point of one literal truth: that there are such things as stories. This tiny area of belief is prevented from shrinking to nothing by the corollaries it yields. The certainty that fictions exist implies that they are somehow important—that for reasons no less real for being laughable, some people feel the need to invent them and some to credit them— and one can therefore conclude that beneath the rich burgeoning of fantasy there must be a seed of truth. To simplify the point, one might say that if a man with Franklin's view of things had paused to ask just why there is such a thing as fiction, he would soon have come to something very like the idea of literature expressed in Irving's tales. Franklin's urbane little sketches—"The Ephemera," for instance—seem quite close to Irving's consciousness: a little less attention to the moral the joke asserts, a little more interest in why it is that joking can moralize, and Franklin's manner would turn into Irving's.

That Irving's view of fiction closely resembles that of later American novelists is illustrated by their attraction to the romance, the tall tale, and melodrama, all of which provide the means for exploring the truth of fiction by emphasizing its apparent falsehood. American forms of romance always seem to require the possibility of a common-sense explanation—that, for example, Goodman Brown was "just dreaming"—and in the tall tale the truth of the lesson or satiric point depends for its force on the fantastic incredibility of the story, while in melodrama interest centers upon the process of recognizing that what at first seemed a "made-up" view is true in a sense that the self-romanticizing characters did not suspect. Thus Isabel Archer is really a prisoner in the Ogre Osmond's dungeon, and Charles Bon and Judith Sutpen must have been the idealized lovers walking together in a garden full of flowers, though their courtship took place at Christmas.[3]

The reader may be disconcerted by my suggestion that Irving justified fiction with reference to something "really real" if he takes this to mean that Irving's tales are important only because their actual subject is a topic as respectable as the nature of myth. Any reader will resist the notion that Rip is not the center of interest and his experience the heart of the story. Such a view is not to be dispensed with, but it does involve a good deal of duplicity. This is not to say that Irving's art is that of presenting fantasy in a way which allows us to enjoy it without shame, but, rather, that his use of fantasy to direct our attention to the ques-

3. I am indebted to Richard Chase's discussion of melodrama and romance in James, though he argues that these are intended to represent a less valid way of interpreting reality than I suggest. See his *The American Novel and Its Tradition*, pp. 117–37.

tion of belief involves us in a process of doubting and believing at once. The possible truth is not, then, just a matter of speculation. We are asked to consider the truth of Rip's story, not of fiction in general. The latter concerns us only by implication—only in that the kinds of truth this fable possesses hint at a definition of fictional truth. The reader's duplicity is that of believing (and wanting to believe) while feeling all the time that he doesn't, since this is just a story. But a story exists for reasons—and not the least of these is that someone wants to tell it and others to listen. Hence the reader, whether as skeptic or believer, is amused by the revelation of his own impulses. He finds that his wanting to believe is a fact his common sense had not taken into account, and he is pleasantly agitated by the feeling that his familiar facts are rearranging themselves to accommodate this one.

Irving, however, is skillful enough to prevent this sense of duplicity from degenerating into an opinion, so that his tale would seem a mere exemplum for a lesson about the way one's mind behaves. Instead, the reader's gaze is directed outward to Rip and the audience he entertains at Mr. Doolittle's hotel, and it is through them that he is made conscious of how subtly doubt and belief support each other. Yet that their reactions depend upon the reader's own is indicated by the darkest of all the hints the tale throws out—the suggestion that Rip's long absence is, after all, not very different from the disappearance of other unhappy husbands. Whenever Dame Van Winkle's name is mentioned, Rip's face takes on a look which "might pass either for an expression of resignation to his fate, or joy at his deliverance." [4] Some of his auditors seem unaware of this disturbing perspective and maintain that he was simply "out of his head" for twenty years. But if his story for them is nonsense, their skepticism seems naïve, and can we then respect our own? We aim at the same sort of common-sense explanation as they, and their blunder is a warning of how quaggy the grounds of common sense can be.

We laugh at the credulous villagers who believe Rip on the

4. *Irving: Selected Prose*, p. 106.

evidence that the thunder is the sound of Hudson's rattling ten-pins, but our logic will not be much better if we confuse the probable with the actual. And some of the believers may not be so credulous as we suppose. Who knows but that their belief is a kind of ironical neighborliness and really more intelligent than the wisdom of the skeptics? It may be one of the social functions of myth to express dangerous truths in a communally acceptable form, in which case the reader who scoffs would show less wisdom than the credulous folk he laughs at.

At any rate, the remark about the thunder makes at least as much sense as the reasonable views, which we have seen ending in confusion. For there is, one feels, a connection between Hudson's men and the circle of old codgers at the hotel. The loafing, the drinking, the smoking, the mental blankness pretending to be meditation, the style of conversation, with its long pauses and portentously worded nothings, all tend to evoke the mood of the ghostly crew at their endless game of bowls. Thus, through the setting, Rip's story takes on a curious historical revelance. One comes to feel that a single mood joins the villagers of his day with the remote founders of the New Netherlands. One says "remote" quite naturally, without reflecting that Hudson's discovery was then less than two centuries in the past. This is an indication of how well Irving has succeeded in giving to the American land-scape such an atmosphere of mellow historicity that Hudson's men seem to loom as fabulous shadows on the horizon of memory. Since the meaning and truth of Rip's story depends upon the effect of a dim, imaginative past, Irving's way of creating temporal per-spective deserves some attention.

On the surface, the story seems to be concerned with the differ-ence between one age and another. The reader is amused at the spectacle of Rip's confusion as he discovers that twenty years have passed since he fell asleep and tries, with all sorts of comic complications, to recognize the village of 1770 in that of 1790. The emphasis on difference is broad enough to satisfy one's taste for such humor. Rip finds his wife gone, his children grown up,

his friends dead or very old, his memory of landmarks confounded by a hundred architectural innovations. These contrasts
are nicely summed up in what seems to be a distinct change of
mood among the villagers: "A busy, bustling, disputatious tone"
has replaced "the accustomed phlegm and drowsy tranquillity." [5]
All this is the work of history, whose power to change things is
summed up in the great political event—revolution.

Throughout the account of Rip's return, however, Irving fosters
our doubts about the reality of change. Politics may have been
transformed from the leisurely contemplation of an out-of-date
newspaper to the partisanship of a noisy election rally, and the old
agrarian economy may have developed toward the commercial-
ism represented by the Yankee peddler who caused Dame Van
Winkle to die of a fit of apoplexy, but there is the same foolish
deference to the village politico and the same necessity for toil.
How slight the apparently great changes are is suggested by the
fact that while the Union Hotel looks quite different from the old
inn it replaces, the sign at the door has only been touched up to
make George Washington out of George III. The Dutch patriarch
Van Vedder has given way to the Yankee proprietor, the tree in
front is replaced by a liberty pole, yet Rip and his friends take
their ease inside just as the elders of yore had done. In short, the
only changes that are more than appearances are natural ones,
those of growing up and growing old. Such alteration is not historic change and certainly not "revolution," belonging rather to
the natural pattern of birth and decay which is always operative
and renders epochs the same rather than different. It is, in effect,
no change at all. Hence Rip becomes a second Nicholas Van
Vedder, and Rip Junior the duplicate of his ne'er-do-well father.

Although nothing has changed, the cloudy remoteness of the
past is impressive. Hudson and his crew are seen dimly across
vast expanses of time, and it is their distance that makes them
legendary. Paradoxically, it is Irving's emphasis upon the sameness of all times that makes Hudson's epoch seem unimaginably

5. Ibid., p. 101.

distant. His method is analogous to the trick in surrealist painting of pushing back the horizon by presenting a ground-level view across terrain so flat that the shadows of objects are preternaturally lengthened. By exaggerating the smooth continuity of the time flow, Irving endows the past with an indeterminate antiquity. Hudson's crew seem remote because in Rip's village nothing notable has happened since; the same events have occurred over and over again in endless repetition since the first Dutch farmer lit his pipe. And, again as in surrealist painting, the abnormally deep perspective depends as much upon the nearness of the foreground as the distance of the horizon.

That foreground is the present of Irving as narrator, and it is essential to his method to hold us to his own point of view. This is achieved by fostering the tacit agreement between the author and the reader that we "know better"—are free to see things as they are—because we stand outside of the system of prejudices and beliefs within which the characters live. We look down upon this world as sophisticates whose vision extends far beyond the limits of provincial experience. Thus the characters' views appear more limited than ours in that they are old-fashioned opinions of an outmoded way of life. We see through and around their opinions simply because we look back; our modernity gives us a knowledge they cannot have. This illustrates the difference between Irving's rural sketches and pastoral. His rustics are not naïve simply because they live in a provincial world and cannot be expected to enjoy the wide consciousness of, say, a Jefferson. Their innocence is historical as well as regional. To live in a simple farm village is, in effect, to live in the past, and Irving's delight in the sleepy hamlets along the Hudson springs from the amused realization of their backwardness. A major source of his humor is the odd persistence of the old ways of thought—the indifference and, often, ignorance which makes the great waves of progress seem ripples on a mill pond. Irving's attitude—and ours, under his influence—is more than a little patronizing. The reader simply joins the author in laughing at the village worthies studying an old newspaper, or at the village historian whose scholarship is so quaintly out of date. Even so, the reader is subtly implicated in the story, for despite the distance of his lofty post of observation, he is forced to join the characters in the risky enterprise of making out the past. As he looks back to Rip's world, he sees that the characters in their turn are looking back. The plot mirrors the reader's own situation, and Irving's style, with its urbane asides implicitly comments on the past and thus symbolizes through gestures of language the same process of retrospection which Rip's return presents as an outward event.

When simply formulated, Irving's time scheme reveals a number of pasts nested, like Chinese boxes, one within the other. As the author and reader look back to Rip, so he in 1799 (granting him time to fix the form of his story) looks back to 1790, the date of his return; and this remembered time contains the memory of 1770 as seen from 1790. The syntax of the sort of remark that one might make about the story manifests the temporal complexity: Irving thinks that Rip thought (1799) that Rip thought (1790) that Rip thought (1770) that the mysterious figures resembled those in an old painting, which had been brought over from Holland in 1635. The last of these past tenses serves as a reminder that 1770 also had a past to look back upon. The multiplication of past times creates the effect of a vast and mysterious temporal distance stretching away from the fictional "now" toward an indefinite antiquity. By emphasizing the fact that every past moment opened, when it was the present, upon a still earlier past, he endows the epochs depicted with extraordinary temporal depth. Hudson's discovery, though but two centuries past when Irving wrote, is made to seem extremely distant in that it appeared remote even from the point of view of a time now long ago.

The "pastness" is not simply an aspect of what might be called setting, for as a condition of understanding events, it enters into meaning. During the progress of the story, events turn into opinions and history becomes historiography. Irving's perspective not only places 1770 at an obscuring distance but, by revealing that epoch as it appeared from a series of intervening past moments, makes every view relative. Each epoch possesses its own unique vision of the past, and the view of any event proves to be inseparable from the point in time from which it is regarded. Rip's tale was "history" to the village antiquarian, and our calling it mere fiction does not dispose of its historical truth. The tale becomes true in a way Rip did not intend, true as a manifestation of real events which led him to tell the story he told. *Something* happened, and in our search for the credible at the heart of the fictive we are led to question what "fact" means.

Significantly, the tale begins with a description of the scenery of the Hudson Valley. The landscape is, as it were, Irving's one certain fact. The reader can at least be sure of the place where past events happened, because it exists as a landscape such as he could behold in his own era, unobscured by time. Irving offers his landscape without reservation, implying no doubt that he speaks of a real place or that it looks otherwise than as he pictures it: "Whoever has made a voyage up the Hudson must remember the Kaatskill mountains. They are a dismembered branch of the great Appalachian family, and are seen away to the west of the river, swelling up to a noble height, and lording it over the surrounding country." [6]

The genial humor here is not just a matter of style. To be sure, Irving seems to be lightly parodying the language of nature literature by the travelogue manner, which is made a bit too insistent —as if the hypothetical voyager could have missed anything so noticeable as a mountain range—by the slight indignity of "dismembered," and by the sequence which moves from "noble height" through "swelling" to "lording it." But such whimsey is felt to be an appropriate response to the scene described; there is a humor in the landscape. A few sentences later this humor is made more explicit by the remark that the Kaatskills "are regarded by all the good wives, far and near, as perfect barometers." [7] Such a practical way of viewing landscape is comic be-

6. Ibid., p. 91.
7. Ibid.

cause it is excessively partial. If the mountains are a barometer, they are also "summits, which, in the last rays of the setting sun, will glow and light up like a crown of glory." [8] Wash-day considerations augment, rather than cancel, the grander effects.

The landscape is funny in that it allows for such an odd assortment of responses and yet absorbs them into a unified impression. Whether considered as the beholder's vision or the object he perceives, it is distinctly itself, but at the same time one feels that it contains innumerable responses or qualities. As a result, while this landscape is a certainty for Irving and for us—we do not doubt that it is *what* we see—we wonder *what* it *is*.

That is why Irving's landscape turns into a fable, and why the fable is comic. The source of fiction is the mystery of fact. Irving moves back into the past as a way of ascertaining and describing the scene before him. The landscape is an instance of immediate, present perception, but the scene is so various and inclusive that to grasp the reality we behold in the present, we must look beyond the moment of experience. The real nature of the landscape eludes every view of it, because through all the shifting lights of imagination and sunshine it remains quite simply itself. Not that it has a purely objective being, but that in experience it persists as itself throughout any imaginable number of views. This simple enduring renders fiction a valid and even necessary mode of landscape description. The story portrays events which transpired in a place that then was just as we see it now; and, conversely, the fable is true because it accords with our vision of the scene.

The way in which Rip's adventures define the landscape is most clearly illustrated at the moment when he falls asleep: "He saw at a distance the lordly Hudson, far, far below him, moving on its silent but majestic course, with the reflection of a purple cloud, or the sail of a lagging bark, here and there sleeping on its glassy bosom, and at last losing itself in the blue highlands." [9] The visual qualities of the scene gradually merge with the qualities of the observer's present state of mind, until the land-

8. Ibid.
9. Ibid., p. 96.

scape's tranquillity and Rip's laziness are one. Unlike the opening description, this picture of landscape is not composed of jarring aspects, unrelated associations. Instead, the qualities of the scene harmonize and the observer's feelings blend into a single mood. More important still, the scene and the mood are united. The enduring sameness of nature and the reflected serenity of Rip's mood do not preclude change but rather reveal it as an unending process. The river's majestic flow, the drift of the boats "sleeping on its glassy bosom," and the slow, sure movement of clouds define change as a pattern which is always the same.

It is natural that Rip's vision of this landscape should initiate a dream in which men long since dead are seen to be still living as they once lived. The landscape picture reveals not only how the dream comes about but the sense in which it is true. As Irving's tale ends in the thought that history is a continuously changing view of fixed events, so landscape is a continuous perceiving of a definite place. Something once happened, something is now beheld, but these determinate events are also indeterminate. They exist in time and are always in a state of becoming, so that the only constant and therefore certain thing is the process of becoming.

Rip is one of those rare and invaluable literary creations, a mythic figure, because his personality is an embodiment of nature. His laziness should not be mistaken for doing nothing; it is merely doing nothing that is purposeful. He exists as nature does, from moment to moment, and thus in him as in landscape all moments are the same. His life is a continuous process rather than a sequence of events leading from a beginning to an end. To live in this way is to live forever: the lazy father perpetuates himself in the lazy son, and one feels that, however markedly society advances, there will always be such people. That thought helps us to place the comedy of Rip's triumph over his wife. His purposeless existing manifests a vitality far greater than the doggedly industrious effort to survive which she represents. In laughing at her as a sour shrew, we also laugh at the society which makes her attitude reasonable. Doubtless it was one of Irving's main motives to question the values of an increasingly commercial society by raising doubts as to the reality of progress.

The comedy of Rip's tale extends far beyond the social context, however. It is, in essence, a comedy of experience, an attempt to express the mysterious character of perception. That Irving treats landscape in a way fundamentally different from Scott is not to be explained by saying that he is more "eighteenth-century" or that his countryside is much less historic. He appreciates and can render what Emerson would later call the "integrity of landscape" as well as Scott, but it is not for him a satisfying conclusion to experience in nature. The merging of consciousness and land-scape strikes him as humorous rather than sublime, because in-stead of allowing thought to come to rest in the sense of some-thing kindred in nature, it raises questions as to what experience itself is, and this comic doubtfulness becomes a quality of the landscape which evokes it.

For Irving, as for American writers ever since, nature experi-ence is unremittingly problematical. Instead of feelings of recon-ciliation and self-fulfillment, it induces detachment and a coolly speculative attitude. Thus at the moments of greatest insight the language tends toward metaphysical wit. One recalls that famous curiosity, Emerson's "transparent eyeball," and in Thoreau's account of fishing at night, the conclusive witticism: "It seemed as if I might next cast my line upward into the air." [10] The same manner is common in writers as diverse as Dickinson, Twain, and Eliot. At the end of "Directive," when he is about to advise the reader to "Drink and be whole again beyond confusion," Frost thinks it entirely appropriate to remark that the cup has been hidden so that "the wrong ones can't find it,/ So can't get saved, as Saint Mark says they mustn't." [11] Gatsby, on the point of incar-nating his dream with a fateful kiss, pauses, listening "to the

10. *Walden*, chap. 9, p. 121.
11. *Complete Poems of Robert Frost: 1949* (New York, Holt, Rinehart, and Winston, 1949), p. 521.

tuning-fork that had been struck upon a star." [12] Such language reflects a perspicaciously ironic attitude which finds nature essentially puzzling. For the nature image is both the merely physical object of present perception and the symbol of a strictly transcendent meaning. While this is also true in the English Romantic renderings of nature with which one inevitably draws comparisons, in American nature description the two aspects of natural images tend to be far more sharply contrasted, and the movement from one to the other is less often a smooth transition than a sudden and witty shift of perspective. This difference of style is the consequence of drawing so crisp a line between the present and other times that the things perceived, the landscape and its contents, direct the mind to areas thought to be distinctly outside of this moment. They refer to realities in past or future, and their meaning is mysterious because, when the real is assumed to be what is now being perceived, existence outside of this limit is a problem to be explained. The more strictly the present is confined to the here-now of sense data, the more arresting the transcendental leap of thought to other times will seem, and the more stylized and consciously symbolic the image initiating this movement will be. Thus American nature descriptions typically focus upon the mystery of how things beyond perception enter into it—of how the scent of lilac brings back the mood of a year ago, or of how a fishing stream in the Pyrenees manifests the wisdom of Ecclesiastes.

In Irving's little narrative the characteristic form of American fiction can be observed at the point of origin. Looking back from "Rip Van Winkle" or "The Legend of Sleepy Hollow," where the fable is even more elaborately conjured from the landscape, one can recognize the fictional process as an extension of the meditative process, as this is delineated in such a work as Anne Bradstreet's "Contemplations." Mistress Bradstreet finds the meaning of her immediate response to landscape by placing the moment

12. F. Scott Fitzgerald, *The Great Gatsby* (New York, Scribners, 1953), p. 112.

within the predestined scheme of history which is God's will. Irving, by comparing epochs as different states of consciousness, develops a general view of the relations between them. But there is, of course, a great difference between the total history he attempts to formulate and Anne Bradstreet's, a difference which can be recognized by recollecting the change in viewpoint Franklin represents. Franklin well illustrates the transition from the view of history as a fixed and static design made known to man by revelation to the view of history as process. He retains the traditional premise of a total design, but assumes that it cannot be seen as such, since every human view, being one from the inside, is limited and relative to the moment. Thus history as it is known is incomplete, a continuous activity rather than an unchanging design. It is but a step from Franklin to Irving and not so large a stride from Irving to Faulkner, as the realization grows that "what really happened" in any given past moment is an event still to be completed.

This view of history provides the basis for a distinctive kind of fiction in which events are so ordered as to reveal a general process, which, it is hoped, may manifest the timeless laws of reality. Instead of a completed action, developing progressively through phases which move from an initial situation to a quite different final one, the story proceeds through repetition, joining events as they are joined in Puritan history, as diverse illustrations of a single mode of happening. The later event is seen as a reenactment rather than an effect of the ones preceding it, and the action moves forward in that each successive reenactment further clarifies the common process, formulating it more obviously or in a new way, and affording, therefore, a more inclusive view. The end is not a different state of affairs, the consequence of an absolute change, but a realization of the situation which has pertained continuously throughout. And of this truth to be found, this actual situation, the symbol is landscape. Thus the setting becomes the standard with reference to which the fictive happenings are to be judged true. The fable is validated in that it accords with the

167

reader's own perceptual process; the way events occur in the story is shown to be identical with the way in which his mind would work were he actually observing the landscape within which the characters act.

The experience of landscape provides the paradigm of literary action, a truth which can be clearly discerned by noticing the distinctive kind of virtue the protagonist in American fiction displays. In *Huckleberry Finn* this virtue is a sort of instinct, which is proved wise and good by the mysterious concord between Huck's evasive, moment-to-moment way of behaving and the endlessly various flow of the Mississippi, while in *Light in August* Lena Grove's journey, from the Advent season of her child's conception to August, when she gives birth, is made analogous to the cycle of the seasons. Since mind and object are united in the event of perception, what is seen "out there" as an activity in nature is also an activity of mind—both of the reader's mind, as he experiences the landscape the author delineates, and of the character's mind. For the character is depicted as a distinct kind of activity rather than a personage composed of intrinsic traits. His selfhood is simply his way of perceiving, what he does being a function of how he sees things. For example, the voyage of the *Pequod* is identical with Ishmael's contemplation of sea and universe; the deeds of Ahab and his men are not just acts known to Ishmael's mind but modes of perception which, taken together in all their interrelations, constitute his identity. James merely carries this method further, converting all important events of plot into moments of perceiving and, by giving greater emphasis to the relativity of points of view, so besetting his characters with difficulties that their actions appear to be almost entirely ways of making things out.

On the surface, fiction of this sort will often appear to be progressive, as if the action were completed and an end such as Aristotle thought necessary had been reached. But the ending is inconclusive with respect to events. After the novel arrives at a point of optimal understanding—at a clear and consistent view of the process the plot enacts—the process still goes on: *there* there is no last phase. Usually the protagonist—Rip, in the person of his son, or Huck, Sister Carrie, Ishmael, or Jake Barnes—is seen at the end on the point of repeating again just such an experience or deed as the novel has depicted. If there is a difference, it is only that now he more fully realizes the pattern of his experience and accepts, usually with a degree of bleak fatalism, the destiny to live on in the same way. For such protagonists, and for the reader also, the apparent progression is an illusion which gradually fades as events force the mind to see that all changes repeat a process which itself never changes.

The effect is scarcely different when the character's story—Hester Prynne's or Gatsby's, for example—rounds to a close. Their journey is no doubt ended, but it can be conceived as a story—as a coherent sequence—only by considering it in the light of psychological and sociological processes which pertain at all times. It is in those processes that such crucial actions as Dimmesdale's confession and Daisy's faithless silence have their cause. The characters are perceptual and behavioral processes, and the dénouements are the largest statements of these processes, not a later consequence of earlier acts. Significantly, Hester lives on in the old way, which is now so familiar that Hawthorne can recount the rest of her life in a few sentences, while Gatsby, though disillusioned, continues to hope for Daisy's love to the moment of his death.

As the novel's action becomes recognizable as an unending process, it often tends to merge with the processes of nature: the cycle of the seasons, birth and death, the flow of the river, the rising and setting of the sun. In this way, the outward movement toward a process which is universal is also rendered as an inward movement toward the reader's immediate present. For a mode of happening which always pertains must pertain in the present moment and must therefore be manifested in the process of the reader's own perception as he views the landscape.

While Irving illustrates how, from the American way of defining the present, and hence experience, the characteristic form of

American fiction is developed, it is in the novels of Cooper that the potentialities of this form are first fully realized. Irving preferred to speak of his tales as sketches such as a man might make on a holiday ramble through the countryside. The metaphor suggests the very tentative belief in fiction which led him to cast his most ambitious narratives in the form of biography or travel literature. By contrast, Cooper allows no hint in his novels that the fable needs to be justified. Apparently he felt that the ethical and social concerns he dealt with provided as reasonable a ground as one could hope to find for the writing of fiction. He assumes that the truth of the novel rests upon its morality, and his social views, as he constantly asserts, issue from this ethic.

But Cooper's morality, when one attempts to formulate it, proves to be inseparable from the natural setting of his novels. It becomes a matter of empty formulas whenever dissociated from the experience of landscape, which explains why value judgments evaporate on the lips of his upper-class characters. If Natty Bumppo's pronouncements seem somewhat more apposite, that is due less to their intrinsic truth than to their truth as things he might say, which, by characterizing his happy adjustment to the wilderness, point to a morality in the land itself. But even Leatherstocking's morals are an inadequate reflection of the setting, so that Cooper can occasionally risk a laugh at his protagonist. No one can state the moral truth successfully, for the morality of nature is different in kind from ethics in the usual sense. It subsists in the experience of nature, and therefore, despite his best efforts, Cooper is unable to make out a better mode of existence than Natty's life in the woods. In Cooper, as in Irving, the fable arises from the scene and is a means of exploring the landscape. His novels are more ample and complex than Irving's tales simply because his ethical concerns made the exploration both more difficult and more urgent.

The Pioneers illustrates the essential design of Cooper's fiction in its clearest form. Even those who would question the judgment that it is probably his greatest work will at least concede that as the first novel of the Leatherstocking series it reveals Cooper at the crucial stage when his art reached maturity. *The Spy,* written just before, anticipates his later fiction in its patriotic and historical concerns, its use of an American setting, and its somewhat too facile devices of plot, but for all this, it is a dull, incoherent production, because, though it assembles Cooper's most propitious materials, they are but loosely held together in the coils of an adventure story. The fault is that the landscape lacks the wholeness required by Cooper's particular kind of fiction; except for a few picturesque views, the setting is an all too "neutral ground," lacking contour and atmosphere. The facelessness which makes Harvey Birch somewhat arresting is a trait indicative of the way the Cooper protagonist depends upon the landscape for any personality he may have. Birch's identity is faint because the landscape is undefined; only the accidents of military history make him a resident of Westchester county. And as the main character is only theoretically present, so there is no significant event to underlie and unite the series of unlikely adventures. By contrast, Cooper's achievement in *The Pioneers* is the result of his full realization of setting. The action is convincing despite the absurdity of occasional episodes, and in Natty Bumppo, Cooper created an enduring fictional personality because, ultimately, the landscape is so effectively pictured that the people and events seen within it become credible. The key to his success is the technique of making the reader's experience of landscape continuous with the characters', so that what we see for ourselves gives validity to what they think and do.

It is with a landscape picture that the novel begins, a picture far more effective than any to be found in *The Spy.* That Cooper here has the advantage of portraying a region remembered from his own childhood indicates the method of his descriptive art. The landscape is placed not only geographically but historically, for in speaking of the location of his story, he finds that he is also speaking of its history. As in Anne Bradstreet's "Contemplations" and Walt Whitman's "Out of the Cradle," to see is to remember, and thus as the landscape is brought into focus, it is transformed from a present perception to a vision of the past. Observing the landscape before one's eyes involves also the process of visualizing how it came into being, for the present objects of sense, particularly those made by men—the "thriving villages," "comfortable farms," "academies," and churches—manifest development. In recognizing *what* they are, the mind makes reference to their origin—to the earlier time, when they were built, and, beyond that, to the ideas behind the purposes which led men to build them. The landscape presently seen contains the scarcely tamed scenery of two decades ago, just as that, in turn, contains those representatives of the virgin forest, Natty and Chingachgook. The perspective of retreating pasts which Irving employs is glimpsed here, and again the movement of the author's thought, as he describes the landscape, foreshadows the pattern of the story he will tell.

While the "neutral ground" of *The Spy* is portrayed through an appeal to such isolated facts of history as one might find in a schoolbook, *The Pioneers* begins with a more definite mode of experiencing—the diagrammatic view of a map: "Near the centre of the great State of New-York lies an extensive district of country, whose surface is a succession of hills and dales, or, to speak with greater deference to geographical definitions, of mountains and valleys." [13] As the eye is brought closer, cartographical features turn into objects directly seen, mountains "arable to the top," vales "rich, and cultivated; with a stream uniformly winding through each, now gliding peacefully under the brow of one of the hills, and then suddenly shooting across the plain, to wash the feet of its opposite rival." [14] And from these items there is a natural transition to villages, roads, and, at last, individual buildings. As the description moves from space abstractly conceived to the human area of motives and beliefs, values which at first seem merely visual—as in Cooper's phrase, the "mighty Susquehanna"—

13. *The Pioneers* (New York, Holt, Rinehart, and Winston, 1962), p. 1.
14. Ibid.

lead into ones which are more distinctly mental—in "comfortable farms," for instance—until, in the notion of "public worship," the transcendent nature of value is made explicit.

As the vision narrows, it expands. The transition from the panoramic view of a map to a prospect such as the bodily eye might comprehend is a movement from objects detached and unvalued to things as they exist within psychological, ethical, and social contexts. These peculiarly human dimensions are as much facts of landscape as the visible mountains and rivers. To behold the landscape is to see farms, academies, churches—things which are symbols not only of the inhabitants' values but of the transcendent ideas of the beholder, who can only perceive these objects by looking beyond them to general meanings. Visible nature makes the same reference in a subtler way, however: the Susquehanna is "mighty," the scenery "Romantic," the streams glide "peacefully." Hence the movement of thought from the scenery to the works of the settlers is but the process of making explicit the way the mind, in perceiving, transcends its sense data.

As the first paragraph ends, landscape opens out upon history: "Only forty years have passed since this whole territory was a wilderness." [15] In fact, one must see the landscape historically to see it at all; what the settled countryside now is must be comprehended through observing the process of settlement. Significantly, Cooper does not present a fully realized scene until he has shifted his point of vantage to the time, some twenty-five years in the past, when Templeton was a new settlement. Though the first few paragraphs, taken by themselves, may not seem very different from the scene-setting usual in European novels of the period, they differ in their function with respect to the whole novel. The process of perception in which Cooper engages the reader through his description of the setting enacts in brief the process by which the narrative will develop. As Cooper places the landscape in space and time, so the novel's action portrays, though of course in much larger outline, the locating of Judge Temple's vil-

15. Ibid., p. 2.

lage in a physical world and a historical perspective which resolve the community's conflicts by interpreting them. The values
intuitively sensed in beholding a landscape are the values upon
which communal life is founded, for the community is in the
physical world in as literal a sense as the visible town is in the
landscape. The action of the reader's mind as he comes to recognize the social scene through the natural scene not only makes the
two kinds of seeing one but unites them with the action of the
characters, whose deeds gradually relate them to the community
by demonstrating that a single order underlies both society and
nature.

In essence the action of *The Pioneers* is the process of discovering the basis of community. Cooper's regret for the passing of the
wilderness is more than sentimental nostalgia; it arises from the
agonizing doubt whether civilization is worth the terrible price
men pay for it. In *The Pioneers* the narrative is the quest for some
solid reality which justifies the settlement of the wilderness, some
value which proves the new community's worth and dignity. That
Templeton exists hints that there must be such a foundation. Simply to hold together *as* a society, it must have an order founded
upon nature—must be natural in the same sense that Natty's way
of life formerly was. The question concerns not simply what a
community *ought* to be but what it *must* be to exist at all. Since
the principle of social order is justice, the representative of the
community is a judge, and the narrative hinges upon the question
of his justice.

The reader is to see justice, then, and since justice is not a
physically visible thing, one might suppose that the novelist's
most promising course would be to depict its qualities behaviorly
through just deeds. But in *The Pioneers* the most crucial act of
justice—Judge Temple's decision to draw up a will guaranteeing
the Effinghams their deserved share of his property—is an event
kept entirely out of sight. Cooper cannot portray the deciding itself, for his conception of experience as an immediate beholding
of things now present requires that the transcendent be revealed

174

through visible objects so that the larger vision may seem to grow directly from sense experience. In Cooper's fiction the action must be an inference created by the mind's act of transcending its present. His events do not add up as phases of progressively developing action, but function as typical and symbolic happenings, whose meaning is their reference to a pattern extending beyond the immediate scene. However many moments of experience are portrayed, each is autonomous, and one always has to look at reality from a present so strictly limited that a direct view of action is precluded. The *transition* from one such moment to another has to be inferred: all the reader can know is that his point of view has changed. The true action is always an inference, always something intuited from the tableau of the presently visible world.

The puzzling structure of *The Pioneers* is the consequence of Cooper's having depended so largely upon the reader's inference. While there are, to be sure, connections of a cause and effect variety between his episodes, the reader who seeks meaning only in their superficial reasonableness will find the novel an aimless, rambling affair. To illustrate with an obvious fact of plot: Natty's final departure from Templeton is the result not of his having been imprisoned nor of Jones' and Doolittle's offensive treatment. To him and to the reader these events are merely representative of a social world unsuited to his style of life, illuminating the reason rather than serving as the cause for his going.

The true action is the growth of awareness of a situation which pertains throughout the novel, and each episode renders an imperfect version of the same set of circumstances, presenting them from a particular point of view, revealing new aspects and thus amplifying earlier episodes rather than developing as a result of what has gone before. For example, the argument over the buck in the first chapter, Natty's trial, and his departure westward all manifest the conflict between the code of the wilderness and the social order, and all conclude with the triumph of the judge's law. The time intervals separating events do not alter the situation;

change consists, rather, in the reader's and characters' understanding of facts which remain constant. The story progresses in that, as events transpire, the vision of the world of Templeton becomes more inclusive and precise.

The form of such fiction is exemplified by the way the novel begins. It is usual enough in first chapters for the reader to feel uncertain as to who the characters are and what their relationships may be, but when one relates Cooper's beginning to the rest of the story, it is clear that he has handled this initial ignorance of the reader's in a way designed to raise doubts rather than provide explanations. The story will be crucially concerned with discovering whether Marmaduke Temple is a just judge, and the way future issues are objectified in the doubtfulness of things that the eye must make out is well illustrated by the account of his appearance. Swathed in heavy furs, the defense of the civilized man who is not really at home in nature, Judge Temple displays, "from beneath this masque," "a fine manly face, and particularly a pair of expressive, large blue eyes, that promised extraordinary intellect, covert humour, and great benevolence." [16] Whether Elizabeth, who is also mysteriously masked, deserves to be the heiress of all that the judge's civilization will bring is another aspect of the question as to whether her father is true to his countenance. Considered as an event, the episode is peculiarly inconclusive. Bullets fly, a buck is killed, and the man called Edwards is wounded, but the ballistical account hardly explains what has happened. What the reader beholds is not essentially a happening but rather a tableau in which the characters are posed as representatives of points of view and "social positions." Judge Temple grants Edwards the buck on mere sufferance, so that the dispute over who rightfully owns the game remains doubtful, and indeed the whole episode, with its freakish shooting accident and uncertainty as to who is who, is indicative of Cooper's focus upon the problem of perceiving things present. Only later will it become clear that the argument about the buck is an instance of the much

16. Ibid., p. 4.

more important conflict between natural and communal law. Similarly, though the reader observes Edwards' sullen and stoical manner of taking the wound, far from identifying him, this calls attention to the doubts as to who he may be, so that the behavior now seen has a meaning which is there but yet to be understood. The same may be said of the entire episode: what is to be discovered is present to the reader's eyes, and although he can only make it out through the unfolding of later events, this means not that it is a reality not yet emergent but, rather, that it is a reality not yet fully perceived.

Cooper's story is an act of focusing upon a situation which subsists throughout the book, a continually deepening perception of what is always there. This is the sense in which I suggest that his fiction grows from landscape. The social and moral situation explored by the novel is a reality taken in a single view, the same momentary vision we have in a view of landscape. Significantly, Templeton does not change in the course of the book, become a more prosperous or united community, or alter any of its social forms. Chingachgook's death and Natty's departure do not affect it, demonstrating merely the fact that it has never included them. The civilizing process is known only inferentially from the facts of village life in a single phase of its development. The reader intuits this process just as he intuits the human dimensions of landscape in the objects it presents to the eye. Thus the reader's response to Cooper's wilderness and his movement along the course of the narrative are not mere parallels: the frontier community is what it is because of its location, and since it exists in a landscape, and therefore in nature, to see it fully one must see the natural order from which it has grown.

The tableau-like confrontation of points of view in the first chapter is an obscure and narrowly angled picture of a state of affairs whose outlines the later episodes will fill in. It is not, of course, an epitome, figuring all future events in a sort of allegorical shorthand, but even so, its details have a remarkable reach of symbolic import. That Judge Temple has the last word in giving away the game that Natty has questioned his right to bestow foreshadows, in a nicely understated way, the fact that his statute law will prevail over the wilderness code. The accidental wound accords precisely but unobtrusively with the injury to his rights which Edwards imagines he has suffered, for this too is the result of chance and misinformation. In both cases the judge did not know of Edwards' whereabouts, failing to see him in the twilight woods as he later fails to recognize his social identity. Edwards insists on taking the buck because he needs it to feed the old Major, an instance, though a modest one, of those principles of property, blood, and loyalty by which the story is meant to reconcile us to the passing of the wilderness. These principles are present and operative within the first event, though not yet seen or understood.

That the form of action in *The Pioneers* is representative of Cooper's method throughout his fiction can be recognized by noting a few distinctive traits which result from shaping narrative in this way. Perhaps the most important is the static quality of the characters. The personages cannot change or grow; instead, they are seen in the process of discovering the truths of their situation in the light of their own beliefs, which remain fixed. For the reader, in turn, the characters grow gradually more distinct. In *The Pioneers* Cooper does not even entertain the possibility of character development. The judge, Natty, Edwards, and Elizabeth are personalities to be discovered, but never persons in a state of becoming. This fixity is natural and proper in Cooper's kind of narrative, and in what seems to have been his only attempt to depict a change of personality, the account of Judith Hutter in *The Deerslayer*, his efforts to show her growing from girlish vanity to moral maturity prove self-defeating. Judith foreswears her dissolute military admirers, but since at the end it appears she has become the mistress of the worst of them, she seems only to fulfill what fate has already made of her. As the child of a fallen mother and piratical father, she can grow only in the scope of her awareness, realizing her inalterable heritage, and Natty's prim rejection of her follows naturally from Cooper's commitment to the static character. That Judith is ruined by just such a seducer as her mother's helps one to appreciate the determinism underlying Cooper's celebration of heredity. Whether in the Hutters, the Effinghams, or the sons of Tamamund, blood perpetuates itself; for blood is nature and nature is always the same. Where the narrative movement is the process of discovery, the characters must remain fixed so that we can circumambulate them; and heredity both arrests them and places them in nature. Thus Cooper's virtuous characters—if they are not aristocrats—must either have no ancestors at all, as in the case of Eau Douce of *The Pathfinder,* or else be descended from yeoman stock which has benefited from good blood through traditional association. While this fixity of character has some laughable consequences, it is also the source of Cooper's finest effects. The magnificent ceremonial of Natty's death in *The Prairie* would be impossible were it not that the aged trapper is so precisely the same person as the youth on his first warpath and the wily marksman of the middle years. It is his static identity which unifies the Leatherstocking novels as phases of a single life.

Cooper's taste for superficial adventure stories is the most obvious trait of his fiction, and in *The Pioneers* the reason for such melodrama is made apparent by the leisurely and episodic character of the narrative as a whole. The very irrelevance and artificiality of the episodes of suspense, which are confined to the latter half of the book, demonstrates that the real action is of a quite different nature. One might say that Cooper tends to an excess of action because, in a more fundamental sense, he can portray no action at all. Since his characters cannot develop, their deeds, however numerous and remarkable, are merely illustrative actions that they might have performed at almost any time. Indeed, the main purpose of Cooper's derring-do is to serve as the means of creating visual panoramas rather than a coherent story.

His main problem in shaping his narrative is to manage the revelations naturally, so that the hidden essentials of his situation seem to rise to the surface of consciousness as if they had always been there and are now in the process of being noticed. The adventure episodes are an expedient called for by the great difficulty of so managing the story. Ideally, the landscape should contain in its visible elements all the social and psychological truths the story will bring into view, but in practice some of the most crucial human factors cannot be so directly conjured from the natural scenery, and it is precisely these factors that the adventure episodes seem designed to picture. The example of Elizabeth's rescue from the panther is a good instance. Cooper wished to demonstrate Leatherstocking's bravery and at the same time portray the value of personal loyalty by giving Elizabeth a sense of obligation in conflict with her father's communal responsibilities, but although the world of Templeton is still close enough to the wilderness to be inherently dangerous, it does not provide occasions for Natty's kind of courage. It is a world whose dangers are manifest in falling trees but not beasts of prey, and the encounter is absurd because either the panther or the ladies ought not to be there. Similarly, because the love of Elizabeth and Edwards is not deducible from the sum of their riches and good breeding, they must be thrown into each other's arms by the forest-fire scene.

This desire to objectify psychological elements and make values physically visible is best illustrated by the elaborate account of the attack on the fortified cave. Old Major Effingham must somehow be brought to light, because he embodies the claims a society must meet if it is to exist at all. But his presence, like Natty's courage, is really more convincing when kept in the background. He cannot literally be an inhabitant of the world of Templeton, yet Cooper feels the need to produce him to complete the social landscape. The Major must appear in the flesh, because the whole situation must be perceived as a visual tableau. And as the organizing symbol in this landscape the Major is perfectly effective. He is perhaps the oldest old man in literature, a pathetic antique, as fragile as a powdering papyrus. For it is by the sense that the past is irretrievably past that its claims on friendship, heredity, and justice are shown to rest on transcendent values and operate in the present as naturally as the growth of plants or the activity of light. The derring-do is designed to effect the tableau in which all the characters are brought together, and throughout Cooper's best novels the adventure episodes are the means of creating such visual realizations.

Beneath the level of the melodramatic adventures, and without their aid, the true narrative progresses at an ambling pace. The novel's events take place during somewhat less than a year, yet significantly enough, nearly half the book is devoted to the first two days of this period. Admirers of plot construction may deplore this slow start, but clearly Cooper abandons the initial moments of his tale with reluctance and only after they have yielded all that they can of social scenery. The true narrative movement develops through a sequence of tableaux by which the vision of the world of Templeton is gradually enlarged and, in the process, explained. The confrontation over the buck, the account of the Christmas Eve service, the tavern scene, which immediately follows, and the trial scene are all pictures of Judge Temple presiding over the assembled community. The only change is that, as we move through this sequence, his justice and the issues it raises become clearer.

Two other sequences, which also originate in the opening tableau, develop parallel to the scenes involving the Judge. One defines Leatherstocking—the turkey shoot, the spear-fishing episode, the slaying of the buck, and the two rather absurd rescue episodes. These reenactments of Natty's frontier prowess clarify the code of the wilderness so that its incompatibility with the social order can at last be crystallized as an issue at law. A third sequence progressively reveals Richard Jones and, through him, the destructive forces of society. It develops from his madcap mismanagement of the sleigh to examples of his officious meddling—in advising the surgeon, for example—and then to the fishing scene, the pigeon massacre, his intrusion into Natty's affairs, and, finally, his experiment in military tactics.

Jones illustrates the remarkable effectiveness of Cooper's method in relating psychological traits to social issues. As the vanity behind the sheriff's follies approaches megalomania, it becomes recognizable as the incipient phase of such social diseases as vandalism, rapaciousness, and tyranny. The early facts about Jones thus broaden in meaning and importance. His relation to the Judge as a cousin comes to symbolize the inevitability of evils inherent in society. That we glimpse Jones' ill-conceived buildings before their foolish architect comes in sight is a good instance of the way Cooper's narrative grows out of his landscape.

Cooper was never again to rely as fully as in *The Pioneers* upon the kind of narrative progression I have described. Whether from an imperfect estimate of where his best talents lay or an immature taste for excitement, he committed himself to the writing of tales of adventure, so that the melodrama used as a last resort in *The Pioneers* becomes a habitual preference in his later frontier novels. Yet these novels also derive whatever value they have from the form of progressive revelation, the adventures being absurd because they are less thoughtfully related to landscape experience. Even in the most factitious of them one can discern Cooper's intention to find the rationale for his events in their relation to setting. Hence spatial relations—as, for instance, the location of the "castle" in *The Deerslayer*—qualities of terrain, weather conditions, and the time of day provide the most usual "reasons why." But when he introduces his episodes by inventing whatever stumps and ravines the events will call for, places the characters where he wants them without much troubling about their reasons for being there, allows the lady whom Leatherstocking has just rescued at the risk of his scalp to wander idiotically outside the stockade the next hour, and has defenseless parties set forth on jaunts which the least foresight would indicate are ill-advised, such faults make it all the more apparent that the action of the Cooper novel is less a story than a perceptual process which, when unskillfully managed, becomes a capricious shifting about of atomistic particles in pure space.

In the novel whose situation remains unchanging, action is most completely a matter of finding things out, and therefore the concealment so obviously employed to create suspense is really essential to Cooper's fiction throughout. *Precaution,* his first novel, demonstrates this with particular force by showing that the main lesson he learned from Jane Austen is the technique of focusing upon the question of just who people are—in respect to their ethics, their histories, their social natures. But while in Jane Austen the revelation of such matters is a developing action—so that Emma's understanding of Frank Churchill and Mr. Knightly reflects the growth of her own character, for example—in Cooper the discovery marks a change not in the character or the situation but in the reader's view of them.

To the extent that Cooper succeeds in engaging the reader's interest in "what will happen next," he achieves suspense, because what is absurd as event is often convincing as vision. His adventures provide the occasion for beautifully realized tableaux, and the best of them are in themselves highly pictorial. It is the precipice that makes the death struggle of Magua and Uncas so exciting. The descent of the rapids in *The Pathfinder,* the description in *The Deerslayer* of Hurry Harry dragged through the water, bound hand and foot, and, in *The Prairie,* the discovery of Inez and the death of Leatherstocking are so impressive as visualized scenes that one forgets, or excuses, their improbability as events. Cooper's novels are narratives of observation, portraying action as a process of discovery, and that which the story reveals has a double nature, existing not only as an object the mind perceives but also as a quality of the mind itself. Judge Temple's last will and testament is inseparable from his justice, and the blood of the Effinghams is their virtue. The outward fact whose revelation makes sense of events is continuous with the psychological predisposition of both character and reader.

A general view of the Leatherstocking series will help to show Cooper's way of uniting the psychic and material worlds. Most particularly, it will emphasize how much the relating of narrative to landscape depends upon Cooper's ability to create a communal point of view.

Significantly, all four of the later Leatherstocking tales are set entirely within the world of the wilderness, with the important consequence that communal forms are present only as a psychological order in the minds of the more cultivated characters. The result is a view of society which is very oblique but none the less effective. Detached from their supporting institutions, the values of the community stand free as merely the beliefs of individuals and can therefore be seen as values set at liberty to prove their own merits. One of Cooper's firmest convictions was that they would meet the test, and it is a measure of his conservatism that he trusted that this proving out of social norms as personal convictions would justify them as proper responses to natural necessities.

One can understand, then, why Cooper could never dispense with his ladies and gentlemen. Since their mental furniture consists of little more than unexamined pieties and allegiance to caste, they are, no doubt, tiresome, but even so, they are necessary to Cooper's wilderness as symbols of the socio-ethical values the narrative is to validate. It is not too serious a fault that they are laughably improbable, because their primary function is simply to be stranded in the woods so that one may discover within the received ideas which make up their personalities what essential truth there may be. Had Cooper's instinct not told him that his Mabel Dunhams and Oliver Effinghams were mere names in a world of empty social abstractions, he would never have left the populous countryside of England or Westchester county.

The educated characters symbolize the problem to be explained, and the fact that Cooper cannot depict them *as people* is a failure that indicates a peculiar kind of success. It is, I would argue, the success of a novelist whose imagination is keen enough to sense the problem of defining personal identity. When we speak of convincing fictional characters, we have in mind distinct individuals, but by the early nineteenth century a novelist might well ask in what sense such individuals may be said to exist. By Whitman's time and, in Europe, that of Flaubert, this question is one we expect will be treated seriously, and it is perhaps our error not to suppose that Cooper also might have been aware of it. For if his gentlefolk and the type characters in their entourage derive from the outmoded will-passion-appetite psychology, his preference for nature over any characters at all indicates that he saw selfhood in quite different terms. Though little interested in metaphysics, Cooper seems to have realized that if one took post-Lockean psychology to heart, one could not understand people without reference to their setting, and that while their setting is society, this in turn cannot be explained in its own terms. For its terms *are* society—as Cooper's "nice" characters are simply the sum of their commonplace opinions—so that one must in the end question not the truth of those terms but their very existence as meaningful words.

After *The Pioneers,* in which he discovers that "owning" is resolvable into subjective predispositions—honor, courage, loyalty, truthfulness—Cooper, in the subsequent Leatherstocking novels, turned to exploring the import of such terms within a wilderness world where they exist without the props of social law. In other words, the later novels fulfill the promise of the first, not just by filling in the outline of Natty's character, nor even by completing the picture of an ever-advancing frontier, but, more fundamentally, by attempting a more exact definition of those terms by which, in the culture of Cooper's America, both social order and personal identity were to be explained. The terms are to be made valid, proved true, shown to have their source in nature, and thus revealed as the terms in which society should—indeed, must—think and judge.

The Leatherstocking series is superior to Cooper's novels of social criticism, because in the former he looks beneath the political and economic issues to the questions of belief which a convincing social theory would have to answer. The Littlepage series, *Wyandotte, Heidenmauer,* and *The Bravo,* which I take to be the best of his other fictions, less often transmute Cooper's legalistic principles into epistemological ones. He assumes that only the ethical foundation of law can give it true authority, but as a rule he proceeds as if the nature and existence of this moral foundation were obvious. Yet it is just the question to demonstrate that such a foundation exists, and it is Cooper's effort to do this in the Leatherstocking novels that accounts for their unity and their grandeur.

Since Cooper's characters, while lifeless as independent agents, are believable as figures in a setting, it is not surprising that Leatherstocking is by all odds the most interesting of them. As the frontiersman, he belongs most completely within Cooper's wilderness landscape. Like Irving's Rip Van Winkle, he embodies the scene, seeming to draw into himself and to generate, as diamonds do sunlight, the elementary forces of nature, so that his universalizing references give him the stature of a mythic hero. Much has been made of Leatherstocking as an image of the American character, but it will never be out of fashion to assert that his undoubted national representativeness depends upon his felt relation to the land. As has often been noted, Natty cannot be imagined in any but his forest setting. Cooper seems to have known this instinctively, since he never risked transplanting Leatherstocking, and, despite two efforts to arrange a marriage, accepted the fact that even domesticity would destroy his hero's identity.

Yet to say that Leatherstocking can only be a person within the wilderness landscape is to recognize the very limited sense in which he is a person at all. Apparently his existence depends upon our perspective, and he is an individual because, whenever we see him, we also see the forest. Though he is one of the most memorable of literary characters, his archaic simplicity defies our idea of characterization as an art of deep psychological exploration. His beliefs, for instance, seem as empty as those of the "nice" characters. His wisdom consists in a stock of just such familiar notions as theirs, his vague Unitarian pieties make no more sense than their churchly views (though Cooper may have imagined otherwise), while such traits as his long, silent laugh and endless talk about "gifts" are typical of the characterizing tags Cooper used to limn his other humble personages. And in his social views Leatherstocking, who knows his place, seems just one more of the crowd. Though he prefers the forest and hunting to the settlements and trade, he never challenges the social hierarchy, urban manners, formal schooling, or upper-class morals. His sentiments are those of the gift books, feelings which Cooper thinks the more respectable in that the illiterate Natty cannot have learned them by reading.

How then, we may ask, can such a bundle of received ideas and attitudes amount to an identity? The answer is that the landscape creates him, just as he, in turn, interprets it. To seek his personality in a catalogue of his traits is futile, because he is not an individual to be considered in himself but a person seen existing within his forest setting. He exists in the affinity between human values and natural forms. For example, his deeds have a moral significance—he acts within a context of assumptions about purposes and values—and this context the visual scene represents. We can conceive of the context, because it is objectively portrayed by the qualities of landscape. Similarly, while the opinions he voices are platitudinous when separately considered, they become true as statements within the world we are seeing. In other words, Leatherstocking becomes a person because we impute to him as moral qualities and psychological predispositions what we experience in Cooper's portrayal of nature as physical realities. This is not to say merely that he exists to us through our own experience as readers, which is, after all, true of every literary character. I mean rather that, guided by Cooper's statements, we unconsciously transfer to Leatherstocking our own responses to the novel's landscape. His behavior as a person acting within the landscape seems to spring from such thoughts and feelings as we

ourselves have in merely looking at the scene. We do not, of
course, fear the Mingos, but since we respond to them as elements of the wilderness world, we assent to his fear as he arms
himself against the evil they threaten, because the forest, with its
darkness and hard exigencies, hints at analogous dangers. In sum,
Leatherstocking's identity is the product of our novelistically controlled view of nature; he becomes a person because his response
to nature is validated by our own.

That Natty is a perfect shot is perhaps his most significant trait.
We learn in *The Deerslayer* that he was renowned for marksmanship even before going on his first warpath, being honored with
the sobriquet "Hawkeye," and the title of the novel is, of course,
the name of the rifle Judith Hutter gives him. Cooper seems to
imply that although one can imagine his hero before he had ever
killed a Mingo or suffered torture, one cannot picture him without his rifle. Thus his childhood, one notes, is but vaguely intimated, while his old age is marked by a shift from shooting to
trapping—his primary resource in *The Prairie* and a sure sign of
his coming death.

Every reader recognizes that for Leatherstocking marksmanship involves much more than a necessary skill. Others shoot
quite well enough to defend themselves and bring down their
dinners, but Natty has raised the art to a cult. He derives from its
practice the satisfaction of essential pieties, because it serves to
express a sanctified relation between the self and nature: he kills
only what he needs, an attitude of reverence toward the life both
of the self and of nature; he kills beautifully and fairly, not just to
assert his skill, but because reality is worthy of an exact "aim." As
in Hemingway's noble matadors, the precision of art is identical
with justness of vision. Shooting, then, is an image of seeing, and
as Natty takes his aim, the reader is to take the landscape. To observe accurately, like the marksman's aiming, is to make the mind
conform exactly to the conditions of nature; and since, for both
the man living in the woods and the audience contemplating a
landscape, nature has transcendent moral dimensions, both kinds
of sight are the result of an ethically correct state of mind.

For Cooper the process of perception unites subject and object, so that moral values are continuous with physical qualities. The spear-fishing episode in *The Pioneers* exemplifies this mode of narrative action quite clearly. We are shown first, by way of contrast, one of those visions of civilized rapacity Cooper was so skillful in creating—the scene in which the villagers under Richard Jones' leadership drag the lake with a huge seine, bringing out thousands of pounds of fish, most of which can never be used. The futility of this waste reflects the crudeness of the method, and, in turn, a primitive state of consciousness. The seine catches only gross, undifferentiated matter; the fish, like Gatsby's shirts, are wealth merely in the abstract, having no relation to human needs or a clear psychological order. What makes this scene brilliant is Cooper's insight that such disordered experience arises not from indifference to values but from a thoughtless and undisciplined response. The fishers seek the life hidden beneath the water, a life remote and alien to human consciousness, but to discover that life without art or purpose is to fail to perceive it. Nearly everyone—even the Judge, for all his interest in conservation—is infected with the frenzy of this rash assault upon nature, and depressed, at last, by the meaningless result.

Prepared by this scene, we are ready to see Leatherstocking's wilderness virtue as a condition of intellectual order. His skill in spearing the one huge trout through the perfect coordination of eye and arm is not just an example of right action in contrast to destructive greed, nor yet of art in contrast to crude practicality. His skill is his vision; its rightness and artistry are aspects of its truth. Natty's aim makes the world coherent and meaningful, because Cooper endows our vision with a similar clarity.

The importance of Cooper's ability to direct our vision is illustrated by his use of light imagery. While the villagers move confusedly in the hellish glare of the bonfire, a point of light appears far across the lake. As it gradually approaches, first projecting a long reflection on the water, then becoming recognizable as a torch, and at last revealing the canoe with its occupants, the reader is unconsciously led into a mode of experience far more precise and clearly focused than that of the villagers. The emphasis is upon efficiency, which is manifested outwardly by the discriminating way the torchlight illuminates only what needs to be seen. This visual precision is continuous with the fishermen's skill, and their skill continuous with traits of mind which are implicitly ethical. To discover the mystery at the heart of the tenebrous landscape and catch, as it were, the ideal trout requires that adjustment of mind to nature which constitutes Natty's unique virtue. Thus the efficiency of the light's selective beams accords with the graceful gliding of the canoe and the restrained and exactly appropriate movements of the men. When Elizabeth sees "thousands" of fish "swimming in shoals along the shallow and warm waters of the shore," one cannot quite dismiss the authorial comment that the torch "exposed all the mysteries of the lake, laying them open to the eye," for in spite of the pretentious phrasing, Cooper has rendered a strangely wondrous quality.[17] A kind of mystery is encountered in looking in upon the life of the wilderness lake, a mystery such as one experiences in seeing a noted cathedral for the first time and discovering "out there" in the world of actual things something that photography has made a familiar sight to the imagination.

Elizabeth expects Natty to dart his spear at random among the swarming fish, but it is of the nature of his pure efficiency to have a single and specific target:

> Elizabeth saw the bright, polished tines, as they slowly and silently entered the water, where the refraction pointed them many degrees from the true direction to the fish; and she thought that the intended victim saw them also, as he seemed to increase the play of his tail and fins, though without moving his station. At the next instant, the tall body of Natty bent to the water's edge, and the handle of his spear disappeared in the lake. The long, dark streak of the gliding weapon, and the little bubbling vortex, which followed its rapid flight, were easily to

17. Ibid., p. 272.

be seen; but it was not until the handle shot again high into the air, by its own reaction, and its master, catching it in his hand, threw its tines uppermost, that Elizabeth was acquainted with the success of the blow. A fish of great size was transfixed by the barbed steel, and was very soon shaken from its impaled situation into the bottom of the canoe.[18]

Because we see all through Elizabeth's eyes, we are obliged to view Natty entirely from the outside, with the result that his character is inferred from her—and our—perceptions. These are markedly objective, tending even to scientific detail, as in the fact that the submerged tines seem pointed in the wrong way or that the spear bounces up by its own reaction. But such visible facts circle back toward subjective response. We do not see the spear strike the fish because Elizabeth cannot, so that our view seems to be from an actual place. When Natty declares he will fish no more tonight because "enough is as good as a feast," we assent to the maxim which, though no less commonplace than those of the other characters, seems true to character because true to the scene.[19] For we have come to know his mind through the harmony between the darkness, silence, and sharply focused light and the graceful efficiency of his actions. These facts of our perceiving are transferable to Natty as moral traits, because they define a skill representing the adjustment of his mind to its setting. He acquires psychological traits because his behavior accords with our own response to the landscape. What we feel in looking at the scene we suppose that he too feels; and since our feelings are real, his seem true. As a reflection of the landscape's noble beauty, his virtue can be credited through our own experience.

The comic rescue of Ben Pump, whom Natty fishes up from the bottom of the lake by entwining his spear in the mariner's queue, affords a glimpse of Cooper's larger intention. He would show us that the virtues of woodcraft are continuous with the social vir-

18. Ibid., pp. 273–74.
19. Ibid., p. 274.

tues, that both arise from the same essential morality. The rescue of Ben foreshadows the rescues of Elizabeth from the Panther and, still later, of Elizabeth and young Effingham from the forest fire. The meaning of these episodes is not simply that Natty is a valuable citizen or good man. Our attention is focused upon the loyalty with which Ben and Elizabeth repay him, which parallels that of Judge Temple to the Effinghams and the woodsmen's to Indian John. Loyalty is the proper response, in the settlements no less than in the wilderness, and its continuing relevance points toward an order of values which endures through all changes. The passing of Natty's way of life becomes acceptable in that its vital merits live on in the civilization that replaces it.

In the fish-spearing episode Elizabeth's role as a point-of-view character is of more than technical significance. We see through her eyes because, as the heiress of Templeton, she represents the social views to be justified. The episode is not uniquely *her* experience, however, for to have a distinctly personal vision, one would have to be more of a person than she. Her identity consists of a few general ideas bound together by a name.

The modern reader is apt to think this shallowness of character a sign of Cooper's incapacity, since it is through the refined definition of the observing character that the kind of *vraisemblance* he admires in more recent fiction is developed. One feels, for instance, that Hemingway manages such scenes more skillfully than Cooper—that seeing Romero in the bull ring is a more fully realized experience, for example, because Jake Barnes is a more definite personality. But perhaps it is this very fact which explains why neither Romero nor any other Hemingway character possesses the mythic stature of Leatherstocking. The more distinct the observer, the more our general views are converted into personal ones. They are not less general for that—Jake's experience is supposed to accord with the wisdom of the Spanish peasant and the "Preacher" of Ecclesiastes—but they are markedly less social. Since Jake is somebody in particular, adopting his point of view means abandoning the position which *anyone* might occupy.

192

By contrast, Elizabeth's transparency allows her to represent anyone's view, and so, possibly, society's. Not that her professed beliefs are really the established principles of society, either in our time or Cooper's, though the novelist wistfully hoped that they might be. Elizabeth and the other aristocratic characters symbolize the communal point of view more subtly by serving as a lexicon of commonplace ideas. They represent the language available to society, the terms in which communal beliefs must be defined. And, like dictionary definitions, their terms are neither meaningless, on the one hand, nor sufficiently intelligible, on the other, so that what they say is not so much false as unconvincing. When they speak, as they commonly do, of honor, courage, piety, and the rest, we know what they mean, in a way, and yet are made uneasy by the feeling that such words have no distinct reference. The terms become valid to the extent that Cooper is able to show their relevance to the world of the wilderness, and there, when tested within our experience of landscape, their validity proves partial. Cooper's fiction wins assent not to Elizabeth's opinions but to the idea that in a limited way her terms are meaningful. Thus, for instance, though she is an Anglican, the novel affirms little more of her faith than a simple monotheism and is much less dependent upon a theology, however vague, than upon an ethical sense so inclusive that it largely accords with the redskin's.

Cooper's narrative, then, is a process of reducing and simplifying the communal language to its elemental terms. The kind of belief which results does not extend very far beyond the idea that value judgments are possible—that there is a moral reality which words such as "virtue," "justice," "loyalty," "honesty" and "falsehood," "law" and "crime" to a certain extent *intend*. Natty's mode of action seems ethically more proper than Richard Jones' and his character is nobler, because, through such scenes as the fishing episode, the meanings of these elemental terms are revealed as existential qualities of landscape.

The terms which emerge from this testing out in nature as valid enough to define a social point of view are rudimentary, no doubt, but the spare quality of this vocabulary indicates the acuteness of Cooper's understanding. He seems to have realized how narrow, by the nineteenth century, the area of communally shared beliefs had become, as the Christmas service at Templeton nicely illustrates. That realization may explain his compulsive didacticism. While the minor novelists of his period proceed on the comfortable premise that there is a morality which all their readers will automatically assume, he must forever reiterate and argue. A trait of temperament, critics say, but perhaps Cooper's dyspepsia was the result of an accurate vision of his difficulties.

Just how far he succeeded in overcoming those difficulties is indicated by the character of Leatherstocking. The woodsman's solid identity is a product of Cooper's point of view, and he is a mythically representative figure because the novelist's style enabled him to focus within his hero some of the real rather than the merely professed assumptions of society. The governing terms are those of Cooper's society, to be sure, but they are so basic, so very modest, so close to the minimal concepts any community must have that they seem to approach permanent principles. Thus, though Leatherstocking is recognizable as an idealized image of American character, his mythic nature transcends his nationality. He may display such traits as Yankee "know-how," but he does so in the manner of Lincoln rather than Ford. He is the American as the representative modern man, whose pragmatism is a form of honesty and whose scientifically precise skills manifest reverence and charity. Just as Cooper's setting, though it is the American wilderness, represents the general conditions of perception, so his hero, who lives only within this world, represents a universal way of perceiving, and so of feeling and thinking. For the style makes Natty's private experience congruent with our public view. By holding us within an official language, the style makes our experience collective; by holding Natty at a distance as an object in a setting, it makes his response to nature an aspect of our response to landscape.

194

One often wishes that Cooper had written more carefully, and there is no denying his frequent clumsiness. But the modern reader is really much less troubled by stylistic slips than by the point of view Cooper assumes. His style is in essence that of official language:

> Elizabeth examined the light ash timbers and thin bark covering of the canoe, in admiration of its neat but simple execution, and with wonder that any human being could be so daring as to trust his life in so frail a vessel. But the youth explained to her the buoyant properties of the boat, and its perfect safety, when under proper management, adding, in such glowing terms, a description of the manner in which the fish were struck with the spear, that she changed suddenly, from an apprehension of the danger of the excursion, to a desire to participate in its pleasures.[20]

The effect of such writing is prolix and ponderous, because the style seems inappropriately detached from the subject. How a girl decides to take a canoe ride is described in the manner of a university president penning a report to the trustees. One objects to Cooper's language because it holds the reader at too great a distance from the event. We "see" the canoe detachedly, as a draftsman might, and since we are given no clear sense of Elizabeth's feelings as an individual, her conversation with Edwards has an air of improbable ceremoniousness. But there are different kinds of immediacy, depending upon one's point of view. Our quarrel with Cooper's language is really a dissent from his way of seeing.

Modern readers may complain that the official language has been hopelessly debased by frequent misuse, but in fact they do not believe that *any* publicly received language can be valid because they reject the possibility of a communal point of view. The modern consensus is that there can be no consensus. Experience is conceived as a distinctly personal affair, from which it follows that a good prose style must be radically subjective, for it will

20. Ibid., pp. 270–71.

195

seem honest only to the extent that it suggests an individual way of perceiving. Thus the contemporary reaction to the prose of the nineteenth century involves a large measure of self-deception. Macaulay, who wrote the official language with much more grace than Cooper, is even less respected, yet in such writers as Emerson or Ruskin the public rhetoric and traditional pieties are viewed tolerantly, because they seem to be used as a means of indicating the tensions and dubieties of an engaged personality. And while the nineteenth-century novelists are far less committed to a subjective style than the essayists, their use of the official language, when not willfully ignored, is forgiven on the ground that it serves them as a source of fictional ways of speaking or a store of masks which allows for a thoughtful kind of role-playing. Thus Thackeray is to be seen as a Victorian Joyce.

The crucial figure in the development of modern American prose style is Twain, whose stern and somewhat adolescent skepticism led him to convert all styles, whether cultured or regional, into social points of view, all of which are more or less mistaken because, to his mind, convention always falsifies perception. Twain's style, when he speaks in his own voice, is that of educated colloquial speech, the informality of which is supposed to betoken freedom from social illusions. While Twain could still speak of "the human heart," the method he inaugurated is one in which the novelist must avoid ever seeming to appeal to received opinion. The big words, if not smuggled in in disguise, as in the case of Hemingway's "nice," can only be uttered by a fictional narrator (or on his behalf), so that the language can be viewed ironically and any false notes charged against his character. Otherwise, the novelist must proceed very indirectly, hinting at the emotional significance of things through what seem to be no more than descriptive statements.

The aim of such a method is to create subjectivity objectively, encouraging the reader to feel that he is responding directly to uninterpreted facts and so can enjoy his own private sensations. Except in more or less "in-character" writing, the norm is a journalistically transparent prose of plain words and unobtrusive syntax, for noticeable mannerisms of any sort would destroy the illusion that no collective judgment is being offered. The later styles most often criticized are those of the novelists who depart from this principle by using language to indicate a conscious public appraisal—Faulkner and Thomas Wolfe, on the one hand, and the writers of novels of social criticism, on the other.

This is not to disparage modern prose styles but to suggest that contemporary assumptions make it difficult to appreciate the rationale underlying Cooper's quite different use of language. I will freely grant that his writing is often awkward even when it functions to express a communal point of view, though the imitation of eighteenth-century prose in *Satanstoe* and the preface to *The Headsman*, together with several passages of incisively candid social commentary, show that he could write gracefully. The merits of any style are inseparable from the mode of experience it creates. If we are to understand why the Leatherstocking novels express what even the harshest critics concede is a profoundly significant aspect of American experience, we will have to give up the notion that Cooper wrote well in an inartistic language, and consider the advantages of a style which, for all its faults, proved serviceable enough to effect this achievement. The traits most often deplored—the stately manner and sententious commentary —are perhaps avoidable but natural results of holding us to a communal view of things.

Cooper cannot allow the kind of empathy modern fiction aims at, because he cannot for a moment permit his readers to enjoy a purely private experience. His objective is quite the opposite: to create the immediacy of direct perception by making it seem that the things viewed exist independently in themselves, quite unaffected by the personality of a particular observer, so that it may appear that what we see are things as anyone might see them. Therefore his manner of speaking must seem detached from the subject, as overt commentary and rhetorical explanation, for it must suggest that the object described simply is, that it can be neither created nor changed by the language, which merely makes statements *about* it. This, of course, is an artistic illusion, and one which present-day philosophy has conditioned us to distrust, but there is as large a measure of feigning in contemporary prose styles, where language is made to seem uniquely personal speech or noninterpretive reportage.

Whichever kind of illusion we prefer, Cooper's has the advantage of affirming what the twentieth century both nostalgically yearns for and resolutely denies—the possibility of a public point of view. The effectiveness of his style is perhaps best illustrated by our habit of discussing Leatherstocking's mythic significance, as if this character enjoyed his own life quite separately from his creator's way of talking about him. Yet if Leatherstocking seems to stand free of the fictional context, as a topic of public debate rather than literary analysis, this is so because Cooper's style has given him an independent life.

Leatherstocking is not the novelist's only success; there are a great many brilliant episodes in which he plays no part. I have invoked him so often because he is for Cooper a main point of focus, and therefore in his character one can most conveniently make out the nature of the novelist's achievement. The question as to why Cooper went on after *The Pioneers* to write four additional novels about Natty Bumppo is obvious, perhaps, but for that very reason interesting, since it encourages us to study the novelist's purposes in the large outlines of narrative. I have answered this question in part by proposing that the series progresses by what in classical rhetoric is called amplification. While *The Pioneers* presents all the elements of Leatherstocking's character, they exist there in embryo, and the later novels may be seen as a means of specifying and elaborating Cooper's germinal conception. For this reason, the later episodes often seem disturbingly explanatory. The almost neurotic detachment which impels Natty to burn down his cabin when his privacy is threatened, for instance, issues into retrospective views of his love for Mabel Dunham and rejection of Judith Hutter. Or, as a further example,

198

his semidivine skillfulness, as of an Hephaestus or Daedalus, is
rather too mechanically explained in the last novel, through the
history of his first warpath. But *The Deerslayer* suggests the
merits of this novelistic method even more clearly than the vices.
In the account of how the young woodsman reverently arranges
the corpse of his first Mingo in a posture of ceremonial enthrone-
ment, for instance, the magnificent ritualism of Leatherstocking's
own death is imaged forth, and the effect suggests what is most
satisfying in Cooper's art. Though the parallel, is contrived
through a mechanical resemblance, it is convincing as a revelation of attitude. One feels that the same awe and reverence per-
vade both scenes, though they mark, quite exactly, the beginning
and the end of Leatherstocking's career.

It should be apparent, then, that Leatherstocking's life is a
point of focus for Cooper's study of history. That is why it has always seemed natural to speak of the series as a sociological study
of the frontier. The frontier as a representation of progress, or
even of mere change, poses the problem of a soul-destroying relativism, and Cooper's moralistic bluster, like Irving's somewhat too
bitterly evasive humor, indicates an awareness of how much is at
stake. It is not just that pure mutability destroys history itself—
since one cannot form an idea even of flux, much less of development, unless there is some constant to recognize change by—but
that personal identity and anything one could call experience become unimaginable if there is nothing permanent. Cooper's snob-
bism and anguished concern for the sacredness of private property
are reflections of the philosophical issue. Status is the social definition of selfhood, and the possession of things the social metaphor
for perceiving them, in the sense that what one "owns" one can
unreservedly "enjoy."

One must make sense of history to make sense at all, and history requires not only a fixed principle of continuity but a fixed
principle of personal identity, for the unity of history lies in its
meaning, and the recognition of history's meaning presupposes a
detachment from the flow of time. However much or little it is

199

emphasized that history is but a limited, human view of events, the constancy which unites happenings as history cannot exist unless the observer remains himself long enough to observe a succession of events.

These points, which I am certainly not offering as subtleties, have a special relevance to the character of Leatherstocking. He is Cooper's most effective symbol of permanence, and it is mainly through reference to his fixed personality that history is made meaningful. While the five Leatherstocking novels portray the hero in every phase of his life, from young manhood to old age, his personality remains unchanged throughout. Physical aging alters none of his essential traits, and though experience presumably accumulates, it only confirms his earliest opinions. Cooper's motive as an artist for continuing the series beyond his first novel is the desire to prove the credibility of this permanence of character—to create, as it were, an image of incorruptible identity.

Leatherstocking's merits are demonstrated by his steadfastness. Absolute virtue, we may say, is a conformity to absolute truth, and the proof of Natty's goodness is that his character embodies permanent principles. Instead of moving down the path of historical change, he stands as a fixed point to which a sequence of epochs are all referable. Being always "Here!" he creates the sequence; each epoch seems to grow organically from those preceding it, because his presence in it manifests the enduring ideas it shares with the past. Thus in *The Pioneers* not only the soundness but the very existence of Judge Temple's village is accounted for through the process of discovering that its basis is the same reality which underlies Leatherstocking's way of life.

The hero's unchanging character is a function of the reader's point of view. Natty's permanence makes us aware of a like constancy in our perceiving. It is always the same process, for throughout a great many episodes and a variety of epochs we are constantly observing the same person. The immutable traits of his

character seem to exist in our experience as constant predispositions, suggesting that beneath his being and our perceiving there
is a ground of eternal values. These values are not easily enumer-
ated: they are not simply the opinions the characters utter, nor is
Cooper's own ethical terminology adequate to express them. But
they give to both varieties of statement a *degree* of reality, since
as values inherent in the experience of nature—in the process of
the subject-object relation—they enjoy a double existence as both
character traits and natural facts. They are realities that can be
indicated only rather clumsily by such hyphenated terms as
"honesty-being," "reverence-efficiency," "loyalty-sameness." The
important point is that they are timeless values; they transcend
all times, and though they are conceived as activities, they always
display the same process.

Cooper's fiction is crucially concerned with resolving the problem of permanence and change, and his method of discovering
timeless principles within the reader's immediate experience by
making narrative grow directly from our response to landscape
reveals close affinities to Puritan meditative poetry, Edwards'
theology, and Franklin's vision of the self. His frontier tales are
designed to produce the growing realization that a series of events
are, in essence, the same event, and that for mankind history displays but one, unchanging spiritual situation. This is not to do
away with change or even to deny that history is going somewhere; for it is the historicity of history that reveals the continuity of what is permanent and so defines man's situation. Further,
it is history which renders that situation a matter of experience.
Because time always brings change, epochs must continually be
accounted for by reinterpreting the past to accommodate the
emerging present, and living is the continual activity of seeking
the permanent in what is always changing. Cooper's enduring
relevance in a period when his art is held in contempt reflects our
sense that in creating the novel of the frontier he touched upon
questions which have since become agonizingly difficult. In a cul-

ture committed to the idea that all things are events—ideas no less than objects—and must be considered in the context of a universe in a state of becoming, the reality of motion itself becomes doubtful. For motion is a meaningless term unless it points to a timeless ground. Even the idea of experience would break down if some permanence were not recognized. An experience must have unity or the word lacks reference; there must be a stable point of view from which its unity is discernible, since it cannot be one thing with reference to merely temporary standards. But for humanity the location of all points of view is the world and, quite literally, the landscape. Because Cooper had the shrewd intuition that even this ground is in motion, his fiction not only records the socio-historical phenomenon of the frontier and suggests its particular meaning to American culture, but constitutes a genre in the fullest sense.

Some readers may deny that thought necessarily intends a timeless ground and may counter my arguments concerning the way unity is implicated in the concepts of experience, event, and process by suggesting that I have mistaken for requirements of thought what are merely artificial structures of language. Not wishing to seem open to Frost's complaint against philosophers, that they always "end up in the universal Whole/ As unoriginal as any rabbit," I would only reply that the idea of fictional truth deserves as skeptical a regard as the idea of unity.[21] To the criticism that—since in fact there is no demonstrable ground and therefore no timeless order of values—Cooper's novels are founded upon an illusion, the proper answer is that fiction is precisely what concerns us. It is hardly reasonable to complain that the art of illusion depends upon illusion. What is real is the illusionary effect or, in other words, the mode of experience the artist creates. Though we often wince at Cooper's crude judgments—as when he declares that old Hutter is "vicious" or Hetty "pure"— we do so because the novelist has created a world where more thoughtful judgments can be expected. His brash opinions are a

21. See "The Lesson for Today," in *Complete Poems: 1949*, p. 474.

result of a confidence with which he imbues the reader, and without really sharing his announced ethics we somehow accept the premise they rest upon: that there are permanent principles. This faith is the essential fiction, which the novelist makes true in that he makes it the basis of our reading experience. That we perceive and therefore judge in the same way throughout the cumulative account of Natty's life is a fact of our experience—whatever the rest of life may teach—and it is a quite effective way of fostering the belief that the conditions of experience are constant.

This belief does not seem uncongenial to the twentieth-century audience, for the prestige of modern psychology and the social sciences appears to rest upon the same assumption. The continuing faith in the doctrine of psychological and social norms may perhaps explain why, when all has been said about his vulgarity, mawkishness, and moralism, Cooper remains an endlessly interesting fact of American culture. It may also reveal why Leatherstocking seems to be broadly representative of the American character and, beyond that, of all humanity, even though the novelistic facts point instead to his uniqueness as an isolated personality, living in a particular locale, in a period of irreversible change. Natty is special as a personality but, through the fiction of his constancy, typical as an object of perception.

The experience of looking at a landscape is one of the most auspicious literary instances of the mind's relation to the world. The landscape symbolizes the world as directly perceived, and Natty's existence as a person always seen within the wilderness setting and always displaying the same traits creates the impression that his virtues must be perceived under the same conditions as the values of landscape. In both cases the reader must account for his own experience of values by discovering what is transcendent in what is now present. "Here!", Leatherstocking's dying utterance, focuses all in a word.[22] It expresses the simple meaning he intends—that he is ready for the summons of the Power

22. See *The Prairie*, chap. 34.

above—and yet it also expresses the "present" of more general application. His readiness for death symbolizes the constancy from which his virtues spring. In that he is *here*, in the physical world, the world directly seen as a landscape, his virtue is as immediate and real as forests, streams, and sunlight.

4
The Death of the Present:
Edgar Allan Poe

The essence of saying is the saying of
essence.

Martin Heidegger

WHETHER or not Poe wrote "The Raven" in the mechanical and
calculating way "The Philosophy of Composition" describes, his
essay gives a very useful account of the poem itself:

> I saw that I could make the first query propounded by the
> lover—the first query to which the Raven should reply "Never-
> more"—that I could make this first query a commonplace one
> —the second less so—the third still less, and so on—until at
> length the lover, startled from his original *nonchalance* by the
> melancholy character of the word itself—by its frequent repeti-
> tion—and by a consideration of the ominous reputation of the
> fowl that uttered it—is at length excited to superstition, and
> wildly propounds queries of a far different character—queries
> whose solution he has passionately at heart—propounds them
> half in superstition and half in that species of despair which
> delights in self-torture.[1]

1. *Selected Writings of Edgar Allan Poe,* ed. Edward H. Davidson (Boston,
Houghton Mifflin, 1956), pp. 458–59. Where possible, references to Poe's writings
are given according to the above text, as an authoritative one which is readily
available.

Considered as a psychic event, the poem is the portrayal of how the self's ordinary reasonableness is subverted by a compulsive desire for suffering. "Despair which delights in self-torture" is the essential emotion of "The Raven," and though the poem is probably not a good poem, the prevalent reason for disliking it—and for disliking Poe's work as a whole—is its emotional destructiveness. That destructiveness seems to parallel and originate in a destructiveness in the poet himself, and criticism of his poems and tales is often unfairly confounded with judgment of the man who wrote them. For it is clear that Poe was a deeply self-divided man, whose inner conflicts can be recognized in his tendency to ruin his own chances—to hurt old friends, create new enemies, discover imaginary offenses, and show a preference for women whose ill health, inappropriate age, or marital status made them unavailable. But we simply do not have the evidence to diagnose Poe's psychological condition, and even if the emotional destructiveness in the poems and tales could be shown to correspond to a neurotic tendency of mind, the questions criticism must answer would still remain. The meaning of particular works would still have to be explored, and what is expressible as a defect of personality in the artist would have to be formulated in literary terms, as an imperfection in the work, a failure to express a meaningful and coherent experience. However, as I shall attempt to show, the destructiveness in the poem or tale is neither irrational as a fictive emotion nor disruptive as a principle of form.

The reader may be willing to grant that no emotion is unsuited to poetic treatment and yet may still conclude that the feelings which bedeviled the man must necessarily have distorted the artist's vision. Thus, though the biographical criticism of Poe may have passed out of fashion in the sense that his works are no longer interpreted as records of particular experiences, the confusion of Poe's subject matter with his own psychological condition still persists. Even so thoughtful a critic as Roy Harvey Pearce characterizes Poe's verse as "neurotic," a kind of "dreamwork," and so, by implication, inferior, since a healthy art must deal with reality.[2]

Yet the question as to what reality is, one trusts, is still open. That Poe gives us mere dreams rather than true visions cannot be demonstrated merely by a covert reference to what we conjecture was wrong with the man. We are to suppose that the mind which produced the poems and tales was capable of recording pathological states of consciousness with perfect accuracy (for Poe's writings are the main evidence of his illness, as the argument runs), and yet on the basis of this perfectly successful self-portraiture we are to conclude that the disease of Poe's mind prevented him from writing well. That readers have felt the need to protect themselves from Poe by such capricious reasoning is a sign both of his purpose and the degree to which he succeeded in fulfilling it.

It is Poe's intent that has proved intolerable. He meant not only to depict the experience of horror but to amplify that experience in intensity to the outermost limits of consciousness. The lover in "The Raven" "experiences a phrenzied pleasure in so modeling his questions as to receive from the *expected* 'Nevermore' the most delicious because the most intolerable of sorrow."[3] And this is precisely Poe's purpose as well: "I first established in mind the climax, or concluding query— . . . that in reply to which this word 'Nevermore' should involve the utmost conceivable amount of sorrow and despair."[4] Poe fails to give more than a meager sense of grief, and for that reason one is all the more impressed by the lover's compulsion, his "phrenzied pleasure" in seeking "the most intolerable of sorrow."

Throughout Poe's work the destructiveness tends to seem even more irrational than the poet intended. One is much less fright-

2. *The Continuity of American Poetry*, pp. 141, 143, 148. Other critical terms, pp. 141–53, passim: "attention-getting," "hysterical," "manic," "helpless megalomania," "wilful demonism," "egocentrism," "agonizingly self-indulgent lyricism."

3. *Selected Writings*, p. 459.

4. Ibid.

ened by the obvious terrors—the premature burials and astronomical catastrophes—and far less moved by the proclaimed sorrows—the deaths of fair maidens and the blights that fall on youthful promise—than by the odd angle of vision from which they are seen. The typical qualities of Poe's horror are sickliness, not pain; lethargy, not violence; and stupefaction, not grief. These are the symptoms of a terror beyond the terror of suffering, a fear that even the consciousness which pain requires will pass away. Annihilation is the goal to which Poe's terror carries the mind, an end so repugnant because depicted so credibly that it may be thought to signify a disease of the poet's mind. Thus D. H. Lawrence, though he credits Poe with important negative achievements, identifies the narrators in "Ligeia" and "The Fall of The House of Usher" with the author in order to show that Poe was possessed by the compulsion to destroy the loved one's identity; [5] and thus Roy Harvey Pearce finds a quick route through the poetry to his conclusion concerning "neurotic" art.

But whatever its psychological causes in the author's mind, the destructiveness in the poem or story is merely a consequence of something more fundamental, a manner of writing which proceeds by expressing things through their opposites. Poe's is a mode of vision in which perceiving, when most complete, most inclusive, most true, is the antithesis of the perceiving that is normal to the self when considered just as itself.

One may best appreciate this with respect to Poe's conception of the nature of poetry:

Regarding, then, Beauty as my province, my next question referred to the *tone* of its highest manifestation—and all experience has shown that this tone is one of *sadness*. Beauty of whatever kind, in its supremest development, invariably excites the sensitive soul to tears. Melancholy is thus the most legitimate of all the poetical tones.[6]

5. *Studies in Classic American Literature,* pp. 76–85.
6. *Selected Writings,* p. 456.

On the face of it, this insistence upon the interdependence of beauty and sorrow seems but another example of an arbitrary preference for the unpleasant and corrupt, an impression which seems to be confirmed by Poe's fantastic conclusion that "the death . . . of a beautiful woman is, unquestionably, the most poetical topic in the world." [7] This absurdity has been the *bête noire* of most readers, and there is no explaining it away, but how Poe arrived at the notion becomes understandable when one notes his remark that "it is an obvious rule of Art that effects should be made to spring from direct causes—that objects should be attained through means best adapted for their attainment." [8] Though the idea of a perfect efficiency of means leads to folly in this one instance, it is, nevertheless a very fruitful concept. We cannot fairly judge Poe's doctrine concerning beauty and sorrow by the foolish inference he forces it to yield; we should consider, instead, what he means by beauty "in its supremest development." For if the object of poetry is the creation of beauty, it is beauty of a certain kind, that beauty alone which effects an "intense and pure elevation of *soul";* and in Poe's analysis of this beauty we see the origin of the destructive effect.[9]

A crucial passage in "The Poetic Principle" declares: "An immortal instinct, deep within the spirit of man, is thus, plainly, a sense of the Beautiful. This it is which administers to his delight in the manifold forms, and sounds, and odours, and sentiments amid which he exists." [10] Man is therefore naturally pleased by copies or reflections of such earthly forms of beauty in art.

> But this mere repetition is not poetry. He who shall simply sing . . . of the sights, and sounds, and odours, and colours, and sentiments, which greet *him* in common with all mankind —he, I say, has yet failed to prove his divine title. There is still a something in the distance which he has been unable to attain.

7. Ibid., p. 458.
8. Ibid., p. 456.
9. Ibid.
10. Ibid., p. 469.

We have still a thirst unquenchable, to allay which he has not shown us the crystal springs.[11]

The Beauty which the poet seeks to create is thus not the beauty of this world, is not, perhaps, even attainable within terrestrial experience. The yearning for Beauty, the "thirst," as Poe continues,

> belongs to the immortality of Man. It is at once a consequence and an indication of his perennial existence. It is the desire of the moth for the star. It is no mere appreciation of the Beauty before us—but a wild effort to reach the Beauty above. Inspired by an ecstatic prescience of the glories beyond the grave, we struggle, by multiform combinations among the things and thoughts of Time, to attain a portion of that Loveliness whose very elements, perhaps, appertain to eternity alone.[12]

It is a "wild effort" because its object is infinitely desirable—and because, by instinct, its existence is unquestioningly believed in—yet "wild" also because its object is impossible to achieve.

One can readily understand, then, why Poe maintains that the Beauty the poet seeks "invariably excites the sensitive soul to tears." Supernal Beauty is at once that which man most desires and that which he cannot have.

> And thus when by Poetry—or when by Music, the most entrancing of the Poetic moods—we find ourselves melted into tears—we weep them—not as the Abbate Gravina supposes—through excess of pleasure, but through a certain, petulant, impatient sorrow at our inability to grasp *now*, wholly, here on earth, at once and for ever, those divine and rapturous joys, of which *through* the poem, or *through* the music, we attain to but brief and indeterminate glimpses.[13]

11. Ibid.
12. Ibid., pp. 469–70.
13. Ibid., p. 470.

It is, then, of the nature of poetry both to depict and cause melancholy. By the glimpses of beauty it affords, it necessarily intensifies man's yearning for the eternal reality, and hence intensifies also his consciousness of estrangement from it.

This theory gives such emphasis to the near impossibility of poetry that it justifies indirection of a very radical kind. Whatever the poet would express must be expressible through "multiform combinations among the things and thoughts of Time," and yet with these he must strive to capture a "Loveliness whose very elements, perhaps, appertain to eternity alone." His best method, it soon becomes clear, will be to hint, and for Poe the most effective mode of hinting is that indirection which seems destructiveness but which is really nothing more than contrariety, the expression of things by their opposites—the beautiful by the grotesque, delight by torture, intelligence by insanity, what is normal by what is pathological, what is most excellent by what is most nearly valueless. To speak generally, the method is that of depicting life through death. If, as Poe insists, man's thirst for Beauty is "inspired by an ecstatic prescience of the glories beyond the grave," then to experience Beauty is to go beyond the limits of life—to enter eternity by withdrawing from time and the world of human experience. Hence Poe's compulsive movement toward a vision of annihilation, not only of the self, but of the cosmos. Since the essential stratagem of his art is that of implying the positive through the negative, the effort to conceive the absolutely excellent—and Supernal Beauty can be no less—must move all the way to absolute nothingness, the negation of consciousness, death itself. The paradox of Poe's aesthetic has as its inevitable consequence this paradoxical technique, by which Supernal Beauty and negation are revealed as two sides of the same coin.

The difficulty is that absolute nothingness is no easier to achieve than Supernal Beauty. It can only be revealed as *something*, and, like Beauty, it must be expressed through the things of time. Thus death also calls for the stratagems of covert contrariety, and Poe indulges his gothic taste for displaying the fair side

211

of horror—the heightened sensitivity of the dying, the bright, metallic colors of decay, the calm at the heart of violence. Moonlight shines beautifully across the malarial swamp, and the room where someone loses his mind or dies of poison is decorated with interesting, not to say "elegant," furnishings. This is a commonplace device of melodrama, of course, and the horrors thus created are not very fearful. It is what they manifest, the intent they reveal, the yearning for death, rather than death itself, which horrifies. And the essence of the horror is that the death wish is really the consequence of the striving for life. One yearns to die through the desire to reach the perfect and unqualified happiness of eternal being. One moves toward the annihilation of world and consciousness in order to enter a better world and higher consciousness.

It should be clear that Poe's view of the human situation, and the literary program he derives from it, have their source in a sense of time based on the same premises as that of the colonial Puritan writers. Here again the self is defined by the limits of its narrow place and time, and the problem of knowledge is conceived as a question of how the mind will transcend these limits. For Poe, as for the Puritans, the alternative to man's circumscribed and imperfect understanding is nothing less than a conspectus of reality as a whole. Once more the truth is equivalent to the eternal—the real order of things—and the mind's quest for the meaning of its personal experience is depicted as a process of enlarging the temporal landscape toward a total history. What makes Poe's vision so obviously different from that of the New England tradition is his intuition that the self must lose its identity in the process of achieving a higher state of consciousness. To enter into the consciousness of the universe is to abandon one's place, one's time, and hence that uniqueness of point of view without which selfhood is not possible. The self dies by becoming a state of mind which both corresponds to and is indistinguishable from reality itself. This, as Poe tells us at the end of *Eureka*, is to be one with God. It is to live forever, but not as oneself.

Instead of conceiving perfect consciousness as an experience in which the self's own present moment is recognized as an epitome of all time, Poe considers the now and eternity as exact opposites, so that vision becomes true to the extent that it ceases to be human—in that the mind has disengaged itself from its place and therefore from its identity. Poe never questions the common-sense view of time as a sequence of discrete moments. Lacking the New England writers' fine sense of the way memory and foresight expand the limits of the moment, he can only suppose that the wider the temporal scope of consciousness, the more the mind is estranged from its place in history.

Nevertheless, Poe's art represents a variant of the literary form which begins in Puritan New England. He was, to be sure, no Puritan, no Yankee. He liked to think of himself as a Virginia gentleman, and this self-image, together with his political views and literary antagonisms, encourages the impression that he is a figure quite distinct from the New England tradition. But his precarious status in the Allan household and therefore in Richmond society symbolizes a rootlessness more characteristic of the urban and middle-class north than of the south of his adoptive class. T. S. Eliot noted that the dominant culture of a people often exists in relation to one or more subcultures which it partially contains and with which it shares a continuing and mutual influence.[14] With respect to literature, at least, the south of Poe's day was a subculture of the literary north, as the facts of his journalistic career illustrate. He wrote, that is, in a cultural milieu in which the Puritan tradition was still dominant, and the very differences which distinguish his work from that of contemporary New England writers reveal a concern for the same problems, a preference for the same terms. Raised in a Presbyterianism scarcely less Calvinistic than the fading Congregationalism of Massachusetts, and finding himself, as Thoreau did, a stranger in a fluid commercial society, he created a mode of vision which,

14. *Notes towards the Definition of Culture* (New York, Harcourt, Brace, 1949), pp. 53–54.

though unlike that of transcendentalism, yet bears to it a strong family resemblance.

The Puritan, or at least Calvinistic, background can be appreciated by noting how clearly Poe's contrariety is anticipated by Jonathan Edwards. "I felt," Edwards recounts in his "Personal Narrative," "an ardency of soul to be, what I know not otherwise how to express, emptied and annihilated; to lie in the dust, and to be full of Christ alone." [15] Though dying to self in order to be reborn in God is an essential theme of Christian piety and has obvious sources in Scripture, one cannot help feeling that in Edwards this paradox is forced far beyond orthodox limits. In his effort to realize and express God's excellence, the nothingness of the self is asserted with an almost masochistic fervor for self-destruction. To break through all boundaries and express the limitless nature of God, Edwards habitually resorts to the stratagem of reducing man to nothingness. For example, in "God Glorified in Man's Dependence," the argument that the glory of God in the gift of his Son is manifest in the degree of human evil and helplessness, the orthodoxy of thought barely conceals the grotesque quality of feeling. "The grace in bestowing this gift is great in proportion to our unworthiness to whom it is given; instead of deserving such a gift, we merited infinitely ill of God's hand" [16]— "infinitely ill" because of estrangement from a goodness which is infinite. As there can be no limit set to God's power, wisdom, and excellence, so there can be, in the other direction, no limit to the evil, depravity, and weakness of man:

> We are more apparently dependent on God for happiness, being first miserable, and afterwards happy. It is more apparently free and without merit in us, because we are actually without any kind of excellency to merit, if there could be any such thing as merit in creature-excellency. And we are not only without any true excellency, but are full of, and wholly defiled with, that which is infinitely odious.[17]

15. Faust and Johnson, *Jonathan Edwards: Representative Selections,* p. 69.
16. *Sermons,* in *Select Works of Jonathan Edwards, 2,* 36.
17. Ibid., p. 38.

214

Once this manner of elaborating the paradoxes inherent in Christianity is established, the transition is easy to the art of contrariety. The familiar "Sinners in the Hands of an Angry God," with its image of the spider suspended by a thread above the all-consuming fire, shows how naturally the effects of rhetorical contrariety can turn grotesque. Actually, perceiving through opposites was well understood by Edwards, who employed it, for example, to clarify what he meant by "being sensible" of something. The consciousness of one thing always involves the awareness of many other things, things related to it by contrast no less than things similar, and the example Edwards supplies makes it clear that contrariety is a crucial aspect of knowledge.

> But yet, in a sense of the terribleness of God's displeasure there is implied an ideal apprehension of more things than merely of that pain or misery, or sense of God's heart. There is implied an ideal apprehension of the being of God and of some intellectual existence, and an ideal apprehension of His greatness and of the greatness of His power.[18]

The damned, by the very torture of their condition, are made conscious of God. Why not, then, of God's condition and attributes? Why not of eternal delight, goodness, beauty? Though Edwards precludes such possibilities by stressing the merely "ideal apprehension" enjoyed by the damned, it is but a step from "Sinners in the Hands of an Angry God" to "The Pit and the Pendulum."

This tale illustrates well the sense in which Poe's contrariety is an extension of Edwards' rhetorical method. If, in the sermon, the utter wretchedness of the sinner who is saved from fire only by the arbitrary and undeserved mercy of God ought to make him sensible of God's power and goodness, then, in Poe's story, the mental anguish of the hero, an anguish caused not only by the slow approach of a horrible death but by the realization of the diabolical nature of minds capable of inventing such tortures, is

18. *The Philosophy of Jonathan Edwards: From His Private Notebooks*, p. 120, Item 782.

the means of realizing what is by contrast infinitely high and good.

It will be recalled that Poe's protagonist is not killed. At the moment when the molten walls of his cell have so narrowed that he will momentarily be forced into the pit, they are rolled back and he finds himself set free. "The French army had entered Toledo. The Inquisition was in the hands of its enemies." [19] It is, of course, not the French army but the dialectic of history which evokes it that manifests the ultimate positive value. It is in the very nature of things that the iniquity of the Inquisition should raise up against itself a countervailing force. Whatever the motives of the French—and we need not suppose them more than moderately admirable—history through them has restored the equilibrium of things. In one sense, then, the dialectic of history is a moral order as well. In the way things happen, in the mere physics of conflicting forces—a physics which the details of the torture chamber give great emphasis—a moral pattern is implicit; and it is a main purpose of the story to the demonstrate the reality—the objective existence—of value.

But the tale does not end happily. Rather, the protagonist's escape reveals a prospect more fearful than inquisitorial torture, though the terror is of a subtler kind. From any human point of view it appears that the hero is rescued by pure accident. The French army could easily have come a moment too late or, what is worse to consider, days earlier, in which case the protagonist need not have suffered at all. By emphasizing the coincidence, Poe compels us to sense the discrepancy between the human world and the real order of things. The dialectic of history is a working out of the relations between broad and generalized aspects of reality, and in this process individuals are averaged away as of little account. Although the universal order is also a moral order, the values it manifests are quite distinct from good when considered with respect to the self's interests. In being saved, the protagonist is really lost through the realization of what his

19. *Selected Writings*, p. 194.

escape signifies. For in the vision of the good with respect to the universe as a whole, the self and its values are canceled. Hence the story ends abruptly with the rescue; after that, selfhood is so illusory that there is nothing more to be said of the narrator's experience.

Though this vision figuratively kills the beholder, it is nevertheless the good toward which his whole life is directed. For life is consciousness, and the will to live is the will to achieve a state of total consciousness and see things as they are. Thus, while in one sense the ultimate vision is annihilation, in another it is the fulfillment of life, the total content which experience at every moment intends to mean. The self ceases to be *as itself* by becoming one with the consciousness of the universe. This logic can be most clearly seen in *Eureka*, where it is expressed in the broad outlines of cosmology and laid out in a simple narrative form as an account of the history of the universe.

In sum, the argument of *Eureka* is as follows. The universe was brought into being by a single creative act, of which all subsequent phenomena are consequences, for since the Creator is perfect in wisdom and power, only one perfectly efficient deed is needed to effect all. The original substance of the universe is God himself, and the universe is created by his act of exerting upon this one unitary being a force sufficient to disperse it evenly throughout an unimaginably vast, though not infinite, space. When the creative act is completed and the original force withdrawn, a counteraction begins; being starts to return to unity. Yet, having been so widely dispersed, its reunification requires what from the human point of view is an inconceivable period of time. Furthermore, another force counteracts the movement toward unity. This is the weaker gravitational pull exerted on a particle by particles lying nearer the sphere's outer edge or at angles to the line from this particle to the center. Though all the particles must inevitably move toward unification, since from every point the greatest mass of particles lies in the direction of the center, the pull in other directions will nevertheless produce resistance. Thus, as soon as reunification begins, a contrary force is also brought into being.

Poe called this force repulsion and identified it with electricity. He contended that it is by the conflict between gravity and electricity, or attraction and repulsion, that the physical world is created. Indeed, matter, as he defines it, is nothing but the coexistence of these forces. The being of which the physical world is an aspect is not, then, reality itself but only a phase of reality, a temporary condition or state of affairs which pertains during the period between the Creation and the ultimate return to unity.

Were it not for space, there would be no matter and no world; unification would be instantaneous, attraction overcoming repulsion immediately, as it will in the end, because it is the stronger force. Yet because of the vast area throughout which God's being is dispersed, its reunification requires a time so extensive that during human history no essential change in the universe is discernible. Time and space are one, then, an insight which has earned Poe some repute as a prophet of modern physics.

More relevant to Poe's literary technique are the paradoxes this cosmology expresses. Obviously his system implies that when the process of unification is completed, there will be no matter—that matter has its existence by the very process which will destroy it. The stars and planets rush together, their catastrophic collisions forming ever larger agglomerations, until at last the few remaining giant particles coalesce. At this point matter itself disappears, for matter is the coexistence of attraction and repulsion, but when all things have become one, neither tendency can pertain. Thus, with respect to the physical universe, unity is annihilation. And yet were it not for the tendency of being toward this annihilating unity, the world would not exist.

In the destiny of the universe Poe finds man's fate writ large. When all entities return to the oneness of God, there can then be no individual selves. Selfhood is separateness: it is created by the walls of distinction which bound off the human individual from the all. Mind is the most advanced stage of the diversification of matter—a complex of the most particular adaptations which matter can assume—and personal identity is the most extreme instance of the dispersion of being.[20] The self lives by its resistance to unity; it exists through "repulsion." (If this term seems odd, it may be helpful to recall the convention, in eighteenth-century psychology, of describing how the qualities of objects are known by the "resistance" they offer to the senses.) The very principle of the self's life is therefore opposed to the course of history and must in time fall victim to it. Man's goal, like that of the physical world, is final annihilation.

And yet the self, like the physical world, has existence only by virtue of the movement toward unity which will at last destroy it. The repulsion which preserves identity is created by the contrary process of merging. *"In the Original Unity of the First Thing lies the Secondary Cause of All Things, with the Germ of their Inevitable Annihilation."* [21] This statement foreshadows Eliot's use of a Heraclitan motif: "In my beginning is my end." The self lives to, lives *in,* the end, and has no reality at all except with respect to this end. Its teleology, and therefore both its value and its significance, is inseparable from that of being as a whole. On the other hand, the self as a point of view is defined by its world; it is just this person because it is just this unique location. Realization of all its relations, consciousness of its entire world, would annihilate its individuality. The perfected consciousness is that of reality as a whole, but to achieve this state of mind is to cease to exist as an individual person; one's world becomes *the* world, and one's mind becomes the universal mind. Actually, in the final unity even mind, in the usual sense, would not exist,

20. "Through the aid—by the means—through the agency of Matter, and by dint of its heterogeneity—is this Ether [i.e. electricity] manifested—is *Spirit individualized.* It is merely in the development of this Ether, through heterogeneity, that particular masses of Matter become animate—sensitive—and in the ratio of their heterogeneity;—some reaching a degree of sensitiveness involving what we call Thought and thus attaining Conscious Intelligence" (*Eureka,* in *The Complete Works of Edgar Allan Poe, 16,* ed. James A. Harrison [New York, Thomas Y. Crowell, 1902], 309).

21. Ibid., pp. 185–86.

because where all is one, there can be no distinction between the mind which observes and the world it has in view. They are united in being of another sort. The Poe character's compulsive desire for annihilation is not, then, a psychological quirk or even, really, a trait of mind. It is a symptom of the self's ontology. The individual is a person only in the process of moving toward that state of consciousness, or more properly of being, which destroys its individuality. As an intent, a desire, this tendency seems insanity. Ultimately, however, it is not a characteristic *within* the self, but the metaphysical condition of its existence.

Poe concedes that innumerable generations will come and go before the return to unity destroys mankind, and he speaks eloquently of the vast distances of cosmic space in order to show how remote the final catastrophe must be. Nevertheless, man must look to the last day and be troubled by its approach because, however remote, it defines the whole tendency and purpose of human experience. Each individual will simply die, in his time; he will not be consumed by the final fires of colliding planets, but the thought that all his strivings for a higher consciousness and securer existence will end by canceling his selfhood is not a happy one. Furthermore, the individual must give up the hope of immortal life. He may believe, as Poe himself probably did, that the soul survives after death, but he knows that it can't survive forever. Finally—and here we approach the heart of Poe's peculiar kind of terror—the self dimly suspects that its very effort to live is really a movement toward its own destruction.

This death, however, is the birth into perfect life. The self ceases to exist in that it becomes identical with God. For God is each man's true identity, the person his intuition tells him he really is. Hence the pertinence of Edward Davidson's illuminating study.[22] Professor Davidson argues that Poe renders the Romantic egocentrism absolute, and demonstrates that it is from the impulse to make the self all that many of the poet's main themes

22. *Poe: A Critical Study* (Cambridge, Mass., Harvard University Press, 1957).

develop. God, having dispersed himself throughout space, "now exists solely in the diffused Matter and Spirit of the Universe." He "now feels his life through an infinity of imperfect pleasures—the partial and pain-intertangled pleasures of those inconceivably numerous things which you designate as his creatures, but which are really but infinite individualizations of himself." To the extent that the individual can grasp the panorama of universal history, his prospect should be a happy one, for he will see that man,

> ceasing imperceptibly to feel himself Man, will at length attain that awfully triumphant epoch when he shall recognize his existence as that of Jehovah. In the meantime bear in mind that all is Life—Life—Life within Life—the less within the greater, and all within the Spirit Divine.[23]

This rhetoric is strongly reminiscent of "Passage to India," and in the total conspectus, as Poe defines it, the experience of evil is to be understood very much in Whitman's manner:

> In this view alone the existence of Evil becomes intelligible; but in this view it becomes more—it becomes endurable. Our souls no longer rebel at a *Sorrow* which we ourselves have imposed upon ourselves, in the furtherance of our own purpose— with a view—if even with a futile view—to the extension of our own *Joy*.[24]

Poe's optimism, however, is mainly theoretical and affords but slight consolation, for although the self may be destined to live forever and in a condition of perfect being, it will not survive *as itself*. Distant as its annihilation may be, it casts across the mind the lengthening shadow of Nemesis. The mind, by its very nature, must necessarily interpret experience according to its idea to the end. To perceive at all is to see the immediately given as existing here and now in time, and thus sensation involves

23. *Complete Works, 16*, pp. 314–15.
24. Ibid., p. 313.

intuiting, however vaguely or subliminally, the history, and therefore the destiny, of the universe. For Poe the final catastrophe is implicit in all experience: the more an experience is understood, the more clearly it is seen in relation to universal history, the more, in consequence, emotion crystallizes into the terror of death, and the more the percipient's view approximates a vision of annihilation.

This movement of mind is the essential drama Poe's poems and tales reenact. Not that they are fictional versions of *Eureka,* for that work, as Poe warns, is to be taken as another poem—a myth formed in the language of science, which is just one possible manner of speaking. My argument is, rather, that the poems and tales depict the nature of experience in the kind of world which, when formulated *as a cosmology,* is the universe *Eureka* pictures.

Characteristically, the persona in the Poe tale or poem dies, whether literally, as in the case of Roderick Usher, or by a change so radical that it signifies the loss of his personality, as in the case of the protagonist of "A Descent into the Maelstrom," or else by falling into a silence which indicates that for him there is nothing more to be experienced, as in the case of Arthur Gordon Pym or the protagonist of "The Pit and the Pendulum." Except in a few instances, Poe does not portray this death as the final catastrophe of the universe, for it does not matter whether a man is actually present at the last day or sees it prospectively. He need only perceive that ultimately all entities will be annihilated to realize that even now his identity is an illusion. The death which *Eureka* figures forth is the truth at the heart of every lived moment, a truth always potentially discoverable, and the shock of recognizing it is a quite credible cause of death, or of the somnambulistic and wraithlike half-existence of what survives of the self. The Poe character dies in realizing that what appear to be many are, from the eternal point of view, one—the realization that his own identity, like that of all other individual things, is but an appearance created by an incomplete view of reality. In a true view, a view of being in all its phases, particular entities prove to be but temporary and incomplete manifestations of the Absolute.

I emphasize the implications of *Eureka* as a way of showing that what readers consider perverse, grotesque, or compulsively destructive in Poe's poems and tales has its source not in the phantasies of a diseased mind but in a metaphysical system reasoned with great subtlety and precision. It is irrelevant that the neuraesthetic tendencies of Poe's mind may have led him to this metaphysical system, or, conversely, that the system may have fostered his melancholy. The question for criticism is concerned not with the origin but with the validity of his beliefs. From a theoretical point of view, and taking into account Poe's place in cultural history, the question of whether the self and the objects of sense are real is hardly a foolish one. Nor is the suspicion that these entities are not real a fantastic answer. A few decades later F. H. Bradley was to reply very much in Poe's manner and adduce similar reasons. The unity which Poe projects as the catastrophic merging of the many into the one is just another version of the Absolute, which, in Bradley's account, "absorbs" all finite entities. That Poe could make fiction of such a metaphysics, employing it to depict and search the reasons for the undeniable sorrow of human experience, is hardly to be accounted a fault. The resemblance to Bradley is cited to suggest, on the one hand, the subtle affinities between Poe and Eliot, and on the other, to show that Poe's beliefs are of a kind which is quite normal within the philosophic context of his time. In fact, they still have a certain relevance today, for the problem of defining personal identity is scarcely passé.

Even more important are the resemblances between Poe's thought and such primary concepts of transcendentalism as: the unity of the self and the universal spirit, of the order of the mind and the order of nature, of the present with all other times. No one is shocked when Emerson writes:

The relations of parts and the end of the whole remaining the same, what is the difference, whether land and sea interact, and worlds revolve and intermingle without number or end,—deep yawning under deep, and galaxy balancing galaxy, throughout absolute space,—or whether, without relations of time and space, the same appearances are inscribed in the constant faith of man? [25]

But his reasoning is in fact shockingly careless, since, if one grants his second hypothesis—that there is really nothing "out there"—then it is a nonsequitur to speak of the "constant faith of man"; in that case there can be no such thing as man, there being no objective world in contrast to which he can know himself or exist as himself. Yet to the extent that Emerson makes sense, he denies the reality of the physical world just as forthrightly as Poe. And, with the world, the self too disappears. Emerson means, of course, that mind and world are both emanations of the Universal Spirit, but even if this be granted, then neither is *ultimately* real. Of this conclusion, which is the same as Poe's, Emerson throws out many hints, especially in his description of the highest state of consciousness: "I become a transparent eye-ball; *I am nothing; I see all;* the currents of the Universal Being circulate through me; *I am part or parcel of God.*" [26] When the self "sees all," not only does it cease to be a self in any meaningful sense, but the universe also moves toward dissolution:

> When the eye of Reason opens, to outline and surface are at once added grace and expression. These proceed from imagination and affection, and *abate somewhat of the angular distinctness of objects.* If the Reason be stimulated to more earnest vision, *outlines and surfaces become transparent, and are no longer seen;* causes and spirits are seen through them. The best moments of life are these delicious awakenings of the higher powers, and the reverential *withdrawing of nature* before its God.[27]

Emerson fails to see that the unity toward which the self moves, the unity in the prospect of which he finds a warrant for

25. *Nature*, in *The Complete Works of Ralph Waldo Emerson, 1,* 47–48.
26. Ibid., p. 10. Italics mine.
27. Ibid., p. 50. Italics mine.

optimism and self-reliance, must necessarily mean the annihilation of the self and the passing of the physical world. But, as has often been noted before, this was plain enough to Melville, who, in the chapter in *Moby-Dick* entitled "The Masthead," indicates quite precisely how the transcendentalist experience must end:

> at last he loses his identity; takes the mystic ocean at his feet for the visible image of that deep, blue, bottomless soul, pervading mankind and nature. . . . But while this sleep, this dream is on ye, move your foot or hand an inch; slip your hold at all; and your identity comes back in horror. Over Descartian vortices you hover. And perhaps, at mid-day, in the fairest weather, with one half-throttled shriek you drop through that transparent air into the summer sea, no more to rise for ever. Heed it well, ye Pantheists! [28]

The mariner may grab hold in time, but this merely serves to show that to go all the way—to commit oneself unreservedly to the transcendentalist dream—is to die. It is no accident, then, that in his sea tales Poe anticipates the ending of *Moby-Dick*. For the truth the white whale symbolizes is a truth at the center of both men's best work. The whale, as its whiteness suggests, is an epitome of all meanings, and one realizes this total meaning only at the cost of one's life.

Such objections as I have offered to Emerson are usually answered by saying that consistency should not be required of the transcendentalists, since they are not, after all, philosophers. Their intentions are of another kind. But if they can be excused in this way, it is hardly fair to judge Poe mistaken because he had the insight to see the end toward which the assumptions of transcendentalism would lead.

Of course, Poe's ideas are of value mainly for the literary possibilities they offer. It is his vision that is important, and this is most clearly expressed in the tales, which, though less radically innovative than the poems, are more successful as works of art. Examin-

28. *Moby-Dick*, pp. 214–15.

ing a few of them may serve to locate the main principles of his writing and the main features of his imaginary world.

The conclusion of one of Richard Wilbur's influential essays on Poe sums up his entire view of Poe's fiction:

> The typical Poe story is, in its action, an allegory of dream-experience: it occurs within the mind of a poet; the characters are not distinct personalities, but principles or faculties of the poet's divided nature; the steps of the action correspond to the successive states of a mind moving into sleep; and the end of the action is the end of the dream.[29]

Wilbur supports this thesis by providing a very valuable study of imagistic patterns, yet his analysis would prove no less illuminating if used to argue quite different conclusions. One is made uneasy by Wilbur's interpretations because, though he takes *Eureka* into account, he does not explain the tendency of that work's reasoning to destroy the very basis of allegory. The whole tenor of *Eureka* is to show the identity of mind and world, and in this one can recognize the philosophic reasons behind the distaste for allegory that Poe's criticism records. Poe can establish no parallel between thought and objective existence, nor therefore between things in the mind and outward characters or events, because for him the two are one. Similarly, the action cannot "correspond to the successive states of a mind moving into sleep," because he believes that actually the distinction between thought and event is false. What Wilbur calls "dream" is to Poe the true view, reality itself—not even a view, really, but a state of affairs.

"A Descent into the Maelstrom," which provides a good instance of the way the thought of *Eureka* impinges upon Poe's fiction, will serve to illustrate what seems to me mistaken in Wilbur's view and, more generally, in any interpretation which defines the Poe tale as a merely "inner" or psychological drama. The

29. "Edgar Allan Poe," an introduction to Poe selections in Perry Miller et al., eds., *Major Writers of America, 1* (2 vols. New York, Harcourt, Brace and World, 1962), 378.

"Descent" bears a striking resemblance to two other Poe fictions, the "MS Found in a Bottle" and his only novel, *The Narrative of Arthur Gordon Pym of Nantucket*. In all three works the hero, deluded by *hubris*, undertakes a voyage which ends when he is swallowed up by some watery Nemesis, and in all three he, in a sense, survives, though horribly transformed. Pym is not talking any more; the hero of the "Descent," whose hair has turned white in a day, is possessed by the compulsion to relate his story, while of the third protagonist only the self-image set down in the rescued manuscript still exists. All three stories portray a catastrophe which, by annihilating, restores—in the sense not of effecting a resurrection but of creating a larger understanding. The new knowledge, a vision of the All in which the self disappears, is brought into being, whether for the protagonist or for those who read of his story.

Just what that knowledge is is made most apparent in "A Descent." The narrator and his brother are themselves the moral cause of their misfortune. They undertake to fish too near the great whirlpool in the hope of a larger catch—in pure self-interest—and it is upon this matter of self-interest that the climactic event turns. The brother, struggling to preserve himself to the end, clings to life so desperately that when he supposes the ring bolt the safest hold, he forces the narrator to give it up to him. "I never felt deeper grief than when I saw him attempt this act— although I knew he was a madman when he did it—a raving maniac through sheer fright." [30] This act is insane, as events prove, because it expresses a false view, even with respect to the self's own interests.

While the brother is drowned, the narrator survives, because he is able to forget himself, passing beyond the ultimate sorrow—"I never felt a deeper grief"—to a mood of serenity and delight. As the boat circles the vortex, his fear gives way to awe: "I began to reflect how magnificent a thing it was to die in such a manner,

30. *Poe's Short Stories*, ed. Killis Campbell (New York, Harcourt, Brace, 1927), p. 190.

and how foolish it was in me to think of so paltry a consideration as my own individual life, in view of so wonderful a manifestation of God's power." [31] And when at last the boat has entered the cone of the whirlpool to spin, suspended, on its inner wall, the narrator is freed from self-interest by feelings of reverential wonder: "Never shall I forget the sensations of awe, horror, and admiration with which I gazed about me." [32]

It is just this power to give himself up that enables the narrator to discover his salvation. He is calm enough to be observant, impressed enough to become curious: "I positively felt a *wish* to explore its depths, even at the sacrifice I was going to make; and my principal grief was that I should never be able to tell my old companions on shore about the mysteries I should see." [33] And because he delights in seeing the forces that will destroy him, he is able to notice that while other objects are hurtling downward, those of cylindrical shape descend very slowly. Lashing himself to a barrel, he leaps from the boat. This act is a perfect figure for the antithetical relation between selfhood and cosmic unity, the individual's human values and the teleology of the universe. The narrator can only save himself by losing himself, survive by giving up his personal interests in favor of the purpose of the universal scheme.

Now, contrary to the technique of allegory, the psychological dilemma here is not merely paralleled or figured forth by the outward situation. The two cannot be separated: the mind is in just this moral situation because it finds itself in just this physical situation and, more broadly, in a world where the Maelstrom exists. Thus the same paradox is embodied in the visual picture of the whirlpool,

> whose perfectly smooth sides might have been mistaken for ebony, but for the bewildering rapidity with which they spun around, and for the gleaming and ghastly radiance they shot

31. Ibid., pp. 189–90.
32. Ibid., p. 191.
33. Ibid., p. 190.

forth, as the rays of the full moon, from that circular rift amid the clouds which I have already described, streamed in a flood of golden glory along the black walls, and far away down into the inmost recesses of the abyss.[34]

As the narrator's mind produces objective observation from the substance of emotional response, so, in contrary fashion, the play of physical forces projects a moral and psychological situation. On this occasion, as at the end of "The Pit and the Pendulum," coincidence proves an advantage. That the moon is exactly above the aperture of the vortex forces us to notice how, in thought, ideas imply their opposites. The image shadows forth the unity of mind and world by revealing one of man's indispensable metaphors, that which expresses good and evil spatially as high and low. At the beginning of the tale the author describes the terrifying height of the precipice to which the narrator has led him before beginning his story. This, we now see, is the proper place for such a narrative, for the meaning of the tale—its significance to the mind—is inseparable from the place—the physical world in which the events recounted transpired. Being is what meaning means, and in the author's sensation of vertigo the union of thought and matter is again made manifest.

In "The Fall of the House of Usher" Poe produced his most precise and elaborate enactment of the return to unity. Wilbur recognizes that this is the story's action, but while he sees that the plot of the tale depicts essentially the same event as that which *Eureka* describes as the history of the universe, he nevertheless maintains that "Usher" is a mere psychological allegory, rendering through make-believe characters and settings Poe's capacity to create a dream by perversely destroying the world. Thus Roderick Usher is "the hero's true and inner self, his purely 'psychal' aspect"; Madeline turns into Psyche (as if, to Poe, universal spirit did not contain all human spirits, all selves); and the reunion of Usher with Madeline "is the end of one night's dream-

34. Ibid., p. 191.

229

journey, a short-term passport to the realms of supernal beauty; and it is also a foreview of the soul's reconstitution and purification in death" (as if that event were not identical with the annihilation of the physical universe).[35] This interpretation retains, though in a subtler form, the habitual premise of most of Poe's commentators, the belief that since his fictions contravene the laws of physics, they are true only as images of psychic phenomena, realities of a quite different order. Since the happenings in Poe's stories consistently show the collapse of mind and the dissolution of material things, Wilbur feels they must be accounted evidence of a neurotically destructive impulse on the author's part, rather than as stories depicting the process *Eureka* outlines in cosmological terms—the process by which consciousness and the physical world both disappear as the universe moves toward its last phase. Yet if Poe's writings have the unity Wilbur assumes, the stories cannot be interpreted in a way which makes them inconsistent with *Eureka,* and there Poe's resolution of the subject–object duality so harmonizes psychology and physics that it becomes unthinkable to suppose physical events could be mere figures for psychic events.

The main reason for failing to see the unity of mind and matter in Poe's tales is the difficulty of understanding a governing principle of his fiction, the idea that when the self has arrived at a certain degree of understanding, when its vision has developed to a certain degree of clarity and inclusiveness, it knows so much that, in effect, it knows all. The self has, in others words, so vivid a sense of the end that by intuition, and in a shadowy but quite sufficient manner, it realizes the whole design of reality. The self, to arrive at this vision, need only observe the *tendency* of things. It need only see how, even in a short sequence of events, objects

35. Introduction to *Poe: Complete Poems,* ed. Richard Wilbur (New York, Dell, 1959), pp. 26, 27–28. See also another important essay by Wilbur, "The House of Poe," in *Anniversary Lectures: 1959* (Washington, D.C., Library of Congress, 1959), pp. 21–38. Often catalogued under Gertrude Clark Whithall Poetry and Literature Fund.

tend to merge and lose their identity. That experience is quite enough to produce the intuition of the final unity, and, from the author's point of view, implying the end in this way is the only possible procedure. Poe cannot depict nothingness itself; that is mere silence, unconsciousness, total blank (an image which often appears at the end of Poe's tales). He must hint at the end by illustrating the movement toward it, revealing the drift by the few straws he casts upon the stream of time.

His straws are real straws, however. The death of the last of the Ushers and the collapse of the family mansion are not mere analogues, nor does either event cause the other. The tale is not an allegory of the mind in which outward events are mere signs for psychic happenings, any more than it is an account of the merely physical processes of death and decay. Rather, the story's events show that the world of mind and the world of matter are in truth one realm, which exists in the process of developing toward an annihilating unity.

That the "House of Usher" is both the family and the building is a fact indicative of the movement toward unity. Unity, it should be clear, accounts in a purely scientific way for the collapse of the mansion, for decay is a form of merging. The fetid tarn absorbs the rotted vegetable matter, and its waters, by blending with the air, form gases which corrode the stones of the building. But the process cannot be conceived as exclusively physical; the chemical simplification contributes to the decay of mind. The commonsensical narrator tries to shake off the depression his first sight of the house induces by persuading himself that "a mere different arrangement of the particulars of the scene, of the details of the picture, would be sufficient to modify, or perhaps to annihilate its capacity for sorrowful impression." [36] But the idea gives him little comfort, for when he looks at the reflection of the house in the tarn—where the arrangement *is* different—he is only the more horrified. Understandably, for the horror has its source

36. *Selected Writings,* p. 96.

in the sense of unity, which is made manifest by the experience of an influence *of any sort* that matter works upon mind, and here the reflection presents the same image in a different medium.

Roderick Usher's belief in the "sentience" of plants and inorganic things prefigures the final catastrophe:

> The conditions of the sentience had been here, he imagined, fulfilled in the method of collocation of these stones—in the order of their arrangement, as well as in that of the many *fungi* which overspread them, and of the decayed trees which stood around—above all, in the long undisturbed endurance of this arrangement, and in its reduplication in the still waters of the tarn.[37]

Eureka argues, in a manner reminiscent of Leibnitz' monadology, that even inanimate objects are "more or less conscious Intelligences; conscious, first, of a proper identity; conscious, secondly and by faint indeterminate glimpses, of an identity with the Divine Being."[38] Usher's belief in this sentience is, then, far from fantastic. It is the first example of his intuition that *in fact* the line between mind and matter is illusory.

The permanence of the landscape impresses Usher even more than its sentience, and this too, in Poe, always signifies the approach to unity. Stasis is sameness, and sameness is oneness. The Usher family has lived in one place for centuries, and the effect of their environment is about to destroy them, not only because of the peculiar nature of this influence but because it is always the *same* influence. The deadly sameness is reflected in the Usher family, which has survived only by direct descent. Of this permanence Roderick and Madeline are the natural culmination. They are identical twins and possess the psychic rapport common among such siblings: "Sympathies of a scarcely intelligible nature had always existed between them."[39] To Roderick, Madeline is

37. Ibid., p. 104.
38. *Complete Works, 16,* 314.
39. *Selected Writings,* p. 106.

"a tenderly beloved sister," and there is a subtle atmosphere of incest which taints their relationship, for they are metaphysically, if not sexually, wedded.[40] It is not incest that horrifies Roderick, but that which incest represents, the merging of two who are already too nearly one, a union so complete that his selfhood will disappear.

Usher explains to his friend that his terror is the fear of fear itself, and, ultimately he himself creates the fear that destroys him. When Madeline is apparently dead, he makes much show of guaranteeing that no mistake has been made. But the deep vault where her body is placed was once a prison and is guarded by a massive door, which he locks securely. As a final precaution against premature burial, he nails her coffin shut. What Usher subconsciously intends, of course, is to keep his identity distinct from hers; and it is her return more than his guilt that at last kills him. He cannot be rid of her, so nearly are they one person. Physically, he "falls" when she falls into his arms; psychologically, he dies from the horror of realizing that they share one self; metaphysically, he dies in that the very means by which his mind has sought to preserve its individuality has turned out to be the means of making his state of mind and hers exactly the same. At the moment when he can no longer find any difference between his consciousness and hers, he dies—his identity disappears.

Usher's heightened percipience is that diversification which, as a counterforce—a reciprocal moving away from the center—the tendency toward unity creates. His senses have become so exquisite that he can only tolerate certain textures and sounds, and his intelligence has grown so keen that he has become clairvoyant—hence his Turner-like painting of the tomb, his fantastic verses, and his "wild" improvisations on the lute. Consciousness drives itself to preternatural vividness in the effort to preserve itself as the movement toward unity accelerates, and, since consciousness is selfhood, the central paradox of *Eureka* is demonstrated by the fact that it is Usher's abnormally overdeveloped consciousness

40. Ibid., p. 100.

that kills him. Because he is so fully aware, he can know exactly what Madeline is feeling and thinking, and to know this perfectly is to be indistinguishable from her. This experience of merging creates a sense so vivid of the tendency of all things toward unity that one can intuit the final annihilation.

It is in terms of such a vision that the "fall" of Roderick Usher and the "fall" of the family mansion are the same event. The reader may well object that the mansion's collapse is merely figurative. Buildings decay piecemeal; they do not fall apart all at once or split down the middle, and the coincidence that the house should fall within a few moments of the last owner's death seems equally incredible. Thus the reader is likely to assume the prevailing critical attitude and reason that these events cannot be taken literally. But Poe would argue that the view of reality in terms of which these happenings seem "unrealistic" is itself false. A coincidence is simply the simultaneous happening of two events which, according to probability, ought not to happen at the same time; but in a true view, as Poe conceives it, all events *are* simultaneous. A true view presents all time and all things in one conspectus, so that all events are one event in that all enact the same drama, the history of the universe. And the history of the universe is the movement of all things into the unity which annihilates them. Taking such a view, one will see the mansion fall in just the way Poe's narrator does; the collapse will be perceived as one event, not as a brick falling, then a rafter caving in, then a chimney toppling. And one will see that the setting moon does shine through the gaping fissure. The moon's setting and the rush of the world of planets toward annihilation are but other aspects of the same event that the fall of the mansion and the death of Usher manifest.

The narrative events which Poe's critics have traditionally regarded as fantastic and therefore merely allegorical with respect to any serious import they may have are, in fact, as literally intended as any fiction can be. According to Poe, they are actual happenings as they would appear to us if we could see phenomena as they truly are. The validity of this vision does not rest upon the truth of the state of consciousness it figures forth. The fiction is not true because it reflects real phenomena in the poet's mind or the human mind in general. Truth of that sort—truth concerning the psyche—is merely a derivative aspect of its validity. Poe intends his fictions to be true with respect to the real nature of the universe, not just that aspect of it we term "mind." One may, of course, disagree with his metaphysical assumptions —indeed, some dissent concerning these would be hard to avoid —but such criticism is bound to be more favorable than the "dream-world" theory will allow, for by leading us to consider what things we can literally believe, it helps us to appreciate the thoughtfulness of Poe's answers.

The narrator of Usher's story illustrates an obtuse, common-sense view, but Poe expects his readers to see beyond that. When the narrator flees at the end, the events he has witnessed are to him sheer mystery and unmitigated horror. Supposing that Usher's death is the final fact, he regards the subsequent collapse of the mansion as a fortuitous arabesque of dreadfulness, and reports it as if to say, "even this had to happen. *C'est trop fort.* The last straw." But this last perverse gesture of the universe signifies a new phase in the movement of things toward unity: if the self is annihilated by merging with the world, then, conversely, the world too loses its former nature. Self and world are no longer so separate: by Usher's loss of consciousness, the universe becomes in some degree more sentient and purposeful. The narrator is horrified by the evidence that the forces of physics have conspired to create that improbable fissure and that the moon is setting at that angle and moment by express intent. His comforting common sense, which keeps entities distinct and holds mind and matter to separate levels, is shaken by the suspicion that the world has a mind of its own. In *Eureka* Poe confirms that nightmarish suspicion by coolly describing how, as entities merge, the multiple selves combine to reconstitute God's personality, which is not a mind distinct from the world but a unitary being that supercedes both. Poe's final coincidence in "Usher" is not, then, designed merely to wring one more shudder from his readers, but to foreshadow, by the tendency it indicates, that final stage of history when mind and world have been replaced by a different kind of being.

Confirmation of this view can be found in an interesting minor tale, "The Colloquy of Monos and Una." Here the two lovers, whose names suggest their psychic oneness, are reunited at a later stage of cosmic evolution, when earth has been destroyed in a planetary disaster. Monos, at the urging of Una, describes his experience of death, reporting that though supposedly dead when he was buried, he retained a measure of consciousness, which only gradually subsided, through phases of increasing synesthesia, until he became both nothing and everything, the selfless because universal principles of nature:

> Many *lustra* had supervened. Dust had returned to dust. The worm had food no more. The sense of being had at length utterly departed, and there reigned in its stead—instead of all things—dominant and perpetual—the autocrats *Place* and *Time*. For *that* which *was not*—for that which had no form— for that which had no thought—for that which had no sentience—for that which was soulless, yet of which matter formed no portion—for all this nothingness, yet for all this immortality, the grave was still a home, and the corrosive hours, co-mates.[41]

Soul has become identical with space and time, the two great actors in the plot of universal history; and history is God in the dispersed phase of his existence.

In depicting the eternal, Poe tends to employ images which are neither strictly physical nor mental but synthesize subject and object in that they exist doubly as both ideas and physical qualities. Music is the most obvious example of this class of images, which also includes the dimensions of space and time, directions

41. *Poe's Short Stories*, pp. 207–08.

—especially inward and outward, upward and downward—as well as ideas of magnitude, speed, and intensity. The purpose of such images is to symbolize the merging of mind and world into a kind of existence which is closer to the final unity. Because, as I have said before, Poe can only depict unity indirectly through the movement toward it, such images are of crucial importance in illustrating the way the particulars of the experienced world tend to break down into more generalized forms of reality. The subject of "The Fall of the House of Usher" is an image or object of this sort. The tale is not the story of Roderick Usher, or of his family, or of mankind, or of the mansion, or even of the physical world, but of the "house"—an entirely different kind of thing.

Poe's tales of detection at first appear to record a vision quite unlike that of the gothic tales, and in his fascinating study, *The French Face of Edgar Poe,* Patrick Quinn argues that the two kinds of fiction express two distinct levels of the poet's mind: "the one obscure in the dark torment of nightmare, the other lucid and enquiring, and eager to explain . . . real and concrete matters of a thoroughly prosaic kind." [42] As one evidence of this, Quinn points out Poe's frequent use of the Doppelganger, but the Doppelganger invites a contrary interpretation. That the Poe character is unable to shake off his alter ego may signify the unity rather than the doubleness of the author's mind. To anyone who joins Quinn in preferring the "other" Poe, who brings news of the terrors of the subconsciousness, the detective stories will seem trivial exercises—the work of "the *raisonneur,* the solver of puzzles." [43] But it may be wiser not to grant the dividedness of Poe's mind, for the tales of detection involve much more than problem-solving, and the literary success of Dupin's ingenious solutions cannot very well be separated from the shrewdness of Poe's idea as to *what* the detective is detecting.

The truth to be found out by M. Dupin is by no means constituted of "concrete matters of a thoroughly prosaic kind." His

42. Carbondale, Ill., Southern Illinois University Press, 1957, p. 201.
43. Ibid.

solution in "The Purloined Letter" requires of Dupin a highly imaginative feat—the uniting of his own mind with that of the Minister D. The maneuver succeeds because Dupin is a poet as well as a mathematician, and the Minister is respected by him for the same qualities (thus it is no accident that their names begin with the same initial). Conversely the prefect of police fails through lack of poetic vision. Having thrust knitting needles into the upholstery and turned over the leaves of all the Minister's books, he has exhausted the possibilities of his premises. He cannot find the letter because he cannot imagine what the real premises of the man who hid it might be. He is unable to suppose a view of reality other than his own. That one must, in a sense, become the criminal to solve the crime is made clear by the lines from Crébillon which Dupin puts in the envelope when he returns it to the Minister's card rack:

> Un dessein si funeste,
> S'il n'est digne d'Atrée, est digne de Thyeste.[44]

Yet to be able to see things from another man's point of view one must abandon one's own—an experience which tends to foster the suspicion that selves are unreal, since a true view would transcend all human views. Appropriately, Dupin, like Usher, is an "isolato," living in a darkened room, having but one friend, and possessing powers of extraordinary clairvoyance. To be sure, this tale does not evoke the horror of "The Fall of the House of Usher." Yet even though the ultimately terrifying fact remains beyond the horizon, it is sensed as a faint intimation, like the flavor of May wine.

Most readers are deflected from the thesis of "The Purloined Letter" by Poe's critical statements about the folly of "attempting to reconcile the obstinate oils and waters of Poetry and Truth." [45] That the items here said to be incompatible are not commensurate is often overlooked but is essential to Poe's meaning. In the

44. *Selected Writings*, p. 225.
45. "The Poetic Principle," ibid., p. 469.

effects they produce, in the *faculties* of mind they engage, in the "*modes*" of their "*inculcation,*" in their *social purposes*, a poem and an essay in discursive reasoning are quite unalike. Poe's point —that a poem's value is its merit as a poem, not as a piece of lucid reasoning, or socially useful rhetoric, or moral instruction— deserved emphasis in the age of Longfellow. It does not follow, however, that the world the poet depicts is a reality different from that which the raisonneur analyzes. Nor can it be assumed that the mental processes of imagination and reason are antithetical. The raisonneur must proceed from imaginatively intuited premises, and the poet, as Poe repeatedly asserts in his criticism, must reason concerning the means to produce his effects.

Poe's view may be summed up by a table of this sort:

The Faculties of Reader's Mind Engaged	Effects upon the Reader	Objects of Reader's Attention	Faculties of Author's Mind Engaged	Object of Author's Attention
Reason	Rational conviction	Truth	Imagination and Reason	Reality
Imagination	Elevation of Soul	Supernal Beauty	Imagination and Reason	Reality
Passion	Stimulation of emotions	Duty	Not discussed by Poe	

Poet and raisonneur have the same world in view, and to the extent that either succeeds, he must fulfill the other's function also. The very real difference between them concerns the objectives intended by their compositions. Since they intend to affect the reader in contrary ways, they depict different aspects of reality. As an effect in the reader's mind or as an object of his attention, truth and beauty are quite unlike, but as aspects of reality itself, they are one and the same. For beauty is harmony—hence the *idée maîtresse* of Poe's criticism is the doctrine of unity of effect—and harmony is identical with consistency, the standard by which the truths of reason are validated.

In *Eureka* Poe makes this point perfectly clear when he asserts that "the sense of the symmetrical is an instinct which may be depended upon with an almost blindfold reliance."

> It is the poetical essence of the Universe—*of the Universe* which, in the supremeness of its symmetry, is but the most sublime of poems. Now symmetry and consistency are convertible terms:—thus Poetry and Truth are one. A thing is consistent in the ratio of its truth—true in the ratio of its consistency. *A perfect consistency, I repeat, can be nothing but an absolute truth.* We may take it for granted, then, that Man cannot long or widely err, if he suffer himself to be guided by his poetical, which I have maintained to be his truthful, in being his symmetrical, instinct.[46]

Shifting from an ontological to a psychological point of view, Poe declares that, just as harmony and consistency or poetry and truth are one, so the faculties of mind which one differentiates as reason and imagination are in essence the same. Imagination is intuition, which in turn is "but *the conviction arising from those inductions or deductions of which the processes are so shadowy as to escape our consciousness, elude our reason, or defy our. capacity of expression.*" [47] Therefore the visionary and ratiocinative aspects of Poe's work cannot be justifiably separated. Imagination is perfected logic, and the world of reason is the world which the poet's eye takes in at a glance.

Now as Dupin declares, the wise mathematician must be a poet also, and his own ratiocinative feats are designed to reveal his poetical nature. His ability to solve a crime even before leaving his study to collect evidence in the world of appearances demonstrates that he can organize the few obvious facts into a system so

46. *Complete Works, 16,* 302.
47. Ibid., p. 206.

harmonious that the truth is revealed. No doubt he must reason step by step, but Poe discovered a principle of literary construction by which the detective's calculations could be given an air of preternatural brilliance. The most striking convention of detective fiction and the one which most obviously originates in Poe rather than in such other early practitioners as Wilkie Collins is that of the detective's concluding summary. As the evidence accumulates, the pattern of the reader's suspicions becomes increasingly tangled and complex, but he is left in the dark up to that satisfying moment when the detective turns to the guests assembled in the drawing room and begins his account of how all the pieces actually fit together. Then the ambiguous events suddenly arrange themselves into simultaneous aspects of a logically harmonious design.

For this miraculous effect, it is essential that the detective's thinking remain largely unknown until that final view is presented, for his correctness depends upon the illusion of his superior intelligence, and, in the last analysis, it is the *speed* of his reasoning that gives him the needful authority. Seeing the main issue at the outset, and swiftly formulating it in a lucid either-or manner, he soon begins to behave oddly, from the reader's point of view, since the one bit of evidence he looks for is a fact the reader cannot even imagine. All the great detectives of fiction are characterized by a certain delicacy of touch, a grace deriving from the speed of their calculations. Poe recognized that the dénouement could be made so suddenly and brilliantly illuminating as to render the detective a poet by endowing him with that power of intuition which alone can prove him right.

A dénouement of this kind will be convincing only to the extent that it is inclusive, and inclusive only insofar as the detective's logic accords with very general laws of probability. The impression must be created that the dénouement presents an overview so complete that nothing of importance has been left out. Poe's art can be distinguished from the mere cleverness of the popular mystery writers by the fact that in his final account, the Poe detective casts a much wider net. To see all the fictional facts at once is a feat requiring but moderate talent; to make it seem that these facts now appear as they would if we could see all the phases of universal history at once is the unique wit of Poe's detective tales. Only Poe has mastered the art of making the detective's summary seem to imply a self-consistent and all-inclusive vision of reality. The movement of the story is not only inward toward the particular truth—the identity of the murderer, for instance—but outward toward a vision of the universe which makes such an event as murder understandable.[48] The detective tales, as Baudelaire's instinct told him, are visionary works, as true to the facts of experience as anything Poe wrote. They will seem rational exercises only to those who cling to the "inner-outer" contrast which in Poe's world is a false distinction—to those who are after "psychological" truths of a sort supposed to be distinct from objective truths.

"How delightful," Baudelaire comments, "is the description of the treasure and what a pleasant feeling of warmth and amazement the reader experiences!" For "the treasure is found! *It was not a dream,* as is usually the case in all those novels where the author brutally wakens us after exciting our minds with tantalizing hopes; this time it is a *real* treasure, and the decipherer has indeed won it." [49] Baudelaire joyfully speculates on the "delusions of grandeur and benevolent impulses" the treasure evokes, but since one can infer that it leads also to feelings much less agreeable, I will stop at this comment that the treasure is *"real."* What delights us most in "The Gold Bug" is that the line of reasoning and the pattern of reality intersect. Legrand can keep the treasure; we rejoice in finding logic relevant to life.

This logic is not confined to the human mind, for at several

48. However, in Poe's detective tales, as in "The Murders in The Rue Morgue" and "The Mystery of Marie Rogêt," what appeared to be murder normally turns out to be something else, a morally neutral event, so far as its cause is concerned.

49. "Edgar Allan Poe: His Life and Works: 1852," in *Baudelaire on Poe: Critical Papers,* trans. Lois and Francis E. Hysop, Jr. (State College, Pa., Bald Eagle Press, 1952), p. 69.

points Legrand's reasoning depends upon mere accident. The logical relations leading to the discovery of the slip of parchment and causing the invisible script to be revealed when it is placed near the fire are not effects of his thought, but betoken a logic subsisting in the total design of things, as unrelated to his deductions as the causes of his recluse personality or his interest in entymology. Yet, of course, the whole meaning of the story serves to imply that these remote things, so accidentally brought together, are strictly—logically—related. Reality is a logic, only a minute portion of which the mind, through reasoning, can exactly duplicate. That is what Legrand does, and it suggests the reason why his name, by another coincidence, proclaims him a "great man." Catching hold of the web of the universal dialectic at one of its tiny filaments, he follows this thread to the treasure—a "*real*" object—reality itself. Little wonder that Baudelaire was pleased. Like Poe, Baudelaire enumerates the whole catalogue of precious objects, riches whose value, as he seems to appreciate, consists of the identity of idea and object, the world of thought and the world of things that the treasure manifests.

The value of the treasure consists not only in what it *means* to mind but also in what it *is*. The treasure is value itself, the motive which impelled Captain Kidd to amass this pile of gold and jewels, and the motive which drives Legrand to search out the past and hidden from the present and apparent. The tale implies that logic should not be considered a value of the intellect only; it is inseparable from emotion, because the order of being is an order of values as well as of ideas and objects. Were it not for the treasure's value, there would have been no pirate, no golden hoard, no treasure-hunter, no event, no story.

We are told that the value of the treasure is more than a million and a half. To Legrand this means the chance of returning to the life of a Louisiana grandee; to the narrator, a similar advantage; to Jupe, a ten dollar tip. Like the doubloon nailed to Ahab's masthead, its meaning depends upon one's point of view. The benefits are undeniable, but they do not reveal what the treasure itself is worth. They show only its value to certain people, in certain circumstances, at certain times in history.

Baudelaire opens a vista that no one in the story seems to have glimpsed. Though "In the chest hidden by pirate Kidd there was certainly the means to alleviate many unknown miseries," to Kidd the treasure was worth more than the two men, whose skeletons are found buried with the chest.[50] While we cannot be sure how much real good Legrand will derive from the gold, one of its values in the past is mysterious only in detail. "Perhaps a couple of blows with a mattock were sufficient, while his coadjutors were busy in the pit; perhaps it required a dozen—who shall tell?" [51]

Legrand thus reduces that mystery to a joke, implying that insofar as a thing is worth knowing, reason can find it out. But the treasure itself is unknowable, since it has the power to create almost anything from a murder to a fashionable bonnet. This ambiguity as to its value is a consequence of the unity it reveals. In the chest Legrand unearths, all things are one, all values identical. The treasure is value itself, embracing all particular values, whether good or evil, just as being unites all things, and the dialectic of the universe, all thoughts. Baudelaire's happy prospect, if one looks to the end of it, terminates in the annihilation of the universe, but then that is a happy event from God's point of view.

The logic behind such seeming coincidences as the scarab resembling a death's head, or the pirate sign that suddenly appears on the reverse of the parchment, exactly opposite to Legrand's sketch of the insect, is now apparent. This paradoxical joining of gold and death, good and evil, is emergent in countless details. It is the bite of the gold bug that leads Legrand to pick up the scrap of parchment and hence, eventually, to win a fortune. His friendly Newfoundland, whose boisterous caresses make the narrator fling his arm out so as to expose the parchment to the fire, is named "Wolf." The skull is nailed to the great tulip tree, a

50. Ibid., pp. 69–70.
51. *Poe's Short Stories*, p. 318.

symbol of vitality, and can be seen only from the "devil's seat" in the "bishop's hostel." What the cypher means by "bishop's hostel" Legrand has some trouble discovering until he learns that Bishop is a family name corrupted to the neutral and meaningless Bessop. Similarly, "hostel" is now "castle," and the place neither one nor the other, but a high rock, while the "devil's seat" is simply the only ledge there resembling a chair. All these instances of the merging of apparent opposites indicate that process of simplification by which diverse kinds of value are united in the ambiguous gold.

Jupe is sure from the outset that the bite of the Gold Bug has driven Legrand insane. His superstitious fear of the scarab appears in comic contrast to his master's intelligence; but we can hardly believe Legrand less mad merely because his calculations prove correct. In the end, Jupe is right. The quest for the treasure is insane, because it can conclude only with the treasure, a value whose worth for man remains utterly indeterminate. Thus Jupiter is well-named, representing not only God as man would have him—the slave of human interests, who is kept to take care of his owner and to make an affectionate but futile show at disciplining the will—but God himself, who knows what Legrand's laborious logic cannot discover: that the bug is solid gold, and its bite is deadly. Legrand is insane in not seeing the annihilation the treasure signifies. He has but faintly disturbing intimations. He knows only that men once died for it and that to find it one must take a sight through the eye of death.

That Poe's poetry, taken as a whole, is much harder to admire than his tales must be conceded. One is disturbed most by the insensitivity of his ear. He is capable of writing of "tears that drip all over," of rhyming "linger" with "sink her," of being both cheaply magnificent—"the night's Plutonian shore"—and laughably bathetic—"take thy form from off my door!" [52] Doubtless

52. See "Dream-Land," line 12, "Ulalume," stanza 6, lines 54–56, and "The Raven," penultimate stanza, line 101, in *Selected Writings*, pp. 35, 39, 41.

Continental critics have had the advantage of not being able to hear the grit in the verbal machinery. Yet the importance of Poe's verse to French poets from Baudelaire to Valéry is a fact it would be rash to ignore. It does not constitute proof that the poetry is better than English-speaking readers may be inclined to suppose. As works of art, the poems are so radically imperfect that a convincing interpretation could hardly serve as a defense. Still, Poe's achievement as a poet is an extremely important, though qualified one, that of expressing a new conception of poetry and illustrating it through poems which, though crudely experimental, reveal its potentialities and exemplify some of its essential techniques. In discussing the poems, I will be primarily concerned with their intention rather than their success. My purpose will be to describe the aesthetic rationale behind the poetry, showing how naturally it derives from Poe's metaphysical ideas, and pointing out the real, though limited, value it gives to particular poems. Whatever the faults of Poe's verse, his idea of poetry is a thoughtful one and worthy of the respect its historical influence on the Continent shows that it deserves. If such a reading of the poems may sometimes seem to impute more merit to them than they possess, it may have the counterbalancing advantage of making their faults more obvious, because more understandable.

For the faults of Poe's verse are almost always the paradoxical consequence of its virtues. His poetry is mechanical because it is precisely mechanics that most interested him. That is, he aimed at a perfect efficiency of poetic techniques, bending every effort to find for his effects the most direct means. Furthermore, he intended not only to achieve such efficiency but to render it obvious, particularly in his later poems, as one can see by comparing the early "Al Aaraaf," which gracefully imitates such poems as "Endymion" and "Prometheus Unbound" with "Ulalume" or "Annabel Lee." In consequence, he writes as if the experience a poem creates is, in the simplest way, determined by its subject—as if, to take the notorious example, the death of a beautiful woman will make for a sad poem because it is a sad event, and a

246

beautiful poem because she is beautiful. The same taste for efficiency vitiates his style. He was so convinced of the value of "music" in poetry that he almost always sacrificed literary "tone" to merely physical sound effects. The more music, presumably, the better. Hence the heavy and monotonous beat of his lines, the obtrusive rhymes, the rigid stanza forms rigidly adhered to. Lines are padded and syntax wrenched to perfect sound patterns which, in their tonal quality, are more often than not at war with the mood and sense. His love of elaborate rhyme schemes—ones often beyond his skill to manage—explains, too, the tendency to fit words in in such a way that none of their normal meanings apply, and sometimes this is the true explanation of what appears as a perverse desire to destroy language. His belief that English metrics can be explained by quantity alone is another source of trouble. For simplicity's sake he founded all the aspects of rhythm upon one physical element—the breathing factor—so that metrics could be rendered scientifically calculable.[53]

Yet efficiency is the governing concept of Poe's poetry, and the very factor which accounts for his surprising repute abroad. What has fascinated foreign writers from Baudelaire onward is, as T. S. Eliot comments, his power to direct attention to the poetic process and to demonstrate that this is itself a proper subject of art.[54] Though most of Poe's poems are failures, in his best verse he succeeds just enough to suggest what a poetry *of* poetry might be. The hint, being just a hint, was perhaps more inspiriting to the emergent symbolist school than a fully successful performance might have been. In any case, the lesson of Poe's poetry was made the more alluring by its exposition in a brilliantly lucid and self-consistent body of criticism. English-speaking readers have been inclined to conflate Poe's theory of poetry with the sterile aestheticism of the nineties, and to conclude that history has proved this theory can only lead to a dead end. But in Europe, Poe's aesthetic helped to open the main avenue, and in

53. "The Rationale of Verse," in *Complete Works, 14,* 241.
54. "From Poe to Valéry," *Hudson Review, 2* (1949), 340–41.

America it foreshadowed the work of Eliot, who derives from Poe indirectly through the symbolists, while developing also from philosophers such as Bradley, whose ideas have important affinities to the thought of Poe.

Even taking Poe's theory at its least attractive—taking it as an aesthetic which could be summed up by the slogan "art for art's sake"—it is not a program for escapism and triviality. Quite the opposite, its fault is that of a too simplistic realism, of making the relation of the poem to the actual world too direct. The basis of Poe's theory is the belief that since metaphysically the poem is a real object, it exists in the real world and the poetic process is therefore an illustration of universal process: the way the poem means is identical with the way things happen in the world. This view of poetry follows logically enough from Poe's more general system of ideas, and by putting his reasoning in the rough and ready language of the classroom, one can see that it has a large measure of relevance, if not of truth. Since we do not know reality directly, but see the world only in experience, to make sense is to bring our random perceptions into self-consistency, harmony, *unity,* and this, in effect, is to make the fragments of thought and sensation into *one world.* Such construction is the work of the imagination, and therefore, to the extent that we make sense, we become poets.

A poem is but a higher and more perfect version of the world which the mind is always creating. There is nothing in experience more immediate, more available for our direct observation and study, than this act of constructing itself. The objects of sense all dissolve into this process when analyzed. They are real to us because of it, for nothing is more certain to us than that we are now having these sensations and considering these thoughts. If our experiencing is a real event, the way it proceeds in constructing our perceptions into the world-as-we-see-it is our surest evidence of the world as it *really* is.

But this process by which the elements of consciousness are organized into an experience is the same as the process by which the elements of a poem are unified, and Poe therefore reasoned that, ideally, the poem's content and form should be one. By an exact and perfectly direct relation of means to ends, he would so manage things that the way the poem happens is identical with the event it pictures. In other words, he sought to make the action portrayed in the poem the same as the process by which the poem itself develops. The fruitfulness of Poe's influence abroad shows the value of this idea of poetry, and though the poems he wrote are marred by serious faults, this does not so much discredit the theory as illustrate a rather too simplistic view of the practical techniques it requires. As a casual reading of the poems will show, their faults are stylistic, and could be described as consequences of the poet's intention only if this were far less reasonable than it seems to be.

The point deserves emphasis, because it is so often argued that Poe's intention is to blame—that he meant to produce poetry that is escapist, irrelevant, purely fictive. For example, Richard Wilbur quotes the Drake-Halleck review as evidence that the poems are meant "to consist of visionary gropings toward imaginary realms":

> If, indeed, there be any one circle of thought distinctly and palpably marked out from amid the jarring and tumultuous chaos of human intelligence, it is that evergreen and radiant Paradise which the true poet knows, and knows alone, as the limited realm of his authority—as the circumscribed Eden of his dreams.[55]

While granting that taken by itself this statement seems to confirm Wilbur's view that Poe severely "contracted the scope and nature of poetry," one may question whether the meaning inferred is that which Poe intended, for in the light of *Eureka* and the criticism as a whole, its tenor appears quite different. Since "Paradise" is understood as living in and to God—participating in his consciousness—the "circumscribed Eden" of the poet's dreams

55. *Poe: Complete Poems*, p. 10; *Selected Writings*, p. 419.

does not fence out the real world, but represents the only view of it with which the poet, *as* poet, is concerned. His purpose is to depict the unity which underlies the "jarring and tumultuous chaos" of mental life, to render through a vision which perforce must be shadowy and inferential the all-inclusive context that particular things exist within the moments of experience approximate. This is "Paradise" in that it is reality, and it is known to the poet "alone" because only the highest imaginative vision can glimpse it. Finally, it is the "Eden of his *dreams*," in that he intuits it, fleetingly, darkly, by faint imitations. In Poe, as often in Romantic literary theory, "dream" signifies imaginative vision, and to misread this term as escapist phantasy is to miss the very problem that it is intended to recognize, to overlook the illusory nature of the world of ordinary experience. Far from recommending going all the way in the withdrawal into autistic make-believe, Poe's aesthetic is based upon a more hard-headed and honestly skeptical view of knowledge than is assumed in comments about his turning away from a real world which is obvious and well-understood.

In terms of the cosmology of *Eureka*, Poe's poetry begins at just the point in history at which the gothic tales end, at the point where mind merges with world and self dies. As the detective stories lead into the tales of horror, and Dupin or Legrand dimly suspects what Usher fully realizes, so the vision that kills Usher is depicted in the animistic landscapes and somnambulistic trances of the poems. Their intended subject, in other words, is reality in a later phase, when the merging of mind and world has advanced so far that the two are scarcely distinguishable and neither seems real except as an aspect of being of a different sort.

Since Poe presents *Eureka* as a poem, it is worthwhile studying his statements about the purpose of this work. "I propose," he writes,

to take such a survey of the Universe that the mind may be able really to receive and perceive an individual impression.

He who from the top of Aetna casts his eyes leisurely around, is affected chiefly by the *extent* and *diversity* of the scene. Only by a rapid whirling on his heel could he hope to comprehend the panorama in the sublimity of its *oneness*. But as, on the summit of Aetna, *no* man has thought of whirling on his heel, so no man has ever taken into his brain the full uniqueness of the prospect; and so, again, whatever considerations lie involved in this uniqueness, have as yet no practical existence for mankind.[56]

But to whirl upon one's heel is to see the visible world dissolved into a blur. An *"individual* impression," or simultaneous view of all things, presents that unity in which the world as we know it disappears. And yet the unity of the world in which men actually live—the uniqueness of its being just *this* world and *one* world, however many spheres of being it contains—is a fact of transcendent importance. We cannot entertain the idea of truth or judge the validity of any statement without assuming that there is a real world which, however complex in design or in the appearances it presents to mind, is nevertheless one world, and uniquely this world that it is. And the unique identity of the universe must have important consequences, since it is the very world in terms of which our human concerns matter. To understand our actual situation, rather than to withdraw from it into a vertiginously thrilling phantasy,

We need so rapid a revolution of all things about the central point of sight that, while the minutiae vanish altogether, even the more conspicuous objects become blended into one. Among the vanishing minutiae, in a survey of this kind, would be all exclusively terrestrial matters. The Earth would be considered in its planetary relations alone. A man, in this view, becomes mankind; mankind a member of the cosmical family of Intelligences.[57]

56. *Complete Works, 16,* 186.
57. Ibid., p. 187.

This statement suggests the mythology of "Al Aaraaf" and the nightmarish dialectic of "The Sleeper." Our attention, though, should not be restricted to the poems' subject matter. The statement points toward an even more important aspect of the poetry —an artistic principle which might be likened to that of the quantum. One will miss the main import of the poetry's dissolutions and mergings if one fails to recognize that their meaning lies in the historical tendency they indicate. Since Poe cannot directly describe the "Eden" of the imagination, for he cannot see it, except faintly, inferentially, he can only enable the reader to *sense* its existence as the end or final state of affairs which events in experience tend toward but never quite reach.

Poe's purpose in his poetry is to bring consciousness as close as possible to a panorama of the whole, and since he conceives the completed vision historically, as the goal toward which the universe is moving, the poet's vision represents a later phase of history. Ideally, the poem should render the penultimate phase, showing being at the point in cosmic evolution just before complete unity is realized.

"The City in the Sea" is perhaps the most impressive of all the poems, and its obscurities are dispelled when it is read with "The Fall of the House of Usher" in mind. In that tale the merging of self and world produces reality of a different order—an area of being which has ceased to be a landscape in that it has taken on sentience and purpose. This area is the poem's subject. It is significant that Poe canceled such earlier titles as "The City of Dis" and "The City of Death," for moral attitudes cannot exist in a world where there is no one to make judgments. The city is not a place, because there are no places, nor an object, because there is no longer a subject to attend to it. It is both subject and object at once—vision and being at a point so near unity that the distinction between them has almost vanished.

One sign of this poem's success in realizing Poe's theoretical objectives is the fact that the very devices of style which seem inappropriately mechanical in the other poems appear quite fitting here. If the emphatic alliteration—for example, "The viol, the violet, and the vine"—is plainly a contrivance, its obviousness is an advantage, for where mind and world have coalesced, speech should seem as automatic and thought as inevitable as the behavior of atomic particles.[58] The automatism of Poe's style enacts the disappearance of selfhood. There is a speaker, to be sure, yet when he exclaims "Lo!" and "alas," his depersonalization is manifest by a tone of indifference which the mechanical rhyming emphasizes:

> For no ripples curl, alas!
> Along that wilderness of glass—[59]

Like a person under hypnosis, the speaker does not speak from himself but submissively echoes the mind which possesses him; and this is not a mind in the usual sense, but a consciousness practically identical with that which we must improperly call the place. The speaker has no thoughts of his own. He exists only as the verbal manifestation of the setting. What might be called the thoughts in his mind are indistinguishable from the things he perceives; thus his feelings are merely reflections of visible surfaces and not primarily his own.

As emotion becomes something else, so things lose their objectivity. The city in the sea is void not only of human inhabitants but of events. Nothing happens, and therefore objects do not exist, since their existence would imply the passage of time during which they endure, whereas here all is static, immutable being. It is a condition of death in that it precludes "living" in any usual sense, but it is also a condition of life in that what immutably is cannot cease to be.

At the end of the poem a faint stirring reveals that the city is sinking, if ever so slowly, into the sea. Evidently the final unification still lies in the future, yet as Poe must have hoped, the poem depicts reality at a stage so close to the end of history that

58. *Selected Writings*, p. 26.
59. Ibid., p. 27.

the last event is almost visible. As the faint movement of the water's surface not only foreshadows the impending inundation of the city, but is actually a part of that event, so the city contains the future by the intimations it affords. Yet in representing the future, it also epitomizes the past by standing as a type for such devastated ancient cities as Balbec, Gomorrah, and Pompeii. Thus foresight is also retrospection, and their unity demonstrates that the change history works in the physical world is also a change in the very nature of consciousness. The movement to a later epoch is not to another time of the same sort, for time itself changes, the present becoming ever more inclusive until ultimately the now, or immediate occasion of consciousness, and eternity, or its total context, are identical. The nearer the approach to the last day, the clearer the goal toward which all moments tend, and the further in the opposite direction—toward the first day, or beginning—the vision extends, for the end is the beginning also, the original unity.

The reader may well feel that the end turns out to be a very distasteful state of affairs, and from the human point of view this judgment is correct, as Poe implies by suggesting that the city is worse than hell. Here not only selfhood and the natural world are annihilated, but even the standards in terms of which this destiny could be evaluated cease to exist. Hell will do the city reverence, because unity absorbs the good, which even hell needs for purposes of definition. Yet though values as such disappear, they do so in taking on a new life and kind of being. It is not to deny or annihilate value to say that it is an aspect of reality rather than a separate object. It is to express an insight which, whether true or not, seems essential to the main themes of tragedy: that value itself is not the same as good from the human point of view, but is rather a higher interest of the self than even its own being. Though less deeply understood, the terror which Poe projects as a static visual tableau is of the same variety as the terror that Job and Lear and Racine's Titus discover through the progressive action of drama.

Granting that by comparison the poems are minor works, such merits as they do have are intimately related to Poe's skill in so handling the time element that action is gradually converted into stasis, with the result that the form of the poem enacts the change of perspective I have just described. At the outset the poem seems to move forward, progressively, as a sequence of perceptions, but slowly, as the details accumulate, they assemble into a fixed picture of a single setting or situation in which different times coexist and the appearance of progression fades away. Since selfhood is existence in history, the fading of times into a single moment is also a process of depersonalization. As history ends in the last day, so the self dies when it achieves "an individual impression" of reality. The familiar argument that the action in a Poe poem consists of psychological events must be regarded as seriously mistaken, because the whole movement of such a poem carries the reader toward the discovery that the mind is ultimately unreal, and that therefore the arena where psychological action could take place does not exist.

With respect to form, the unity in which the self disappears is to be made manifest by the unity of the poem. The latter, Poe tells us, is a unity of effect—a unity, then, known in the reader's own experience. Though Poe thought poetry a higher form, his ideas concerning prose fiction cast much light on his poetic technique. Poe believed that, in fiction, plot is the most obvious manifestation of unity. Plot "is *that in which no part can be displaced without ruin to the whole*. It may be described as a building so dependently constructed, that to change the position of a single brick is to overthrow the entire fabric." [60] Plot, then, is not just the design of incidents; it is the whole work, considered under the aspect of action. An image—a descriptive detail, for instance —is thus an element of plot, for its appearing to the character's consciousness, and to the reader's also, are events in the fullest sense.

The purpose of unity of plot is to approximate the unity of the

60. "Night and Morning," in *Selected Writings*, p. 424.

real. Poe is not being at all figurative when he speaks of the universe as a "plot of God." Since to omniscience all times are present, the more nearly literary action approximates this unity, the more events will seem to be simultaneous. In "The American Drama" Poe contends that this simultaneity is indeed the goal toward which the writer should work:

All the Bridgewater Treatises have failed in noticing the *great* idiosyncrasy in the Divine system of adaptation. . . . I speak of the complete *mutuality* of adaptation. For example:—in human constructions, a particular cause has a particular effect —a particular purpose brings about a particular object, but we see no reciprocity. The effect does not re-act upon the cause— the object does not change relations with the purpose. In Divine constructions, the object is either object or purpose as we choose to regard it, while the purpose is either purpose or object; so that we can never (abstractly—without concretion— without reference to facts of the moment) decide which is which.[61]

It follows, then, that

The Pleasure which we derive from any exertion of human ingenuity, is in the direct ratio of the *approach* to this species of reciprocity between cause and effect. In the construction of *plot*, for example, in fictitious literature, we should aim at so arranging the points, or incidents, that we cannot distinctly see, in respect to any one of them, whether that one depends from any one other or upholds it. In this sense, of course, perfection of plot is unattainable *in fact*—because Man is the constructor. The plots of God are perfect. The Universe is a plot of God.[62]

In the tale entitled "The Power of Words" the source of "reciprocity" is shown to be "retrogradation," or God's "faculty of referring at *all* epochs, *all* effects to *all* causes," and to see things in this way

61. "The American Drama," in *Complete Works, 13*, 45.
62. Ibid., p. 46.

is to view a conspectus of all times.[63] This inclusive vision, so obvious in "The Gold Bug"—where nearly half the tale is devoted to Legrand's retrospective explanations—is more subtly depicted in the poems, which commence at a later phase of consciousness, so that the panorama is not as distinct from the movement toward it. "Ulalume" and "The Sleeper" illustrate Poe's favorite device of beginning with a moody bit of scene setting, so ominous in its effect that the action which wells from it seems illusionary from the outset. The initial landscape expresses a consciousness so close to the final vision of death that the characters living in this "place" have but a wraithlike existence.

Baudelaire's epigram that all of Poe's ideas, "like obedient arrows, fly to the same target," is especially true of his critical opinions.[64] The target is unity and, with respect to literary form, the unity of the poem's action with the historical process it enacts. In view of this conception several ideas which otherwise seem faddish or cranky fit together and make sense. I would point out three such ideas as indicative: Poe's concept of "indefinitiveness," his emphasis on the value of music in poetry, and his arguments against the creativity of the poet's imagination.

"Indefinitiveness" is the quality Poe praises in Tennyson, the poet he grew to admire most, and the quality he cultivates in his own verse, because it is the main stylistic effect expressive of merging, the blur one sees by whirling on one's heel. And of "indefinitiveness," music is Poe's favorite manifestation, because it reflects the unifying process within the very language of poetry. Sounds and rhythm, being more generalized than words and grammar, are more nearly simple elements of matter, and yet, at the same time, music seems freer from particulars and more purely formal than literature. By the striking way it synthesizes the formal and the material, music symbolizes the merging of thought and the physical world.

Floyd Stovall argues that Poe's remarks on the creative imagi-

63. *Poe's Short Stories*, p. 416.
64. *Baudelaire on Poe*, p. 79.

nation should be discounted on the ground that he disagrees with Coleridge only to make a vain display of his originality.[65] But that the imagination does not create is a significant and inevitable principle within his system: "Novel conceptions are merely unusual combinations. The mind of man can imagine nothing which does not really exist." [66] Later in the same essay, however, Poe seems to reverse his position, conceding that the artist's mind makes novel combinations, and that if the "absolute 'chemical combination'" be strong enough, the poet may even produce "something that shall have nothing of the quality" of the objects constituting it. But this creation is not really the mind's, for though the mind does combine things, it is the fact of their being combinable that creates such unification:

> From novel arrangements of old forms which present themselves to it, it [the imagination] selects such only as are harmonious; the result, of course, is *beauty* itself—using the word in its most extended sense and as inclusive of the sublime. The pure imagination chooses, *from either beauty or deformity,* only the most combinable things hitherto uncombined.[67]

The poet's selecting, then, is no free act of the self; his choice is dictated by the nature of the things. To be sure, the imagination's "materials extend throughout the universe"; but to create the harmony of art requires just such an alignment of mind with reality as Legrand achieves.[68] The poet's art is that of discovering what is already there, neither imitating nor reflecting, but *bringing out,* to some degree, the harmony of the universe. Thus, while the poet's combinations are novel in that no other artist has discovered them, the combining is not strictly his. The things combined merge in the same way and by the same law as all things in their movement toward unity. The poetic process is the

65. "Poe's Debt to Coleridge," *University of Texas Studies In English,* 10 (1930), 70–127.
66. "N. P. Willis," *The Literati,* in *Complete Works,* 15, 13, n. 1.
67. Ibid.
68. Ibid., p. 14, n. continued from p. 13.

historical dialectic, and to the extent that the poem approximates the plot of God, it is the universe in small.

To appreciate how radically Poe altered the concept of poetry, one need only survey the consequences of his disagreement with Coleridge. It will be remembered that Coleridge defines the "primary Imagination" as "a repetition in the finite mind of the eternal act of creation," and concludes that the "secondary" or poetic imagination is "identical with the primary in the *kind* of its agency . . . differing only in *degree,* and in the *mode* of its operation." [69] Though Coleridge could regard the failure of his own powers as the effect of a loss of rapport with "the eternal action of creation," he tended to place greater emphasis than Poe on the freedom of creativity which the imagination's divine origin would seem to betoken. Poe reasoned that this freedom is illusory, for since the poet creates by imperfectly repeating the process of divine creation, it is God who writes the poem. As he acidly remarks, if the imagination could create something which does not already exist, "it would create not only ideally but substantially, as do the thoughts of God." [70] Coleridge writes that the imagination "dissolves, diffuses, dissipates, in order to re-create." [71] Poe would say that it dissolves, diffuses, dissipates in order to discover.

Poe reinterprets the Coleridgean imagination in such a way as to produce most of the changes which separate modern poetry from Romantic. By substituting discovery for creation, he shifts attention from the poet to the poem, from vision to craftsmanship, and from poetic sensibility to literary effect. The poem is no longer an expression of an event in the poet's mind, developing with an organic naturalness from his perceptual act: it is itself the event to be considered, and when viewed as an experience, it is the reader's, not the poet's. The poem does not record the poet's feelings or intuitions on the assumption that the reader will auto-

69. *Biographia Literaria* (London, J. M. Dent, 1947), pp. 145–46.
70. "N. P. Willis," *The Literati,* in *Complete Works, 15,* 13, n. 1.
71. *Biographia Literaria,* p. 146.

matically participate in them, but is designed to produce these feelings and intuitions as effects in the reader's mind. In consequence, the poet's imagination is relegated to a secondary role, as Poe makes clear in arguing that a man of "metaphysical acumen" will write a finer poem than a man of extraordinary imagination:

> For a poem is not the poetic faculty, but the means of exciting it in mankind. Now these means the metaphysician may discover by analysis of their effects in other cases than his own, without even conceiving the nature of these effects—thus arriving at a result which the unaided Ideality of his competitor would be utterly unable, except by accident, to attain.[72]

This argument proposes not that the imagination can be dispensed with, but that it is not, strictly speaking, the poet's. To the extent that *his* vision is true, and therefore imaginative, it turns into reality itself, and in the process ceases to be a vision or the experience of any particular person. This change is the action of the poem—not only the event the poem *depicts,* as a painting depicts recognizable objects, not only the self's depersonalization, and the annihilation, through merging, of the objects it perceives, but the development of the poem itself.

The poem begins by moving forward, chronologically, as it were, through a sequence of moments and psychic states. Yet when this progression has reached a certain point, it becomes obvious that the movement, being always the same, developing always according to the same process, is not really movement at all, but stasis. For if the same things happen at every moment, all moments are one; and if all psychic phases illustrate the same thinking and the same thoughts, they are all versions of a single state of mind. At the point when this is realized, the poem ends. Though in fact Poe may never have quite achieved the dénouement he intended, theoretically, the poem has arrived at a perfect unity of effect by acting out, in small, the essential process of

72. "Drake-Halleck," in *Selected Writings,* p. 421.

universal history. As in the summarizing explanations of the detective tales, the ending's conclusiveness depends upon the effect of simultaneity. Like the last phase of history, the ending contains all the phases in a unitary moment.

It is perhaps in "To Helen" that Poe's essential action is most gracefully managed, a success attributable to the fact that the symbolic process provides the poem's subject as well as its form. The immediate object of experience is transcended at the outset, for it is Helen's beauty, not Helen herself, that arrests the speaker's attention. To see the lady is to see something more general and evidently more real, something which leads the mind into an ever-widening circle of associations. At first, these seem historical, evocations of a past which carry thought to earlier times, but as memory proceeds, the past becomes indeterminate, a direction rather than a destination. The speaker is carried back, like Odysseus, "the weary way-worn wanderer," to "his own native shore." [73] But the journey backward in time soon becomes a journey out of it, to the glory of Greece, the grandeur of Rome —the timeless realities rather than the particular places or epochs. Because Helen's beauty is the same as that revealed by classical statuary, it has the power to evoke the primal myth of antiquity, leading the mind to ideas which transcend the civilization they created. Yet, having gone so far, the mind can hardly stop there. Since the meaning of Helen's beauty is an ever-widening area of experience in which an increasing number of things are harmoniously combined, beauty itself must be identical with the process of unification. The "home" or destination toward which thought tends is unity, the "Holy-Land" from which even Spirit or Psyche is derived; it is, in other words, that which philosophers sometimes term the "ground"—pure being. Thus Helen, standing "statue-like" in the window-niche, merges with Psyche, the girl in Apuleius' tale, and both of these personages merge with Psyche in the more general sense of "soul," which contains also the soul of the speaker, who finds that to see

73. Ibid., p. 23.

Helen's beauty is, in effect, to see the self in its original oneness with all things.

The last lines transmute progression into stasis by showing that the speaker's journeying is illusory. What appeared to be several thoughts in sequence are, in the final perspective, versions of the same thought. The beauty which set thought in motion is really the unity in which it comes to rest. The object "here" directly before the speaker, let us even say before Poe as he admired Mrs. Stannard, disappears along with the observer when what it is is fully realized. But the moment of realization is not a later time, actually, though it may seem so from the human point of view. It is rather the same moment more fully understood, or, to put the matter in another way, the actual present which the speaker's experience of the present meant to be from the first.

In poetry of this kind the symbol functions in a special way, a fact which can be appreciated by noting the difficulty of interpreting Poe's literary allusions. Interpretations of "Nicean" and "Hyacinth" have proved inconclusive, and a scrutiny of the references to Psyche and Helen would open further doubts, since Apuleius' maiden drives Cupid away when she strikes a light, and Helen lures Odysseus away from, not toward, his "native shore." But the artificiality of such puzzles in exegesis suggests that they are based on a misconception concerning the way the symbols symbolize. It will not do simply to say that Poe's symbols make freely associative references rather than conscious ones, for it is really a question whether they "refer" at all. At any rate, they refer so indiscriminately that they appear to mean almost anything they are able to bring to the reader's mind. They are extremely vague with respect to the "things" they mean, but are precise as images of the process by which things are related to each other or, in psychological terms, of the way experience reaches beyond itself to an ever-widening horizon. The meaning of the symbol in Poe is what it does, and its behavior, like that of atoms or thoughts in Poe's cosmology, is that of merging. The symbol becomes a symbol by blending with something other than itself, an event which betokens its movement toward the final unity.

To the extent that the symbol has meaning, it is no longer a distinct object. Thus, at the beginning of "To Helen," what Poe sees has already ceased to be the lady herself and become her beauty, something more general. Yet, in saying that the symbol "becomes" or changes nature, one must keep in mind the distortion caused by the human need to see things sequentially from within time. Actually, any given thing includes its relations to other things, and it is related to every other thing. Thus, in Poe's view, all symbols must ultimately have the same meaning: unity. But the very simplicity of this doctrine has the effect of complicating symbolic meaning, for since, from the human point of view, the symbol's meaning is but partially glimpsed, the poem can depict many symbols moving to the same end along diverse paths, forming a variety of combinations, suggesting a multiplicity of particular meanings. For all the faults of Poe's poetry, it has in some measure the mystery and suggestiveness the symbolists valued, and these merits are a consequence of conceiving the symbol as something in process, so that its meaning is shaded, transitional, and surprising in its capacity to yield new implications.

The merging by which the symbol's meaning develops is also the process by which the speaker is depersonalized, since in observing the way the objects he directly perceives are absorbed into a larger reality, he arrives at the intuition that, since all things are one, his identity is an illusion. This is well illustrated in "To Helen" by the passivity of the speaker, who does not so much think about Helen's beauty as observe its effects and detachedly report the way his thoughts develop. His somnambulistic manner and air of fatigue dramatize the involuntary, even mechanical nature of his responses. In later poems Poe sought to heighten this effect by making the prosody automatic as well, so that the reader could join in the persona's hypnotic suspension as he watches the symbol unfold its meaning, slowly, inexorably, as if by a will of its own. Indeed, in a poem by Poe there is little for the mind to do but watch, since the meaning is in the symbol, whether recognized or not, and to the extent that the mind discovers it, the mind is at one with universal process and not free to shape meaning at will. Further, it should be noted that in Poe's world no object, and therefore no image, can avoid being a symbol also, for to be mentioned in the poem, an object must be known to consciousness, and since the awareness of it relates it to other objects, it is already representative of things beyond itself and already united in some degree to them.

While the curiously blurred effect of the diction in Poe's verse has often been accounted a result of his desire to "destroy" language, the behavior of his words is a natural consequence of his metaphysics. There is an intentional effect of vagueness, which serves to render a very precise experience, just as a misty seascape by Turner presents a precise visual image. Such vagueness, which both Poe's aesthetic and his subject matter demanded, must be distinguished from the vagueness resulting from Poe's failure to use language effectively. I will consider his faults of style later, but in order to describe the real confusions in his verse, I must first give an account of that very different variety of "indefinitiveness" which is proper and essential to his best poems. Since words are symbols, their destiny, in the Poe poem, cannot differ from that of other sensible objects. Poe meant to "destroy" language only in the sense of depicting words ceasing to exist in the process of becoming what they mean. To recall *Eureka* once more, the principle by which anything exists is also the principle that will destroy it. As the self dies through the development of the very consciousness which constitutes its identity, so a word is destroyed by the meaningfulness which makes it a word. It is the word's meaning that distinguishes it from a mere sound or visible object, yet in becoming a word, it has already started to merge with the reality it signifies.

Poe's raven does not mean anything by the word it utters. It croaks "Nevermore" by rote. Apparently, then, it is the lover who gives the word meaning by the questions he frames, yet as the poem progresses, one comes to see that the word dictates the questions to him. While it is true that the meaning the lover finds—the agonizing despair—is created by his own particular situation, he must find *his* meaning within the area of objectively possible meanings. If the raven had uttered another word, the lover's thought would have taken another direction, but in fact it cried "Nevermore," and the view of his situation to which this word leads the lover is correct, in that this view is the consequence which in fact resulted from the actual event.[74] The apparent subjectivity of the meaning the word has for the lover is due to his unique selfhood and circumstances, and it may be granted that whenever a word is used, the occasion, being particular, gives it a unique significance (even if its uniqueness is usually too faint or uninteresting to discern). On the other hand, a word has its own range, so that while its meaning varies according to the occasion, it lies within certain limits. It has the kind of meaning dictionaries intend by defining what, with respect to the present state of language, the word always means. There is, then, an inevitable contrast between the word's general meaning and that which it has on a particular occasion. To Poe this contrast is a matter of perspective, a contrast between a narrower and a broader view of a single occasion, what the word now means and what it always means differing only to the extent that one fails to see the present in the context of reality as a whole. In "The Raven" the lover's attitude changes as the word "Nevermore" causes him to define his situation in an increasingly inclusive way. At first, he sees merely his immediate circumstances: the location is the room where he sits, the time a winter evening; but gradually, as his perspective changes, he comes to see his situation as a lifetime, and in asking at last whether he will meet Lenore in Paradise, he recognizes his situation as the universe,

74. Not that the incident occurred in "real life," but that the word "Nevermore" is an actual word and its effects on the lover are, given the fictional event and circumstances, the real effects that follow from the word's real nature.

and his occasion as history as a whole. There is no longer a discrepancy between the particular and general meaning of the raven's word, and thus there is no way of keeping the limits of the word's meaning distinct from the meanings of other words. As the lover's question about ever seeing Lenore again illustrates, the word forces thought to entertain ideas it seems to exclude. "Nevermore" premises "always": one has to consider time as a whole to form the idea of something that will never again occur. The meaning of "Nevermore" is the sum of the ideas it evokes, and since it even evokes the meaning of contrary words, it merges with them and exemplifies the way language as a whole fades away by uniting with the world. Ultimately, "Nevermore" means the final unity, which is death to the self and the cause of the lover's despair in losing Lenore, but also the timelessness of the reality in terms of which the loss is significant—the reality which makes words vain, but which, as their meaning, creates them. Of course, from the human point of view "Nevermore" has a more specific meaning and words do not all mean the same thing. Yet if the limits of man's situation preserve the distinct meanings of words, it is also these limits that make death real and love temporary by virtue of their power to give the self its finite identity. To be finite is to be mortal. "Nevermore" means sorrow to the speaker because he cannot escape living in a world of distinct things, where his own individuality is a cause of suffering.

In terms of Poe's cosmology the end of history is the end of language also. In unity there can be no more difference between the word and what it means than between the mind and the world. The indentations or hieroglyphics which Arthur Gordon Pym finds in the black rock near the South Pole exemplify language at the point of disappearing. They have a meaning, of course; they read "to be white," yet the significance of this phrase depends upon the context of the series of chasms spelling "to be shady" in Ethiopian, upon the larger context of the black land, where the natives detest whiteness, and even more generally, upon the context of Pym's whole experience, in which events continually illustrate the merging of opposites. The inscription is an example of the way this paradoxical process enters into the nature of language.[75] As "to be white" is lettered in the black rock, so language exists only in that it stands out against the otherness of reality; yet it is the nonverbal things which words mean that give language its being. Whiteness symbolizes the unity into which Pym will soon disappear, and the hieroglyphics represent language at the stage just before it, too, is absorbed in the all. "To be white" predicates nothing—is not a sentence—names a general quality rather than a more particular object, employs a verb lacking tense and number, and is recognizable as language only in that it contains words and a syntactical form. At the last phase of history even this vestigial language disappears. The manuscript is broken off; Pym will say no more.

Poe's use of language in his poetry is designed to enact this process by presenting words in the act of merging and as already so indistinct that their meanings have faded, blurred. The familiar criticism that Poe uses words in such a way as to deprive them of all their normal meanings is self-contradictory, since it is only in terms of the context that particular usages seem abnormal, yet the context would not be clear if the words were not. One must discriminate between actual imprecision and the "indefinitiveness" which dramatizes the process of merging. Since unity is the central fact in Poe's world, his vision will seem true and his language precise to the extent that his words appear to enact the movement toward unity. It is the fictional appearance that matters, just as it is the convincing quality of the poem's meaning that constitutes its value. Whether Poe's words actually behave as his theory of language assumes or merely seem to do so is beside the point, since the value of a poem is not the correctness of the view of language it implies but its total meaning, the whole experience it expresses.

While there is a good deal wrong with the language of the

75. *The Narrative of Arthur Gordon Pym of Nantucket*, chap. 23 and note at the end of the novel, in *Selected Writings*, pp. 390–95, 406–07.

poetry, most attempts to explain its faults have an air of irrelevance because they premise the quite questionable idea that when language is precisely used, the meanings of words are stable and can be thought of as distinct entities. This is not only to miss the point of Poe's intention but to overlook obvious difficulties. Since the meaning of a word is largely determined by its context, it is transitional, altering as the poem develops. Or, if one thinks of a word's meaning as the "thing" it refers to in the real world, what that object is is affected by its relations to other things, and the relations, like those pertaining between words in a poem, are always changing. Thus meaning appears to be a developing event, whose final content is a process as well as an object. I mean not that, in fact, a poem has more than one meaning, but that Poe's use of language creates the fictional appearance that the poem's meaning is in process, developing toward a total significance which can only be obscurely intuited. Indeed, by shifting attention from the things words mean to their way of meaning, Poe foreshadowed a main tendency of literature since his time, and few would willingly maintain that to depict meaning as process is to be imprecise.

In certain poems, and occasionally in passages scattered throughout his poetry, words merge according to the theory I have described or at least give the fictional effect of behaving in this manner, as Poe intended; and in articulating his stylistic principles, I have attempted to show that whenever language accords with theory, his style is precise, appropriate, and successful, even though its merits may not be of the very highest order. But in turning from Poe's theory to his practice, one finds more to condemn than to praise, and since, as I suggested earlier, his faults are a consequence of his virtues, these faults need particular attention if we are to avoid discounting Poe's undoubted historical importance on the ground that his whole aesthetic is mistaken and that the world view it projects is simply "wrong." The faults are the consequence of the virtues in the sense that when Poe errs, it is always by attempting to fulfill his intention in too simple and direct a manner. The result is that, far from making words merge and flow into each other, his methods in fact create disunity rather than unity. The connotations of words, though they are intended to harmonize, in fact contradict, and in the absence of clear argument, which Poe's kind of fiction precludes, the tenor does not conceal the irrelevant ideas evoked, so that every false note is a loud one. The second stanza of "The Sleeper" illustrates the jolts which comically interrupt the poem's intended mood:

> Oh, lady bright! can it be right—
> This window open to the night?
> The wanton airs, from the tree-top
> Laughingly through the lattice drop—
> The bodiless airs, a wizard rout,
> Flit through thy chamber in and out
> And wave the curtain canopy
> So fitfully—so fearfully—
> Above the closed and fringéd lid
> 'Neath which thy slumb'ring soul lies hid,
> That, o'er the floor and down the wall,
> Like ghosts the shadows rise and fall! [76]

The sleeping Irene is threatened by some unnameable danger, and the vagueness of the speaker's premonition is meant to show the blending of his mood and the setting, where all is silent, tenebrous, vague in outline. But the tone of the question with which the stanza begins suggests a scolding duenna, fearful of merely practical dangers—a bad cold, for example—rather than evils to be feared for their elusiveness. The sequence "wanton airs," "bodiless airs, a wizard rout" blends the fitful stirring of breezes and drapery with ideas of caprice and stealthy intent, an effect which is then abruptly canceled by the phrase "in and out," which emphasizes precise, even calculated action. Similarly, "hid" is a jarring conclusion to the sequence "fitfully," "fearfully,"

76. Lines 18–29, in *Selected Writings*, p. 28.

"closed," "fringed," "slumbering," because it is too definite, too suggestive of a nut tucked into its shell. The bathos of "down the wall" results from the implication that just where the shadows fall is important, whereas the passage as a whole emphasizes swarming darkness, uncertain limits, shifting perspectives. Many such errors of style result from straining for rhymes, thus giving a false emphasis to secondary images and coupling them, through rhyme words, in laughable combinations. But this is to say how Poe blundered rather than why his mistakes are blunders, and the essential fault is that of disunity, irrelevance, or formlessness, though from the biographical point of view we may say that it is caused by Poe's attempt to depict unity by means that do not succeed.

Thus, instead of discounting Poe's entire poetic program as wrongheaded because it led to bad writing, it would be wiser to conclude that the poet erred in applying his theories too narrowly. In attempting to understand the practical consequences of his belief that cosmology and poetry could be synthesized, he seems to have been misled by a naïve materialism into supposing that the merely logical connection he intended between words or sentences would suffice to create a larger relevance of association, and that if words as pure sounds rhymed and measured out the line exactly enough, the effect would be harmonious. It was the error of conceiving the analogy of atoms and words too simply, as if words were unicellular particles rather than aggregates of considerable complexity—more nearly like organisms than like molecules—and as if their meanings were multiple only with respect to their potential variety of future references rather than also manifold in their already established meanings. He ignored the connotative range of words, and in contriving musical effects, he all too often produced strains far from melodious because he ignored the way verbal sounds are modulated by nonauditory associations.

While the frequent crudeness of Poe's language cannot be excused, the influence of his poems abroad indicates that they have values of an important kind. T. S. Eliot has perhaps provided the fairest judgment in remarking that having once read the poems, one can never forget them.[77] This is an oblique tribute, which makes a large allowance for memorable absurdities, yet I think Eliot mainly intended to point out a permanence that only richness of meaning can give. The memorable poem, like the memorable experience, is continually renewed in meaning, revealing ever new kinds of significance as experience alters one's perspective. This is the kind of meaning Poe intended, a meaning revealed by the behavior of words, which, as they merge, acquire a more broadly inclusive import and a more fully realized context. In Poe's practice, however, the words tend to have a merely logical consistency, one not of tone and association but of idea alone. Thus a much better case can always be made for the rationale of a Poe poem than for its style, and quotation is the apologist's greatest gamble. It is tempting to contrast the excellence of Poe's conceptions with the clumsiness of his style—to say, for example, that "The Raven" is a brilliant study in linguistics but a badly written poem; yet since it is only through the words that the ideas are revealed, the style must have its value. Prose sense is always poetic in some degree; the consistency of thought on the level of tenor or denotation always implies a larger vision, however faintly, and records an attitude potentially dramatic. It is a question of degree whether the poet's conscious reasoning is exact and inclusive enough to define a world and constitute an experience. Poe seems to depict a possible experience which his stylistic blunders betray, a potentiality of meaning that Continental poets could, perhaps, apprehend more sensitively than we, because to foreign ears the false notes are less audible. As a poet who had little time to spare for the art, Poe succeeded just sufficiently to alter the whole idea of poetry.

77. "'A Dream within A Dream,'" *The Listener*, 29 (Feb. 25, 1943), 244.

5
The Poetry of the Present and the Form of the Moment: Walt Whitman

Our first thought is rendered back to us by
the trumpets of the Last Judgment.
                    Ralph Waldo Emerson

THOREAU states, perhaps as exactly as anyone has, the problem of Whitman's poetry: "By his heartiness and broad generalities, he puts me into a liberal frame of mind prepared to see wonders—as it were, sets me upon a hill or in the midst of a plain, stirs me well up, and then—throws in a thousand brick." [1] Modern readers are more likely to be heartened by the brick than the generalities, which today seem either untrue or excessively elastic, but they will agree that there is in Whitman's poetry an odd vacillation between the level of abstract ideas and the ground of solid particularity. Whitman's mind moves easily in both these areas, yet while it is possible to admire his opinions or his images, or even both at once, it is difficult to see them in relation. This seeming irrelevance is no doubt the source of many weaknesses—the "yawping," the vagueness, and the prolix itemizing which, when Whitman fails, make the failure all too apparent—but the same contrast informs the best poems. It is of the essence of his art, the

1. F. B. Sanborn, ed., *The Writings of Henry David Thoreau, 6* (20 vols. Boston, Houghton, Mifflin, 1906), 296.

consequence of the mode of experience that art records and without which it could not exist. Unless the relation of ideas to things, and the roles Whitman would have them play in his poetry, are understood, his work cannot really be seen as poetry. He can only be applauded as an astute reporter of facts, for all his vaporish philosophizing, or praised in Thoreau's and the nineteenth century's manner, as a man of inspiriting ideas, whose pronouncements keep being drowned out by the thunderous depositing of brick. Lawrence comments: "Esquimos are not minor little Walts. They are something that I am not, I know that. Outside the egg of my Allness chuckles the greasy little Esquimo. Outside the egg of Whitman's Allness too."[2] Lawrence is scouting Whitman's claim to be at one with all human beings, but while he disposes of the idea neatly enough, one feels he has not touched the poetry. His irrelevance is the result of answering the idea as if it existed in isolation. He asks whether this idea is generally true, and in replying " 'Tis not!" he reads Whitman in much the same manner as those admirers of the "philosophy" who say " 'Tis so!" One cannot view Whitman's ideas so simply, as notions which are to be taken as in themselves true or false. They are generalities uttered from within experience—dramatic statements—and though he voices them with the air of one delivering final truths, their actual truth, for both Whitman and his readers, is that which the experience of the poem gives them. I do not mean to warn against reading "out of context"; my point is rather that in Whitman ideas have a status which makes the usual truth valuations particularly unhelpful.

Encountered in an actual passage, the idea Lawrence ridicules is not really the *same* idea.

> Agonies are one of my changes of garments.
> I do not ask the wounded person how he feels, I
>   myself become the wounded person,

2. *Studies in Classic American Literature*, p. 179.

> My hurts turn livid upon me as I lean on a cane and
>   observe.[3]

The "proof" Whitman offers to show that he can be one with the
wounded man is the vividness of his perceptions: he sees the
other person so accurately that one is persuaded he shares that
person's thoughts. This is odd indeed, for the wounded man is
described entirely from the outside: instead of giving us the man's
thoughts, he notes the "livid" wounds, the rueful leaning on the
cane, things which are seen by the poet as a distinct spectator.
Yet the details of the man's experience are convertible into his
thoughts; they have the power to express just what it feels like to
be the wounded man. In fact, unity depends upon separation.
Whitman becomes the wounded man because he gives equal
emphasis to that person's and his own existence as distinct individuals. Such unity is perceived, and in Whitman can only be
perceived, against a background of disparity. Perhaps assertions
of unity always involve such a double view, since to speak of
things being one involves the thought of them as several. This
merely logical requirement can be concealed, but Whitman's
method requires that it be emphasized. For it is by stressing his
distance from the other person that the power of Whitman's own
perceptions to suggest that man's thoughts becomes proof of their
common selfhood.

This is not the unity Lawrence finds absurd, because it includes
separation also. The meaning of Whitman's poetry is not a digest
of his opinions but the state of consciousness he depicts—a condition in which unity and separation are simultaneously perceived.
The idea is but a part of this experience and one means of creating it.

Of course, Whitman believes his opinions and would like the

3. "Song of Myself," sec. 33, in *Complete Poetry and Selected Prose*, p. 52.
Wherever possible, quotations from Whitman's writings are given according to
this Riverside edition (see Introduction, p. 3, n. 2), which reproduces the
1891–92 or "deathbed" edition.

reader to agree. But the truth of his "endless announcements" does not consist only in their validity as statements about reality. As generalizations, they advance the claim that they are true to everyone, everywhere, at all times, but this general validity rests upon—is to be proved by—their status as statements presently being made. They are true as they now exist, as the ideas that come to the poet's mind as the truth of the experience he is now having. They not only have a relevance to that experience but, as it were, exist within it.

If this seems a subtle distinction, its importance for Whitman's poetry can be demonstrated by many typical passages, as, for example, the following from "Starting from Paumanok."

> Victory, union, faith, identity, time,
> The indissoluble compacts, riches, mystery,
> Eternal progress, the kosmos, and the modern reports.
> This then is life,
> Here is what has come to the surface after so many
>   throes and convulsions.
> How curious! how real!
> Underfoot the divine soil, overhead the sun.[4]

Most readers will feel that this is an example of Whitman at his worst. The ideas seem at once too obvious and too nebulous, with the result that the generalizing is so free as to approach an ultimate vagueness, where even predication disappears and there is only the naming of topics—faith, identity, time, and so on. The incommensurate items named are then haphazardly gathered up in the comment, "This then is life," and, finally, as if to make incoherence complete, Whitman irrelevantly remarks that the sun is overhead and his feet are on the ground. Such nonsequiturs seem to produce nothing beyond the sense of an inarticulate, because amorphous, enthusiasm. But the effect of irrelevance is the result of the reader's expectation that the ideas will "follow"

4. Sec. 2, ibid., p. 15.

logically as a sequence of propositional statements. One supposes that when Whitman mentions "victory, union, faith," he means to go on to say something about them, and finding that they receive a bravo rather than a predicate, one is led to speak of Whitman's disorder, carelessness, and vaporish emotion. But if instead of assuming that the poet intends to make assertions about "victory, union, faith," one recognizes that he would comment upon their existence as ideas now present in his mind, then his casual way of surveying them will seem far from imprecise. For Whitman's ideas are specimens of intellectual materia—of "what has come to the surface after so many throes and convulsions," and he is interested not merely in the external objects to which such words as "victory" refer but in their presence to consciousness, or, more precisely, in the experience of knowing them as ideas which now come to mind. Indeed, the objective reality of "victory, union, faith" is proved by the poet's present thought of them, and to speak truly is not to make statements about the objects, as things in themselves, but to describe the sensation of having ideas. That the ideas are so very general makes the passage precise rather than vague, because it sharpens the contrast between universals and particulars, or concepts and sense data. "How curious! how real!" that ideas derived from the past and applicable, by their generality, to any and all time should exist to me here in the present in which I find myself feeling the sun's rays and the pressure of the earth beneath my feet.

Such passages record an emotional experience of a very precise kind—an experience of the being or actual reality of ideas. One can understand why Whitman must shun the sort of rational connectedness which would make his philosophizing seem more sensible. An orderly line of reasoning would divert attention from the way concepts rise to the surface of consciousness. And one can understand, too, Whitman's taste for abstractions. The more general an idea is the better, for it is its application to all moments that makes its presence in the now most remarkable, and through this presentness demonstrates the transcendental power of the mind by opening to it the whole panorama of past and future.

The passage from "Starting from Paumanok" is crucial, for it is the pivot upon which Whitman turns from retrospection to prophecy. He looks next to the future and the "Succession of men, Americanos, a hundred million" advancing in the van of progress, but "With faces turn'd sideways or backwards towards me to listen,/ With eyes retrospective towards me." [5] Whether or not the prophecy is artistically successful, taken by itself, it is very convincing as a dramatization of the way the transcendent vision emerges. It is Whitman's recognition of the concepts implicit in his present experience, his ability to be aware of them as the thoughts he is now having, that sets his mind free to journey across the expanses of space and time. The journey is toward generalization, but the panorama the poet generalizes upon grows out of—and is, indeed, a realization of—the present moment. What the idea asserts *about* reality is true and meaningful only in that it is the thought he is now having.

One should not conclude that for Whitman any idea will do, or that his subject is epistemology alone, which one opinion can illustrate as well as another. Whitman's ideas are undoubtedly those that seem the truest and most important within his world, for only such ideas can be present to his mind as actual, can appear to him as "what has come to the surface" of present reality. Close reasoning is unsuited to Whitman's subject, because it involves entertaining opinions not believed, and while a man can consider these, he cannot think them as events of his full consciousness. They do not grow out of his current perceptions and lead directly to every part of the world he knows. For Whitman, finding the truth is a matter not of relating ideas to each other but of observing the process by which they come to mind. It is the natural way they emerge in his present experience that reveals their meaning and proves them true. Hence he does not wish to win for his beliefs a merely rational assent. The poem as an act of

5. Ibid., p. 16.

communication no less than as a record of experience requires that an idea's truth be grounded in its existence as a now-transpiring thought. The reader will accept Whitman's beliefs only to the extent that he too can see them developing, as if inevitably, from his own perceiving.

The disconcerting contrast between the level of generalities and the level of minute particulars becomes understandable when Whitman's subject—and his meaning—are recognized as neither the system of beliefs nor the often tediously catalogued sense data but the process by which they are related. Like the poet and the wounded man, the two levels must seem to be separated by an impassable gulf in order that their unity may be depicted as an event.

The present is the only arena in which such an event can take place. Ideas are true in that the self is now thinking them, and objects are real as things he is presently seeing. The cosmic vision and the generalities describing it grow out of the poet's experience here and now. Whitman's poetry is, above all, a poetry of the now, a poetry which not only depicts the present moment but makes the poem itself exist as that moment and portrays all events, objects, and thoughts as things now appearing to consciousness.[6]

That Whitman conceived the poem in this way may seem to many readers either doubtful or unimportant, for as a subject, the present seems to have mattered to him less than the things it contains. Compared to the values which have traditionally been recognized and praised in his poetry—his delight in the natural world, his robust sensuality, his patriotism and celebration of American democracy, his faith in the future, his keen eye for the details of the contemporary social landscape—the art of render-

6. There are, of course, several Whitman poems which narrate past events in chronological order and seem to develop progressively. But as a rule, these poems exist as parts within poetic cycles, as, for example, "The Centenarian's Story" in *Drum-Taps*, or, as in the case of "There Was a Child Went Forth," the narrative is contained within the speaker's present occasion and functions as a realization of the landscape he now sees.

ing the present may appear a coldly technical affair. Notions of poetic method and craftsmanly contrivance do not seem to be in keeping with Whitman's naturalness, enthusiasm, freedom from "formules." But granting that his methods may have been largely instinctive, the truth of his ideas and the value of his facts depend upon his ability to depict the now. For these things are real in that they are present, are good in that they now exist in his experience. As he asserts in an important passage in the Preface of 1855:

> The direct trial of him who would be the greatest poet is today. If he does not flood himself with the immediate age as with vast oceanic tides . . . and if he does not attract his own land body and soul to himself and hang on its neck with incomparable love and plunge his semitic muscle into its merits and demerits . . . and if he be not himself the age transfigured . . . and if to him is not opened the eternity which gives similitude to all periods and locations and processes and animate and inanimate forms, and which is the bond of time, and rises up from inconceivable vagueness and infiniteness in the swimming shape of today, and is held by the ductile anchors of life, and makes the present spot the passage from what was to what shall be, and commits itself to the representation of this wave of an hour and this one of the sixty beautiful children of the wave—let him merge in the general run and wait his development.[7]

The moment of experience is not a mere container; one cannot separate the objects and thoughts Whitman values from their reality as things now existing. And, with respect to Whitman's methods or those of any poet, one cannot value the experience his poems express as if this were not dependent upon the art which expresses it.

Whitman, to be sure, presents all experiences as his own, and it is true that when he attempts to define the purpose of his poetry,

7. Preface to 1855 ed. of *Leaves of Grass*, in *Complete Poetry*, pp. 424–25.

he speaks much more often of portraying himself than of rendering the now. He declares, for instance, that *Leaves of Grass* is "an attempt, from first to last, to put a *Person*, a human being (myself, in the latter half of the Nineteenth Century, in America,) freely, fully and truly on record." [8] Or he asserts that he has tried "to articulate and faithfully express in literary or poetic form . . . my own physical, emotional, moral, intellectual, and aesthetic Personality, in the midst of, and tallying, the momentous spirit and facts of its immediate days, and of current America." [9] Yet one notices in nearly all these statements of purpose that expressing the self involves seeing it within its world and time. This is a natural consequence of Whitman's belief that while, in one sense, he is "a single, separate person," his selfhood is at one with the universal spirit and therefore with the whole of his world. Indeed, only as the self who sees this world, can the personality Whitman would portray be revealed. And Whitman's world is the world he now finds himself in. To show the self, he must show its "immediate days."

It should be clear that Whitman's purpose was not to be achieved simply by writing in the present tense, as poets, and especially lyric poets, have done in every age. The statements of a poem follow one another, so that even though every statement is cast in the present tense, the poem will still move forward as the present turns into a new now, and then yet another. To arrest this natural progression so that the whole of the poem would constitute one moment required innovations of a more fundamental kind. What is unique in Whitman's art can only be appreciated in terms of the radical way in which he has changed the very nature of poetry. Nor will it suffice to define Whitman's break with the literary past on the level of conscious beliefs alone. For his ideas, when considered by themselves, are hardly original. Those which do not have their source in Zeno or Lucretius are more lucidly expressed by Jefferson, Coleridge, or Hegel. They are Whitman's

8. "A Backward Glance O'er Travel'd Roads," ibid., p. 454.
9. Ibid., p. 444.

only in the sense that he has made them seem true within the imaginative world of his poetry. But even granting that he has created an original synthesis of familiar ideas, one must still ask why his synthesis is more valuable than the numerous other lay philosophies of the period. For myself, I do not see how a case can be made for the demonstrable truth of Whitman's beliefs. The poetry itself is the only demonstration. One cannot say why one feels he is "right" in principle, one cannot even say just what he means, without reference to his imaginative vision. One is brought back, always, to a way of seeing and, hence, to a mode of art.

What is unique in Whitman is the ordering of the poem. All the other kinds of originality depend upon and derive from this. To recognize that this is so, one need only consider why it is that Whitman's locomotives, canals, sailships, red-brick factories, and pioneer farmsteads have not taken on the quaintness of Currier and Ives but retain a contemporary look even a hundred years later.

To capture the now is not a new enterprise, but one which begins to appear in the literature of seventeenth-century New England. To Anne Bradstreet, as to Whitman, the self's true nature is to be found by finding its relation to eternal spirit, and the self's present condition—the way the mind now works—is the primary evidence. Yet "Contemplations" is so fundamentally unlike such a poem as "Crossing Brooklyn Ferry"—differs from it in ways which the Anne Bradstreet's differing idea of God and manner of speaking reflect but do not explain—that one may fittingly take advantage of the dissimilarity to bring out Whitman's new method. The crucial difference is one of point of view—not of the point of view of the poet at his desk, environed by his opinions, but that of the poet as character in the poem, uttering the lines. In "Contemplations" the poet and character are distinct. Mistress Bradstreet looks back toward herself in the moment of experience, speaks in the past tense, employs a poetic stanza so formal that her present way of speaking cannot be taken for speech spoken from within the occasion. The saying is not at one with the seeing. She can do no more, by way of placing herself in the character's present, than to quote what she then said to herself.

Whitman, of course, is separated from Mistress Bradstreet by the Romantic movement, and it may be granted that in Romantic poetry the poet as narrator and the poet as character are brought closer together, so that the poem's progression dramatizes, in an important degree, the development of the experience it describes. But usually the Romantic poem retains the status of a report, and when this is not so, it will, in any case, progress, thus portraying a change rather than a static duration.

It is not really until Poe that the narrator's and character's experience coexist in a present which constitutes the whole poem. Yet Poe regards the present as unreal; it is an appearance which turns into all times when its content is realized. The action of the Poe poem consists, therefore, in the destruction of the present by its conversion into eternity. It remained for Whitman to make the poem itself constitute a determinate present moment, so that all statements have the status of speech now being spoken, and all things perceived seem to exist as objects now appearing to consciousness.

That this was Whitman's essential purpose is evidenced by his awareness of how radically the new American poetry he attempted to write must differ from the literary modes of the past. "The expression of the American poet," he announces, ". . . is to be indirect and not direct or descriptive or epic." [10] The latter qualities are those of traditional poetry, and by habitually contrasting earlier forms with his own, he tries to show that the difference is one of method rather than merely of subject matter. He believed that the distance of the traditional forms from the facts of today is evidence not only of their being out of date but of their detachment from the present as it existed in any time. The result is an art of retrospection, an art which portrays the

10. Preface to 1855 ed. of *Leaves of Grass,* ibid., p. 413.

"mythical" in preference to the "demonstrable," an art which, though the best possible in its time, was never satisfying, because it fails to recognize that men "make their mark out of any times." [11]

Whitman's hostility to traditional forms is thus, in essence, a quarrel with an uncongenial sense of time. Epic, the archetype of narrative literature, disconcerts him because it carries the mind through a succession of moments, so that at each point the present is different, and other moments lie off as purely future or past. And "descriptive" poetry, though one cannot be sure just what he meant by the term, suggests talking *about* things as a process distinct from presently perceiving them. Without quite realizing it, Whitman insisted upon the difference between his art and that of the earlier poets, because he sensed that their methods precluded his own.

In the main, however, the contrast with the literary past is rhetorical, and Whitman has more success in explaining his art when he speaks of its effects upon the reader. He emphasizes, above all, the democratic nature of the new poetry. It is a poetry in which the excellence of all things is celebrated, a poetry about and addressed to the common laborer, a poetry announcing the gospel of spiritual brotherhood toward which mankind and the entire universe are tending. From these democratic purposes, it follows that the poem, as an act of communication, must function in a democratic way. In characterizing the new poetry as "indirect," Whitman means to say that instead of communicating through the poet's picturing and interpreting of reality, it will reveal reality itself, and the reader will know the poet's meaning indirectly, as the meaning which comes to him from the things he himself perceives. As Whitman instructs us early in *Song of Myself,*

> You shall no longer take things at second or
> third hand, nor look through the eyes of the dead, nor feed
> on the spectres in books,

11. Ibid., p. 412.

> You shall not look through my eyes either, nor take
>   things from me,
> You shall listen to all sides and filter them
>   from your self.[12]

It is not really as peculiar as at first appears that Whitman
should declare the reader's independence in sentences so obviously meant to tell him what to think. For it is in a poetry designed to let the reader have his own reactions that the poet's
overt explaining will be most apparent. Whitman's bold direct-
ness in addressing the reader reveals his desire to make even his
explanations seem items or data to which each reader may react
according to his own lights. The open road is Whitman's favorite image for the kind of experience his poetry offers, because it
symbolizes the reader's free participation. He himself travels the
road of the poem, and the things Whitman depicts are perceived
as if from his own immediate contact with the world.

> Not I, not any one else can travel that road for you,
> You must travel it for yourself.[13]

Of course, the road is actually of Whitman's construction; it
passes through his world, and the poet's firm guidance is not to be
escaped. Yet though the theory is questionable, the poetry often
makes it seem true. When Whitman is successful, the seeing is so
vividly a present event that we mistake it for our own.

This immediacy depends upon the illusion that the experience
is now transpiring, that the words are addressed directly to the
reader, and that the things and events of 1860 are immediately
before the reader's eyes. To achieve this effect, the poem's natural
progression must be arrested or concealed so that the present will
seem to remain the same moment throughout. If the passage of
time is at all noticeable, the whole character of the poem
changes. The poet and his day slide into the past, for the things

12. Sec. 2, ibid., p. 26.
13. Sec. 46, ibid., p. 64.

he names are not identical with the things the reader is now perceiving.

Whitman could believe that a perfect sharing of experience is possible, because he retained always at the back of his mind the belief that poetry could somehow present the objects themselves which are its subject. That notion receives its boldest statement in his remark that "the United States themselves are essentially the greatest poem." [14] The extravagance of the claim may well put us off, but it is really just another way of indicating the immediacy he sought. "The greatest poet," he explains, "has less a marked style and is more the channel of thoughts and things without increase or diminution, and is the free channel of himself." [15] The difficulty here is that if actual things are poems, then the best art is no art, and there is no room for poetry in the usual sense. But Whitman was saved from such despairing conclusions by his sense that things exist for us in the event of our experiencing them. Though as poet Whitman conceived of himself as a mere channel for "thoughts and things," he never forgot that these existed to him as a person, and his purpose was to make them exist as vividly to the reader. The objects a poem portrays, which, in a sense, *are* the poem, are not distinct from the self; they exist in the experiencing.

The poet's experience and the reader's can be identical because, as Whitman believed, the sense faculties and, indeed, the whole bodily nature of human beings are the same in their functioning. Hence his curious faith that the things he knew could be conveyed through the channel of his mind exactly as they are, unaltered by the poet's interpretation. "What I experience or portray shall go from my composition without a shred of my composition." [16] And it is significant, though generally overlooked, that Whitman believed he could depict himself with the same objectivity. "Walt Whitman, a kosmos, of Manhattan the son"

14. Preface to 1855 ed. of *Leaves of Grass,* ibid., p. 411.
15. Ibid., p. 417.
16. Ibid., p. 418.

may compass the whole universe and be God, but the poet is no more than the "free channel" through which this remarkable personality, like all other things, is conveyed. Whitman is the most impersonal of poets, an artist completely concealed by his fictive character, Walt Whitman, Poet, and a man who delighted in his own experience because he supposed it was absolutely everybody's.

To make the poem an image of the present, Whitman effected so radical a revolution in the basic arrangements of poetry that his innovations are not yet fully understood. One may best begin to describe this achievement by clearing away some likely misconceptions. First, one should grant that portraying the present amounts to a good deal more than simply proposing a new opinion about the nature of time. On this subject Whitman's beliefs are not, in fact, remarkably original: his sense of time is at most a variant of that which appears in the conscious theory of the transcendentalists and has its origin in the main tradition of American thought from Puritan New England onward. Moreover, Whitman does not deny the reality of linear time, and in studying his methods one must keep in mind the fact that temporal arrangement can be used to express almost any view of time. Thus some authors employ flashbacks to emphasize rather than arrest the smooth forward movement of time, while others use an exact chronological arrangement to cancel temporal progression by implying that since all moments are the same, time does not advance.

Whitman's innovations are not, then, to be lumped together with other striking experiments simply on the ground that all involve a radical reordering of the temporal elements. Sterne, Joyce, and Proust, to cite the three obvious examples, treat time quite differently from Whitman. For all Sterne's intricate confusion of past times, *Tristram Shandy* progresses through a sequence of moments in which Tristram composes it, becoming, toward the end, the narrator's diary. At no point is the whole novel viewed as the content of a single moment of consciousness.

Much less can it be said that the novel itself comprises a single moment. On the contrary, the present is always changing as the realization of the past widens Tristram's understanding. Joyce's *Ulysses* and *Finnegans Wake* are even more clearly novels of progressive action, whose unusual construction is due to the principle of "slow motion" concealed beneath the fantasia of linguistic experiments and variations. And it should scarcely need pointing out that Proust's novel is not the record of a single moment. Though its ultimate purpose is to reconstitute the past in the present, this is a goal toward which the novel advances, and Proust can make it known only by moving through numerous phases—often widely distant in time—as the final view is progressively developed. Since these notable experiments in literary time have been performed to such different purpose, Whitman's methods cannot be explained simply by observing that he too rearranges the temporal elements.

Nor can his method be understood as a mere alteration of the chronological scheme. It matters little how frequent or extensive are the elements of past and future introduced in the course of a work, for so long as it does have a course—so long, that is, as the work is conceived as an account of a movement from an initial moment to a later one—the form will be progressive, since there will be a changing present. In the poetry before Whitman the subject was a completed action or determinate sequence of events, which, as the Aristotelian formula happily describes it, has a beginning, a middle, and an end. An action of this sort is the natural subject of literature, because it accords with the sequential nature of language. A story, like a rational argument (which also expresses itself successively as a sequence of thoughts), moves forward as language does, by a sequence of sentences; it starts at one point and develops until another is reached, a new situation and a later time.

Whitman saw that the completion of the work need not coincide with the completion of the action. He doubted the necessity that the action should come to rest or that the reader must see its beginning in order that the poem may be unified and complete. Instead of an event, his subject could be an activity or continuing process, and the poem could then end, not when the action is completed, but when its meaning and significance are so fully realized that no more need be said.

In seeing matters in this way, Whitman did no more than bring to full consciousness and into the practice of poetry a principle which seems always to have been implicit in American literature. Such diverse works as Franklin's *Autobiography*, Cooper's *The Pioneers*, and Thoreau's *Walden* (or looking ahead, *Huckleberry Finn, Sister Carrie*, and *The Sun Also Rises*) do not come to a conclusion in the sense that events have rounded to a close. Even when the protagonist's story seems done, this story is but an example of an action which continues; it only holds together *as* a story when the events are generalized into a process—and the end is conclusive as the recognition of this process rather than as a last event.

Such characteristic American works achieve their effect by going with the forward movement of language, yet normally their method is that of "running on"—of repeating the same process in episode after episode, as the Puritan historians did, until, through an increasing explicitness and elaboration of parallels, the essential pattern of the process becomes clear. Time does not stand still. It flows forward endlessly, and only because this movement shows the same event occurring over and over again does the reader come to rest in the conclusion that any moment is an epitome of all the rest. *Walden* well illustrates this paradoxical conclusion. The "auroral hour," which Thoreau describes as the moment of perfected consciousness, and which corresponds to Whitman's "today," is the potential of every moment; but to reveal the "auroral hour," Thoreau must lead the reader through a sequence of phases, the psychic states represented by the seasons, to the final phase, which stands at the end as the goal at last achieved.

Whitman's problem was to find the means of concealing the

forward movement of literary time, so that it might appear that the present at every point in the poem is the same present. But in fact time does pass in the poem, and there is no way of stopping it. Not only do words and statements follow chronologically, but the reader too must move forward. He must know more at the end of the poem than at the beginning, and the development of his knowledge must be a temporal event, transpiring in phases as he moves from the first line to the last. To make the whole poem seem to be but one present moment is therefore to create a fiction —an illusion, if you will. And despite Whitman's intention to present things themselves, rather than images and interpretations, it is far less unreasonable to recognize his fiction-making than to suppose that there can be a poetry without illusion.

All modes of art involve feigning, make-believe, of course; otherwise, there would be no way of distinguishing works of art from other sensible objects, or the images they present from the realities imaged. That Whitman's feigning has rarely been discussed, that we find it hard to imagine that his poetry depends upon a fiction, that illusion seems entirely inconsistent with his whole view of poetry are indications of how far his fiction has succeeded. Perhaps his methods are so congruent with prevailing assumptions that we cannot recognize them as artistic techniques. Perhaps, too, Whitman himself was to a large extent unaware of the feigning his methods involve. For there is no reason to believe that in the writing of poetry only the conscious and calculating mind is engaged.

Since "Song of Myself" is the first of Whitman's major poems and, if not his greatest single work, at least his most ambitious one, it illustrates both his methods and his difficulties in a crucial way. The sensible reader will cling to a paradoxical opinion of this work. He will not let go of the belief that "Song of Myself" is a great poem. And yet he will not for a moment deny the feeling that there is something wrong with it. No viable interpretation can ignore either the greatness or the imperfection. To see that this is so, one need only consider the question of unity. It is impossible to determine whether "Song of Myself" is really one poem or a series of loosely related lyrics—a poetic cycle, one might say. The work is unified to such a degree that the lyrics lose much of their beauty and meaning when read separately. But while certain clusters of lyrics—27, 28, and 29, for example— obviously fit together, one feels that many others could be rearranged without serious loss. One cannot say that "Song of Myself" is so diffuse that it lacks design; but one cannot say, either, that it is as unified as it ought to be. Whitman apparently did not quite achieve his intention, yet the difficulties of "Song of Myself" are to be blamed less on his failure than on his readers' misunderstanding. The poem can make little sense unless its intention is understood, and to grasp what Whitman here attempted one must free one's mind from the idea that he meant to depict a progressive action. Criticism, however, has always tried to find the principle of unity in development of some kind.

The earlier critics usually attempted to define this pattern as an argument or progression of reasoning. They assumed that Whitman's ideas carry the poem through a dialectic from premises to conclusions. While such an approach will always be alluring to those who value Whitman mainly for his social and moral theories, its results are disappointing. To read "Song of Myself" in this way is to study the generalizing passages at the expense of the passages of vivid immediate picturing. If the ideas are regarded as the primary value, the images are, perforce, treated as mere illustrations. Since one illustration will do as well as another, the attempt to find the unity of "Song of Myself" in a philosophic rationale can only end by making this work seem hopelessly disorganized. For to grant that the poem is largely made up of random examples is to give the game away. Then, too, the generalizing in "Song of Myself" is so repetitious and so obviously lacking in logical order that discovering a line of reasoning involves a great deal of special pleading.

More recent critics have usually looked for a progression of action rather than of argument. James I. Miller, whose interpretation is the most interesting modern one, proposes that "Song of Myself" should be understood as a dramatization of mystical experience.[17] While granting that it is an "inverted mysticism"—a merging of the self with deity through carnal delight and vitalistic enthusiasm rather than self-denial—he nevertheless maintains that the poem depicts the self passing through the phases of the mystic's journey to God. To read the poem in this way is to regard its subject as a dramatic action and find its unity in the progression of events from an initial to a final state. But regardless of what mysticism truly is and of whether "Song of Myself" depicts it, it does not follow that because the experience is mystical, the poem presents the successive phases by which the mystic arrives at this experience. In fact, it would seem that to the extent that Whitman's experience is actually mystical, it could not be expressed as action. "Inverted mysticism" is merely an inconvenient definition, but dramatized mysticism is a contradiction in terms.[18]

The search for a progression, whether logical or dramatic, is defeated by the poem's circularity and repetitiousness, for the intended subject of "Song of Myself" is an activity rather than an action, and the various parts are joined together in that the same process is shown transpiring throughout them all. The poem begins by rendering the familiar duality of consciousness, the odd contrast between the self's sense of existing here in this particular place at this particular moment and yet, by the mind's power to

17. "'Song of Myself' as Inverted Mystical Experience," *PMLA*, 70 (Sept. 1955), 636–61.

18. Malcolm Cowley presents a more persuasive interpretation of "Song of Myself" as a poem of progressive action. "Its real subject is a state of illumination induced by two (or three) separate moments of ecstasy. In more or less narrative sequence it describes those moments, their sequels in life, and the doctrines to which they give rise; but the doctrines are not expounded by logical steps or supported by arguments. Instead they are presented dramatically, that is, as the new convictions of a hero, and they are revealed by successive unfoldings of his states of mind" ("Walt Whitman's Buried Masterpiece," *Saturday Review of Literature*, 42 [Oct. 31, 1959], 13).

entertain general ideas, existing also in all places and times: "I lean and loafe at my ease, observing a spear of summer grass," Whitman says, but he introduces this specific act of perception by a broad generalization: "every atom belonging to me as good belongs to you." This, in turn, initiates thoughts of the poet's past and of past generations before him: "Born here of parents born here from parents the same, and their parents the same." [19] Section 1 is programmatic, yet to understand the program it announces, one must understand the process by which the percept and concept, the present experience and generalization, are related. The first lyric is the nucleus of the entire poem, the first brief record of a moment which the other sections explore. In other words, the whole of "Song of Myself" is a picture of Whitman's state of mind as he loafs on a bank contemplating a spear of grass.

It is by virtue of the mind's transcendence that all the other sections and the diverse experiences they record exist merely as aspects of this experience or as views of the content of this one moment. To have an experience is to locate oneself in a here and now which can only be known with reference to other places and times. And, conversely, the here and now of one's immediate sensation imply a real world and history, which extend beyond the horizon of sense data. Whitman, as he loafs on the grass, is a person with a mind, and what he knows at this moment amounts to a good deal more than the place where he is and the objects he now looks at. To say, "I am here" implies some knowledge of geography. To say, "This is a spear of grass I see," implies knowing not only genera—plants as opposed to animals, for instance—or species—grasses as opposed to mosses—but the ideas of genera and species, and beyond that, an idea of a natural order. And to say, "I am I," implies the ability to bring all one's knowledge to bear at once.

Section 1 depicts the psychic activity of now having an experience. It presents, on the other hand, the process of locating the

19. Sec. 1, in *Complete Poetry*, p. 25.

self by moving in from general concepts to the particular objects of the present and, on the other hand, the complementary process of moving outward from the sense data to a transcendent vision of the world in terms of which the data are recognized *as objects*. These processes are interdependent. Neither precedes, or exists for the purpose of, the other. They are two aspects of one activity, two sides of consciousness.

"Song of Myself" portrays a series of transcendental journeys, each of which brings into view a different aspect of Whitman's world. This outward journeying is what the reader sees, the activity continually repeated, but it was Whitman's purpose to employ the journeying as a means of returning to the center. That is, the transcending is supposed to be an exposition of the thoughts involved—the areas of consciousness implicit in his present as he looks at the spear of grass.

While the poem does not quite fulfill this purpose, for reasons to be considered later, that it clearly was his purpose is evidenced by a memorandum for a lecture which describes certain exercises he would practice to put himself in a suitable frame of mind:

> First of all prepare for study by the following self-teaching exercises. Abstract yourself from this book; realize where you are at present located, the point you stand that is now to you the centre of all. Look up overhead, think of the space stretching out, think of all the unnumbered orbs wheeling safely there, invisible to us by day, some visible by night; think of the sun around which the earth revolves; the moon revolving round the earth, and accompanying it; think of the different planets belonging to our system. Spend some three minutes faithfully in this exercise. Then again realize your self upon the earth, at the particular point you now occupy. Which way stretches the north, and what country, seas, etc.? Which way the south? Which way the east? Which way the west? Seize these firmly with your mind, pass freely over immense dis-

stances. Turn your face a moment thither. Fix definitely the direction and the idea of the distance of separate sections of your own country, also of England, the Mediterranean sea, Cape Horn, the North pole, and such like distinct places.[20]

The resemblance of this passage to the panoramic visions of "Song of Myself" is sufficient to show that in the poem Whitman meant to capture the same sort of consciousness. What is most significant about the "self-teaching exercises" is that they reveal Whitman consciously training himself to see the remote as a function of the immediate. Thus, if in the course of "Song of Myself" he seems to have moved very far away from the moment of section 1, it is nevertheless from this point of view that all the distant places and times are perceived.

The Whitman poem typically begins with an introductory section in which an epitome of the whole poem is presented. In the maturer and more firmly structured poems this preface is clearly marked. The long, one-sentence opening of "Out of the Cradle" and the first four sections of the Lincoln elegy illustrate well, because they so obviously precede the narration of the past remembered. In the first five sections of "Song of Myself" the same sort of introduction is to be found, though its outlines are fainter. After the picture, in section 1, of the poet loafing on the grass, the next three sections are composed of announcements which describe his present attitudes, beliefs, and feelings in a highly abstract manner. These generalizations have the purpose of sketching the broad assumptions the mind brings to the moment and finds confirmed there. They can also serve to announce the poetic program, because the premises of Whitman's experience are the premises of the poem as well. The ideas emerge from section 1 by a process of amplification. "I permit to speak . . . Nature without check with original energy" turns into the passage beginning

20. *Walt Whitman's Workshop*, ed. Clifton Joseph Furness (Cambridge, Harvard University Press, 1928), p. 189.

"Urge and urge and urge," while "what I assume you shall assume" is amplified by the advice to the reader at the end of section 2.

To the extent that there is any vivid imagery of things outside the present in these sections, it has the rhetorical status of mere illustration. Most especially this seems true of the scene in section 3 in which Whitman pictures himself in bed in the morning after his lover of the night before has departed. Yet illustrating is a faint version of transcendental journeying. Though to visualize the rooms of houses and "the bank of the wood" is to depart from the now, the reader does not at first notice this departure, because the things pictured are only typical and are confusedly generalized.

In section 5 the transcendence becomes explicit, as Whitman recalls a particular experience in the past. It is a love experience and is not only more elaborately detailed but placed and identified as that one specific past event. This act of remembering presents the first full dramatization of the self's ability to project itself from the present into a distant place and time. Yet "project" is not really the proper word. Whitman finds himself in the past experience by virtue of living in the present one. As he now lounges on the grass, he remembers a similar occasion, and what he then felt and learned crystallizes and interprets his present mood. Looking back from section 5, one can see that all has tended toward this act of memory, that the confused blending of nature imagery and erotic sensations has anticipated the recollected love scene, just as the generalizing has prepared the way for the sonorous announcement that love is the kelson of the creation with which section 5 closes. That declaration summarizes not only the meaning of the moment remembered but of the present moment. To realize what he now means to say is, for Whitman, a process of realizing what other moments of experience meant and mean. Like the first description of the thrush in the Lincoln elegy, section 5 brings the introductory portion of the poem to a close. The whole poem has been presented in small, and the rest of "Song of Myself" is a realizing, through amplification, of the experience here portrayed.

This is not to say that after section 5 Whitman merely repeats himself. As the process of transcendence is continually reenacted, it takes a great variety of forms. There is cataloguing of a simple kind—as in section 15, where perceptions are merely itemized—and there is a more elaborate cataloguing, which has the effect of creating a landscape panorama—as in section 8—or a historical tableau, sometimes one which reaches back into prehistory—as in section 31. Then there are passages in which the poet pauses to sketch a picture: sometimes a mere vignette, such as that of the wounded soldier, sometimes a more detailed portrait, like the one of the runaway slave in section 10. And at least once, in the story of the "old-time sea-fight," the poet interpolates an extensive narrative.

Such variety not only serves to mitigate repetition, but has the more important function of illustrating the many different ways in which the act of transcending occurs. Though it remains essentially the same process, it takes different forms, and through Whitman's variations the reader is made aware of the multiplicity of perceptual modes which consciousness involves.

One of the most effective variations of transcendence is given in the account of the rich lady and the twenty-eight bathers. She stands "aft the blinds of the window," secretly watching the young men (whose number corresponds to her age), yet through her intense longing she is with the bathers also.

> Where are you off to, lady? for I see you,
> You splash in the water there, yet stay stock still
>   in your room.[21]

Her presence is revealed through her absence; it is the sharp and absolute distance between her window and the shore that makes her unity with the bathers a poignant psychological truth. The episode would be far less effective if it were only the woman who

21. Sec. 11, in *Complete Poetry*, p. 31.

existed doubly, but the poet, in visualizing her, repeats the same process in a more subtle way, entering into her consciousness, becoming both the lady at the window and the lady in the water, while as spectator, viewing the scene as a whole, he too remains detached—"aft the blinds" of his own window.

By turning from this elaborately developed episode to a sequence of briefly noted experiences, the reader can appreciate the different, yet equally brilliant, effect Whitman can produce by a sharp focus:

> The little one sleeps in its cradle,
> I lift the gauze and look a long time, and silently
> brush away flies with my hand.
> The youngster and the red-faced girl turn aside up the
> bushy hill,
> I peeringly view them from the top.
> The suicide sprawls on the bloody floor of the bedroom,
> I witness the corpse with its dabbled hair, I note
> where the pistol has fallen.[22]

The first of these little sketches has a beautiful immediacy. Seeing the baby seems a matter of pure sensation. No ideas, no thinking "about" what Whitman sees, seem to be involved, and poet and baby merge by sharing a mood of innocent, simple presentness. The concepts participating in sensation—the ideas of delicacy and helplessness, for example—are as faintly subliminal as the impulse to brush away flies. By contrast, seeing the "youngster and the red-faced girl" is quite a different experience, one in which reasoning is more explicit, and the facts discerned are more clearly mental events. The very distance of the poet, as he voyeuristically watches the couple disappear, demonstrates the transcendence by which, in thought, he enters into the urgency and guilt of their desire. The suicide scene, with its melodramatic, detective-story evidence, illustrates transcendence in still another form. Here the inferences by which the poet understands

22. Sec. 8, ibid., p. 30.

what he sees are made by the calculations of conscious reason. Such transcending makes not for a finer type of experience but for one which may be shallower, less complete, yet it is a different mental activity, another potential of thought. Taken together, the three scenes illustrate the way Whitman's perspective continually alters, even in a short passage, so that each object seen seems to dramatize a new way of seeing.

One cannot, then, speak of Whitman's cataloguing as if it were always done in the same way and required no more skill than the composition of a laundry list. The catalogues have been deplored ever since Thoreau dropped the remark about a thousand brick, and it may be conceded that often they are prolix recitations of items cited at random. But it does not follow that cataloguing is wrong on principle; much less, that it is an artless procedure. Many of the catalogue sections in "Song of Myself" are brilliantly successful, and the best of them render kinds of experience which could not be expressed in any other way. The following passage from section 15 will serve to show how skillful the choice and arrangement of items can be:

> The bride unrumples her white dress, the minute-hand
>   of the clock moves slowly,
> The opium-eater reclines with rigid head and just-
>   open'd lips,
> The prostitute draggles her shawl, her bonnet bobs
>   on her tipsy and pimpled neck,
> The crowd laugh at her blackguard oaths, the men
>   jeer and wink to each other,
> (Miserable! I do not laugh at your oaths nor jeer you;)
> The President holding a cabinet council is surrounded
>   by the great Secretaries,
> On the piazza walk three matrons stately and friendly
>   with twined arms,
> The crew of the fish-smack pack repeated layers
>   of halibut in the hold . . .[23]

23. Ibid., p. 35.

The reader must be refused any explanations which would relate items in a reasoned way in order that he may perceive the subtler connections between the bride's rumpled dress and wedding-night nerves and the prostitute's rag of a shawl and shrill defiance, between the scoffers surrounding her and the cabinet members surrounding the president and the twined arms of the matrons circling each others' waists. There is a delicate modulation from restless calm to torpor and then to violence, from official dignity to the serenity of an evening stroll, and at last back to calm again, the stillness of the packed fish. The disorder of the bridal costume turns by degrees into the order of the halibut.

Such connections are, as it were, nervous events. The items catalogued are distinct from the self, as individual objects, but in their relations to each other, as things perceived, they contain the mind; they embody the pattern which is the observer's thought. Since the self is its consciousness, the way in which the diverse things it knows relate to each other illustrates a form of transcendence. For as the reader sees the items listed developing toward a pattern, he recognizes the presence of mind "out there" among them. Thus the catalogues are often formed on some obvious principle of association—lists of sounds, parts of the human body, animals, objects found in a particular region, phases of a historical event, or examples of religious creeds, professions, biological species, and the like—so that all seem both to emerge from and return to the idea in the observer's mind.

While the catalogues are often pertinent and brilliantly managed, this is not always so, and some of Whitman's lists represent well the diffuseness which has led many readers to conclude that "Song of Myself"—and, indeed, the larger part of his poetry—is formless. The frequent failure of the catalogues to function as they should is but a consequence of a more general failure—a failure in the whole conception of the poem. "Song of Myself" is designed to give the total content of present consciousness, but that consciousness has no clear limits. Everything the poet can bring to mind is potentially relevant, and Whitman would entertain us by showing how wide a circle we must draw about the now. Yet if this moment is not defined clearly enough, if it is not objectified in a set of immediate sense data, there can be no standard of relevance, no way of discerning what the multiplicity of other experiences are relevant *to*.

Charles Feidelson describes the problem with consummate precision when, in speaking of Whitman's indeterminacy, he observes that by transforming the poet from "a contemplative eye" to a "voyaging ego," Whitman effects a "large-scale theoretical shift from categories of 'substance' to those of 'process.'" [24] "A poem, therefore, instead of referring to a completed act of perception, constitutes the act itself, both in the author and in the reader." [25] The poet, he concludes, cannot very well avoid "diffuseness and arbitrary choice of materials," since "whatever the nominal subject, it is soon lost in sheer 'process'; all roads lead into 'Song of Myself,' in which the bare Ego interacts with a miscellaneous world. . . . When the subject is endless, any form becomes arbitrary." [26] The poet's difficulties, then, are the result of having abandoned the usual means of outlining his subject.

Whitman's subject is not, as Feidelson correctly observes, a "completed act of perception," but it does not follow from Feidelson's astute analysis that no other subject is possible. In fact, Whitman sought for and soon found a new principle of limitation in the concept of the present itself. For him all is process except the experiential moment. The now abides, and indeed it is only because of its fixity that process can be perceived, either in a Whitman poem or any other context. Since process is temporally indeterminate—a continuous activity which never comes to an end—to conceive of a process one must form the idea of a present duration, for if time passes during the present, any activity must reach conclusion and constitute an event, not a process, while

24. *Symbolism and American Literature* (Chicago, University of Chicago Press, Phoenix Books, 1959), p. 17.
25. Ibid., p. 18.
26. Ibid., pp. 19, 25.

processes in past or future presuppose what is then the present, a now of the same kind.

As a span of time which the mind defines by the walls it constructs against past and future, the present limits experience and renders it determinate, despite the endless variety of other experiences which are implicit in its content. For Whitman the reality of the present seems to be beyond question. Its "constructed" character does not trouble him, if, indeed, he is aware of it, yet pointing out the subjectivity of the now does not really disprove its usefulness as a principle of form. Logic suggests that the present is only a point moving along a line, and theoretically every moment identified as now is divisible into smaller units, but in experience the duration of the present proves very real. We live in it as we live in a house, occupying the whole of its time at once, even though actually located in but a portion of that volume.

Because time is a dimension of reality, not a distinct object, the now can only be defined with reference to the sense data it presents. Just as a person knows where he is in space in terms of the objects about him, so his present location in time is indicated by the things he now perceives. But in "Song of Myself" this immediate landscape is not distinct enough. Whitman supposed that the moment could be symbolized by a single object, the leaf of grass, and hence he returns to that image frequently, repeating it yet once more at the close of the poem:

> I bequeath myself to the dirt to grow from the grass I love,
> If you want me again look for me under your boot-soles.[27]

Yet the leaf of grass does not seem continually present, and Whitman's far-ranging thoughts merely leave it behind, rather than developing from his perception of it.

Not that the image itself is unsuited or uninteresting, but no single object can suffice to represent the moment. A set of related images is needed, since the present is a situation—a landscape

27. Sec. 52, in *Complete Poetry*, p. 68.

and a system of circumstances. The absence of these is grievously felt in "Song of Myself." "The past and present wilt," Whitman concludes: "I have fill'd them, emptied them,/ And proceed to fill my next fold of the future." [28] Clearly, we are meant to feel that his present state of consciousness has been filled and emptied too—that through the poem the moment's entire content has been realized. But it is rather too like a glass of water without the glass. Since the present has no clear bounds, its elements are not sufficiently unified. Hence the "running on" and the effect of prolixity.

The poem holds together because, to a remarkable extent, Whitman has succeeded in creating the impression that at every phase the same activity is proceeding. But it is impossible to maintain the highest intensity throughout a poem of such length, and the plebeian passages create pauses, so that the next rise to intensity suggests movement to a later moment. For this reason there is an appearance of progression, yet since the poem is designed to circle rather than advance, the forward movement reaches no destination, but meanders in random loops as it doubles back upon itself.

Because the reader is inadvertently led to expect a kind of development Whitman did not intend, he is apt to think the poem far less unified than it actually is. To say that "Song of Myself" is unorganized and inchoate is to comment on the poem's architecture, yet in any work the grand design—the pattern one sees by viewing it panoramically as a whole—is but an outward form whose meaning and value grow out of the more fundamental unity one discerns in the ordering of language in particular passages. The ultimate source of form is style. It is through his way of combining words that the poet so synthesizes opinion, feeling, and point of view that a mode of experience is created. And while style is form seen close up, this local ordering is not confined to the passage in which one finds it; it is also projected outward. The moments of highest consciousness in a poem not only focus

28. Sec. 51, ibid.

but radiate meaning, infusing their significance into the other passages, which they interpret by the perspectives they create. True, each center of energy is acted upon by the others as well as acting upon them, but it is qualified in the same way that it qualifies. That is, the local ordering is what creates these relations between passages, and the sum total of such relations is not the same thing as architecture, which stands merely as a symbol of them, rationalizing as a logical scheme (and always a rather simplified one) the unity they present as an experience.

The most vivid moments reveal the form of a whole work. They are, in fact, the true source of any unity a work can have. What they reveal is not a grand design but the way of experience which makes that design convincing. That is why a Shakespearean soliloquy, an episode from *The Prelude*, or a stanza of Yeats' is hardly meaningless when read by itself. Though much is lost, so much still remains that the passage appears a poem in itself, having its own completeness and order. Were this not so, quotation would be a vain practice, but the imaginative reach of a single line or even a phrase indicates that there is a unity which subsists beneath the grand design and yet is different in kind.

This is not to say that architecture is of no importance. The reader must visualize the unity of the work as an all-inclusive pattern as well as an ordering of language, because as he reads a poem or novel, he is engaged not only with the page before his eyes but with the whole work. The transcendent and immediate views are equally necessary. But an architecture which is irrelevant is worse than none at all. If the grand design is a pretense, if it only misrepresents the form seen in local passages, it becomes perfunctory, like the neat tying up of plot ends in a novel by Scott. That in Romantic literature the traditional genres have already lost most of their authority and are made pertinent mainly as parodies or mere parallels to the true form of the work is a sign of the growing irrelevance which led Whitman to scrap them altogether. "Song of Myself" is a work without architectonics, and lacking a grand design to symbolize its unity in an outward and obvious form, it seems much more incoherent than it really is. It has an exclusively inward life, which one is conscious of but cannot fully recognize—a synthesis of feeling and perception which is ever-varying, yet always consistent. It is perhaps all to the good that the greatest American poem must be appreciated by responding to its essential and poetic rather than its merely rational form.

Whitman's development after "Song of Myself" is toward a poetry which explores a determinate present. The problem he faced in 1855 was that of finding a way to keep the moment continually before the reader, so that the transcendental journeying would depart from and circle back to the same present and identical experience. To achieve this effect, he created three main kinds of poetic form, which, for lack of more suitable terms, I shall denominate the meditation, the song, and the imagist poem. Not all the poems written after 1855 are to be so classified, but there are few valuable ones that do not tend to one or another of these forms. A reasonable estimate of Whitman's achievement must, I think, concede that a large portion of *Leaves of Grass* is not very good. To make a case for the artistic success of the whole body of his work is a futile undertaking and can only end in the devaluation of what is best in his poetry. Like Wordsworth, Whitman must be judged by his finest poems, not ignoring the tracts of dry and uninspired stuff, but not assuming, either, that his poetry is formless (or, as the social critics would have it, that form does not matter anyway), because one cannot find a form which gives artistic validity to all the poems. Much of his verse is formless, yet every fault in poetry, Whitman's or any other poet's, is a case of formlessness.[29] There is no other way to fail; and conversely, a poem succeeds only through a realization of order.

29. All other kinds of failure are instances of formlessness, because all are failures to achieve the degree of coherence necessary to constitute an experience. The bad poem does not hold together (is self-contradictory) because it has not found a footing in the phenomenal world, and vice-versa.

In Whitman's finest poems the design tends to take one of the three forms I have indicated.

The song is the simplest of these. In such poems present experience is symbolized by a single object—the redwood tree or the military drum, for example. The song consists of the associations this object brings to mind, and which, by appearing to consciousness, manifest the transcendental activity. If not the least effective way of organizing a poem, it is the one most liable to the vagueness typical of Whitman's failures. Since the associations the symbol evokes need not be relevant to each other but are united merely by their common reference to the object which suggests them, there is a centrifugal tendency. Whitman supposed this could be overcome by returning, again and again, to the governing image, but too often the reader has a sense of being dragged back. The intention of the song is to portray the experience of now perceiving some one thing—of focusing upon the object before one's eyes—by the process of realizing its total context, and in the best of Whitman's songs this sort of drama is very neatly brought off.

"Song of the Broad Axe" is a superb example of the song poem, though even here the danger of formlessness is apparent:

> The shapes arise!
> Shapes of the using of axes anyhow, and the users
> and all that neighbors them.[30]

The seeming casualness of such lines is appropriate to the poem's rationale. The lines exemplify Whitman's central argument that seeing the axe involves the awareness of its functions, the places in which it is found, the meanings it has had in various other times. And in demonstrating the way the geographical and historical contexts arrange themselves around the object now perceived, the poet shapes his associations with great skill. The first section presents an epitome of the whole poem. The opening close-up view—"Weapon shapely, naked, wan"—quickly expands to a

30. Sec. 9, in *Complete Poetry*, p. 141.

306

scene, as the object is spatially located—"Resting the grass amid and upon,"—and then turns into an indefinitely broad panorama.[31] From this point on, the poem continually alters perspective between the inclusive and sharply focused view, as when the ranging survey of lands in section 2 suddenly narrows to the picture of a farmstead.

As the cataloguing of the present uses of the axe opens into an analysis of the psychic traits of the users, their intentions, and what the ideas which motivate them intend, the reader comes to realize that just as the shapes the axe now cuts are continuous with the more general forms in terms of which men think and act, so the whole form or order he recognizes as the present is only to be perceived by seeing also the shape of history and that dialectic of which the modern age is the latest phase.

Throughout the poem's development there is a continual variation between particular object and general concept, the form of the axe and the form of the world in terms of which it is an axe. The poem concludes on the highest level of generalization— "Shapes bracing the earth and braced with the whole earth"—but Whitman would show that the most abstract statement can yield the most specific meaning.[32] An axe has its own very definite shape, but to make an axe or to recognize one when one sees it is to discover the form of the universe in the particular object, and the whole of history within the moment of experience.

The great defect, or at least limitation, of the song is its dependence upon a single symbol, for this isolated percept cannot create a picture of the speaker's present situation. Who, for example, is the speaker in "Song of the Broad Axe"? What are the circumstances within which he speaks the lines? One can only answer that he is the bard and speaks out of duty, as the spokesman for all humanity. But a spokesman for all humanity tends to be no one in particular. His vision is so nearly limitless that one cannot discern the personal point of view which is supposed to be

31. Sec. 1, ibid., p. 133.
32. Sec. 12, ibid., p. 142.

its center. When selfhood becomes so indeterminate, Whitman smilingly dissolves into the annihilating unity which terrified Poe. It is a matter of emphasis that makes saying "the present is really all times" different from saying that "all times are really present." Whitman favored the latter statement, and that makes all the difference between his vision and that of *Eureka*, but when he errs, it is frequently by a twist of the tongue which turns his statement back into Poe's. When his skill began to leave him in later years, the failure involved, if it did not result from, merging personal identity so fully in universal sympathy that he became that formless cloud-shape, the Good Gray Poet. This depersonalization is always the danger in the song poems, most regrettably in "Song of the Exposition," which begins rather well.

On one occasion, however, the depersonalizing effect of the song poem proves an advantage. In "Beat! Beat! Drums" the speaker's situation is precisely that of having no situation, of having lost his identity. The poem depicts the intrusion of general circumstances upon personal ones, which they cancel and replace. The onset of war overrides all private concerns, negates the self's intentions, feelings, and beliefs in favor of communal ones. By its power to redefine other people's situations, the marshaling drum also redefines the poet's role. His aloofness is in fact his involvement. He becomes a mere voice—the voice of the community which has preempted his selfhood—and in proclaiming the dissolution of all warm, human ties, he says not what he would but what he must. Thus the fading of his identity is itself the central fact of his personal experience. The depersonalization of war is universal, and to hear its inaugural drum is to experience the death it brings to every man, for that is the drum's meaning to every man who hears it. Yet many are deaf, and the poet must shout to the drums to beat still louder. Paradoxically, the deafness by which a person seems to preserve his identity destroys it, for by failing to see that war cancels selfhood, he ignores a fact of his own situation and is false to his own experience.

What I have termed the meditation is a far richer and more satisfying poetic form than the song, because in it the self's immediate percept is an entire setting or landscape. Many images that comprise the present vision may serve as symbols, but they all coexist as elements of a larger whole, and it is the total landscape that symbolizes the now. Such a landscape is by nature a situation—a dramatic situation, the situation of the persona as an individual, the world in which he now finds himself, and whose contents, various but unified, are the things he now perceives.

"Crossing Brooklyn Ferry" is the first of the great meditative poems. It was published but a year after "Song of Myself" and so indicates how quickly Whitman solved the problem which beset him in "Song of Myself." Instead of a spear of grass, "Crossing Brooklyn Ferry" presents an entire landscape. Whitman depicts the process by which his immediate perception of the scene leads him to place it with reference to other times—most specifically to the future, in which other voyagers will see the same landscape. The transcendental voyaging by which he comes to share the experience of future generations and of his reader, however distant in time, develops directly from the objects before him. The objects begin to relate to each other as the poet draws off; and they form into an elaborately detailed scene only when he has so far transcended his own time as to see the panorama through the eyes of future men. Though eventually he seems to depart from the scene altogether, this proves to have been no absence at all, for when the landscape description is recapitulated at the end, it becomes clear that his journey was but a circle around the present—a tracing of its psychic horizon, one might say. And within the landscape all things circle because all are cyclical. The flowing river, the shuttling ferry, the rising and setting sun, the circumnavigating merchant ships, the circling gulls—all manifest the indeterminate happening which merges present and future, while as separate objects now seen, these images distinguish the two, so that times stand apart and the journey from present to future is possible.[33]

33. See James W. Gargano, "Technique in 'Crossing Brooklyn Ferry': The Everlasting Moment," *Journal of English and Germanic Philology*, 62 (April 1963), 262–69.

"When Lilacs Last in the Dooryard Bloom'd" is essentially the same in its form as "Crossing Brooklyn Ferry." Both poems explore a present whose symbol is an entire situation, and in both, this situation is at once a landscape and a set of personal circumstances. The elegy appears to be a more consciously "symbolic" poem, because the key images seem to make a more definite kind of reference. Their greater explicitness is partly a result of the poet's movement backward into the past rather than the future, and partly the consequence of treating a familiar public occasion. Considered by themselves, past events seem determinate and fixed. But of course they should not be considered by themselves, for they cannot be separated from consciousness. What happened is the emergence of a meaning as well as the transpiring of an outward event, and the meaning is still in the process of developing as consciousness itself develops—a process which cannot reach conclusion until the last day. For consciousness is never strictly personal: the more fully it is realized, the more it tends to include and merge with the experiences of other selves. Even so, past events do seem to exist in their own right, independent of thought. They are, we say, facts of history, and it is the public view, the view projected by written history, that objectifies them and thus holds them confined in a past epoch, where they must perforce exist as merely completed events. Thus in one sense the public view contravenes experience, where past events still transpire as elements in the process of presently developing thought. But without the public view there could be no personal experience, for the self must take its vision as a vision of the real world, and the real world is real as the world of everyone's experience. Because Lincoln's death is a public and therefore historical event, it poses in the most explicit form the problem inherent in all the objects of experience—that of reconciling the community's view, which objectivity predicates, with the self's personal response.

Indeed, the public character of the event is an essential aspect of the poet's own response to it. The conventional attitudes are partly his, and so, in the elegy, the symbol must include the fixities of popular opinion, combining them with the poet's purely private associations. The shadow covering the land is the blackness of funeral drapery and serge suits as well as the cloud enveloping the poet's mind; similarly, the lilac appears as a sprig placed on the coffin along with senatorial wreaths.

The relation of private to public fact suggests still another quality of the poem, its traditional character. "When Lilacs Last in the Dooryard Bloom'd" is not only an elegy but, by its apotheosis, invocations, floral offerings, and concluding consolation, announces itself as a specimen of this conventional genre. For this reason also, its symbolism appears to be more definite. While the images are things the poet perceives and which have a symbolic meaning within his own experience, they also have the status of public symbols, which the conventions of the elegy give a fixed meaning. For instance, the poet saw the star "drooping" in the western sky just before Lincoln's death, and therefore it becomes for him a personal image of the dead man. But it also has this meaning with respect to the system of public recollections we call the elegy, where the star has always served as a traditional symbol of the person mourned. At times the public and private views coincide, and the star *is* Lincoln. But just as often the star is quite separate from the man, as we see in the last lines. Whitman's symbolism is far less schematic and fixed than the parallels to literary tradition make it appear. When the star is not Lincoln, its meaning is no more specific than those of the landscape images in "Crossing Brooklyn Ferry."

The point, of course, is not that the traditional symbolism is false, but that only a private symbolism can make it true. The poem is an original work rather than a magpie's nest of conventions, because the poet's own psychological process gives the old genre validity. Interpretations usually err because they attempt to explain the poem through fixed definitions of its symbols. Star, lilac, bird, and cloud are not objects having separate meanings; they are things perceived in experience, and their meanings (so shifting and elusive) are to be discerned in the particular moment when the images reveal their meanings. If in order to compass the conventional public view of Lincoln's death, Whitman has restored a conventional literary form, he has done so by destroying its conventionality—by rediscovering the symbols of tradition in sense data. It is the self's moment of consciousness that gives the public view whatever truth it may have. Considered in this light, the governing images lose their rigidity: they are objects of sense first, but in that they refer the mind of the perceiver to realities outside of the now, they reveal the power of transcendence which enables it to possess the present—to look down from above upon its own state of mind and see what the symbols can mean there.

It might be said that the subject of the elegy is the odd fact of memory. Like "Crossing Brooklyn Ferry," the elegy begins with the report of present experience, and what is now happening is remembering:

> When lilacs last in the dooryard bloom'd,
> And the great star early droop'd in the western sky in
>   the night,
> I mourn'd, and yet shall mourn with ever-returning spring.[34]

That Whitman grieved for the dead president is shown by his memory of having grieved. In the recollection of mourning he mourns again and realizes he always will mourn, for present remembering makes certain a repetition of the act of remembering.

> Ever-returning spring, trinity sure to me you bring,
> Lilac blooming perennial and drooping star in the west,
> And thought of him I love.[35]

One should note how inconsiderable the more specific meanings of lilac and star are at this point in the poem. Here they are symbols only in that they belong to spring, and it is the present as a whole that symbolizes the moment remembered. That the poet will always remember is assured by the fact that spring will al-

34. Sec. 1, in *Complete Poetry*, p. 233.
35. Ibid.

ways return. Thus though the lilac, with its sweet blossoms and "heart-shaped" leaves, suggests love—and more specifically, Whitman's love for the great man departed—it is symbolic first because it is "perennial." It will always bloom because spring will always return. The same may be said of the evening star, whose setting suggests Lincoln's death. Not the qualities of objects but the certainty that they will return each spring is the source of their symbolic meaning. For spring is the permanent aspect of the moment remembered, and the sense objects it brings have the power to evoke memory, because they are now just as they were at the time remembered.

Lincoln died and the poet, now either in the next spring or imagining he is, finds he must mourn anew. Memory brings back the past, and to understand his present state of mind he must relive the experience of a year ago as if it were the present. Thus he is overwhelmed again by the blind sorrow of that time:

> . . . O the black murk that hides the star!
> O cruel hands that hold me powerless—O helpless soul
>   of me!
> O harsh surrounding cloud that will not free my soul.[36]

And again the events of a year ago are presently happening. The coffin passes across the land now, just as the lilac blooms and the thrush sings now. Until the fourteenth stanza, past and present events transpire together as present happenings, for such is the power of memory that there is no clear division between the two. The moment remembered is an aspect of the present, because he is now remembering it.

The development of the poem is not, then, progressive but exploratory. It is a realization of the present moment effected through the process of continuously enlarging the consciousness of what that moment contains. While the first four stanzas may be taken as a simple present—the spring a year after Lincoln's death

36. Sec. 2, ibid.

—even there the enlargement is seen. The lilac, by stanza 2, is more definitely placed—"In the dooryard fronting an old farm-house near the white-wash'd palings"—and details of shape, color, and smell are recognized.[37] The poet breaks a sprig from the bush, repeating, though he does not yet recall it, his tribute of a year ago. And when he again hears the bird singing in the cedar swamp, we see that his memory has developed a great deal further—so far that specific lessons emerge to consciousness. The song, he tells us, is "Death's outlet song of life," and in this para-dox the resolution that the entire poem moves toward is con-tained.[38]

The first four stanzas are, then, a paradigm of the whole poem, containing not only a first glimpse of the main images and a first hint of the essential thought of the moment remembered, but, as it were, a brief enactment of the way the poem develops. The enlargement of memory, the increasing awareness of what it con-tains, is the main principle of form; the rest of the poem is but an ampler and more explicit portrayal of the moment seen here in small. It may be asked how a poem so constructed can ever arrive at a conclusion: the answer is to be found in the process of mem-ory itself.

In remembering, the poet may relive the past as if it were now transpiring, but he is also aware of the whole course of that expe-rience at once. He is conscious of the "powerful western fallen star" and "Death's outlet song of life" simultaneously, whereas in the original experience he perceived the first before the second. As a record of remembering, the poem must therefore combine these two views: what happened must unfold temporally as a story, because that is the way it originally transpired; but it must also be seen as a whole, in one instant.

The skill with which Whitman makes memory appear at once chronological and simultaneous is the most remarkable aspect of the poem and his greatest formal achievement. The early remark

37. Sec. 3, ibid.
38. Sec. 4, ibid.

314

that the thrush's song is "Death's outlet song of life" is a clear token of his method. The poet tells the story of how he came to terms with his grief and at the same time constantly reminds us that he is already reconciled to it. The bird's aria in stanza 14 is but an ampler statement of the acceptance of death which the poet has voiced much earlier. "Not for you, for one alone," he chants, placing his sprig of lilac on Lincoln's coffin:

> Blossoms and branches green to coffins all I bring,
> For fresh as the morning, thus would I chant a song for
>   you O sane and sacred death.[39]

And by his repeated addresses to the bird—"I hear, I come presently, I understand you"—he sustains this awareness of what the song means throughout the narrative of his search for that meaning. In other words, the poem can end, because the memory explored contains its own conclusion. In reliving his suffering, he also rediscovers the wisdom that resolved it.

That the mourner is also the elegist furthers the union of the simultaneous and chronological views:

> O how shall I warble myself for the dead one there I
>   loved?
> And how shall I deck my song for the large sweet soul
>   that has gone?
> And what shall my perfume be for the grave of him I love? [40]

These are the questions the elegist faces, but clearly they also express the questions of the mourner of today—and of a year since. The elegist's search for form enacts the same paradoxical hunting for what he already knows that we have observed in the mourner's search for meaning. As Feidelson has pointed out, the poet is writing the poem at the same time that he tries to decide what sort of a poem it will be.[41] One can understand, then, why

39. Sec. 7, ibid., p. 234.
40. Sec. 10, ibid., p. 235.
41. *Symbolism and American Literature*, pp. 21–23.

Whitman thought it important to emphasize the traditional quality of his symbols. As elegiac conventions, they are symbols of the poetic process; and by his use of them, the poet creates the effect of knowing throughout the poem the literary form he seems, at the same time, to be in the act of discovering.

The search for meaning and the search for form both have as their object the thrush's song. The aria symbolizes both the bard's poem and the mourner's meaning. Yet if, as I have argued, the song in both these aspects is something the poet knows all along, why is his realization of it delayed for some thirteen stanzas? This question can be easily settled by considering the kind of meaning the thrush offers. His song comes as a resolution of the poet's sorrow. It is an elaborate lyric celebration of the thought of death as "sane and sacred." Death is "soothing," a "Dark Mother" who comforts, and a "strong deliveress" who redeems. While such an attitude toward death is not difficult to understand or express, it will only seem convincing if the poet can show that it is justified by the mourner's experience. If, taken alone, the aria recommends rejecting experience by an escape into comfortable unconsciousness, then instead of voicing the significance that the poet seeks in his past, it is merely a giving up of the quest and can tell us nothing either of Lincoln's death or the poet's life. The song is meant to tell us *what* to think, rather than *not* to think—to determine our feelings, not to negate them—and it can only do this when it is perceived within the experience which it at once crystallizes and resolves.

Since this experience is the extremely complex one of remembering, the cedar swamp must be approached through the circuitous route of the first thirteen stanzas, in which Whitman's winding course enacts the process of memory. Hearing the thrush at spring's return, the poet discerns in its song the meaning he heard the year before: memory makes the song what it now is, but to hear the song truly he must rediscover the memory it wakes. And so too must the reader. To be told flatly that death is good is not enough; he must be given a vision of a world in which such a statement is true.

What transforms the song from mere noise or any tune into the particular melody the poet hears is, then, the process of memory, and in stanzas 5 through 13 this process is traced through the gradually widening view of the moment remembered. The lilac soon ceases to be the particular bush in the dooryard. It blooms throughout the spring landscape which the funeral train crosses, and, as the poet's offered sprig, takes its place as a somewhat whimsical item in the panoply of official mourning. Similarly, the star is now seen within the completed recollection of how the poet watched it sink lustrous beneath the horizon one evening the April before, a sight he now beholds again, just as he again looks about him at the flowered countryside. By these stages our vision is widened until, from more and more widely focused scenes, we at last come to see the whole spring landscape spread before us, and the poet's gaze now includes all that he then looked out upon.

Of the landscape scenes, critics have generally said little, yet they are of the greatest importance in bringing the poet's meaning forward. He offers them in answer to the question of what "pictures" he should hang on the walls of Lincoln's tomb. Being both mortuary ornaments and "pictures of growing spring," they manifest yet more broadly the paradox Whitman hinted at in speaking of "Death's outlet song of life" and in describing the funeral train "passing the yellow-spear'd wheat." [42] Into these landscapes the key images merge and disappear. The lilac is absorbed in the burgeoning greenness, the "drooping" star is replaced by the setting sun, and the black cloud becomes identical with the shades of evening and morn. For these images hold attention by their reference to the past, and as memory recovers it, reference fades and the symbol returns into its oneness with the

42. Sec. 11, in *Complete Poetry*, p. 235; sec. 4, ibid., p. 233: sec. 5, ibid., p. 234.

thing symbolized. When the past is fully present to the mind's eye, there is no need for symbolism.

The landscapes present not only a wider view than the preceding sections but a more precise one. In seeing a larger number of things, one is enabled to see them more exactly, for only in such a panoramic vision are the total relations of objects discernible. Of these relations, that which seems to govern and explain the rest is the mutability of all the things. "The indolent, sinking sun," "the workmen homeward returning," "the sparkling and hurrying tides," "the gentle soft-born measureless light" of dawn, and every other object perceived are changeable things, poised delicately at the moment of passing away.[43] But the flux has its permanence, and things are not active at random: there is a cosmic routine in the commuting, blooming, and stellar rotation. Things become to cease and depart to return. Every aspect of landscape is embraced in this basic cyclical movement, an effect greatly aided by Whitman's swift changes of time from sunset, to dawn, to noontide, and thence again to "eve delicious, the welcome night and the stars." [44] The beauty of the last phrase shows how skillfully he has managed to make the landscape itself express the resolution of his grief. The black cloud, when at last seen in experience, is the darkness of night, the death which leads back to life, a necessary phase in the eternal process of becoming.

Such a resolution seems facile when stated thus baldly, but in the poem it becomes convincing because there the reader is shown how the poet arrives at it. In seeing how the past is repossessed at the advent of "ever-returning spring," we come to recognize the cycle as an event of consciousness. That Lincoln as Lincoln will return to life because the lilac blooms every April is an idea tactfully avoided. The resurrection is only that of life itself. The poet can repossess the life of his past in the present because death has made that past memorable. One is consoled, then, not because the life cycle assures immortality, even of a very impersonal sort, but because without death there could be no life. To

43. Sec. 11, ibid., p. 235; sec. 12, ibid., p. 236.
44. Sec. 12, ibid.

live is to experience the present, and there can be no present without a past, and hence without the passing of time which brings all things to death. Doubtless Whitman goes as far as his discretion will allow in implying more optimistic conclusions: that since life can never really end, death is but a rest and the soul somehow endures. In the world of the poem these are by no means dismissible notions, but the ground of whatever truth they here may have is present experience, the moment of full, delighted, and loving perception. To realize such consciousness is to win a great deal from death. The victory is achieved by remembering. Memory, by showing how death makes the present what it is, reveals death as itself the condition of experience.

It is in stanza 14 that the past is at last fully repossessed:

Now while I sat in the day and look'd forth,
In the close of the day with its light and the fields of
    spring, and the farmers preparing their crops

· · ·

I saw the ships how they sail'd,
And the summer approaching with richness, and the fields
    all busy with labor,
And the infinite separate houses, how they all went on,
    each with its meals and minutia of daily usages,
And the streets how their throbbings throbb'd, and the cities
    pent—lo, then and there,
Falling upon them all and among them all, enveloping me
    with the rest,
Appear'd the cloud, appear'd the long black trail,
And I knew death, its thought, and the sacred knowledge of
    death.[45]

That the poet here retrieves the ultimate memory, the precise moment when he saw the full meaning of death and could accept it, is beautifully evidenced by the way that the shifting and vari-

45. Ibid.

ous landscape views here become fixed and definite. The preceding scenes are composed of rapid glimpses, but now all things exist within a single view and are seen as if from a single point of vantage. Further, the time of seeing, which before was rapidly altered through the phases of day and night, is here arrested at the moment of sunset. The perfecting of the visual focus is identical with the perfecting of thought; the unity of life and death implied by the previous landscapes is consciously perceived. The shadow of night falling across the land is seen, now, as identical with the shadow of grief, which seized the nation a year ago and now holds the poet again—the shadow of the funeral train winding across the April landscape, the shadow enveloping the star. Since death is universal—like night, it covers all cities and people —it is the source of that sympathy which causes man to mourn, of the love which creates grief. And since death is a function of time, without whose passing there could be no past with respect to which the present exists, without death there could be no experience either. Through memory, the poet has regained "the sacred knowledge of death," the knowledge of its necessity to life.[46]

Only after his eyes open to this vision can the poet listen to the bird, whose aria at last bursts forth upon the night, celebrating rapturously the feelings of calm acceptance and relief from pain. These emotions can only seem ethically right or intellectually meaningful when death, like night, can be viewed as a phase in the cycle of life.

One should note, also, that only when death is so viewed can the public and conventional attitude toward it become acceptable. The nation buried Lincoln as a president and war leader, whereas Whitman mourned him only as an individual—"the sweetest, wisest soul of all my days and lands." [47] The offering of the lilac sprig seems, therefore, an eccentric gesture in the ceremony of public mourning, and it is not until the bird's aria has been heard that the poet can combine the public view with his

46. Sec. 14, ibid.
47. Sec. 16, ibid., p. 239.

own, seeing Lincoln's death as a valid symbol of the war and realizing that the agony which is real and must now be accepted is that not of the fallen but of those who live to mourn them. The vision of the battlefield is the last-presented evidence of the reconciliation the poem offers, because it is the most general—the evidence which the community shares and its historians record. Whitman's ability to come to terms with his own grief is both a cause and an effect of discovering his solidarity with the people of America, through sharing in the common grief. In finding that death creates love, which in turn overcomes it, he finds the basis of community, which is also the basis of communication and therefore of poetry.

The poem ends in a beautiful diminuendo. The images from which Whitman's experience developed fade from consciousness as the moment of remembering is completed. Lilac, star, and bird are "twined with the chant" of the poet's soul.[48] The chant is the poem, and uttering the poem's lines is the same as the remembering that the poem depicts. No poem could be more conclusive, and the artistry of its ending shows more clearly than anything else Whitman's ability to organize time in such a way that the poem exactly coincides with the moment it portrays.

At the crucial moment the poem takes a peculiar turn. Until stanza 14 everything is reported in the present tense, but when death is at last understood, Whitman shifts to the past. Some readers may take this as evidence that the poem is progressive in form, after all, but I think a different and quite significant conclusion should be drawn. Let us say that when a memory is fully developed, the mind can see and accept the pastness of the time remembered. The present is not the past or any other time. It is solely the moment it is, and its reality depends upon its separateness. It is the vague, half-formed memory that seems to make the past and present identical, and active remembering begins at just this point. Confused, overmastered, oppressed by inexplicable feelings, the mind starts trying to remember what it remembers.

48. Ibid.

One restores the limits of the present by reestablishing the distinction between remembering and what it reveals. To fully understand one's present experience is to recognize that the past is really past except as a memory. Whitman's shift to the past tense signifies his full realization of the now. Grammar parallels vision; the past falls back into its proper place just as the shifting imagery at last composes into a single and coherent landscape. Realizing the meaning of "the thought of death"—the mere idea, on the one hand, and the mere feeling, on the other—the poet possesses the "sacred knowledge of death," the understanding that "tallies" the thrush's song. He can now look back, for the present is restored; therefore he can also foresee, and the poem ends with a look toward the futurity in which he will continue to remember. But this is to return to the beginning, to the poem's very first sentence: "I mourn'd, and yet shall mourn . . ." One can appreciate the difference between the poem of realization and the poem of developing action by considering what we know when we read the last sentence that we did not learn from the first.

The third kind of poetic form which Whitman used most effectively is that which is to be found in what I have termed the imagist poem. But before turning to works of this type, it will be best to take a look at certain characteristic techniques. Most of these are obvious and have long been recognized, yet they continue to seem somewhat idiosyncratic because their relation to form remains obscure. My point will be that their expressive function and propriety, as elements of Whitman's idiom, become clearer when they are understood as devices meant to create an effect of presentness.

The most striking technique is that of giving the symbol an exaggeratedly "symbolic" character. This is mainly achieved through naming the symbol frequently and in more or less identical language. Thus lilac, star, and bird not only function as symbols but seem to announce themselves as such, so that we are certain of their symbolic character long before we can discover what they symbolize. The effect is to make the symbol persist as something we are constantly perceiving. It becomes a static point of reference which conceals the poem's real progression by anchoring all its phases to the first phase of experience.

The "framing" of the great meditative poems is the most ambitious application of this technique. By describing the landscape at the beginning and then repeating the description almost verbatim at the end, Whitman makes the poem seem to conclude where it began, thus disguising the poem's inevitable forward movement so that it seems only to be realizing things present to consciousness throughout.

The symbolic function itself becomes a symbol, and this accords perfectly with the elaborate confusion of times in the Whitman poem. As the now comes into focus, the poet shifts by carefully masked gradations into a number of other moments, while at the same time remaining in his original present. A time past or future becomes the present, and the earlier present is viewed as a moment remembered or foreseen. *Out of the Cradle* illustrates this perspectivism in its most complex form. It contains at least eight distinct levels of time. Among other curiosities to be observed there, one can see a moment which is future from one point of view and past from another, uniting with a moment future in both respects. This merging is meant not to destroy temporal distinctions but, on the contrary, to prove them real. The poem is to be made identical with the present it explores. Hence the poet's now and the reader's must unite, an event which presupposes a distance between them. The two nows unite not as the same time but as the same experience in the same world, a world whose historical phases are different, so that times are distinct, yet a world which is always realizing the same meaning, so that each present contains the other.

The transcending, the crossing from one present to another, is outwardly symbolized by Whitman's addresses to the reader. Our present and his are united in that the poem is what he now says to us. They are also given this immediacy by Whitman's technique of making a prominent symbol in the poem a symbol *of* the poem also. The thing we perceive, the thrush's aria or the sea's whisper, becomes identical with the poet's chant, so that the symbol—the song or the whisper—is the poem.

Though the ways in which Whitman's style serves to render the present are often obvious in principle, close examination shows them to be subtle and various in application. For example, it was no remarkable insight on Whitman's part to realize that speaking always in the present tense would be the proper procedure, yet his handling of verbal forms shows great artistry. Consider, as an instance, the first of the lyrics in *Children of Adam.*

> To the garden the world anew ascending,
> Potent mates, daughters, sons, preluding,
> The love, the life of their bodies, meaning and being,
> Curious here behold my resurrection after slumber,
> The revolving cycles in their wide sweep having
>   brought me again,
> Amorous, mature, all beautiful to me, all wondrous,
> My limbs and the quivering fire that ever plays through
>   them, for reasons, most wondrous,
> Existing I peer and penetrate still,
> Content with the present, content with the past,
> By my side or back of me Eve following,
> Or in front, and I following her just the same.[49]

The effect the participles create of a continuing action expresses perfectly the union of personal and historical views. Whitman's presently seeing the world is the same as seeing it at its first moment, because the world in his perceptions is as fresh as the original garden. By a broadening inclusiveness, the participles issue into phrases rendering the poet's sense of his body. Since he sees the world through his sense faculties, his body creates the world seen. At the center of the now the completed action which sums it up is expressed in the present indicative: "I peer and

49. Ibid., p. 69.

penetrate still." The lovely garden is seen to be identical with the act of love, by virtue of the creativity of sensation; and when the participles resume, opening outward again in the listing of things seen, Eden is Eve, and the poet simultaneously her mate, her descendant, and her heavenly father, as we see him in Adam, walking with her in Paradise. The present cannot always be made to depend so entirely on verbal forms, but this short poem reveals how much the simple act of predicating that an event "happens" or this "is happening" can do to create duration. Whitman relies upon the use of the present tense very heavily, and almost always the other verbal forms are found in the subordinate elements of sentences in the present indicative.

Closely allied to this manner of using tense is Whitman's obvious taste for parallelism, a device he exploits in every imaginable way.[50] Not only individual words or phrases but syntactical forms are repeated, providing one of his most effective means of making the sentence hover and delay so that its meaning seems to expand rather than advance. Most of his catalogues are conducted in this manner. Phrases of identical syntax, all being tied to the same element of the main clause, seem to unfold from it when it comes first, and hang awaiting its explanation when it brings the sentence to a close.

Indeed, Whitman is the master of every trick for concealing the forward thrust of sentences. By inverting the normal word order, confusing tenses, separating the main elements, smothering the grammatically important under the subordinate, confounding participle and gerund, noun and verb, appositional phrase and subject, he makes the sentence itself seem suspended in midcourse.

Whitman's distinctive use of rhythm and meter manifests the same intention. The extremely long line he favors has the effect of forcing the reader to linger over it as if it were an independent unit rather than a phase in a succession of units. And within the

50. See Autrey Nell Wiley, "Reiterative Devices in *Leaves of Grass*," *American Literature*, 1 (May 1929), 161–70.

line the feet are so varied in length that the dominant beat does not habituate the mind to a uniform pace; one is hurried or delayed rather than smoothly carried along by a recognizable cadence. These effects of stasis are further augmented by end-stopping, which is to be found in all but a very few of Whitman's lines.[51] End-stopping, when combined with the other rhythmic qualities, creates the impression that each line is a fresh version of the previous ones, expressing the same point in a different form instead of introducing distinctly new material. Any one of these rhythmic devices could be used to quite different effect, of course, but in combination with each other and with Whitman's special subject matter and point of view, they function to express continuous duration in the movement of language itself.

The vacillation in Whitman's language between a high and low style reflects and is to be explained by the contrast, noted at the beginning of this chapter, between the excessively general and the minutely particular. The former tends to be allied with the bardic manner, the prophet's style, grandly resonant, dignified, rhetorical, embellished at times with an elegantly traditional word or phrase: "To me the converging objects of the universe perpetually flow." Yet in the next line the elevated language is replaced by a markedly colloquial style: "All are written to me, and I must get what the writing means." [52] This pair of lines from "Song of Myself" illustrates Whitman's habit of juxtaposing the two. Often, as here, the effect is somewhat comic, but humor is just one aspect of the tone such contrasts create. In these lines from "Starting from Paumanok" there are frequent shifts from the high to low style, yet the effect is not bathetic:

> Having studied the mocking-bird's tones and the flights
> of the mountain-hawk,
> And heard at dawn the unrivall'd one, the hermit
> thrush from the swamp-cedars,

51. See Robert D. Faner, *Walt Whitman and Opera* (Philadelphia, University of Pennsylvania Press, 1951), p. 192.

52. "Song of Myself," sec. 20, in *Complete Poetry,* p. 38.

> Solitary, singing in the West, I strike up for a
>   New World.[53]

The styles, then, are high and low with regard to their perspectives, not their emotional freightage.

Since it conveys a strong sense of the past, the bardic manner suggests traditional pieties, general knowledge, and abstract ideas. It is the language of oratory and Pisgah visions. It represents the poet's transcendent self, the self who surveys reality broadly from a remote point of vantage, from which he can look down the vistas of time to first and last things. Playing against this, the colloquial manner depicts the poet as he is engaged—standing in a particular place and time, talking as people do in their personal relations and practical affairs. The sudden shift from one manner of speaking to the other enacts the change in point of view—an event which is, of course, of the greatest importance to the whole meaning of the Whitman poem, for in such a movement the transcendental process is revealed. The rise from the colloquial to the bardic manner portrays the enlargement by which the mind ascends from the scene immediately before it to those broader views in which other times in their relation to it can be seen. Conversely, the swift drop from the high to low style, dramatizes both the mind in its return to the landscape and its present and the merging of transcendent realities into particular sights. For example, in the following lines on the mocking-bird the colloquial tone of the clause—"it came to me that what he really sang for"—serves to anchor the general to the immediate.

> As I have walk'd in Alabama my morning walk,
> I have seen where the she-bird the mocking-bird sat
>   on her nest in the briers hatching her brood.
>
> I have seen the he-bird also,
> I have paus'd to hear him near at hand inflating his
>   throat and joyfully singing.

53. Sec. 1, ibid., p. 15.

> And while I paus'd it came to me that what he really
>   sang for was not there only,
> Nor for his mate nor himself only, nor all sent
>   back by the echoes,
> But subtle, clandestine, away beyond,
> A charge transmitted and gift occult for those being
>   born.[54]

How else but by the grit of ordinary speech could the ponderous latinity—"clandestine," "transmitted," occult"—be sustained? By blending the bardic and colloquial ways of speaking, Whitman unites the all-times of the seer with the right-now of the earth-bound individual.

The Romantic poets also worked to bring the elements of time to unity, of course, and in their poetry, no less than in Whitman's, the merging of times reflects a concern to show the unity of things in experience. The marked differences of style result from the more fundamental difference between his sense of time and theirs. For the kind of time a poet assumes largely determines his use of language by defining the speaker and his world. Through its radical influence upon the relations between thought and its objects, and more importantly upon the relations between events in the mind, the poet's time establishes the laws of psychological process and thus the stylistic decorum—both the words, or diction, and the way words behave. In a representative passage from *The Prelude* we see Wordsworth working to suppress the very contrasts Whitman's style depends upon.

>   . . . But, ere nightfall,
> When in our pinnace we returned at leisure
> Over the shadowy lake, and to the beach
> Of some small island steered our course with one,
> The Minstrel of the Troop, and left him there,
> And rowed off gently, while he blew his flute
> Alone upon the rock—oh, then, the calm

54. "Starting from Paumanok," sec. 11, ibid., p. 19.

> And dead still water lay upon my mind
> Even with a weight of pleasure, and the sky,
> Never before so beautiful, sank down
> Into my heart, and held me like a dream! [55]

This exquisite rendering of a nature experience depicts transcendental unity, to be sure, but the event is of a kind which would be grievously distorted by the shifting perspectives Whitman favors. Here mind merges with landscape through a language of double reference. "Calm" and "still" denote mental and physical qualities at once, and Wordsworth's psychological terms rather strongly suggest the language of physics—the "dead still water *lay upon my mind . . . with a weight* of pleasure." This merging has been carefully prepared for in the preceding description of the landscape, whose physical reality is seen, not in sharply outlined objects, but in physical qualities—"night-fall," "the shadowy lake"— and in objects which are so generalized that they suggest formless substances—"the beach," "the rock," "dead still water." The suppression of the particularity of objects—the hypothetical "some small island" is a charming instance—does not make the objects seem less physical. If anything, their solid immediacy is emphasized by blurring their outlines, since this tends to unite them as parts of a single scene. At the crucial moment mind and landscape merge through the mediation of the most unformed of visible things—water and sky—physical qualities so generalized that they seem ideas also, and therefore qualities of mind.

The event Wordsworth describes is not a sudden realization; it is a smooth, progressively developing flow of perception into meaning. The effect would be destroyed by any hint that the present is a distinct duration. For to Wordsworth time is a continuum in which the past evenly advances toward the present, like a rising wave. The past and present are united, as parts of the stream of time, different sections of the same river. Though Wordsworth liked to argue that in retrospection one can under-

55. *The Prelude*, Bk. II, in *The Poetic Works of Wordsworth*, p. 644.

stand what in experience one merely feels, the emergence of understanding is portrayed by retracing, in thought, the smooth progression of some portion of the past toward the present.

To create this effect of continuity, it is essential that the past be kept at a distance from the present so that the flowing of the one into the other can be seen. Wordsworth does not project himself directly into the time remembered or relive it as if it were the present; he sees it as what it *was*. Thus his manner of speaking must be sufficiently elevated to represent the poet's detachment from the time he looks back upon and to convince us that he has a broad enough view to see a moment so far off. In such poetry it would be unfitting to allow the humble vocabulary Whitman prefers, as, for instance, "row-boat" for "pinnace" or "flute-player" for "minstrel," since colloquial terms imply too close a view. Instead, the manner of dignified and philosophic generality must be sustained throughout, in order that the poet's point of view may remain on fairly high ground. For the effect of smooth continuity Wordsworth requires, there must be a steadiness of tone which Whitman's sharp contrasts and shifts of perspective would deny.

For Whitman, however, the unity of time is always curious, because the present is so distinctly walled off from other times that their implication in it appears to involve, always, the mind's miraculous overleaping of the wall. Instead of a temporal continuum, there is a continuous movement on the part of the poet, whose present perceiving commits him to endless commutation between the now and other times markedly distinct from it:

> In vain the speeding or shyness,
> In vain the plutonic rocks send their old heat against
>   my approach,
> In vain the mastodon retreats beneath its own powder'd
>   bones,
> In vain objects stand leagues off and assume manifold
>   shapes,

> In vain the ocean settling in hollows and the great
>   monsters lying low,
> In vain the buzzard houses herself with the sky,
> In vain the snake slides through the creepers and logs,
> In vain the elk takes to the inner passes of the woods,
> In vain the razor-bill'd auk sails far north to
>   Labrador,
> I follow quickly, I ascend to the nest in the fissure
>   of the cliff.[56]

It may seem unfair to compare this passage with the one from Wordsworth, because here Whitman is not viewing a particular landscape or recollecting a particular experience. But the difference has its source in the two poets' differing views as to what in fact a landscape and a personal experience are—as to how they should be delimited. Whitman would say that a landscape contains everything the mind's eye can see at the moment of perception. Thus the prehistoric mastodon and the contemporary auk are coexistent, since, through the mind's transcendence, the extinct species can be seen within the visible panorama. Yet while the remotest things imaginable can be brought into the present, Whitman can only show them as immediately here by emphasizing their remoteness. They are not seen in process, developing toward the realities of today, but are present in that we see how the poet transcends the now in the act of bringing them to mind. Thus Whitman uses collage rather than blending. Even his most fully visualized landscapes are composed of sharply outlined objects in distinct times and/or places, and the moment of such experience is exclusively present rather than a time segment in which the present shades off imperceptibly into the past.

Climbing the auk's nest illustrates the difference well, since it is such an un-Wordsworthian example of merging. It is the distance of things in space and time that reveals their unity in experience.

56. "Song of Myself," sec. 31, in *Complete Poetry*, p. 47.

Here all the objects illustrate the "speeding or shyness" which, when the poet sees it in the commonplace snake, he also sees it in the mastodon "beneath its own powder'd bones." The paradoxical presence of things remote is a consequence of the poet's point of view: he sees things both within a limitless panorama and very close up. Hence the style is marked by a sharp contrast between the generalizing, prophetic manner, with its elevated diction—"plutonic rocks," "manifold shapes," "I ascend"—and the colloquial idiom—"stand off," "lying low," "takes to."

The parallelism expresses this double perspective rhetorically. Whitman's view is so broad that only a few sample items of all that he sees can be named. On the other hand, each of the objects listed is viewed so closely that the view of it excludes the rest. The incantatory repetition of "In vain" suggests the elevated tone of the seer, yet the equality of the parallel phrases creates the impression that each line reports a momentary personal gimpse. Wordsworth's flowing blank verse, in which enjambment serves to make the lines run smoothly into each other, would have the effect of concealing the gulfs of time that Whitman's mind overleaps. Each of Whitman's lines is a capsulated perception, whose air of independence plays against the unity the parallelism creates. Whitman's is not a late Romantic style which has merely been "brought up to date" by colloquial mannerisms and references to things modern but a fundamentally different style which is designed to render organic development through process in a static present rather than through temporal continuity.

If the difference of style shows Whitman's distance from the Romantic age, it also serves to illustrate the respects in which he anticipates the poetry of the twentieth century. We have seen that his way of using language is very largely determined by that duality of consciousness which commits him to view all things simultaneously from the point of view of eternity and from the present moment. Logically, these points of view are absolutes: the transcendent view can include no less than all things in all times (in a "cosmic vision"), while the close view can present only immediate sensations. But neither way of seeing exists by itself, and Whitman's essential program may be described as a demonstration of their coexistence and implication in each other. Just because this is so, Whitman could at times throw his weight entirely to one side of the contrast. If either mode of vision contains the other—if the vision of the all is a definition of the now and vice versa—then by portraying one, the other will also be depicted.

Whitman was inclined to push this logic rather far. For the sake of argument, suppose that such reasoning carried him to the point where transcendence became pure consciousness. At that point the self would no longer range the universe freely but know all of it at once, and thus, just as in Poe, cease to be a self by becoming indistinguishable from the universe. Or supposing that a like extreme were reached in the other direction, so that sense became absolute and the self disappeared into its perceptions. In either case, Whitman would then have arrived at a poetry in which there is no ego to perceive and no objects of perception, a poetry of pure sensation, whose meaning seems entirely contained within the sensation itself. These suppositions show how swiftly Whitman's line of reasoning leads to imagism—a doctrine that I take for granted is impossible for poetry, and one long since abandoned, but that is nevertheless important because it made explicit certain assumptions which continue to flourish.

In proposing that the purpose of poetry is to render pure sensation, imagism expresses, though perhaps too narrowly, the prevailing modern belief that the vision poetry gives must have its origin in immediate experience and, in turn, be validated there. While immediate experience is personal experience, of course, in sensation the personal is objectified: feeling and thought are transferred from the observer to the things he experiences—the objective correlatives. Thus imagism stands as a good example of the way the effort to achieve immediacy puts the self's identity in doubt. How urgent the problem has become of finding for the self a new basis of identity is revealed by a number of characteristically twentieth-century notions—the mask, the finite center, the ordered experience, the collective unconscious, and the mythic character—all of which serve as attempts to reconcile personal identity with the fact of its dispersion outward into the things perceived, things which are not, of course, really things any more, but percepts.

Most poets who tried imagism soon abandoned it because they quickly discovered that it was not possible to write poetry of much value without implied commentary and judgment. The effort to exclude these merely made them indefinite and groundless, so that the advantage of putting people back in poems was soon recognized. But the characters that now appear are of a different kind. They are not selves in their own right but percepts. That is, they exist either as persons known to the invisible observer or as his self-images—fictional versions of his real personality. Thus the poem composed of the perceptions of an imaginary personage or of the poet in one of his masks can make more sense than the imagist poem of pure sensations only to the extent that somehow it gives an account of the perceiver of the perceptions. Such poetry locates value in immediacy, and the more it elevates the thing-as-seen as the most absolutely real phenomenon, the more it tends to depress the perceiver. His identity is reduced to what he perceives; he becomes no more than the consciousness the poem expresses. He is, in Whitman's phrase, "both in and out of the game," but so far in that he is just one of the objects he observes, and so far out that he disappears into the firmament of possible points of view.

This "invisible poet," as Hugh Kenner terms him in speaking of Eliot, is really Whitman's dualistic ego developed to either of the logical conclusions I have described: become either all-inclusive consciousness or no more than the sum of its perception. This self is not, of course, the actual Eliot or Williams or Stevens or Frost, but the perceiver implied by the percepts, and poets such as these are not so much concerned with autobiography—the apparent egotism of some of them being really a consequence of the way the known self has turned into a mere character—as with the problem of how any selfhood is possible. Having assumed that the percept is the ultimate reality, they find the experiencing self scattered throughout space and time, and seek to reconstruct a mosaic portrait of it from the shale-heap of its accumulated perceptions. But the little squares of immediacy only exist when looked at closely, and as one draws back to view the face they delineate, it disappears. Like Whitman, the modern poet must therefore commit himself to a double view and depict percepts of a kind that indicate the immediate and transcendent modes simultaneously.

As a very simple instance, consider the following poem by William Carlos Williams:

BETWEEN WALLS

the back wings
of the

hospital where
nothing

will grow lie
cinders

in which shine
the broken

pieces of a green
bottle [57]

In the immediate view the transcendent view is implicit. Recognizing that the blind court is a place where nothing will grow involves the thought of places burgeoning with vegetation; seeing the "shine" of the coldly glittering glass involves comparing it with a sprouting plant. There are sunny meadows "between the walls," after all. The symbolist poetry of Eliot and Yeats represents the dominant mode of poetry in the first half of the twentieth century, because its method is the most consciously and obviously designed to present symbols which express both the

57. *Selected Poems* (Norfolk, Conn., New Directions, 1963), pp. 57–58.

immediate, momentary perceiving and a meaning which is time-less. For only such percepts can provide the present with a past and future and the naked eye with a historical body.

How close Whitman came to the situation in which the best modern poets have found themselves, and how relevant his art therefore is to the poetry of our time, is best illustrated by his short imagist poems. Most of these are to be found in poetic cycles such as "Children of Adam" or "Drum, Taps." "Cavalry Crossing a Ford" is probably the finest example:

> A line in long array where they wind betwixt green
>   islands,
> They take a serpentine course, their arms flash in
>   the sun—hark to the musical clank,
> Behold the silvery river, in it the splashing
>   horses loitering stop to drink,
> Behold the brown-faced men, each group, each person
>   a picture, the negligent rest on the saddles,
> Some emerge on the opposite bank, others are just
>   entering the ford—while,
> Scarlet and blue and snowy white,
> The guidon flags flutter gayly in the wind.[58]

Despite the exhortations to "behold" and a faint element of com-mentary, Whitman's essential method is the imagist technique of conveying, or seeming to convey, meaning through sense data alone. All the sights and sounds are contained within a single scene and so within a single moment of experiencing. There is no overt reference to anything beyond the present either in space or time. Instead, the details create an instinctive awareness of things remote, whose relation to the sense data gives the scene its special significance. The river, for instance, is not merely a visible reality, for to see it as a river is to intuit its entire course and bring to mind places far beyond the range of sight. Similarly, the troops'

58. *Complete Poetry*, p. 215.

"serpentine course" depends upon the intuiting of their journey as a whole. As they cross the ford, the cavalrymen are seen in an isolated moment, yet by their positions—"some emerge on the opposite bank, others are just entering the ford"—all phases of the crossing are observed at once. The march is a certain event, though even from a Union balloon only one phase of it could be seen at one time. The river's flowing and the cavalry's advance symbolize the wholeness of time and space. Whitman stresses the arrested quality of the objects seen—the men's faces are picture-like, the horses pause—to demonstrate the implication of other times in the present and other places in the visible scene. But the unity one intuits by locating the landscape within wider ranges of space and time is also a unity of values. Though within the scene all is sunshiny, musical, relaxed, it contains the grim reali-ties lying beyond the horizon. The march, the battle, and the war are aspects of immediate sensation. At the end their presence is crystallized in the image of the gayly fluttering guidon flags, whose function it is to point the way toward the bloody fields ahead. The flags define purpose, and though they are merely guidon flags uniting the cavalry troop by pointing to its particular purpose, the proximate military goal cannot be separated from the commanding general's intent, nor that from the nation's pur-pose, which, whether right or wrong, is ultimately moral. To per-ceive is to evaluate: as one sees the scene by intuiting its relation to the world of space and time, one intuits its place in the world of values also, and if the intuition reveals some sad truths, the process of recognizing them bears witness to the reality of values.

Such a poem represents the consummation of Whitman's effort to allow the things of experience to reveal what he believed were their own intrinsic meanings. But if one asks where the self—either as poet, character, or reader—is to be found, one must answer that it has melted away, disappearing into the particular object seen, on the one hand, and into the world as a whole, on the other. To arrive at the immediacy the poem achieves is to arrive also at the situation of the modern poet, who is faced with a terrifying depersonalization and must seek, always, a new basis for believing in personal identity.

Whitman's guidon flags have the outward status of symbols—symbols for the cavalrymen as well as for the poet and reader. Like the spear of grass or the lilac in the dooryard, they are symbols of symbolizing. But to a greater or lesser extent the same is true of all of Whitman's images: the way they mean is always an important aspect of them, because Whitman's perspective is such that every object in the poem is to be considered as an event of perception whose meaning is inseparable from the way it happens.

For this reason Whitman should be placed in the American symbolist tradition with Hawthorne, Melville, Poe, and the transcendentalists, yet such a judgment will not be very useful unless one has an idea of where the tradition itself should be placed. Did it simply spring up in a quite untraditional way? And did it come to a close with the nineteenth century? The example of Whitman affords some answers to these questions. Unlike Hawthorne or Emerson, he does not derive directly from Puritan tradition; unlike Poe or Melville, he grew up in a milieu in which the institutionalized culture of library, church, and classroom did not press so heavily upon the mind. Thus the symbolist nature of Whitman's art seems largely the consequence of instinct and a habit of mind. The same is probably true of American symbolism in general. It seems to have developed from prevalent assumptions of the American mind rather than strictly literary influences. And when its relevance to the literature of the present century is considered, though it seems dead or moribund as an influence, it is very much alive as a state of mind. Again Whitman illustrates the point well. Considering his achievement, his influence upon later American writers is remarkably slight. Ezra Pound, Hart Crane, and William Carlos Williams acknowledged a debt to him, and in *Four Quartets* the recollections of *Leaves of Grass* are extensive and subtly pertinent, but only special pleading could make a case for the thesis that Whitman is a primary source of modern American poetry.

Nevertheless, it is equally foolish to ignore the many respects in which Whitman's work anticipates and resembles the best American poetry since his time. For Whitman expressed one version of a mode of experience which still prevails in America. "Ahead of Whitman, nothing. Ahead of all poets, pioneering into the wilderness of unopened life, Whitman." [59] Lawrence's praise may turn out to be nearly true. If the reader regards his grandiose philosophic statements as dramatic utterances rather than axiomatic beliefs and has the courage to judge the poems, so that in his mind the many inferior ones do not damn the rest, he may discover that Whitman's advice is still timely:

> Failing to fetch me at first keep encouraged,
> Missing me one place search another,
> I stop somewhere waiting for you.[60]

59. *Studies in Classic American Literature*, p. 183.
60. "Song of Myself," sec. 52, in *Complete Poetry*, p. 68.

6
Selfhood and the Reality
of Time: T. S. Eliot

From this—experienced Here—
Remove the Dates—to These
Let Months dissolve in further Months—
And Years—exhale in Years—

Without Debate—or Pause—
Or Celebrated Days—
No different Our Years would be
From Anno Dominies—

Emily Dickinson

A YEAR before the publication of *The Waste Land* T. S. Eliot observed that Poe "demands the static poem; that in which there shall be no movement of tension and relaxation, only the capture of a single unit of intense feeling." [1] This is a preference which Eliot found natural both to himself and to the modern reader. As he goes on to say, "We are, most of us, inclined to agree with him: we do not like long poems." [2] But our premise, that to be intense a poem must be brief, is hardly supported by the greatest long poems: the *Odyssey*, the *Aeneid*, and the *Divine Comedy*, "have, in different degrees, the movement toward and from intensity which is life itself." [3]

It is with the static poem that Eliot began. Probably he did not at first think it appropriate, or even possible, to attempt more than "the capture of a single moment of intense feeling." Yet the course of his career is a development from the poem of a single

1. "Prose and Verse," *Chapbook*, 22 (April 1921), 5.
2. Ibid.
3. Ibid.

moment to the poem of movement. That goal he never quite reached: the static poem remained the most natural; so that while in his last—and longest—work he succeeded in uniting four isolated moments as phases of a single action, it was still through moments that he worked, and their succession as a sequence is designed to show their coexistence within a single moment of higher consciousness. Even so, the poem of movement was Eliot's objective. The odd and increasingly devious stratagems of his art bear witness to the difficulties he encountered and the maneuvers he found necessary in attempting to escape the confines of poetry of the present.

Although in trying to return to the portrayal of literary action, Eliot seems to reverse the tradition we have been considering, the elaborate nature of his methods and their rather desperate daring are our surest evidence that he belongs within it. My thesis will be that Eliot has extended the tradition of Edwards, Poe, and Whitman; that his departures from this tradition grow naturally from the assumptions he seems to deny; and that in his poetry we find the latest and perhaps the fullest expression of a way of thought and of art, which was naturally his by birth, and whose very nature fostered his desire to transcend it.

Eliot's view of the self provides the most crucial instance of his American character. It is inevitable that this should be so, for selfhood has been the great argument of American poetry since its beginning in Puritanism, which, through its doctrine of grace, defined literary action as self-examination. By the mid-nineteenth century the changes wrought by the age of Edwards and Franklin had had their effect, and the question of the self's election had been transformed into the scarcely less urgent or interesting question of its reality. In Poe and Whitman alike, this is the issue upon which all others depend. That it was a metaphysical issue makes it no less a poetic one as well. The kinds of experience their poems portray are determined by the self they imagine as having experience.

For both poets, as for the best American authors before them,

342

the self is revealed in a present whose nature is manifest through its commerce with the eternal. Poe's and Whitman's conclusions were exactly antithetical—as answers to the same question often are—and Eliot could be satisfied with neither, because he could not respect the simple monism which makes it but a step down the open road from the now of solipsistic egotism to the always in which consciousness melts away. Yet Eliot's answers proceed from the same question. His concept of tradition, when we study its origin in Royce and Bradley, proves to be but another means of mediating between an irreducibly immediate present and an exclusively transcendent eternity. In Eliot, as, again, in Poe and Whitman, it is the failure to *feel* that history organically unites these opposites which compels the poet to make of history a metaphysics. Thus, in his last major poem, the terms of Puritan meditation are scarcely less apparent than in Bradstreet or Taylor. It is still a question of the eternally real and the momentarily experienced, of the intersection of the timeless and time, of the eternal plan which contains the present and yet is contained by it.

Before observing the way in which Eliot's poetry develops from the problem of personal identity, we must dispel some doubts which are bound to be raised by the enterprise of placing him within a national tradition. That Eliot abandoned his country, both by his permanent remove to England and, more ungratefully, by adopting social views uncongenial to the liberal democratic tradition, is a fact which will not trouble us if we recall James, on the one hand, and Cooper or Twain, on the other, as reminders that foreign residence and doubts about Jeffersonian principle are normal enough in American literary careers. And if it seems odd to place in a narrowly American tradition a poet who drew the bounds of what *he* called tradition so amply that they embraced the Hindu scriptures, we may consider whether his catholicity is not, in the end, one more, and perhaps our surest, evidence of his nationality. While "the mind of Europe" is by no means exclusive, it does not seem so very expansive either, when set beside the cosmology of *Eureka* and the past where Whitman "slept through the lethargic mist,/ And took [his] time, and took no hurt from the fetid carbon." [4] Again, in Eliot, the past turns out to be a function of the self, for his tradition is the past as it is known and (what to Eliot is always an aspect of cognition) potentially knowable. To narrow tradition would be to diminish the self by constricting the field of consciousness. Eliot's tradition, then, is another version of the indefinitely expansive historical panorama by which the American poet has always attempted to compass eternity. And as such, it is also the medium of self-realization. One enlarges the temporal horizon in order to focus more sharply on the self as it just now is—to give the self a wider consciousness that it may become more fully itself.

If the un-American character of Eliot's sources seem troublesome to the reader, he may find reassurance by recalling that even in such a "native" writer as Mark Twain it would be hard to prove the predominant influence of American literature, while with respect to native "schools," the sources of any make a reading list more largely European than American. Nor does it seem reasonable to regret that one does not find in Eliot's poetry the sights, the sounds—the experience, some may say—of American life, less because there are in his poems many glimpses of St. Louis and Boston, than because this objection results from the effort to weigh subject matter by the pound, a method by which much of Emerson could be denationalized. And if, finally, it is argued that what one means by American experience consists of characteristic ideas rather than visible details, then surely the point has been conceded: that what is constant in the American tradition is a mode of experience, not native scenery—though that is a likely evidence—nor a set of books, though these, no doubt, reveal it.

To grasp this mode of experience as it appears in Eliot—to see his personal variation of it—will require considering first in just what sense he found the self real. A comparison of "Prufrock"

4. "Song of Myself," sec. 44.

with a poem of Frost's will serve to reveal Eliot's odd assumptions about identity, and by turning, then, to consider what Eliot learned from Royce and Bradley, the reader will be able to appreciate that they were not such odd assumptions after all, especially when they are viewed also in the light of the state of poetry at the time when Eliot began to write. The latter portion of this essay will then trace the main phases of the development of Eliot's poetic method. I shall undertake to show that in the poems up to and including *The Waste Land* Eliot's main concern is to achieve a convincing portrayal of the self as it exists in the one moment of its present consciousness. And then, by surveying his later poetry, I shall trace the line of development by which his view of selfhood led him from the "static" poem to the poem of action. The metaphysical ideas he most favored and drew upon—especially those concerning time—must inevitably be invoked, but briefly enough, I hope, for the subject here is Eliot's poetry, not his beliefs, though by observing a few of these, one gains assurance and, if one feels one needs it, a sort of biographical proof.

"A Servant to Servants" may be said to pivot upon one line, which Frost's harried woman quotes as the advice of her husband: "He says the best way out is always through." [5] Doubtless Len meant this remark as we, reading it alone, are apt to take it—as a call to persevere and accept one's commitment to live. And it is perhaps the central point of the poem that Frost's woman takes this advice quite differently; that for her it offers a sanction for the compulsive self-denial which drives her toward insanity. The madness she fears is really but a mask concealing the madness she desires, for what in the end she most wishes is to be "kept"—as her mad uncle was in a cage in the family barn, or in the asylum where she has already sojourned, or, less obviously, in the prison of her dependence upon her husband. And in that prison she already lives, as her attempt to make Len's opinion her own law illustrates. This submission is of a piece with the self-pity which leads her to cast herself as a mere servant to servants,

5. *Complete Poems of Robert Frost: 1949*, p. 82.

the sufferer rather than the actor, fated to a routine of "doing/ Things over and over that just won't stay done." [6] But nothing will do; the more extravagant her efforts to destroy her individuality, the more intensely she becomes a "character"—a person. For Frost, as for the woman, the way through is self-realization, and the way out can only be the triumphing in one's doom to be *someone*. Let us not confuse this triumph with the merging of self with world, as in Poe or Whitman. It is rather the celebration of an irreducible independence. That is why Frost's heroic self-sufficiency is tinged with regret. The price of so assured an identity must be loneliness. Success, by confirming the ego in its strength, tended sometimes to blight Frost's later work, for it made the poet so complete in himself that there was the danger the world might seem no more than a subject one talked about. But the fatality of selfhood casts its shadow from the first poem of Frost's first book, a poem in which we find him imagining that if the dark woods stretched to the edge of doom, he could journey through them to prove at the end to all those he cared for that he was not "changed from him they knew/ Only more sure of all I thought was true." [7]

If the way out is always through, however, the way through may be that of self-abnegation as well as self-reliance. What was for Frost an occasional experiment—as in "A Servant to Servants" or "The Old Man's Winter Night," the experiment of putting the self through a course of deprivation that we may see what is left when everything removable has been stripped away—is Eliot's normal procedure. His humility may be quite unlike Frost's robust confidence, but as in Edwards and Poe, it is a means of self-realization. One insists on the self's nothingness only to prove that it is in the end something indeed: that the self lives eternally in God's eternal will. It is a humility made "endless" by the ambition it expresses.

Hugh Kenner, one of Eliot's most understanding critics, has

6. Ibid., p. 83.
7. "Into My Own," ibid., p. 5.

termed him "the invisible poet," which is an apt way of pointing out that what, morally speaking, we call self-abnegation is, from the literary point of view, the method of Eliot's "impersonal art." [8] One must take care not to mistake Mr. Kenner's meaning and suppose that this invisibility is no more than a screen to conceal a poet who does not particularly want to reveal himself. It is a method of art because it is a condition of belief. Man's moral depravity, which Eliot presents as a final fact in his social criticism, is seen always in his poetry as a condition of imperfect consciousness. Like the Puritan's "natural man," the self in Eliot is sinful because incomplete.

But to speak in this way of the self's incompleteness is to move from the moral to the metaphysical aspect of identity. What is wrong is evil because it is unreal. Thus an imperfect identity seems a contradiction: if the self is incomplete, we must ask whether it exists at all. This, for Eliot, is the central question. He cannot simply posit the identity of a character, since it is the main task of his poetry to show us the ground of its identity; nor can he speak in his own person as "the poet," for again, who is he? In what respects is anyone a credible person? Eliot's depersonalization and his humility bear witness to the urgency of his desire to find the self real. In general, his answer is that selfhood is always relative—a degree of consciousness and a more or less improved moral nature, which, in one sense, create and, in another sense, result from a degree of identity. If at its worst the self is still somewhat alive, at its best it cannot be quite real.

"A Servant to Servants" opposes to this the idea of an irreducible identity, and we may find some instruction in noting why Frost's fable does not seem pertinent to Eliot's world. The woman's isolation is the prominent fact: when she tries to surrender her own opinions, there are only her husband's to fall back upon, and these in turn exist without reference to any others. Eliot could not have created such a character, because he could not imagine a person whose opinions do not lead us beyond her circle to a soci-

8. *The Invisible Poet: T. S. Eliot* (New York, Citadel Press, 1964).

ety, the history of a culture, a language. Frost locates his character quite precisely enough: she is the wife of a man who runs a string of tourist cabins near a New England fishing resort. We can infer the larger social scene beyond her place in the world, while her distinctive speech relates her to other levels of culture and phases of history. Yet her isolation remains. She lives quite separately in her own time, as in her remote corner of the world. She is just such a unique specimen of "the mind of Europe" as exists at this special place and moment. One cannot avoid concluding that the moment depends upon the place: that the region matters very much here, as it commonly does in Frost's poems.

By contrast, J. Alfred Prufrock has no determinate location. On the other hand, he is significantly more informed. Books provide him with a source of ideas no less accessible than the conversation of his acquaintances. We may place him in a social milieu, but if his class is his only specification, he will prove a mere type rather than a person. He does, in fact, turn out to be nobody in particular, which, in terms of morality, is what is "wrong with him." The poem is his utterance, and the impossibility of deciding when, where, or to whom he speaks symbolizes in a formal way the elusiveness of one who is less than a real person. At every point the self he seems to reveal dissolves into an assumed role. Mr. Kenner helpfully points out the derivative quality of Prufrock's language. Prufrock's statements turn out, upon examination, to be a series of familiar stylistic gestures, which do not so much express his thoughts—whether badly or well—as display ways of thinking anyone might pick up in the course of normally wide reading. When he asks, for example, whether he should "force the moment to its crisis," the manner being familiar (as Marvell made it), we are deluded by the belief that the question asked is meaningful.[9] But in considering what forcing the moment to its crisis might involve, we find that it suggests nothing more definite than being like "Lazarus/ Come from the dead," and

9. *The Complete Poems and Plays: 1909–1950* (New York, Harcourt, Brace and World, 1952), p. 6. All quotations from Eliot's poetry are taken from that edition.

348

when we question what being Lazarus would be like, the only answer discernible is that it is such a role as Prufrock cannot play, because he is not like Hamlet.[10] Since both Hamlet and Lazarus were forceful enough to do something, it is reasonable, though uninteresting, to conclude that, in saying he is unlike them, Prufrock confesses his weakness. But it is his manner rather than his tenor that convinces. Failing to find any idea that does not collapse into a mannerism, or any language that is his, we begin to doubt Prufrock's existence. He seems totally unreal because he at no point transcends imitation through an act of personal choice. He is powerless to move from the hypothetical to the actual. He cannot act because he does not exist, except as an assumed self in a supposed moment of experience, confronting merely typical circumstances in terms of merely possible thoughts and feelings.

Yet this merely hypothetical self is a good deal more than nothing at all. There must be a real identity behind the series of illusionary self-images, a supposer to do the supposing. In calling Prufrock a nonentity, one has the odd sensation of describing him as a person. Actually, his derivative thoughts seem his because they fit together as parts of a system—hence the elaborately interrelated imagery—of clothes, music, aliments, for example— and the way thoughts cluster, like steel filings, about such magnetic ideas as seduction, heroism, and metamorphosis. Since criticism has already surveyed these kinds of design, one may grant the poem's orderliness and consider, instead, the principle of order. For it is a question not of how the literary allusions become relevant to *each other* or of the way in which an image manifests an idea, but of how the elements are made to exist as parts of an experience. Everything is Prufrock's thought, yet how can we say Prufrock's? What is this self? What right has one to assume him? The answer, I believe, is that he is the center with reference to which all thoughts and things appear. Though all is derivative, there is just this set of elements in just this arrangement. Pru-

10. Ibid.

frock's identity, then, is a point of view. The self is the location from which these, and only these, objects are perceived in this particular system of relations.

For Eliot this point of view is a point in time. To be sure, identity means living in a place as well as a moment, and it will become clear later that higher states of consciousness are expressed through a more fully realized landscape; but the relations which most interested Eliot are those between the now of experience and other times.[11] The space which individuates the Frost character by isolating it cannot serve as the ground of selfhood for a poet whose teachers convinced him that the problem of identity is one of uniting the moments of living in a single life; that hope and memory, by positing future and past, construct the physical world.

The self is its point of view, and its point of view is a moment. Thus Prufrock becomes real to us in the process by which his percepts place him in time. For example, though the mermaids of the final lines are clearly derived from the *Odyssey*, they exist to Prufrock's mind within the perspective of Keats' "Ode to a Nightingale," Arnold's "The Foresaken Merman," and a number of poems by Tennyson, Morris, and Swinburne. Their song is modulated by the chant of "The Lotus-Eaters" and blends the strains of certain familiar nineteenth-century sentiments: that death is "easeful," that one ought to surrender to "enchanting" music, be "ravished," die to the world of practical cares. While "Do I wake or sleep?" is so nearly a statement that Prufrock cannot be blamed for making it one, his doing so illustrates his falsehood. He does not really drown, any more than he has really heard the mermaids "singing each to each" (in quaint Pre-Raphaelite phrase); he merely talks about these things, because the poetry he knows

11. Eliot's emphasis on the temporal is well expressed by a memorable sentence of Royce: "Space furnished indeed the stage and the scenery of the universe, but the world's play occurs in time" (*The World and the Individual*, 2 [New York, 1901], p. 125).

supplies the metaphors. And it is just this past, this alignment of literary texts, which locates his identity. Eliot is able to make the characterization precise by providing a number of such perspectives: of the Sistine frescoes as seen with reference to the talk of a Beacon Street "at home"; of Wordsworth's evening ("silent as a nun"), qualified by the fogs of a Whistler landscape, the shirt-sleeved poor as the Barbizon school liked to paint them, the science of anesthetics, and the feline sphinx (of ambiguous questions) lurking behind Poe's black cat. Not that the poem alludes to these items specifically, but what is more remarkable, that it makes us sense Prufrock's culture as a familiarity with art works of these particular kinds.

Such vistas seem to open out from a center very spacious indeed: from an epoch—the Edwardian age, let us say. But if Prufrock is no more than his time, how is he to be distinguished from Russell, Bergson, or Teddy Roosevelt? True, his slavish conformity has reduced him to little more than an image of prevailing conventions, but Prufrock has not quite killed himself, and, indeed, he cannot. His identity proves as durable as that of Frost's lonely woman. It persists, however diminished, because his present is unique. Russell and Roosevelt are contemporaries of Prufrock only with reference to a public calendar, while Prufrock's present belongs within a private view of time. I do not mean that Prufrock is aware of Russell, but that if he were, the philosopher, like any other object of Prufrock's thought, would exist to him as seen from the personal present which seeing just these objects in just this temporal order creates.

Prufrock is not Russell because his view of the past (and hence of the future he anticipates) is not Russell's. Conversely, he is Russell to the extent that he shares the same elements of consciousness—in that they both have read *Hamlet*, for example. A measure of common experience, however slight, makes it impossible to distinguish Prufrock absolutely from any other person; and since the differences which individuate the self are but relatively

351

great, selfhood is always a partial thing. On the other hand, self-hood is not an illusion, since there is always some measure of difference to preserve it.

The uniqueness of Prufrock's sensibility, however, would seem to depend on our ability to date him by the public calendar. Though he is an individual because he takes the past in his own way, his view can be recognized only by reference to a real past of which his is one interpretation. And yet how is this possible? For surely our assumed past is just another view. If in this relativism there is no ground for preferring one view to another, how can we understand Prufrock, much less judge him? And if judgment is not possible, how can the poem itself have meaning?

Eliot found his answer in the fact that a view of reality, however false, however distorted by the viewer's limitation, *intends to be* reality. It is actually an appearance, the world as seen, but for the self it is the real world. When we judge that Prufrock is deluded, we assume a world he mistakes—not reality as *we* see it, but reality *as it is*. Thus, though each self is locked in its own private world (as Bradley asserted in a passage made familiar by the notes to *The Waste Land*), the real world forms a basis for communication, not as known and commonly acknowledged, but as intended by all experience.

The intending of reality makes views continuous: one comments upon the other and supplements it; the more coherent a view, the more it will include, by explaining and making sense of, other views. For all intend one world, and the better view is that which can bring more of experience into a single order. Thus, with respect to Prufrock's view, in the act of recognizing it as a view, we already begin to understand and judge it. For we contrast it with the order and unity which the real world must have. It is not our perceptions which judge his, but a sense of what his perceptions *ought to be*. And to some extent this "ought" is not just abstractly known. The contrast between the objects of his consciousness and these objects as we see them reveals similarities, defines a ground of common experience, which is truer because it includes several views, and creates, in this way, some sense of what reality itself must be like. For example, one may understand how Prufrock takes Keats' question, "Do I wake or sleep?", and yet object that Keats meant something more complicated than an invitation to "easeful death." This is not to offer one's own interpretation but to acknowledge that there is an objectively right meaning, which Prufrock has misapprehended.

Eliot's method is best understood by noticing that while the poem is entirely Prufrock's utterance, it judges him in a way quite different from his judgment of himself. Swift and Twain, in their best satiric moments, manage to transmute the character's naïve remarks into the author's commentary by a sort of double entendre. " 'Good Gracious! anybody hurt?' 'No'm. Killed a nigger.' 'Well, it's lucky; because sometimes people do get hurt.' " [12] The sharp wit of this results from the clash of two distinct meanings for "anybody." Huck and Aunt Sally mean one thing, the reader is to understand quite another, so that a statement about the characters seems to be made which can only be attributed to the author. But in "Prufrock" his meaning and the reader's are not so neatly polarized, but differ by faint shadings. The character himself is an ironist, and one judges differently only because one is able to see that his ironies extend further than he intended. The result is just the effect of impersonality Eliot aimed at and, indeed, required, in order to define selfhood as the center of a state of consciousness. By contrasting a view with what it intends, he creates the illusion that the poem speaks for itself, as if its meaning emerged simply from the nature of things. This meaning cannot be assigned to an author, because there is no way of drawing a line between Prufrock's thoughts and the poem's meaning. Yet there is as real a difference as between upriver and down.

The difference is a relative one, however, a matter of tendency, and it would be a most serious mistake to suppose that in Eliot's poems the character is totally distinct from either the poet or the

12. *The Adventures of Huckleberry Finn* (New York, Holt, Rinehart and Winston, 1958), p. 222.

reader. To some extent, Prufrock intentionally expresses meanings which are true meanings of the poem as a whole, and in that degree his voice is identical with the poet's. To some extent, too, the reader agrees with meanings Prufrock intends to communicate—as, for example, that his concern with manners fetters him —and in sharing his opinion the reader in some measure shares his identity. In his fine study *The Poet in the Poem* George T. Wright has given a salutary refutation of the old habit of regarding the persona's statements as simply the author's own opinions, but his argument simplifies Eliot's aesthetic by making the merely relative difference between persona and poet absolute:

> Not what the personae say, nor what they embody, but what the poem *is*, is the point. Instead of presenting an instance of human experience, the poem provides an experience, is, in its role of artifact undergone, an experience itself. Poet and reader have the experience together; and it is in the having of it—not in the seeing of it, as in Browning, nor in the pretending to have someone else's as in the Romantics—that the poet and reader coincide.[13]

As a description of how poet and reader "coincide" or, as I would express it, share in some degree a common identity, this statement is admirable, yet one must notice the sacrifice of the character that Wright's line of reasoning requires. Since the character's experience is an element in the total experience the work provides, the reader must partially share this experience. He must, for example, see the same objects the character has in view, though in a more or less different way. The very mistakenness or confusion of the character's vision can only be recognized by seeing things in his way, and such notoriously mistaken characters as Shakespeare's Iago are in error because the poet has enabled us to behold the world through their eyes. Hence the significance of the epigraph to "Prufrock," which, by asserting both the poet's and the reader's

13. *The Poet in the Poem: The Personae of Eliot, Yeats, and Pound* (Berkeley, University of California Press, 1960), p. 86.

complicity in the character's error, serves as a reminder that these three selves are only relatively distinct.

Understanding Prufrock and judging him are the same process, for a self is real only to the extent that his view of things is right and therefore coherent. We may, then, observe the ethical side of Eliot's method by noticing the way in which Prufrock's mild self-disparagement turns into an incisive criticism. When he indulgently mocks his fastidious habits of dress:

> My morning coat, my collar mounting firmly to the
> chin,
> My necktie rich and modest, but asserted by a simple
> pin—[14]

we see that he knows better than to be deluded by the self-confidence the clothing ads promise. And there is a nice humor in his sense of Polonius' moral confusions: ". . . rich, not gaudy./ For the apparel oft proclaims the man . . . To thine own self be true." But at the end it is still for him a question of whether to wear his trousers rolled. In short, Prufrock knows what he does not know, a trait common to all Eliot's characters. He is not to be blamed for living in his own time or because he has failed to make the most of it—has never read Cardinal Newman, for example. His guilt is manifest in the ease with which he dismisses what he does know. The knowing better always comes to naught, because what he believes is less believable to him than what others think. This modesty is a sort of egotism. He would be just himself and is paralyzed by reconsiderations because he aims at perfect self-expression—would take every possible view into account, while there is always "so much more." Thus he sins by rejecting, on the one hand, his own finitude, and on the other, by refusing to admit that his world is not uniquely his but is continuous with other private and public worlds. Hence the fastidiousness, which is so pronounced that Prufrock seems to have reduced himself to mere manners. For manners, or appearances, are all that there is

14. *Complete Poems and Plays*, p. 4.

left to perceive of the perfectly isolated selves Prufrock assumes. Though the problems of the wardrobe are trifling enough, clothing is associated with his sharpest pangs, and we can move easily from his doubts about his cravat to his terror at the "universal question." He foresees that asking it will be forestalled by such stage business as "settling a pillow or throwing off a shawl." [15] "Is it perfume from a dress/ That makes me so digress?" [16] This prideful display of fine sensibility is intended to hold the world at bay, but its real effect is to submerge him in a depersonalizing convention. He knows that the standards of his world of novels, teacups, and "skirts that trail along the floor" are false, but this is not for him a judgment at all.[17] It is a finely wrought bit of porcelain within that world.

Even so, the judgment is known to him, as the purgatorial death by water is suspected by Madame Sosostris and as "Christ the tiger" is known to Gerontion. In this partial knowing or faint, half-conscious recognition, one can see the poetic method by which Eliot is able to establish the moral responsibility of his characters. There is a potential of truth within consciousness which the character, through neglect or sloth or coldness of heart, is disinclined to notice, and this turning away, being a choice, has ethical meaning. Thus, for instance, though Prufrock only parodies humility, he suffers real humiliation and to some extent knows the proper attitude through the false one. That is why the figures with whom he contrasts himself are persons like Hamlet and John the Baptist, who represent the anguish he suffers as well as the commitment he shuns. There is always this doubleness within the objects of his consciousness, so that the reader's mind glides naturally from his relatively false opinion toward a true one. When he declares, "No! I am not Prince Hamlet," we must take the remark as a certain truth, though he believes it but half-heartedly.[18]

15. Ibid., p. 6.
16. Ibid., p. 5.
17. Ibid., p. 6.
18. Ibid., p. 7.

That Royce's thought should have some relevance to the young poet who wrote "Prufrock" while specializing in philosophy at Royce's Harvard is made apparent by the following passage:

> Deep emotional experiences give the sense of a new or wavering selfhood. There are many people, of a fine social sensibility, who are conscious of a strong tendency to assume, temporarily, the behavior, the moods, and in a measure, both the bearing and the accent, both the customs and the opinions of people in whose company they spend any considerable time. I have known amongst such people those who were oppressed by a sense of insincerity in consequence of their own social plasticity. "I almost seem to have no true Self at all," such a sensitive person may say. "I am involuntarily compelled to change my whole attitude towards the most important things whenever I change my company. I find myself helplessly thinking and believing and speaking as the present company want me to do. I feel humiliated by my own lack of moral independence. But I cannot help this fickleness. And the saddest is that I do not know where my true Self lies, or what one amongst all these various selves is the genuine one.[19]

I do not wish to offer this as the source of "Prufrock," though it seems hard to doubt that Eliot had read Royce's paragraph; my purpose is to show how accurately he reflects Royce's view of the problem of identity, and how probable it is that he was already familiar with the main features of Royce's theory of the self. Eric Thompson, in his useful study of Eliot, shows us how much harder it is to doubt than believe this when he confesses his astonishment that before Eliot had read Bradley, he should already have adopted a Bradleyan position.[20] Royce and Bradley have so

19. *The World and the Individual*, 2, 253–54.
20. *T. S. Eliot: The Metaphysical Perspective* (Carbondale, Southern Illinois University Press, 1963), p. xx. Though Mr. Thompson does not consider the probability that Eliot's Bradleyan ideas may first have come to him through undergraduate reading of Royce, he offers some interesting comments on Royce's influence.

357

much in common that what seems Bradleyan in the early poems can be thought Roycean as well.

It is mainly through arguments concerning time and duration that Royce accounts for selfhood. His arguments are briefly as follows: The self is not empirically "given"; when a person looks within himself, he cannot see himself, but can see only his perceptions, while any self which he may find there is not the true self but, necessarily, another perception, for it does not include the thinker who perceives it. The world the self sees when it looks without is not purely subjective, however. It is the world as perceived by this particular mind, surely, but the mind conceives it objectively, as the same world in which others live. And without this reference to other selves—without positing their existence—neither self nor world would exist. For the self has both its origin and its being in the contrast between its own and other selves. Self-consciousness develops after and from consciousness of others. For example, the self is created by its acts of imitation. By imitating others, it notices that the imitation is not the same as the act copied, but an act of its own. And, similarly, by measuring itself against the standards of others, it distinguishes between wish or opinion, as interior, and reality, as objective. What is empirically known is a contrast between the self and others, a contrast which keeps shifting as occasion and the intention of thought demand. The known self, then, is pragmatic and incomplete, while the selfhood of another person is even further removed, being, for the observer, a set of perceived aspects assigned to a postulated identity.

It follows, then, that finding identity within these shifting contrasts requires a self to which all its moments would belong. This leads naturally to Royce's theory of duration. For what is real is what is perceived, and a self can be real only if all its moments can be seen simultaneously within a single conspectus. Ultimately, God alone possesses a consciousness capable of such a view. But duration rather than deity is the governing idea: without a present, no experience; without duration, no present. Though abstractly considered, the now has no duration, every moment being infinitely divisible, in experience we find that duration does exist—that while, during our present, time moves forward, we can, even so, view this present as a whole. Duration is illustrated by our consciousness of a line of poetry, which we grasp as a single present whole, even though, within the line, the words exist in sequence. Clearly, the duration of a present varies: in the discourse of geologists, for instance, "now" indicates an extremely long period; in practical affairs it can mean a decade or a moment. For the self its own identity is obscured by the mind's inability to grasp more than a very limited duration as its present. The moments before appear as in an irrevocable past, and those which follow as still unknown. Yet the fact that, even so, the self is convinced it is the same person that it was in the past bears witness to the fact that the self would be real if seen within reality as a whole. To God the real self appears; he not only sees the whole of its life as a single unit, which is the self, but he sees it in all its relations to all things. The self, then, is not "absorbed" into reality, as Bradley argued. Royce's theory is designed to preserve the self as a perfect individual, which exists within reality in its own proper time and place, as a word exists in a poetic line. There is, in this theory, a peculiar complication. In one sense, the only real self is God. The individual is but an imperfect realization of him; a person approaches selfhood when, through loyalty and vocation, he intends the world which, as a whole, comprises God's consciousness. But in another sense, a human self is a discrete entity existing with all other selves and things in the temporal sequence which composes God's duration.[21]

21. "Our idealistic theory teaches that all individual lives and plans and experiences win their unity in God, in such wise that there is, indeed, but one absolutely final and integrated Self, that of the Absolute. But our idealism also recognizes that in the one life of the divine there is, indeed, articulation, contrast, and variety. So that, while it is, indeed, true that for every one of us the Absolute Self is God, we still retain our individuality, and our distinction from one another, just in so far as our life-plans, by the very necessity of their social basis, are mutually contrasting life-plans, each one of which can reach its own fulfillment only by recognizing other life-plans as different from its own" (*The World and the Individual*, 2, 289; for a convenient summary of Royce's theory of selfhood, see 2, 135–37).

The past (and the future) is constructed from the self's present, as that which leads up to (or must follow) from what one takes to be immediate reality. Clearly, the past one sees depends upon the scope and content of the duration one assumes. In "Prufrock" this theory is perforce seen in reverse, since Eliot's object is to show us his character's present condition through what his sense of the past tells us about him. But that the poet's view of selfhood is fundamentally like Royce's can be seen even more clearly in the fact that the poem's form is grounded in Roycean epistemology. We have seen that Prufrock's identity is created by our inference; that our view, being continuous with his, implies a real world where the self, which his distorted self-image intends to be, exists. It is in just this contrast between views that Royce finds the origin of selfhood.

To appreciate the effect of Royce upon Eliot's poetry, we must notice particularly that in Royce views are always temporal views. Experience is a duration defining the whole of reality as a temporal sequence; the empirical self—as opposed to the real self—is he of whom the sequence he assumes makes sense, so that he will be the more himself the more complete and coherent his view of time is. Yet his perceptions are never just his own; his and those of others interpenetrate. For example, history as he sees it is created by its contrast with the community's sense of the past, just as his identity is created through the contrast with other selves. That explains a well-known feature of Eliot's thought: his interest in the misfortune an individual suffers if he lives in a community which is unconscious of its tradition. But again like Royce, Eliot seeks to overcome this difficulty by defining community in the broadest possible sense. It is not, he would say, the gross average of living people, nor is it limited to those now alive, but, like the invisible church, it exists as a society in which selves of all epochs are united. When Royce speaks of loyalty, he means not allegiance to established laws and preferences but the act of willing the kingdom of God; and though it be conceded that Eliot is a good deal more complacent about the stock exchange than the Fabian Society, his social theories have the same basis.

Eliot's poems reflect what one would expect in a poet who had assimilated the thought of Royce: they are built upon the contrast between diverse temporal systems; they assume that reality is a conspectus in which the whole of time is simultaneously presented to consciousness; they portray every form of human experience as but relatively true, because always an incomplete version of this perfect consciousness; they value thought according to the coherence of the time system it implies; and they present themselves as poems which are objective and real in themselves, rather than being the author's state of mind or the reader's response, because they have the status of being truer than the views they include, and hence closer to a conspectus of the whole.

F. H. Bradley's influence is not less important than Royce's. It is of a different and, perhaps, more crucial kind. If we ask why it was that Eliot could not rest satisfied with the method of "Prufrock"—still his most popular work—we will find the answer, I think, in the minor nature of that poem's mysteries. It is not mysterious enough; that is, its assumed reality is too close to what any sensible person ought to know. The reader is allowed to feel that he is "right"—that he knows quite well enough the things of which the character is ignorant. There is only one way to respond to Prufrock's desire to be a pair of ragged claws, and a large part of his thought is even more easily dismissible. Worrying about whether or not to eat a peach is exposed as folly by mere common sense. Thus, when one is mystified, one feels one oughtn't to be—that only a lout would miss a point so plain. This effect—as of a narrowly elegant and snobbish wit—brings the poem rather too close to *vers de société*. The reader is apt to feel that if he were sufficiently cultivated, there would be no mystery at all. Yet surely the ideas of Royce we have noted demand a poetry in which the real is not just unknown but unknowable. The poet and reader should see further than the character, not because they perceive the real situation, but because they have a wider view. The ultimate effect should be to create the feeling of a reality which transcends all possible views, and which, although the comparison of views affords us a few certainties—that Prufrock is vain, for instance—extends beyond experience. For this purpose mystery is essential. The reader must be made to sense that reality exists, by sensing it through the tendency of perceptions to form into an order, but if, as in "Prufrock," this reality seems accessible, it will seem less than real. I do not mean that the poem, in this respect, fails, but that, having succeeded to some extent, Eliot had still before him the problem of making thoughts seem to emerge as dim intimations coming to us from the Absolute, not as facts a knowing poet has held back.

Though we have seen the basis for such a poetry in Royce, his manner of writing does not foster the requisite skepticism. For one thing, metaphysics is not usually the central subject in his books; a far greater amount of space is devoted to working out the ethical, social, and religious implications of his premises than to elucidating them. And in this operation, Royce proceeds with such confidence that in their total effect, his arguments seem to end by merely confirming our belief in the world of common sense and justifying a very commonplace liberal Protestantism. Though he acknowledges that God alone sees reality as it is, the human world, as Royce depicts it, is orderly, reliable, and largely true, a place where trust seems much more reasonable than doubt. Now Bradley is quite different in these respects: he continually holds our attention to ultimate questions, subordinating, always, the practical working-out of an idea to its function as illustration or proof of major principles. By being more consistently theoretical, he is both more precise and more suggestive. The relevance of his ideas to life is left largely to implication, for in the end this relevance is partial and to be felt rather than explained. In this we can sense how his skepticism could lead into Eliot's kind of mystery. Bradley differs from Royce most in thinking that far less can be known about the Absolute. On this point Royce is explicit: he objects to Bradley's conclusion that in reality all finite things are transformed. Bradley maintained that every entity except the Absolute itself is an appearance. The main argument, though rather technical, is essentially this: that the many, since they are unified in the one, cannot really have individual being. Space, time, nature, self, and every other such object of human thought is constructed for practical purposes by selecting from experience certain features to serve the mind as aspects of an individual thing. But this thing, being one among many in the world, is logically contradictory. Its relation to other things is a part of its being, but if this be granted, the relation is then a third element, and we must find another relation to conjoin these three, which, in turn, calls for yet another, and so on to infinity. This infinite regress shows that the thing has no final limits and thus has, in fact, no identity.

Now Royce intended his theory of duration as a means of solving this dilemma. While agreeing with Bradley that reality is an experience in which all things coexist, he asserts that they survive there as discrete entities. The motive of Royce's argument is revealed by its effects. Royce desires to maintain the reality of finite objects, because he wishes to show that there is a fairly clear and dependable relation between the Absolute and human experience.[22] That things are "absorbed" and "transformed" in the Absolute he finds absurd on logical grounds, yet his objections are sound only if the limits of human understanding are wider than Bradley would grant. Bradley does not claim to know just how objects really exist. He goes no further than to insist that logically they must have their being in the unity of the whole, and that

22. Thus in the important Supplementary Essay at the end of Volume 1 of *The World and the Individual*, he writes: "Defining and defending a conception of the Absolute as 'one system,' whose contents are 'experience,' Mr. Bradley, to whose well-known book, *Appearance And Reality*, I am here referring, has, nevertheless, maintained that we are wholly unable to 'construe' to ourselves the way in which the realm of Appearance finds its unity in the Absolute. *He rejects, in consequence, every more detailed effort to interpret* our own life in its relations to the Absolute" (italics mine). See also James Harry Cotton, *Royce on the Human Self* (Cambridge, Harvard University Press, 1954), and chap. 4 of Gabriel Marcel, *Royce's Metaphysics*, trans. Virginia and Gordon Ringer (Chicago, Henry Regnery Co., 1956).

since we perceive them as sundered individuals, their true nature cannot be as it appears in our experience. This is not at all to assert that reality is the undifferentiated white something before which Poe and Melville trembled. We cannot know the Absolute, and to say that Bradley's arguments make it a blank is an indulgence in metaphor which illustrates the mind's limitation. As Eliot said of this objection, "The fact that we can think only in terms of things does not compel us to the conclusion that reality consists of things." [23] So much emphasis has been placed upon Bradley's skepticism that we are inclined to ignore the realism it supports. Appearances, though that is all men can know, are appearances of the real, and to have any experience at all is to experience, in some measure, what is real.

It is Bradley's sense of the shaded, qualified, and incomplete nature of human knowledge that most appealed to Eliot. For, as poet, Eliot confronted the problem of making reality real by making it transcendent, an effect not to be achieved simply by throwing dust in the reader's eyes. Something must be known: there must be an order unifying the poetic elements; they must seem to exist in a system and as parts of a single consciousness. Yet if a poem is to portray experience—if it is to dramatize a credible state of mind—there must be a contrast between what is perceived and what is. Unless the truth is kept beneath the horizon, it will not seem convincing. We must sense its existence and a part of its import, without clearly apprehending it. This kind of vision, with its dubieties, its faint glimmerings from an area beyond human consciousness, its sense of the illusions of common sense, and its leap from the discontinuities of experience to the mysterious unity logic demands, was Bradley's gift to Eliot.

The importance of the debt is best appreciated by noticing that it was from Bradley that Eliot's crucial concept of the unity of thought and feeling is derived. Royce also maintains that the real world unites emotion and idea—that the world of appreciation,

23. *Knowledge and Experience in the Philosophy of F. H. Bradley* (New York, Farrar, Straus, 1964), p. 165.

the warm, felt reality of personal experience, is the object of knowledge. And in analyzing the intention of thought, he insists always that ideas are instrumental, being brought into play to satisfy human needs. But in Royce feeling is mainly a matter of the will's conscious calculations. He is interested in emotions as the stimuli to purposeful action. Suffering, in both the large and narrow sense, is but the negative which generates willing. Thus he does not often consider states of consciousness in their wholeness. For Bradley the unity in the Absolute of what we call emotions, on the one hand, and objects, on the other, is the main fact. The Absolute is Experience, and human experience is always at a remove from it, since consciousness begins when, by a process of abstraction, reality is organized into self and world, so that feelings appear to be somewhat separated from the objects they are "about." To Bradley's doubt "Whether there is a stage at which experience is merely immediate," Eliot answers: "here, I feel sure, he has understated his case, and we may assert positively that there is indeed no such stage." [24] This remark signifies clearly the ground of Eliot's relativism: without artificially constructing the subject-object scheme, there could be no consciousness, but this necessary ordering, by nature, somewhat falsifies the immediately given. And one does so again when one thinks of cognition as a development through a series of phases in time, so that the immediately given seems to be *prior* to knowledge, for in any actual event of knowing, all the phases coexist. Eliot quotes as "the words with which the whole theory is summed up," the statement that experience "is not a stage which shows itself at the beginning, and then disappears, but it remains at the bottom throughout as fundamental. And further, remaining, it contains in itself every development which in a sense transcends it. Nor does it merely contain all developments, but in its own way it acts as their judge." [25] Clearly, thought both grows out of and always tends toward this background Experience. It is the reality our

24. Ibid., p. 16.
25. Ibid.

experience is about, what thought would bring into focus, the felt unity which "judges" and "contains" all thoughts as that which they intend. But this immediate Experience cannot be grasped by thought; it extends beyond consciousness. That is the most crucial fact for those who would understand Eliot's belief that thought and feeling should be one. They *are* one in the ground Experience. In Royce's and Eliot's view the higher the state of consciousness, the more nearly it approaches Experience, and the more thought and feeling are united, but to Bradley, with whom they most significantly differ on just this point, Experience cannot be regarded as the consciousness even of an omniscient observer, for it is logically prior to the subject-object scheme, without which no consciousness can exist.

Bradleyan Experience differs from a person's experience in that the latter is finite, a result of "constructing" a world by selecting elements from Experience which are assigned either to the self or to a hypothetical objective reality. Thus, whenever it is known, experience is incomplete, no longer Experience, but a view of reality enjoyed by a self from its own point of view. Yet while a person's experience is incomplete, it points beyond itself to reality as a whole or, in other words, to Experience, the Absolute.

Bradley's concept of Experience casts a glaring light upon many of Eliot's most enigmatic ideas. One thinks first of his comment that while the Victorian poets "do not feel their thought as immediately as the odour of a rose. A thought to Donne was an experience." [26] A little reflection will reveal the Bradleyan assumption behind the "dissociation of sensibility, " the "objective correlative," and the theory of the poet as catalyst, transforming private feelings into "impersonal" poetic feelings "which are not in actual emotions at all." [27] But one ought to be more concerned with Eliot's poetic achievements than with his aesthetic principles, and it is in this respect that Bradley's influence is most sig-

26. "The Metaphysical Poets," in his *Selected Essays: 1917–1932* (New York, Harcourt Brace, 1932), p. 247.
27. "Tradition and the Individual Talent," ibid., p. 10.

nificant. It helps to define more precisely than before two of the poet's most powerful effects: the sense of mystery and the fine-drawn wit. Both are aspects of the delicately controlled gradations of knowing which Bradley's metaphysics fostered. The nature of the debt can be sufficiently grasped by noticing two of Eliot's most suggestive remarks:

> We never know, in any assertion, just what, or how much, we are asserting.[28]

> It seems to me that beyond the namable, classifiable emotions and motives of our conscious life when directed towards action —the part of life which prose drama is wholly adequate to express—there is a fringe of indefinite extent, of feeling which we can only detect, so to speak, out of the corner of the eye and can never completely focus; of feeling of which we are only aware in a kind of temporary detachment from action.[29]

Those puzzled by the first may consult the footnote Eliot appended; those who wonder how wit can enter into the state of mind both suggest may be satisfied with the thought that wit gains its keenness from surprise, which is never stronger than when the mind discovers that what it did not know was just what it unconsciously expected.

Royce and Bradley mattered to Eliot as guides in the development of belief. Let us take care, then, not to think of them as two capacious old trunks in which the poet discovered a store of costumes and dramatic scripts. Nor were they tool boxes. Eliot had to start by wondering whether he had anything to say, and his undergraduate interest in philosophy shows that he thought this question involved answering a larger one: Just what is believable? Successful poetry, if not true, must at least have the power of seeming true. One may relate what Eliot derived from Royce and Bradley to his sense of the literary situation by observing

28. *Knowledge and Experience,* p. 166.
29. *Poetry and Drama* (Cambridge, Harvard University Press, 1951), p. 42.

why it was that he thought the then received poetic manner no longer viable. Romantic poetry took the unquestionable fact to be the self. One wrote about experience because, being one's own, it must be real. The philosophic bent of the Romantics was toward explanations of this fact, not questions as to its truth. The decline of Romanticism was effected through its extension. The more the experiencing self was embraced as the one certain reality, and the more rigorously it was examined, the more it tended to dissolve into its perceptions. I have tried to show that in Poe and Whitman both the Romantic premises have been so uncompromisingly applied as to transform Romanticism itself into another kind of poetry. By enlarging the self's experience to include all reality through all history, they tranformed the person acting into the activity, which, when fully realized, is seen as the world's, not the self's. The self, then, disappears, either by melting into the world it knows or by losing its identity in universal process. Eliot is clearly within this American tradition, of which the Unitarianism of his forebears is but an earlier phase. Yet Eliot's dilemma does not necessarily have to be explained with reference to American poets who did not, in fact, greatly interest him. For English poetry had arrived at the same point. Looking back from the 1940s to his college years, Eliot recalled that "The question was still: where do we go from Swinburne? and the answer appeared to be, nowhere." [30] He would later praise Swinburne for the "completeness and self-sufficiency" of his world, and yet conclude that language and the object "are identified in the verse of Swinburne solely because the object has ceased to exist, because the meaning is merely the hallucination of meaning, because language, uprooted, has adapted itself to an independent life of atmospheric nourishment." [31] Now a world where language refers neither to objects nor to feelings, a world which, as Eliot declares, "is impersonal," yet which "no one else

30. "Ezra Pound," *Poetry, 68* (Sept. 1946), 327.
31. "Swinburne as Poet," in *Selected Essays,* p. 285.

368

could have made," [32] is quite the same sort of place as Poe's "City in the Sea."

However, this problem—a problem from which American poetry derived its most auspicious themes—the Victorians blundered into and never clearly understood. *In Memoriam* is a crucial instance of their difficulties. As Eliot remarked, the merit of this work rests upon the brief moments of feeling it records, rather than on its general argument; and this is an instance of what he meant in complaining that the Victorians cannot think and feel at once.[33] It was Tennyson's conscious intent to develop his poem dramatically through a sequence of reasoning which would carry the self from an initial to a final attitude. But the self this journey assumes is a purely separate person observing an objective world, whereas the self of the poem's best moments is continuous with its world and cannot develop beyond a single view of things. Tennyson seeks the meaning of Arthur Hallam's death in his own experience; but this experience, it turns out, is not specifically *his*. It lacks definite bounds, fades off into thoughts which might be anyone's, so that the poet is constantly diverted by general issues:

> Are God and Nature then at strife,
>> That Nature lends such evil dreams?
>> So careful of the type she seems,
> So careless of the single life . . .[34]

The banality of this results less from the commonplace nature of the ideas than their disengagement. They do not seem to exist as the thought of a particular person; they are not placed either in the history of a mind or in its immediate landscape. Yet the vagueness—the failure to convince us that the question raised really matters to the person speaking—results from what Eliot

32. Ibid., p. 284.

33. See "In Memoriam," in his *Essays Ancient and Modern* (New York, Harcourt Brace, 1932), p. 196.

34. Sec. 55, in *Complete Poetical Works of Tennyson*, Cambridge ed. (Boston, Houghton Mifflin, 1898), p. 176.

praised as the "quality" of the poem's "doubt." [35] Tennyson's question is surely pertinent: it is one the speaker is aware of, even if only as something another person *might* ask. But if whatever the self *could* think about is a part of personal experience, just where do his experience and his selfhood end? Tennyson's consciousness proves indefinitely expansible. The result is a wavering identity, for where the experienced world has no limits, it is hard to find the self at its center.

The assurance behind Tennyson's philosophizing manifests a feeling that there is no need to distinguish between the self's personal concerns and those of anybody else. Hence he finds the commonplace true and can play the Laureate for whom cannon "volleyed and thundered." The automatism of cliché often makes the Tennyson character Prufrockian by inadvertence: "I will take some savage woman, she shall rear my dusky race . . . Fool, again the dream, the fancy! But I know my words are wild . . ." [36] This posturing, however, has its source in the poet's sense that every possible thought falls within consciousness, a sense which enabled him to merge the private in the public mind and speak with effect as the voice of community. His "Ode on the Death of the Duke of Wellington" is a success of a rare and valuable kind, a good occasional poem. Tennyson's best practice brings us close to the point at which Eliot started. In "Ulysses," for instance, selfhood is a matter of outlook; the character is revealed entirely through his own sense of the past he recollects and the future he foresees. By rereading "Journey of the Magi" with "Ulysses" in mind, one can observe a kind of borrowing which is so natural that it seems largely unconscious.

If Swinburne and Tennyson define the state of poetry in the 1900s, Browning serves best to show us why Eliot's view of the self proved an effective means of developing beyond it. When the Bishop of Saint Praxed speaks of a lump of lapis lazuli, "Blue as a vein o'er the Madonna's breast," he means to express the qualities

35. "In Memoriam," in *Essays Ancient and Modern*, pp. 200–01.
36. Lines 168, 173, in *Complete Poetical Works*, p. 94.

of the stone—its color, beauty, value—but to us the descriptive function of his words is of little account. Rather, we take them as an instance of a peculiarly Renaissance mixture of earthiness and superstition. We think the stone beautiful and precious as it exists within his world, which, if we find it gorgeous, pleases as much through its deep tints of corruption as through the objects the Bishop admires. This discrepancy between the Bishop's meaning and ours exemplifies the unpassable gulf separating character from reader. The Bishop's metaphor displays piety as a mere reflex; what is faith in his world seems superstition to us. It is a faith whose truth for us consists of the fact that it was *then* believed. Since the Bishop is sealed off within his remote historic period, Browning cannot really judge him as a person. We are to consider the Bishop in terms of our judgment of the age which created him. Thus, while granting that the poet has succeeded in showing us a common humanity through the odd knots history has wrought in it, we must wonder whether his method allows for clear discrimination. For all his probing of guilt and psychic grotesquerie, Browning seems complacent because he embraced his own age as a sure standard of right thinking. Quatrocento faith is thus measured by Victorian piety, and Browning's nearly always historical characters are made significant by their place in a history which produced the normative present.

In "Prufrock" Eliot brings character and reader into a relation which is more credible, not because Prufrock's failings confirm our doubts concerning the superiority of the present or because he is a man of our age, but because Eliot's method makes Prufrock's selfhood accessible. By reducing the self to its point of view, Eliot allows us to enter into its consciousness. Prufrock is a point of view where we may stand. And yet our very power to imagine how things look from there creates the contrast between our vision and his by which we judge him. It is not, as in Browning, a matter of measuring the character's view by our presumably true one. We can be as fallible as our skepticism requires us to suppose we are. Whatever we assume, by its difference from what the character assumes, creates a real world which, though we cannot see it, forms a background against which both his insights and his errors stand out. Eliot's view of selfhood offers two antithetical but complementary advantages: it makes the reading experience more immediate, involving us more intimately in a character's state of mind, and it makes the poem more objective, for its meaning appears to be neither the poet's intention nor the reader's response, but enjoys the status of a reality toward which all views are directed. To be sure, this objectivity is a fiction or poetic seeming. Whether and in what way a poem objectively exists are questions awaiting the advent of a final metaphysics. But as a literary effect, this objectivity is quite good enough: it convinces.

In the period between "Prufrock" and *The Waste Land* Eliot sought to perfect his method by making the real seem truly transcendent, divorcing it, more completely than he had been able to do in "Prufrock," from mere common sense, on the one hand, and, on the other, from anything the reader might be inclined to identify as an idea the poet "had in mind." The slightness of the poems written during these years indicates their experimental nature, and we may best understand the method he developed while composing them by recollecting that this was also the period in which his speculations crystallized into a set of critical premises, whose grand theme is the need for an adequate sense of the past. That tradition, as an "ideal order" of literary works, is the main standard of judgment in his critical system is a fact which directs us to time as the governing concept in his poetry.

Since it was from Royce that Eliot had derived the idea that the self is the center of its own time system, it is natural that, in trying to improve his technique of indicating the real through the contrast of points of view, he should have proceeded from contrasting selves to contrasting time systems. In his poetry "real time" may be said to correspond to tradition in his critical theory. Both are aspects of the Absolute, real time being what experienced time intends, just as tradition is that which the critic's sense of tradition (which is altered with the advent of a truly new work) approximates. And since literary works exist in the medium of time, Eliot seems to have decided at an early date that he had best work with the grain of his material, learning to indicate the Absolute through its temporal aspect, suggesting a real time as that which a set of experienced time-systems intend.

The four "Preludes," the first two of which were composed during the year when "Prufrock" was begun (1909–10),[37] show an early and fairly simple instance of this method. These poems are united as a sequence of moments moving from night to morning and back to night. We have, then, an objective natural or clock time, but the poetic cycle does not develop because this time moves forward. Rather, clock time is created by the progressive development of consciousness. In each of the poems one sees the self realizing its identity by observing the time of day. That is, one sees, in four experiences, how the awareness of self and the awareness of the present moment arise together. There is in the "Preludes" a time progression—so that morning comes after the first evening, and the second evening follows morning— because in the series of experienced moments there is a nicely managed increase of definiteness of thought and feeling. The self becomes more keenly aware of its identity and conceives the world more objectively. Thus, for instance, it is only at the end that a general thought or idea appears: "I am moved by fancies . . ."[38] The same development is manifest in the gradual emergence of personal pronouns. In the first "Prelude," where the self is indistinguishable from its perceptions, one finds only the pale collectivity of "your." In the second, as feeling begins to crystallize into a figuratively *meant* image—"the hands/ Raising dingy shades"—there is a more definite "One thinks . . . "[39] In the third this generalized identity is then organized into the "I . . . You" relation of the self to some one else, whose state of

37. My authority for this date is Kenner, *The Invisible Poet*, p. 33.
38. *Complete Poems and Plays*, p. 13.
39. Ibid., p. 12.

mind is set off as the object he contemplates. The process is that which Royce had traced: by conceiving another's experience, the speaker is able to recognize his own *as* experience and so distinguish himself as a person separate from the world he observes. As the streetwalker's vision of the street is not one the street would understand, so in the final "Prelude" the speaker at last finds himself in a world objective enough for *thoughts about it* to be considered and generalized. Time comes into being in the process by which immediate experience is organized into self and world.

But clock time, as Eliot doubtless felt, is not an adequate image of real time. It probably did not require attending Bergson's lectures (1910–11) to make Eliot aware of its artificial character. Yet only at the very end of the last "Prelude" does time seem anything more than the common-sense system of minutes and hours. When the speaker has achieved an explicit and nameable feeling, "The *notion* of some infinitely gentle/ Infinitely suffering thing," clock time begins to turn into something else.[40] For his feeling has its own logic and carries him further. He realizes that as a feeling it is a fancy, hence "out there" one sees only mechanical routine: the poor women revolve like the planets. But to see this blind whirling is to see it *as* blind. One protests that the women are not just specks in space. Pathos turns to bitterness, by becoming more intensely felt as *my* feeling about a world which has no feeling. And just as one is outraged that the women are reduced to material objects, one is forced to account for this feeling. How does one know that they *ought to be* more? The question leads us beyond merely naturalistic theories of time to a sense that the wheels of clock time must be turned by the cogs of a greater wheel. Yet this intuition is perhaps too faint and, coming at the end, has the air of a truth at last found, whereas Eliot's purpose is to make the real seem implicit in every phase of the poem.

Though Eliot would return to the method of contrasting phases in the consciousness of one self, a more promising method proved to be that of comparing various selves, whose differing time-views

40. Ibid., p. 13.

are so related as to sustain the impression of real time throughout the poem. Eliot's purpose remained the same. He would show that the self is real to the extent that its view of time approaches real time. For real time, like all time systems, defines a point of view and hence a self, God, or perfect consciousness. This theory must be borne in mind, because as we move from "Prufrock" to *The Waste Land*, we observe what seems to be an increasing depersonalization. The apparent disappearance of the persona results from Eliot's radical program. He would show us the self entirely through the world he knows, so that we perceive no more of him than the order of his own state of consciousness can imply.

"Mr. Apollinax" differs from earlier attempts to combine several points of view—"Portrait of a Lady" or "La Figlia che Piange," for instance—in its concern with *kinds* of experienced time. The relative simplicity of this experiment is shown by the survival of a rather too intrusive observer: "I thought . . . ," "I looked . . . ," "I remember . . ." create selfhood by grammatical fiat. Though we are getting only the speaker's impressions, these are presented as the truth itself. Eliot tried to establish his persona's authority by making him wiser than either Apollinax or his American hosts. He can appreciate Apollinax, whereas the Cambridge folk remain unaccountably disturbed. And he is wiser than Apollinax as well, for he amusedly realizes that the man is not only too great for an academic tea but too great to be a person. Apollinax is a sort of Falstaffian fool—everywhere, like Whitman, but for that reason nowhere and nobody, since he lacks the poet's power of reconstitution. We may grant that "the society of Boston was and is quite uncivilized but refined beyond the point of civilization," and grant, too, that the Channing-Cheetahs have so reduced themselves to a social convention that in them the self is a mere inference—the person who owned the teeth that bit the macaroon; yet Apollinax shows that one may die by expansion as well as by shrinkage.[41] He disappears in the Whitmanesque "procreant urge"; one expects to find his head "rolling under a chair,"

41. "The Hawthorne Aspect," *Little Review*, 5 (Aug. 1918), 49.

because he is murdered by his own vitality, just as Orpheus is decapitated by the Bacchantes. In Apollinax intellect and appetite are two spokes in a single wheel. His conversation "devours" the afternoon and blurs to the "beat of centaur's hoofs." [42] The difference between him and the Bostonians is thus absorbed in a broader similarity. By their retreat into manners and a merely "improving" culture, they too end in animalism—mere eating and swallowing. If Apollinax, in a complaint they would be likely to make, has forgotten "where he is," they have forgotten a great deal too. They do not know what to make of pointed ears. We must charge it to the speaker's credit that he does know. His wisdom is his knowledge of the past. But this history is that which every undergraduate should know, as we see in the facile contrast between Bostonian and Hellenic culture. Thus the juxtaposition of the "wrong" Apollinax and the "wrong" Channing-Cheetahs points only to a common-sense world in terms of which they appear foolish. The trouble is that the speaker's history must be taken as the past itself. This not only makes the speaker too nearly "right"—a "wiseacre," one feels—but by conflating personal and public views, it prevents us from seeing him as a self at the center of his own unique vision.

The great step from poems of this sort to the art of *The Waste Land* seems to have been made in writing "Sweeney among the Nightingales." The change is clarified by a later article on Pound, where, in praising the "Seafarer," Eliot declares it evidence of an "extensive historical sense, the extent of which implied that the point, the only possible point, upon which such various historical interests could converge was the present." [43] Yet in the same article Eliot complains that two of Pound's pieces "irritate in a way in which poems should not irritate; they make you conscious of having been written by somebody; they have not written themselves." [44] A third statement brings these two together:

42. *Complete Poems and Plays,* p. 18.
43. "The Method of Mr. Pound," *The Athenaeum* (Oct. 24, 1919), p. 1065.
44. Ibid. The poems thus described are "Mr. Styrax" and "Nodier Raconte."

> As the present is no more than the present existence, the present significance, of the entire past, Mr. Pound proceeds by acquiring the entire past; and when the entire past is acquired, the constituents fall into place and the present is revealed. . . . It is a method which allows of no arrest, for the poet imposes upon himself, necessarily, the condition of continually changing his mask; *hic et ubique* then we'll shift our ground.[45]

The poem which writes itself and the present revealed only by the past meet in the invisible poet. *He* does not write the poem; his view of history declares his state of mind. And though invisible, he is not nonexistent. He is to be seen in the succession of his masks. He is the center of consciousness which we discover through the multiple points of view he can observe from his own. This way of portraying the self is the essential method of "Sweeney among the Nightingales" and of *The Waste Land* after it. To grasp Eliot's radically new technique, we should notice what is implied by the mild sarcasm of his remark that Pound "proceeds by acquiring the entire past." By 1919 Eliot appreciated the need to make every view of the past seem incomplete, so that real time could appear to exist.

Sweeney and Agamemnon are neither masks nor "characters" of the usual kind. Their traits do not directly engage us. Rather, we see them as personalities because they represent ways of viewing the past. Sweeney seems to be a man without history because his sense of history is so slight. But if history is a pattern of events—the way things happen—then we cannot deny him some historical perspective. As he looks in through the window of the pub, he smiles at the way matters have turned out, satisfied that he judged the course of events correctly. And while Aeschylus is far wiser than Sweeney, what are we to say of Agamemnon? We cannot credit him with the wisdom of the playwright. His faith in Clytemnestra rests on the bland supposition that the past can be forgotten or at least left behind. The mysterious dialectic of his-

45. Ibid.

tory by which, in the suffering of generations, an original wrong is righted is Aeschylus' insight, not his. Agamemnon's "tragic mistake" forces us to dismiss the thought that Eliot's poem does no more than contrast modern squalor and classical wisdom. Agamemnon is the more guilty in being a person of dignity in a culture less chaotic than Sweeney's, while the Convent of the Sacred Heart stands as a valid interpretation of Sweeney's world, even though Sweeney is unaware of it. Let us grant Agamemnon's greater humanity—that he is capable of sin, and that, as Eliot wrote in his essay on Baudelaire, "it is better, in a paradoxical way, to do evil than to do nothing; at least we exist." [46] But it is still a question of how to get from wrong to right. Right seems to lie in the direction of the convent, and we may recognize Judas' betrayal of Christ as an analogue of the treachery Clytemnestra and Sweeney's women symbolize. Yet Christianity does not appear as a final truth. It is but another view of reality, and if it seems a higher or more complete view, that is so because it makes more explicit a pattern the other views adumbrate.

Like Agamemnon, Sweeney is damned by his ignorance. He has not escaped the dialectic of sin, death, and atonement. His smiling image at the wisteria-wreathed window, like a rosy apotheosis by Rubens, makes his success the measure of his failure. He can be no more a person than his vision of reality will allow. He escapes the death Agamemnon suffers because he is too unreal to die. For to see history in his narrowly mechanistic way is to reduce oneself accordingly. Sweeney succeeds within a world too simplified to be a place fit for human life, a world where the pattern of events is as calculable as the behavior of billiard balls, where evil is a "gambit," moral cause the "motive" of detective stories, and ethics the science of knowing when to walk out. Anyone who insists that Sweeney remains very much alive is of course right in this sense: that Sweeney is a person to

46. "Baudelaire," in *Selected Essays*, p. 344.

378

us, that he exists within that wider consciousness which enables us to realize that the pub is just down the street from the convent. The song of the nightingales, like that which the nightingales of the pub sometimes "sing" to the police, is the same song they sang in the bloody wood. The permanence of natural forms manifests the eternal order. The same song is heard in all experiential worlds, because all are versions of reality.

Eliot was doubtless satisfied that this poem had "written itself." There is no observer to relate modern London and fifth-century Athens; rather, they relate themselves to each other because, as time experiences, they imply a single real time. The analogy between Sweeney's experience and Agamemnon's is just apparent enough to persuade us that they are connected. In trying to make out the common pattern which joins them, the reader has no course but to adopt a view of history similar to that which the anthropologist assumes in formulating cultural norms from the comparison of diverse societies. Only such a view seems inclusive enough, but one would hardly want to think it superior to the vision of Aeschylus or Saint Benedict. It is relativistic; it converts value into something less important and is, in that respect, closer to the modern pub than the antique stage. But it is one of the great virtues of Eliot's method not to impose on his readers the impossible duty of being "right." The anthropological interpretation is quite good enough, since it reveals what is most important —one's motive for having favored it: the necessity of postulating a real time order if one is to bring diverse views of time into a single system. This necessity indicates the Absolute, giving thought reference to a real world beyond itself. It is a positive advantage that this view seems incomplete. The sharp discontinuities of subject, place, and time show us that things have not fallen into a final pattern but exist in the process of formation. The effect is to intensify the need for order and completeness so that the real is *felt,* and one becomes aware of it as a goal toward which all thought tends. Thus the poem begins by describing the moment. The discordant jarring of astrology and meteorology bespeaks a real time in which Sardis and Greenwich would be reconciled.

There is no observer in "Sweeney among the Nightingales," because there is not an order complete enough to afford one. Selfhood requires existence within a time system which more nearly approaches real time. Yet there is a consistency of attitude —a feeling projected by a tone of voice. One is aware of a wraith-like presence behind the poem. And though it is no more than the shadow of personality, it is a selfhood more real than that which we find in Prufrock, whose words are, in the end, all echo. In "Sweeney among the Nightingales" Eliot at last succeeded in relying on the courage of his metaphysics, making the self emerge entirely from the elements of its world. Though the result is a merely subliminal identity, what there is of it is real; it is necessitated by its percepts and is only so much of a self as they can create.

The Waste Land represents an extension of this method so radical that difference of degree becomes difference of kind. The most notorious of the footnotes to this work informs us that all of the elements of the poem exist in relation to a single center of consciousness: "Tyresias, although a mere spectator and not indeed a 'character,' is yet the most important personage in the poem . . . What Tyresias *sees*, in fact, is the substance of the poem." Obviously Eliot failed to make of Tyresias what he intended: it is impossible to conceive all the episodes as his experience, or all the voices as audible to him, while if "*substance* of the poem" is to be taken in a philosophic sense, we must ask why his view should be considered more typical than those of several other characters. The truth is that no identifiable personality can serve as the poem's central intelligence. The world depicted would not be a wasteland if the self at its center were so fully a person as even the changeable Tyresias. The persona must elude us because the disorder of his world is the disease of consciousness and limits him to a minimal identity.

The advantages of *The Waste Land's* wide inclusiveness are readily grasped. The method of "Sweeney among the Nightingales" is extended to the portrayal of a far greater variety of objects and events. Instead of a few carefully aligned contexts, we see a world crowded with people and furnished with a bewildering assortment of things. The mere quantity makes for an effect of *vraisemblance;* like the world of ordinary experience, this one seems to contain more than the mind can ever comprehend. But if Eliot had done no more than provide a great number of things for us to observe, Yvor Winters' criticism that the poem expresses confusion through confusion would be more pertinent than it actually is.[47] Granted, mere "cataloging" will not do. Still, the more plentiful the elements, the more complex the relations the poet can develop between them. The wealth of things perceived may be accounted Eliot's means of so elaborating the field of consciousness that the self at its center can be more precisely defined. That this self escapes our best efforts to find him is not proof to the contrary. Eliot intends not a character study but something more desperately necessary—a demonstration of the self's mere existence. His procedure is still that of affirming by negation: actuality is revealed through illusion, and the self through its dissolution. To say, then, that the poem portrays an unhealthy state of consciousness is to grant Eliot's success, for such a comment shows that the poem refers us to the idea of a better state.

Nor should we conclude that the persona of *The Waste Land* has no discernible character just because we cannot clearly see him. If the real is the experienced and a poem is true in being the experience of someone, then the self that that person might see is the only "I" the poet can show us. But the self one sees as himself is an object of thought which does not include the spectator. To be sure, the speaker's sickness prevents him from forming a distinct self-image. But that is hardly worse than having, as Prufrock does, a false notion of who he is. The speaker of *The Waste Land*

47. See "T. S. Eliot: Or the Illusion of Reaction" in *The Anatomy of Nonsense* (Norfolk, Conn., New Directions, 1943), p. 164.

seems absent because our view of him is so largely internal ("You! Hypocrite Lecteur . . ."). We observe what he is like through the kind of experience which results from being such a person.[48]

Eliot's chief means of placing us thus within his state of consciousness is that of temporal perspective. Whereas "Sweeney among the Nightingales" presents a view of history as one looks in a single direction, here vistas open into the past on every side. By greatly multiplying the characters and episodes, the modes of time experience are made so numerous that they become temporal volumes extending outward from our present. For there are too many systems to allow the reader to consider them as such; he cannot pause to draw the line between the past, as it appears to each of the characters and cultural groups, and these diverse views as he is aware of them. Thus he seems to stand within a multidimensional time, whose various kinds of past and future moments are all simultaneously related to the present he assumes. That is why, though *The Waste Land* is not a long poem, it has the peculiar spaciousness of epic poetry.

The peculiar power of Eliot's language is due, in large part, to the indefinitely vast temporal volume within which his words are sounded. As a very simple instance, consider the line: "Come in under the shadow of this red rock." [49] Its effectiveness cannot be explained by searching within the line. The words, so simple, even spare, seem to drop like pebbles on packed earth. Yet somehow, the sound they awaken persists, as if, though starting as speech, the language acquired an existence of its own. A sound, not quite the original sound, continues to reverberate and boom, like an echo which cannot end because the surface reflecting it is so far off that the sound is forever returning. In part, this effect is to be explained by references the line makes to other parts of the poem: to "Belladonna, the Lady of the Rocks" and the desert scenery of "What the Thunder Said," for example. And, in part

48. *Complete Poems and Plays*, p. 39.
49. Ibid., p. 38.

also, the resonance arises from literary allusions that the line effects. Surely Isaiah is a source, but if this be granted, why should we stop there? Can we exclude Christ's characterization of Peter as the rock upon which the Church will be founded? If not, we must go on to the rock from which water sprang at Moses' command, the stone rolled aside on Easter morning, and the rock on which the wise man will build his house. When interpretation has advanced this far, we begin to feel that its path is leading us away from the object of perception. The references, both external and internal, suggest various things the rock "stands for," but do not reveal its objective being. And for the reader this being is within a line having a particular quality of language. Now if we conceive these references in a different way, if we think of them as specimens of speech uttered from other points of view and therefore representing other modes of time experience, the stylistic effect becomes understandable. By its references, the line exists within these multiple kinds of time. Being present in such diverse systems, its sound transcends the speaker's utterance, just as its meaning transcends what *he* meant.[50]

What matters most to style as well as to meaning is this placement of the line in a temporal manifold. The specific meanings deduced either by making out literary allusions or tracing thought to points elsewhere in the poem are there, of course. But these references are even more important as means of symbolizing time systems and in this way creating a sense of the real time these systems all approximate. Therefore, beyond a certain point the searching of Eliot's sources becomes futile. One is tempted to it because Eliot seems to mean something, and, being unable to say just what, one would like to identify his meanings in his sources, which are definite and can be looked up. But it was

50. Though the following passage deals with verbal symbols, it clarifies Eliot's general view of symbolism. "No symbol, I maintain, is ever a mere symbol, but is continuous with that which it symbolizes. Without words, no objects. The object, purely experienced, and not denominated, is not yet an object, because it is only a bundle of particular perceptions; in order to be an object it must present identity in difference throughout a span of time" (*Knowledge and Experience,* p. 132).

Eliot's achievement, as it was his purpose, to write a poetry in which experience has no such terminal meanings but extends beyond all particular interpretations toward the Absolute. The references are not, then, meanings in any final sense. They are tentative and incomplete views of meaning, which, in combination, show us how, through the diverse viewpoints in consciousness, experience faintly intimates reality.

Furthermore, the reality intimated is not a reality which exists independently of consciousness, already there, awaiting discovery, like a cat in the dark. In the dissertation Eliot takes pains to reject this notion:

> The process of development of a real world, as we are apt to forget in our theories, works in two ways; we have not first a real world to which we add our imaginings, nor have we a real world out of which we select *our* "real" world, but the real and the unreal develop side by side. If we think of the world not as ready made—the world, that is, of meaning for us—but as constructed, or constructing itself, (for I am careful not to talk of the creative activity of mind, a phrase meaningless in metaphysics) at every moment, and never more than an approximate construction, a construction essentially practical in its nature: then the difficulties of real and unreal disappear.[51]

Therefore the meaning of a symbol is not ultimately a referent—a particular idea or the object it signifies—but a sensation of meaningfulness which is unique only with respect to the path of particularized associations by which the reader arrives at it: an awareness that there is a reality toward which words reach; that the speech of one moment exists also in every other moment, because all are views of what is. The learned allusions are auxiliary meanings. They indicate just enough significance to make the real meaning exist for us as a *felt* reality in our experience. I do not see how the alternative opinion can be upheld, for it commits us to

51. Ibid., p. 136.

the hopeless task of reconciling meanings which cancel each other. If the red rock symbolizes Christ by virtue of the allusion to Isaiah, it also symbolizes sin by its reference to the disobedience of Moses and to the desert landscape of life without faith. By calling the rock an ambiguous image, we name its quality but not its meaning. Unless we rise above these recognizable meanings by postulating the Absolute, and regard them as partial views of this, how can we claim that such contradictory ideas are all joined together into one meaning?

But as views, our references are time experiences. The logic enabling us to account for meaning is, then, the same as that by which Eliot's language acquires its peculiar resonance. As its reference to the Absolute makes an utterance seem relevant to innumerable other experiences, so it makes the uttering echo, however faintly, within the diverse worlds of these experiences.

I am describing, of course, the optimal effect, which most passages show only in degree. It would not be desirable for the poet to hold to his most richly orchestrated sound throughout, even if he could, since all depends on a dramatic movement to and from intensity. The sudden conversion of plebeian tones into deep reverberation—the way that speech which seems shallow matter-of-fact takes on a sudden portentousness and that a note of reminiscence sounds faintly beneath a casual phrase—illustrates how important flat, even relaxed language is to the subtle suggestiveness of Eliot's style.

Eliot's conversion to Anglo-Catholicism is marked in his poetry by a movement from negative to positive states of consciousness. Our attention is turned from the "dry brain in a dry season" to the more salutary vision of a self struggling up the twisted staircase of belief.[52] But we must not suppose that Eliot thought he had found in faith a reliable literary program. His remarks indicate that as poet he stood where he had before. Thus, in replying to I. A. Richards' comment on the despair of *The Waste Land,* he

52. See "Gerontion," p. 23, and "Ash Wednesday," p. 63, in *Complete Poems and Plays.*

asserts that "doubt and uncertainty are merely a variety of belief," [53] and in his analysis of Pascal he describes that author's despair as "a necessary prelude to, and element in, the joy of faith." [54] Where doubt can thus confirm, assurance will seem dubious. If anything, Eliot's faith increased his sensitivity to the need of discriminating between degrees of belief. To profess a creed sincerely is to commit oneself to the struggle to believe what one believes. By its emphasis upon the limitations of the human point of view, Christianity makes faith and doubt continuous, and fosters the conviction that the best states of human consciousness are far from perfect. There was, then, no necessary contradiction between the dogmas Eliot now embraced and the metaphysical ideas he had previously favored. Rather, as we can see in his relish for T. E. Hulme's statements about innate depravity, the creed and the metaphysics agreed; the distinction between divinity and humanity corresponds to that between the Absolute and finite consciousness. This equation, adopted by Royce and very common in philosophical idealism, was hardly new to Eliot. But the change in belief is no less real for being a matter of degree, and the effects of this change upon his poetry are equally substantial.

From belief in God, it follows naturally that there are "states of improvement and beatitude," and a poet who wishes to render religious experience rather than bare dogma might well find his procedure in the reverse of this argument: "if certain emotional states, certain developments of character, and what in the highest sense can be called 'saintliness' are inherently and by inspection known to be good, then the satisfactory explanation of the world must be an explanation which will admit the 'reality' of these values." [55] This statement indicates nicely the way in which Eliot's later poetry extends his earlier method. Reality is still to be intimated only through experience from points of view. The

53. "A Note on Poetry and Belief," *Enemy*, 1 (June [Feb.], 1927), p. 16.
54. "The Pensées of Pascal," in *Essays Ancient and Modern*, p. 160.
55. Ibid., p. 153.

difference is that *in turning from lower to higher states of consciousness, Eliot requires subtler means of distinguishing experience from reality.* For since the higher states afford a truer vision, there is the danger that they will be mistaken for reality itself and God will lose his divinity. The real must transcend consciousness, or the saintly character would have no experience at all.

The dilemma is crucial with respect to time. The better personality is the more real, and the more real is he whose time system more nearly coincides with real time so that his present is a moment in actual history. Thus to portray a healthy state of consciousness, Eliot must render the self in action. His happiness will be shown by his living in real time. But Eliot's theory of the self has the effect of immobilizing his characters. So long as he dealt with diseased states, this was no problem—rather, an advantage. The characters who could only reflect, wait—fish—manifested their sickness through their passivity. Nor need the poem describing such states develop through progressive action. Though, on the one hand, the earlier Eliot is close to Poe in depicting the Absolute negatively through the disintegration of personality, on the other he finds it natural to develop the poem in a way fundamentally like Whitman's—as the realization of a single moment. At the end of *The Waste Land* the speaker remains in the desert, and his situation has altered only to the extent that it is somewhat more clearly understood. The "fragments I have shored against my ruins" are the initial "heap of broken images" brought to a degree of order.[56] There is only a potential of change, revealed by a potential of significance. After 1922 the static poem would no longer do. Eliot now required a progressive form in order that the character may seem to act.

How action could be reconciled with the self as the present at the center of his own time system, Eliot seems to have learned from his study of Dante. In discussing the *Paradiso*, he praises it for the effect it creates of "the mystery of the inequality, and of the indifference of that inequality, in the blessedness of the

56. *Complete Poems and Plays,* pp. 38, 50.

blessed." [57] This seems to have suggested the kind of action he now begins to employ in his own poetry. While continuing to view personality as a static state of consciousness, he could find in the relations between different states a movement upward through the spiritual hierarchy from lower to higher states. This movement could be traced through a sequence of several different characters, or it could be developed through several phases in the life of one person, whose diverse selves were, in this case, united as one person by being referred to his transcendent identity, as an individual in God's sight. The inequality between states makes action possible; the indifference to that inequality gives the action meaning. It dramatizes the characters' humility and their faith in the possibility of spiritual growth, feelings which will be strong according to their degrees of happiness. So that even though Eliot's characters live in this world, they resemble those of the *Paradiso* in their sense of salvation.

The kind of poetic action Eliot developed after 1922 is most simply illustrated by the *Ariel Poems*. These are really parts of a single poem portraying a movement, through a sequence of experiences, from lower to higher states of consciousness. Eliot could not depict a simple progress from biblical to modern times. That would only beg the question, since real time is not just the calendar of the history books, though it validates that. To show us that there is progress, that time has moved forward, Eliot must demonstrate that time exists. And because he is committed to working entirely from within states of consciousness, he cannot assume a pattern of history which his characters do not know of. Rather— and this is the essence of his method—he must render history through their views of it. The four poems illustrate how radically *known* history is altered by a change of point of view.

In the Mage and in Simeon the self's nature is determined by the history it is able to know. Since both live in the special period between the Nativity and the Resurrection, there is a sharp contrast between their view of history and ours. They have "seen"

57. "Dante," in *Selected Essays,* p. 226.

God but are ignorant of the nature of his salvation, and are therefore terrified by the change the Incarnation has wrought. For the
Mage, Christ's coming has invalidated the old dispensation, making him irreconcilably discontented with the life he has known,
while for Simeon, whose vision is somewhat more acute, the Incarnation foreshadows only the calamities God's judgment will
bring upon Israel. Both desire a death of mere release, yet in their
despair the hope of Christianity is implicit. The Mage can at least
imagine a death which would also be a birth; while Simeon,
through his attempt at self-justification, expresses a yearning for
atonement.

Both are "characters" of the sort Browning depicts in his dramatic monologues—distinct personalities whom we view as from
the outside, even though, as monologists, they allow us to over-
hear their thoughts. In the second pair of *Ariel Poems* the situation is otherwise. The speaker of "Animula" is a very different sort
of personage. One hesitates to call him a character at all, he is so
much less obviously the subject of the poem. In describing the
life of the "simple soul," he defines man's situation, not just his
own, and though the phases of experience he describes are embodied in his own personal memories, these are generalized. His
role is closer to that of the poet commenting than the character
acting. He is just such a self as we find in the earlier poems, a
person made real by his perceptions. That he remains shadowy,
unlocated, signifies an unhealthy state of consciousness.

In what sense, then, does "Animula" carry us beyond "A Song
for Simeon" to a higher spiritual condition? The answer is to be
found in the difference between the old and new dispensations.
"Animula" depicts experience in the light of grace, and if the
speaker's misery is intense and his selfhood doubtful, that is so
because revelation has so enlarged man's vision that life is to be
judged by a higher standard. While Simeon believes that he can
be justified by his own good works and only fears earthly misfortunes, the sour discontent of "Animula" arises from the feeling
that only through grace is human life redeemed. The speaker is

less a person with respect to a wider view. That in his prayer the possibility of immortal life is assumed manifests a change in the whole conception of history. By asserting the soul's eternal nature, Christianity makes God's relation to men in all times exist within a single order, the Divine plan. Future times and those preceding chronicled history are thus brought within man's purview—hence the panoramic effect of this poem. Its reference to the *Encyclopædia Britannica* and other contemporary items tempt us to think that it records a distinctly "modern" experience, but these images are combined with oddly archaic ones. Boudin, the victim of an artillery shell, is aligned with the tapestry-like image of Floret, "by the boarhound slain between the yew trees." [58] Though a blend of images implies the sameness of all times, the anachronistic effect suggests a somewhat disordered state of consciousness. The present of "Animula" cannot be tagged as the twentieth century, but, then, it is not any other particular time. We cannot realize it as a moment of experience, just as we cannot bring the speaker into focus. Faith has given his vision breadth but not coherence, and the lack of clear order seems to result from the unhealthy detachment taking so very wide a view involves. He sins in his desire to stand outside of life, for this is really to reject it altogether and conclude, as he does, in the heresy that one does not live at all until the moment of death.

Yet if his despair is more reprehensible than that of the Mage, this is so because under the new dispensation the possibilities of consciousness are far wider. He is unhappy in the awareness of salvation, and in his greater knowledge he is more nearly saved than the Mage or Simeon. How Eliot would show the justice of this, I will attempt to explain later. Let us first consider the final phase of Eliot's poetic action.

"Marina" seems oddly out of place with the other three poems: its mood is so much happier and its subject so much more narrowly personal. These differences point toward a larger one: the fact that the experience depicted is both poignantly immediate

58. *Complete Poems and Plays*, p. 71.

yet impossible to place. Though the speaker exists in a landscape and the poem itself may be said to portray the process by which he discovers "where he is," there is no way of deciding in what century or even millennium his experience falls. Nor can we find its place in our geography, even though Eliot has drawn some visual details from his memory of the New England coast. But this vagueness of location is quite different from that of "Animula." The place is vivid and real; the time a unique moment. Instead of detachment and a panoramic view, Eliot depicts a consciousness totally immersed in its place and time. That the speaker exists just now and just here makes him fully himself. He possesses his point of view. Thus he is both real and happy. For when we say that we cannot locate him, we mean that his place is not to be found within time and space as we know them, whereas the poem portrays that place from the point of view of the personality who exists at its center. It is according to its own coherence and meaningfulness that the moment is actual, the landscape real. But coherence and meaningfulness are aspects of the Absolute. What Eliot has undertaken in "Marina" is the portrayal of a moment of real time. That is why it presents an experience we may imagine taking place in any historical period. In its approach to the order underlying all times, experience becomes universal.

The subtle beauty of "Marina" arises from the delicate shading off of things sensed into concepts assumed. George Williamson supplies a helpful term in speaking of the character's awakening as an experience of "orientation." [59] As in Thoreau's *Walden*, awakening represents the perfecting of consciousness.[60] The self

59. *A Reader's Guide to T. S. Eliot: A Poem-by-Poem Analysis* (New York, Farrar, Straus, 1953), pp. 185–87.

60. See chap. 2, pp. 61–62, and chap. 16, p. 193 of *Walden*. The following quotations illustrate several striking parallels: "To be awake is to be alive. I have never yet met a man who was quite awake. How could I have looked him in the face?" (p. 62). "After a still winter night I awoke with the impression that some question had been put to me, which I had been endeavouring in vain to answer in my sleep, as what—how—when—where? . . . I awoke to an answered question, to Nature and daylight" (p. 193).

is seen at the point of acquiring identity through establishing its location with reference to points outside its own position. Thus no line can be drawn between sense objects and transcendent meanings. The perceiving of things in the landscape is not a merely physical response to unvalued items in pure space. It is a valuing and interpreting or it would not be a perception. "What seas what shores what grey rocks and what islands . . ." ? [61] In asking the question, the mind is already formulating its answer. That is, the naming of objects is also the act of assuming a conceptual system. Since the percepts are valued objects—things having emotional qualities—the world in which they are perceived is an order of value as well as an order of nature.

Marina's name suggests the unity of the two. She is the "genius" of the scene; its beauty is a diffusion of hers: "this grace dissolved in place." [62] The grace of sensible forms points toward the grace which, through love, gives being to the observer and his world. The odd sense in which she is present illustrates her creative role. She is not, like Shakespeare's Marina, present to her father in the flesh. Her real presence is shown by her literal absence. It is by seeing how her father's relation to her creates his world that we are made to feel that she is "there." She is part of him—of his own flesh—as the beloved daughter of an earlier love —"the pulse in the arm . . . more distant than stars and nearer than the eye." [63] Her remoteness is a condition of her reality; she is distant as another person, as the most valued of the objects of thought, without which there could be no consciousness. Royce's theory that personal identity develops through the consciousness of others is here extended to show that the fullest selfhood exists in the preferring of another person—in loving. As the existence of others leads one to intend the real world, so preference for another commits one to belief in a transcendent order of values.

It should be clear that the idea of Incarnation lies behind the

61. *Complete Poems and Plays,* p. 72.
62. Ibid.
63. Ibid.

poem. Marina, like the ladies of *Ash Wednesday*, tends toward identification with the Virgin Mary. But we cannot say that the speaker makes this reference. There is no evidence that he is a Christian or even that he lives in what we call the Christian era. To him Seneca and Shakespeare do not exist; it is only with reference to the poet that one can speak of literary allusions. We see, then, an important difference between this poem and *The Waste Land*. There the character is aware of the allusions as such; here he echoes them inadvertently. When he speaks of resigning "my life for this life, my speech for that unspoken," his meaning extends only so far as the life of the next few generations, and we should not suppose his hope involves more than the feeling that life will go on, offering still the possibility of the love he now feels.[64] But the new life transcends that of any individuals, and the "speech unspoken" points beyond the words of love Marina may someday utter toward the Word. In *Ash Wednesday* we see this larger meaning made explicit. The gesture of the lady in the garden, who "bent her head and signed but spoke no word," is an approximation of "the Word unheard," which is present, though unrecognized by mankind.[65]

> If the unheard, unspoken
> Word is unspoken, unheard;
> Still is the unspoken word, the Word unheard,
> The Word without a word, the Word within
> The world and for the world;
> And the light shone in darkness and
> Against the Word the unstilled world still whirled
> About the centre of the silent Word.[66]

Without disparaging *Ash Wednesday*, which is a different kind of poem, one can say that "Marina" would be spoiled by such explicitness. Its beauty depends upon the obscurity of general

64. Ibid., p. 73.
65. Ibid., p. 64.
66. Ibid., p. 65.

meanings—their seeming to exist as subliminal aspects of perception. The "speech unspoken" is *not* the Word, but continuous with it, just as in the other direction it tends toward the speechlessness of "those who suffer the ecstacy of the animals." [67] The wood thrush's song spans the whole diapason.

By diapason I mean a continuum of feeling. Eliot would show us that in the highest states of consciousness the whole moral order is implicitly *felt* within the moment's particular emotion. Love of Marina is not a parallel or analogy for love of God. It is an imperfect enactment of the divine process, creating the self and its world as God does. Thus it is that the speaker's first thought of Marina brings to his mind the modes of sin from which his love of her releases him. And thus too the relevance to Seneca's *Hercules Furens* is made understandable. Hercules, in awakening from madness to discover he has killed his children, is not the antithesis of Pericles. His horror contrasts with Pericles' joy as its negative potential—the terminus, in the other direction, of the same continuum of feeling. Hercules could only suffer to the degree that he loved. The happiness of "Marina" is the approach of experience to the real order of things, which includes both blessedness and agony.

The way in which, as a higher state, "Marina" concludes the action of the *Ariel Poems* can best be understood by turning to a troublesome question I mentioned earlier. Is it just, one may ask, that the Mage should be thought inferior to the speaker of "Animula" or of "Marina" merely because fate placed him in an earlier period of history? The question assumes that calendar time is real time. Eliot's characters are not arranged along a single historical curve. Each exists in—and, indeed, is—just such a person as it is possible to be within his own kind of time. The new dispensation is not a later epoch in the same history; it differs from the old in being a different view of time. It is *later* because it is better; it is more coherent, more complete. Though real time transcends all views of it, its existence and something of its move-

67. Ibid., p. 72.

ment is revealed in the contrast between them as narrower or wider views, lower or higher states of consciousness. Real time passes through levels of value or degrees of development rather than a sequence of indifferent moments. Thus, if it is argued that "Journey of the Magi" precedes "A Song for Simeon" because the Nativity precedes the Circumcision, we may answer that both these events exist as experiences. The one is prior to the other as an earlier phase of consciousness. A passage from Eliot's dissertation illuminates the issue:

> In order to conceive the development of the world, in the science of geology, let us say, we have to present it as it would have looked had we, with *our* bodies and our nervous systems, been there to see it. To say that the world really was as we describe it, a million years ago, is a statement which overlooks the development of mind.[68]

To speak of the injustice done those born too soon involves conceiving history in the manner of the Mage and Simeon. Their simple and compact identities exist within time as a continuum. The self, so viewed, is merely its lifetime, a segment of the temporal stream. They live up to just this point; death is a ceasing to be. But the continuum is a self-contradictory idea in that it assumes a principle of permanence—the sameness of the time process. (That, perhaps, is why poets have always favored the paradox that the river flows into the sea.) "Marina" depicts the process by which higher experience transcends the continuum through the realization of the sameness of all times. Personal experience is always a relation of the self to reality. Grace, then, is the potentiality of every moment; earlier times are less complete experiences. Socrates is not barred from Paradise because from our point of view he lived too soon. His place in real time would

---

68. *Knowledge and Experience*, p. 22. Thus we cannot assume (1) that our own time system is objectively true, (2) that past epochs are as we imagine them, or (3) that the states of consciousness of other persons really are as we perceive them.

depend on his state of mind. Not that time and history are illusions, but as they are known, they change *not only their content but their nature* when we shift our point of view. By showing us this, Eliot would persuade us that real time is an order of relations to the real, a hierarchy of moral states. By making the highest state unlocatable in our calendar, he makes it a moment which includes all history. Yet real time progresses. It is not just a static now. The Mage's experience is as truly in the past as the Brontosaurus. One cannot return to it once one has entered the world of "Animula."

Turning to "Marina" from *The Waste Land* causes the same odd disappointment we feel in turning to "Crossing Brooklyn Ferry" from "Song of Myself." In each case the later poem displays a perfection which seems to have been won at too heavy a price. Both are landscape poems in which all the elements seem to grow out of and return to a single scene. Both start with a "funny feeling," find the meaning of sense data in the self's relation to a person or persons absent, and recapitulate the initial notation of landscape at the end. They are poems handicapped by their purpose: to render an unmitigated happiness. In theory the closer the self is to blessedness, the more it rejoices in its single place and time. Hence the landscape—one place, one moment, one identity. However, such simplification is not a literary advantage, and one misses, in both poems, the tension of life in a world too complex to fall into order. Where experience is so orderly, much less needs to be taken into account, since nearly everything can be *assumed*. Granting the jewel-like formal perfection of "Marina" and its delicate suggestiveness, we can still understand why Eliot did not again attempt to render beatitude. He realized that the relation between "improved" states was a more promising subject than the highest state by itself, so that while defining reality as the stillness at the center of the turning wheel, his poetry is increasingly concerned with the wheel's rotation—with action.

In the *Ariel Poems* action is the movement through a series of different selves, or states, which are, in themselves, static. But while Eliot was composing this poetic cycle, he was also engaged in writing *Ash Wednesday*, which traces the movement of a single self. Though here, also, Eliot works through fixed moments, they are shown as experiences of one person, so that the character is portrayed in process, moving forward in time from an earlier to a later condition. We see living as development rather than realization, though it is by realizing that the character changes. *Ash Wednesday*, with its single character living through an hour or so of time, leads to the *Four Quartets*, where we see the poet during approximately a decade of his life, just as the *Ariel Poems*, with their contrast of several personages, lead to the kind of play Eliot would soon begin to write.

But how, it may be asked, can Eliot show us the self in action without abandoning the idea of selfhood upon which his earlier poetry is based? Has not Christianity forced upon him an entirely different view of personality? For if the self is still the present at the center of its experience, its movement to a new moment will make it another self. How are these moments to be connected as phases of a single lifetime? The solution to this problem becomes clear when we recollect that Eliot formerly dealt with despairing persons whose sinfulness makes them only minimally real. The disease which estranges them from the Absolute prevents them from accepting their place in real time. It is we who place them. By inferring a past and future they do not know, we postulate a real time within which their lives must fall. This point leads to an even more crucial one: that the self transcends time. The self seen in the world, the self Eliot depicts at the center of its own experience, is an approximation of its real identity. The latter is thus always a thing inferred. Self-consciousness involves transcending the immediately given by the act of supposing a self who was the same person in the past and will be the same person in the future. But this involves believing much more than can be empirically known. It is an act of faith. And to join thus the Whitmanesquely various selves of our innumerable moments into one person is not an isolated act. The real self is intended by supposing a real world. We must postulate an eternal order, the Absolute, or else we cannot attribute diverse states to a self which remains itself though passing through them all. Yet the transcendent self is not merely a Platonic form. Nor is the Absolute. Reality is Experience. We need not attempt to construe the metaphysical explanation of just how the transcendent and momentary selves are related. Eliot himself did no more in this way than to suggest, in "Leibniz' Monads and Bradley's Finite Centres," that our necessary shifting from one discursive point of view to another creates the problem.[69] Reality is Experience. The real self, one's own or another's, exists in being postulated by someone from a point of view. What matters in Eliot's poetry is the *intending* of transcendent selfhood. That is the dramatic action. And what matters most of all is that in intending this real identity, the self intends reality as a whole.

It is, then, through the power of his faith that the speaker of *Ash Wednesday* is able to survive as himself through a sequence of moments. They are, for him, moments of *his own* experience, because in all of them he postulates the same self by postulating the same reality. And this reality is manifest as a time: Ash Wednesday. The title is the key to the poem. The self is still defined as the present at the center of its own time system, but *Ash Wednesday* differs from *The Waste Land* because, since this system is much closer to the real order of time, the character's lived moments are more nearly moments of real time.

The action of *Ash Wednesday* may be measured by observing the difference in thought and feeling between the initial line and its repetition toward the end. The change from "Because" to "Although I do not hope to turn again" is the result of the discovery that a truth which seemed primary is really subordinate.[70] As the summarizing "Because" indicates, the speaker at first assumes that his futile "turning" to and from God provides the whole

69. Ibid., pp. 205–06.
70. *Complete Poems and Plays,* pp. 60, 66.

398

formula of his condition. From this opinion the poem moves toward a realization that his turning is but a consequence of a larger event. For it is through time that God works man's salvation. The known experience, the turning, points beyond man's willfulness to God's will. How else but by reference to the divine plan could this turning be known as such? To quote Eliot's dissertation once again: "Experience is certainly more real than anything else, but any experience demands reference to something real which lies outside of *that* experience." [71] The speaker makes this reference from the beginning, and we see him change by coming to realize what it implies, by discovering that error, without ceasing to be error, is but an aspect of the process in which God is made known to the self. Sin is thus, at last, understood as an improper response to the good; and though life in time leads to "turning," it is found good as the medium through which grace is recognized and redemption effected. The beauty of the "lost lilac" is not the less positive because in the mind it sounds the prelude to rebellious feelings.

At the beginning, however, the speaker seems to think so. His initial despair arises from the belief that he must make a simple choice between the world and God. Faith, he imagines, requires an unqualified rejection of life in the world. His effort to turn to God therefore leads to a sour regret for the world he must leave behind. And since his denial is neither possible nor right, it results in mere passivity and the indulgent self-pity of the image of the "aged eagle."

Forced to its conclusion, this straining to reject the world ends in a masochistic phantasy of annihilation. That the vision of the Lady and the leopards in the second section represents a seriously imperfect kind of piety is made plain by the comic effect of its "chirping" bones and after-dinner satisfactions. The perverse rewording of Ezekiel with which this vision ends shows the speaker the precise nature of his error. He has, like the speaker of "Animula," confused sacrifice with mere negation. All human experi-

71. *Knowledge and Experience*, p. 21.

ence is categorically rejected. Yet one should not repeat the error by considering his mistake complete. His view is but relatively mistaken and includes, also, a degree of wisdom, so that the spiritual insights implied by Eliot's echoing of Scripture, Dante, and Saint John of the Cross are not merely caricatured. I emphasize his mistakenness, perhaps unduly, as evidence that in this phase of experience his understanding is still markedly incomplete and his condition seriously imperfect.

It is appropriate at this point to note that what I call views or approximations correspond to what Hugh Kenner terms parodies. Because Professor Kenner regards Eliot primarily as a craftsman —"not a poet" (for a poet "constructs an action") but a "superlative writer of poetry" (who "perfects a surface, or rotates an intuition")—he reasons that only in the later poetry does Eliot come to realize that parodies are the only means of discerning the real, rather than merely ignoble illusions.[72] Yet on the evidence of Royce's influence, it seems clear that Eliot always worked from this insight and regarded the aesthetic and moral as uniting in and deriving from the metaphysical. The issue posed by the pejorative connotations of "parody" is therefore a crucial one: whether Eliot's is simply a self-sustaining craftsmanship or whether his craftsmanly success depends upon the verisimilitude he achieved by employing techniques grounded in a persuasive and therefore artistically useful metaphysics. Whether or not the metaphysics seem true as metaphysics, Eliot's poems are much more dependent upon his metaphysical assumptions than the word parody implies. For his way of writing poetry loses point— indeed, becomes itself a mere parody of writing—if separated from the rationale which makes it also a way of belief.

Part II of *Ash Wednesday* is a good instance of parody in Kenner's sense and yet also of the point I would make in emphasizing that for Eliot experience is never just parody, since even the most disorganized experience points, by its very mistakenness, to the truth it fails to reach. One has to recognize the absurdity of Part

72. *The Invisible Poet,* p. 217.

II, with its simple-minded denial of the world, to see why the persona must advance beyond this vision to explain sin in a more thoughtful way. He now conceives his turning as the process of a spiral ascent. The image of this—the staircase—proves more valid than that of the complacently punitive leopards, because it gives to his past a place and purpose in the scheme of salvation. But like evolution, turning points beyond itself. While the speaker thinks he has left his earlier selves behind, twisting on the stairs below, the view from a "slotted window" displays the desires he hoped to have abandoned. On the other hand, the stair itself is not the ascent; the "strength beyond hope and despair" by which he climbs comes to him from above.[73] There persists the sharp separation between the world and God—and hence, also, the false choice.

To overcome the dilemma, the self must recognize that God's presence in the world redeems it and justifies life in time. And of God's presence, the Incarnation is the primary instance. Thus from the last words of Part III—"Lord, I am not worthy/ but speak the word only"—he moves to a meditation upon Christ as the "Word unheard," as the center of the "unstilled world." [74] But it is through the memory of another word unspoken, that of a Lady in a garden, that the "Word" of Part V comes to consciousness out of the "word" of Part III. His love of the Lady was the response to a love immanent in the world and having the power to give it reality, meaning, and beauty, as Marina does the seascape.

Thus Eliot gives the meditation on the Word a ground in personal experience. It is not just a notional statement of faith by one who understands Church doctrine, but a thought that grows dramatically as a truth felt in the memory of a past moment, which, above all others, made life in time valuable. Dialectic is presented as psychological dynamics. The felt meaning of the Lady in the garden can be made explicit in doctrines and formal

73. *Complete Poems and Plays,* p. 63.
74. Ibid. and p. 65.

prayers which, though known at the beginning of the poem, only now seem fully true. For to the speaker, in his devotions, it is a question of believing what he believes, by discovering once again (since one is forever turning) that the purposiveness of life in time which the Church teaches is a truth known in his own experience. At the end he has reached a state of much more fully confident faith than he enjoyed at the beginning. Not that he feels he has at last vanquished sin: he anticipates turning again, as "the weak spirit quickens to rebel/ For the bent golden-rod and the lost sea smell." [75] His having outgrown the delusion of total reform, which can only rest on a heretical self-sufficiency, is a sign of his wider consciousness, of his sense of dependence upon grace.

This simplified account of the poem's argument may suffice to show that in *Ash Wednesday* there is psychological change of a sort. But it may be asked whether there is any real difference between this poem and Eliot's earlier ones. Here again there is the germinal presence of later thoughts in earlier ones and the reappearance, at the end, of initial images. How, then, can it be said that *Ash Wednesday* depicts an action rather than presenting one more instance of the realizing to be found in "Gerontion" or *The Waste Land?* The answer, I suppose, may be found in the marked difference between the initial and final states. But I would point rather to a difference in Eliot's use of the *reprise*. "Teach us to care and not to care/ Teach us to sit still" is an instance of the poet's new manner. Instead of the tenuous echoing of *The Waste Land,* we find here a deliberate repetition. While some images, like the sail ship flying before the wind with "unbroken wings," recall ones appearing earlier in the poem as by a kind of subliminal suggestion, more often the references to previous lines are ones that the speaker himself seems to intend, as in his mention of the yew tree, for example. This deliberate intending symbolizes the fixed order he assumes throughout the poem. And it is, one may say, his capacity thus to refer thought to the same world at

75. Ibid., p. 66.

all points which unites the moments of his experience into one sequence and makes change possible. That he really changes is shown by the change in what the same words mean to him. "To sit still," by which he first meant a despairing passivity, comes at last to mean placing his trust in God's will.[76] To be sure, the first sections depict him striving for the self-denial this involves, and always the later meaning is implicit in the earlier. But realizing the later meaning involves movement in time. The mind approaches it through a sequence of phases.

It is because his words endure, because they remain the same words, that he can recognize the phases as different times. Furthermore, these words lose certain aspects of meaning as their fuller significance is realized. In The Waste Land it is a system of key images rather than a language which endures. For there the speaker lives within several competing language systems. It is just his "fix" to have no reliable vocabulary. The lack of one both causes and results from his inability to intend a fixed order throughout a time sequence. Instead, he passively observes the way in which his percepts tend to form themselves into a pattern, as voices, not his—he only overhears or echoes them—name the same objects from different points of view. There is a series of language systems, not one language, so that the real subsists in a shadowy way beneath certain images which keep turning up. In Ash Wednesday the persistence of the same words manifests the intending of the same reality and so, also, the power of the Eternal Word. I do not mean that the speaker's terms are absolutely valid. Their truth is relative and is to be believed on the evidence of their power to unify the self's moments as phases of one person's experience.

Let us consider as the most crucial of these terms, Ash Wednesday itself. It is a day because it is something more: a phase of revelation from which revelation as a whole is viewed. This is in some degree true of any day in our ordinary calendar. It presents the whole of history from a certain point of view. We intend that

76. Ibid., pp. 61, 67.

any past or future event could be dated by the system we assume in saying, "This is Monday, the twentieth of July." But the secular calendar implies neither end nor beginning. Nor does it give any day a unique significance with reference to the whole. Having no limits or interpretative functions, such time is inherently absurd. One can hardly think it is something, since by infinite regress it eludes all definition. In fact, our faith in it seems to depend on the belief that nature is getting somewhere. We trust to an end without naming it. But to be conscious is to be temporally located, to exist in relation to a definite beginning and end. The higher the consciousness, the more unique the day, and the more real. Human life is real to the extent that the experiential moment has a unique place within the whole of time. We grant this in insisting that just this July 20 will never come again, but in thinking thus of the whole of time, as we must in order that today may exist, we have already passed beyond time to an order which does not change. It is a primary purpose of *Ash Wednesday* to dramatize the process by which God creates life by creating time. The stark simplification of language which will appear in Eliot's plays and the *Quartets* begins here—in the faith that the reality our words intend will make them meaningful over a period of time.

The way the stability of words allows the speaker to change by discovering what his words mean helps us to resolve the problem of just how the various ladies in *Ash Wednesday* are related. We seem to face a hopeless choice between viewing them all as really one person and concluding that they are several, Mary being just one among the rest. But these persons exist to consciousness: that is, they mean something and are real to the extent that their meaning is clear. As God's presence creates the world, so the Virgin symbolizes the reality within which the other ladies have life. They are real because she is; in one sense they are incomplete manifestations of her; but they are not identical with her, being in various degrees less than she is. From the beginning the speaker's meditation includes the thought of her. The Lady of the leopards, the lady in the garden, and the "veiled sister" come to

404

his mind as a sequence of approximations to Mary, just as the various views of self-denial are phases in his movement toward a correct attitude. They exist to him through the thought of Mary, in the same way that the day becomes real through the thought of the year. The first, the Lady of the leopards, is the faintest, a pictorial image such as one might see in a tapestry of the lady and the unicorn; the lady in the garden is a much more real person, a woman he once loved but who is present to him now only in memory. The "veiled sister," the most "otherworldly" of the three, is a nun whom he addresses directly in asking to be remembered in her prayers. It is the way they come to mind that matters most, the way his thought of the Virgin carries him from the aloof beauty of the first lady to the warm personal love of the second, and from that to the religious devotion of the third. Since it is through the thought of Mary that they appear, he prays to Mary throughout the poem, and they seem to turn into her. As approximations, they manifest, in experience, the reality of the Incarnation.

This movement of a character in time is not to be found in Eliot's plays. It was, rather, from the sort of action we observed in the *Ariel Poems* that he turned toward dramatic poetry. I say "toward" to suggest that for Eliot drama was a form attempted rather than achieved. This is not to deny the merit of his plays but to question whether they are plays in any full sense. Here he must deal with several personages who stand free instead of existing as people within an all-inclusive consciousness. Only the person who enjoys a high state of consciousness can act, since only he has view of time close enough to real time. But since this person—whether Becket, Celia Copplestone, Harry, Lord Monchesey, or Lord Claverton—is just one among several others, the latters' behavior cannot be reduced to an aspect or element in his own. Their views compete with his, rather than being included within it. The audience sees all the characters from the outside, and thus as separate and competing views, so that it cannot, by the nature of things, observe any one of them moving in time. For

405

that would require seeing the rest only as he does, from his point of view. Thus the characters must be static and represent fixed states of consciousness. The only kind of action that was possible to Eliot was that of a gradual clarification of the relationships between unchanging selves.

Instead of movement along a continuum of phases, we learn, always, of a change which has already taken place. Becket is seen not in the act of changing his mind but as a series of states. He is in one, then suddenly in the next, without our having observed the transition. We only infer that he has moved by recognizing his new position. And this position differs from the previous one in that it is a completion of it, not a new state. The sum of Becket's speeches is an exposition of his first word, "Peace." We see realization rather than development within the character; and in the play as a whole, action is really the discovery of a pattern which was present at the first moment.

Becket, while the most obvious instance, is typical of all Eliot's dramatic characters. Eliot cannot achieve psychological change because he shares Becket's belief that what we see as action is an appearance emanating from the eternal order of things. The human deed is secondary, derivative. The real event is God's willing, an action both beyond experience and not, in itself, an event. Thus the event is known by report as a *fait accompli:* "Now is my way clear, now is the meaning plain." Monchesey and Sir Henry Harcourt Riley make similar announcements. Though Eliot's last two plays reveal an effort to achieve smoother transitions, their inferior quality shows us how uncongenial such action is to the poet's mind. By multiplying the steps, or states, he is prevented from giving Sir Claude or Lord Claverton that totality of vision which makes the Eliot character convincing.

Eliot's remark that "character [in drama] is created and made real only in an action, a communication between imaginary people," illustrates well his belief that events on stage are a matter of outward relationships rather than inward change.[77] The plays

77. "The Three Voices of Poetry," in his *On Poetry and Poets* (London, Faber and Faber, 1957), p. 95.

have the appearance of real drama because the deeds are credible; behavior springs from relationships which make sense. But being just outward events, they produce a disturbingly flat effect. This Eliot seems to have preferred as a means of stylizing and thus of ritualizing. It is an effect quite in line with his admiration for "Everyman" and Jonson's comedies. In praising that dramatist, he writes

> Volpone's life . . . is bounded by the scene in which it is played; in fact, the life is the life of the scene and is derivatively the life of Volpone; . . . Whereas in Shakespeare the effect is due to the way in which the characters *act upon* one another, in Jonson it is given by the way in which the characters *fit in* with each other. The artistic result of *Volpone* is not due to any effect that Volpone, Mosca, Corvino, Corbaccio, Voltore have upon each other, but simply to their combination into a whole.[78]

The same "fitting in" is the essential action of Eliot's own characters. What matters, then, is far less their action than the spectator's realization. They are seen "composing" in the manner of Fenimore Cooper's people—as elements of a fixed situation, not participants in a transpiring event. The action is the coming to see that what appears as an event is really a situation. That is why Eliot is so naturally attracted to the device of suspending above his own play a classic of the Athenian theatre. The ancient play is an epitome of the one Eliot writes. To recognize its relevance to the business on stage is to perceive action as pattern and see the events unfolding before us as emanations of a timeless pattern. This device serves both to justify and to conceal the lack of psychological action. It encourages the spectator to agree that events are really relations between the characters' fixed points of view. And it so engages him in the activity of inferring connections between the play and its mythic parallel that he overlooks the characters' inability to do more, themselves, than infer.

For Eliot not only the character but the play itself exists as a

78. "Ben Jonson," in *Selected Essays*, p. 133.

single, unchanging state of consciousness. That is why he describes "the whole of Shakespeare's work" as "*one* poem" and praises him for most nearly fulfilling the condition that a great dramatist's work should be "united by one significant, consistent, and developing personality." [79] The true action is not within the individual play but in all the plays as phases of the playwright's career. And it follows that the characters should dramatize, "but in no obvious form, an action or struggle for harmony in the soul of the poet." [80] Not that dramatic meaning is autobiography, self-expression. "The world of a great poetic dramatist is a world in which the creator is everywhere present, and everywhere hidden." [81] The play portrays a *world*, not the dramatist whose world it is, yet he is "everywhere present" as the consciousness of the whole. But this world, this total meaning, reduces dramatic action to the status of appearance.

The same fixity must result from Eliot's belief that a play should present a whole of feeling. "It must have a dominant tone; and if this be strong enough, the most heterogeneous emotions may be made to reinforce it." [82] This is to require much more than emotional consistency; it is to demand that whatever development of feeling occurs must somehow be contained by a more inclusive emotion, which persists in the same way at every point in the play's progress. And so there is to be a static emotional condition to deny the apparent movement of feelings, just as there is an eternal order of reality to prove the course of events illusory.

It is in the *Four Quartets* rather than his plays that Eliot created his most effective poetic action. These poems, considered together, are also his most thoroughly communal work, not in being popular to a wide and diversified audience, but in the profounder, though more limited, function of validating the common lan-

79. "John Ford," ibid., p. 179.
80. Ibid., pp. 172–73.
81. "The Three Voices of Poetry," in his *On Poetry and Poets*, p. 44.
82. "Philip Massinger," in his *Selected Essays*, p. 190.

guage. To grasp Eliot's intent, one may best begin by surveying some of the obvious ways in which the *Four Quartets* differ from *Ash Wednesday*. The most important of these is in their greater temporal scope. *Ash Wednesday* depicts the self during the experience of a brief hour—perhaps, as has been persuasively argued, during the time of his attendance at Mass. The *Quartets* represent a sequence of experiences in the course of a decade, and that period is a distinct one—1930–40. This leads to a second distinction—that the *Quartets*, unlike *Ash Wednesday*, treat history in the ordinary or textbook sense. One reason for the breadth of Eliot's canvas is the possibility it affords to place the self within its historical epoch. And since the substance of the history we have in mind when we speak of epochs is public events—the happenings in the life of a nation and a civilization—this locating of the self in history is also the process of establishing its relation to the community. The self as poet is therefore a prominent theme; his vocation is his public identity. And to some extent, his life as a whole is also public, for his personality is revealed in its origins, which lead us back to the earlier phases of the culture that produced him. Finally, in his last major poem, the speaker emerges as that publicly known personage, Mr. T. S. Eliot.

That the "invisible poet" can at last step forth as himself is a sign of his power to compass the world of common sense. He is not merely surrendering to it, like a stage manager emerging from the curtain to make an important announcement. The point to be grasped—for it is the crucial point in the argument of *Four Quartets*—is that the world of common sense is made real through our consciousness of its source in the Eternal. There would be no history, no society, no public for the poet to address, and no meaning to the phrase "Mr. T. S. Eliot" were it not that the common-sense view of things intends to be reality itself. Eliot is a real person to us because he exists somewhere within our common world and common history. But how are the communal geography and history made actual? How can one trust in their being more than views? In exploring his own life Eliot is also

409

seeking the answer to these questions. For the personal and the communal are interdependent. Eliot's private life would not exist at all except in the communal world which makes it also a public life. Eliot's view of the self has not altered. The persona here, as in the earlier poems, is the center of his own view of time. But it is also a communal view of time. He depicts himself living "now and in England"—now, by the public clock, in an England which is the same place to everybody.[83] And the place is really a time also: England is defined by its past.

The *Quartets* follow naturally from *Ash Wednesday*, where, as we have seen, the self is made real by its ability to live in real time. The closer a person's own experienced time approaches real time, the more inclusive and therefore public his time system becomes. For the self's view of time and the history of the history books intend the same reality; they mean to unite with each other in that both approximate the eternal order or real time. As Royce argued, it is the community which creates the self. But Eliot also credits the opposite view: that it is in the willing of innumerable separate persons that the community is born. In the life of the saint and in the rare moments of illumination which come to ordinary men, the community as well as the self has its origin. That is why the poet's journey ends "where prayer has been valid"—at "Little Gidding," the place of faith. There the England of 1940 was born as what Royce calls a community of Interpretation, and a religious community also, since the thought of England, the thought which creates England, exists in the intending of the eternal order, or God's consciousness. But in another sense Eliot is the creature of his society, and the quest for the meaning of his life leads him back to East Coker, Dry Salvages, and Little Gidding, as places symbolic of the past from which he grew.

That self and community are each prior to the other as cause, in one sense, and subsequent as effect, in another, directs us toward the central difficulty of the *Four Quartets*—Eliot's view of time as both circular and progressive. The circular aspect is rep-

83. *Complete Poems and Plays*, p. 139.

resented by history as a cycle, which does not advance, but endlessly repeats the same sequence of phases. Thus all action is really one action, the beginning the end, the end the beginning. This view accords with Eliot's suspicion, as a man growing old, that his life may not, after all, have any meaning, and as a citizen of London during the dark days of 1938–41, that history may have no significance, for it seems again to have led but to the same old disaster. Time's cyclical nature is made manifest by that of the *Quartets,* which, by the correspondence of their general design and the repetition of common themes, imagery, and metrical effects, tend to suggest that each quartet is a version of the others and all enact the same event. But just as "Little Gidding" is really different from "Burnt Norton," so the idea of time as a cycle is not, by itself, credible. For cyclical time is not really time at all. Since the cycles, whether of epochs or moments, are the same, there can be no before and after, no succession, and hence no time.

Without progression of some sort, time could not exist. And in the *Quartets* the reality of time's passing is just as strongly asserted as the absence of discernible progress. If history returns us to the old disaster, it also fosters an agonizing regret for things lost. In the sadness of men's losses they find proof that time has indeed passed. Time destroys by leaving the past behind, and death is therefore a function of temporal progress. Thus the *Quartets* not only record the sorrow wrought by time's passing, but move forward from the narrowly personal experience in the rose garden to the broadly communal occasion of London during the blitz. Yet progressive time is as absurd as cyclical time. While it presupposes an end toward which time moves, every last moment implies another beyond it.

Eliot can combine progressive and cyclical time and, in doing so, free them from absurdity by seeing them as aspects of another sort of time. An end is required, and the reader's problem arises from mistakenly thinking that the last day is just another day of the same sort—a caboose to the temporal train. Calling it the Day of Judgment is a way of describing the end as a point of view, a point from which the whole of history can be seen. The last day, then, is a state of consciousness, a perfect state, God's consciousness. It is, in short, the conspectus Royce proposed, a view in which all things exist temporally in series and yet are simultaneously present to consciousness. Thus the last day and the day of Creation are identical. If cyclical time is expressed in the thought that the end is the beginning, progressive time is also, for the end, the divine conspectus—is that which all systems of experienced time move toward, try to become. One has to keep constantly in mind the thought that experienced time is just a view of reality. Since its end cannot therefore be found within it, experienced time moves forward endlessly. In that the divine conspectus includes all other time systems, experienced time is cyclical, the same recurrent pattern of events. But because in the divine conspectus all things exist in series, in an order, as Eliot learned to say from Royce, there is real progression also, though not that which one can fully understand.[84]

This theory points up the main difficulty of *Four Quartets:* the paradoxical claim Eliot makes that in experience there is both advance and mere repetition. The advance is manifest in the change in experienced time. As in the *Ariel Poems*, each of the four quartets presents a new time system:

> For the pattern is new in every moment
> And every moment is a new and shocking
> Valuation of all we have been.[85]

Yet in such progress we see also how time circles back to the old disaster. The disaster of the primitive life forms on the beach. There are, Royce argued, time systems utterly beyond our imagining, an idea Eliot reflects when he writes of "time not our time, rung by the unhurried/ Ground swell." [86] Not only is human time variable, but it exists within a continuum of unnumbered other

84. See *The World and the Individual,* 2, 137–38, 231–32.
85. *Complete Poems and Plays,* p. 125.
86. Ibid., p. 131.

time systems which are relatively more or less real. And it is only in the contrast between them that we are persuaded that there is a real time: that the individual's life does progress; that history is going somewhere. In the wreckage on the beach development is manifest: "the gear of foreign dead men" is mingled with "hints of earlier and other creation:/ The starfish, the hermit crab, the whale's backbone"—earlier because lower in value, in organization.[87] Through a like development from a markedly confused experience to a more ordered, significant, and therefore more valuable experience, the action of the *Four Quartets* is revealed. One sees that time has passed, not what it really is. And its passing, without mitigating the pain of human losses or the futility of history's circling, bears witness to an end in which these things make sense.

I would stress at this point the need to take great care in distinguishing Eliot's view of time from those more commonplace time theories which are illustrated by loose talk about the "eternal now" and the "timeless moment." Morris Weitz exemplifies the dangers when, in his generally thoughtful essay, he describes Eliot's theory of time as "Neoplatonic" and declares it "an Immanence doctrine according to which the Eternal or Timeless is regarded as the creative source of the flux or temporal." Though Mr. Weitz emphasizes that Eliot does not deny "the reality of the flux," it is difficult to see how, in his account, time can be more than an appearance and thus not ultimately real.[88] Yet to Eliot, as to Royce, the temporal and eternal are coequal and interdependent. That is why the *Quartets* describe the moments of highest human consciousness as both "in and out of time," an idea that would hardly hold true if time itself were but a Neoplatonic emanation of the deity. The point is that God in his own nature is temporal as well as eternal, for God is perfect consciousness, and in his consciousness the elements are arranged temporally.

87. Ibid., p. 130.
88. "T. S. Eliot: Time as a Mode of Salvation," *Sewanee Review, 60* (Winter 1952), 52.

That is the import of the theory of duration by which Royce intended to refute Bradley, and even in Bradley time is not regarded as less real than any other entity. "The Eternal," as Mr. Weitz uses the phrase, plays a double role: if "The Eternal" is understood as simply another name for God or the Absolute, then it is indeed the source of time, but as a name for eternity it is not. Both time and eternity are aspects of God, and therefore each is the source of the other. Thus the equation of the temporal with the flux is inadmissible, since no such thing as the flux exists. Every time is a state of consciousness, and even in the lowest state—the most blurred experience—time is not mere change, but reveals some meaning, just as objects disclose some truth.

The danger implicit in Mr. Weitz' discussion is that one will come to think of Eliot's theory as not very different from those which deny the reality of time, an error illustrated by Lewis Freed when he asserts: "The present, with Bradley [whom Freed regards as the source of Eliot's ideas], is not time opposed to past and future. It is the negation of time. The present is a duration in which reality is directly apprehended. What is present is not time, but the content of consciousness, which is out of time. Consciousness is an event in time, but its content is universal." [89] This formulation errs through a failure to distinguish three varieties of present: (1) that which the self takes the present to be; (2) the present Mr. Freed attributes to Bradley (a duration in which all the self sees as present, past, and future coexist); and (3) the present Mr. Freed refers to when he states that the event of consciousness is in time. The third is the true present, a moment in real time, but Freed conflates it with the second variety of present and forgets the first. Clearly, the result does not accord with Bradley, who would not agree that the content of consciousness is out of time and universal, except in some partial degree. For the content of consciousness is something less than reality, an incomplete view, as Freed himself grants in saying that con-

89. *T. S. Eliot: Aesthetics and History* (La Salle, Ill., Open Court, 1962), p. 140.

sciousness is an event in time. Furthermore, as this chapter has argued, Eliot is not completely in accord with Bradley, as the *Monist* essays, together with certain comments in the dissertation itself, demonstrate.

One must insist upon Eliot's belief in real time, because without a time which is real, progress also becomes a mere appearance, and without progress, the two main subjects of the *Quartets* —history and biography—not only cease to make sense but, quite simply, cease to exist. Eliot is committed to portraying progress, not of course "mere sequence" or a "development" fostered by "superficial notions of evolution," for the latter are "a means of disowning the past." [90] Instead, he wishes to describe a progress which is cumulative and restores the past by discovering its meaning—a progress which brings forward the very times it advances beyond. A progress of this kind must also be communal, amplifying personal consciousness by gradually uniting it with the consciousness of the community, because to realize one's own present more fully is to grow in understanding the history within which the community and its present also become real.

For Eliot the ultimate question concerned the end of history, and the goal toward which the action of the *Quartets* moves is the recognition of God as the end. This goal is most satisfactorily summarized in a passage near the end of "Little Gidding":

> We shall not cease from exploration
> And the end of all our exploring
> Will be to arrive where we started
> And know the place for the first time.[91]

Here cyclical and progressive time are reconciled. The end is the beginning, but also a new experience, a fuller understanding of what was but dimly known before. An earlier version of this passage appears in "Dry Salvages":

90. *Complete Poems and Plays*, p. 132.
91. Ibid., p. 145.

> We had the experience but missed the meaning,
> And approach to the meaning restores the experience
> In a different form . . .[92]

And Eliot explains here that the form differs because

> . . . the past experience revived in the meaning
> Is not the experience of one life only
> But of many generations—not forgetting
>
> . . .
>
> . . . the backward half-look
> Over the shoulder, towards the primitive terror.[93]

If the first-quoted passage expresses the central idea of *Four Quartets*, these lines show us most clearly the kind of experience in which Eliot has embodied his idea. It is, I suggest, the experience of moving outward from a private to a public view, of seeing one's own life, with its personal joy and loss, within the life of the community. At the end of "East Coker" one finds yet an earlier version of the passage from "Little Gidding":

> Home is where one starts from. As we grow older
> The world becomes stranger, the pattern more com-
> plicated
> Of dead and living. Not the intense moment
> Isolated, with no before and after,
> But a lifetime burning in every moment
> And not the lifetime of one man only
> But of old stones that cannot be deciphered.[94]

The "old stones that cannot be deciphered" are the gravestones of Eliot's ancestors in East Coker, but also the remains of much earlier human societies. In "Dry Salvages" the old stones include also the great rocks off the New England Coast, symbols of a past be-

92. Ibid., p. 133.
93. Ibid.
94. Ibid., p. 129.

fore human or, indeed, any life. On the other hand, "East Coker" refers us to "Burnt Norton": the "intense moment,/ Isolated, with no before and after," which has now changed into a "pattern more complicated," is the moment in the rose garden. The narrowly personal experience of the first quartet becomes, in the second, an experience within the textbook scheme of history, as the poet revisits the village of his ancestors. In the third quartet his experience is radically enlarged into just such a panoramic view of all time as "Animula" presented. And the last quartet, like "Marina," portrays the experience of one committed to living in his immediate present, the precise historical moment in which he finds himself, the time of London's ordeal in the Battle of Britain.

The roughness of this outline will seem the most objectionable in the way it pictures "Burnt Norton." The rose garden experience, it may be said, is by no means a narrowly personal one. The garden is Eden, in a sense, and the symbols—rose, water, bird, lotus—so obviously archetypal that they universalize in an emphatic way. But if one recollects that *selfhood is location,* this universality will appear as an aspect of intense privacy.

The experience is that of remembering an earlier one which is never mentioned. We see the lovers in the garden in winter, disappointed, childless, unhappy in their marriage, being made aware, through their present disappointment, of "what might have been," the happiness which they might have had implied by their sad acknowledgment of "what has been"—thus the bird's deceitfulness, the laughter of children, the water and flower which suddenly appear in the empty concrete pool. And yet Eliot may be thought to speak to the public at large rather than to his wife. There is really no way of distinguishing the two, or locating the poet, who is interchangeably husband and public figure. The self is vague because the moment is unspecified. It has no clear place in history, because it is defined only with reference to the poet's own lifetime. It seems symbolic of everyone's experience, because, as merely his own, it is not the experience of a fully real person, of anyone in particular. But the moment's incompleteness is one of degree. It is placed at Burnt Norton, a point in the public geography; it announces the theme of the later quartets: that "Only through time time is conquered"; and in its reference to love "unmoving," it foreshadows the concept of God as the end.[95]

Yet one must recognize the failure in order to understand the way the later *Quartets* trace a progress of enlightenment from that which was present, but misunderstood, in the rose garden of "Burnt Norton" to what is at last perceived in "Little Gidding." The failure can best be observed by noting that the ambiguities of language in the first *Quartet* point in two directions—to the persona's conscious interpretation of his experience at the time, and to the fuller understanding to be achieved in the course of the later *Quartets*. For example, "only" in line eight can mean either "merely" or "exclusively." The persona seems to mean that "what might have been" does not remain a "perpetual possibility" —indeed, does not exist at all—"*except* in a world of speculation"; but by the end of "Little Gidding" the reader should be able to see that the statement asserts something much more positive than the speaker intended—that "what might have been" is real and that only, *exclusively,* "in a world of speculation" does it seem to be no more than a "perpetual possibility." Following the lead of Agatha Christie's *The Secret of Chimneys* (1925), Eliot develops the idea that the bricked-up passageway is the route the persona actually takes to the rose garden and its secret, but the persona himself regards the passageway as one he can pass through only in imagination. The laughing children and the scornful bird function in a similar way. The persona views the children both as offspring he might have fathered but did not, symbols of the happiness of "what might have been," and as the earlier selves of himself and his wife, like the ghostly young lovers—"our guests." But in the perspective of "Little Gidding" the children represent the new life promised by the discovery that the end of life is also the beginning.[96] Similarly, the bird's

95. Ibid., pp. 120, 122.
96. Ibid., p. 118.

warning—"human kind/ Cannot bear very much reality"—dispels the persona's vision because, as he thinks, reality is too painful for more than a fleeting glimpse, but in retrospect the reader perceives that the vision passes, not because it is too painful, but because the persona's faith was too weak to recognize it as more than an illusion.[97] The persona of "Burnt Norton" cannot discern the reality of the vision, just as he cannot yet credit the reality of "what might have been," and the failure of consciousness is made explicit at the end of this *Quartet*. For surely selfhood and meaning demand a stronger sense of time's purposiveness than the ending of "Burnt Norton" allows. To make sense of a lifetime or a nation's history, one cannot rest in the belief that except for a few vivid moments, all is a "waste sad time/ Stretching before and after." [98]

In "East Coker" the landscape becomes more real in the process of being viewed as a *historic* place, and we see the poet more distinctly as a figure within it. He is the tourist in his ancestral village, and he is also, much more obviously than before, Mr. T. S. Eliot, the poet of the *entre-deux-guerres*, speaking of his technical problems in writing rather than of an ideal stillness of poetic form. Whereas in "Burnt Norton" there is no clear relation between modern experience—the benightedness of the people in the subway—and the self-denial of the dark night of the soul, here purgatorial pain is expressed through the distinctly modern hospital metaphor. Loss is no longer just a personal regret. The poet's own suffering is included in the ruin which death brings to all humanity. All go into the dark, as William Cullen Bryant's "Thanatopsis" declares.

By contrast, "The Dry Salvages" is the most impersonal of the quartets. Eliot himself is not to be seen within its vast temporal panorama, where even human history disappears within the unimaginable wastes of the tolling buoy. Here the poet's vocation dwindles to a faint shadow beneath the reference to various kinds

97. Ibid.
98. Ibid., p. 122.

of sortilege, as the poet is reduced to a voice, sometimes prophetic in tone, more often plangently discursive. Yet his detachment and the abstract quality of this quartet—the place is not
quite a place, and not one he individually remembers—follows
from the movement which brought him to East Coker.[99] In attempting to place himself in a merely human history, he has necessarily committed himself to seeking his place in time as a
whole. For the life of the race, like a single lifetime, is not complete in itself. And in "East Coker" the conflict between cyclical
time and progression is so sharpened—the beginning is the end,
but then, "We must be still and still moving/ Into another in-
tensity/ For a further union"—that resolution must be sought in a
wider context.[1]

Like "Animula" the third quartet presents the "right" answers,
but only on the level of theory. The poet realizes that human time,
the river "within us," implies eternity, the sea "all about us."[2]
But this eternity is not the Absolute; it is a pure abstraction. It is
that endless expanse of time, that infinite series, which necessarily
follows from our clock time. "There is no end of it," just more and
more, a continual washing away.[3] For time, when thus abstractly
considered, is assumed to be a thing in itself. We cannot find its
end within it, because we have started by assuming that it is *just*
time and nothing else.

Yet this abstract time is not really *just* time; it is also the sea.
The requirements of thought force us to conceive it as something
more definite, even if only such an indistinct and unstable thing
as water. And this logic within experience shows how the abstract
concept points toward reality.

"We *cannot think* of a time that is oceanless." To have the idea,
we must embody it in the phenomenal object, and in doing so, we

---

99. In fact, Eliot had seen the place and draws upon his memory of it, but in
the poem he is not depicted remembering this place.
1. *Complete Poems and Plays,* p. 129.
2. Ibid., p. 130.
3. Ibid., p. 132.

necessarily evaluate, as well as perceive, even if only by a negative judgment:

> We cannot think of a time that is oceanless
> Or of an ocean not littered with wastage
> Or a future that is not liable
> Like the past, to have no destination.[4]

Thus an end is implicit, even in our vision of the failure of life in
time to reach it. Human failure is transcended by the same logic.
Of the fishermen, Eliot writes:

> We *have to* think of them as forever bailing,
> Setting and hauling . . .
>
>   . . .
>
> Not as making a trip that will be unpayable
> For a haul that will not bear examination.[5]

To deny the end would be to reject our own empirical experience.
In that we perceive time as futile and are touched by the pathos
of the fishermen whose life-long toil time seems to cancel, our
emotions bear witness to the end. The fishermen exist—*are fishermen* and are known as such to us—with reference to their purpose, their fishing, and their living, which are real despite the
death time brings. Similarly, our thought that time gets nowhere
is only possible with reference to the reality of an end it fails to
reach. Thus time's symbol, the bell of the seamark, is also the bell
of the Annunciation. Its doleful clang announces the reality to
which we must refer to hear the bell at all. And so futility and
defeat prove no less purposeful in human experience than joy.
That is why Eliot goes on to explain that "the past experience re-
vived in the meaning" includes, also, the "primitive terror." [6] The
rock in the sea, which "in sombre season/ Or the sudden fury, is

4. Ibid.
5. Ibid.
6. Ibid., p. 133.

what it always was," is as much a part of reality as the joy regret-fully glimpsed in the rose garden.[7] Agony and ecstasy are one. Their unity is manifest in the Incarnation. This is "The hint half guessed, the gift half understood." [8] In the Incarnation "past and future/ Are conquered and reconciled," because it is both the per-fect joy which men's happiest moments approach and the good which makes their bitterest failures real.[9]

In "Dry Salvages," however, this insight is mainly notional. The quartet's truths tend to be ideas rather than immediately felt real-ities. By standing, as he does, outside of life and viewing time as a whole, the poet perceives a merely general suffering, not his own, nor that of his particular time.

In the last quartet, as in the last of the *Ariel Poems,* we see the self immersed in its immediate present, because committed, as it was not before, to faith that life in time is meaningful. And to possess one's present is to be oneself. Thus far "Little Gidding" and "Marina" are the same. But they differ in two significant ways. The last quartet does not depict a state of unqualified hap-piness, while, on the other hand, the personal experience it re-cords is defined by its place in a known public history. The com-mitment to the present unites self and community; it involves rec-ognizing that one's own lifetime and the history of one's nation exist together within real time. Textbook history is true not in it-self but in its reference to reality. That history and personal expe-rience both intend the same thing makes them both actual. In the London blitz Eliot's life and England's both seem to have come to failure; the present, in each case, brings us back to the old disas-ter. England's greatness perishes in the Battle of Britain. The poet during a walk in the blackout—his present is the same as Eng-land's—learns from his master, a "familiar compound ghost," that his poetry is a thing of the past and he must now face an old age which mocks all he thought was public achievement or private

7. Ibid.
8. Ibid., p. 136.
9. Ibid.

virtue.[10] But in England's fate he can see his own writ large, and he can recognize there that disaster, if understood, is purgation. England's present agony is made meaningful by reference to that of the Civil War, not because seventeenth-century errors are to be thought the *cause* of today's misfortunes, but because the past event shows the same intention as the present. England's real being, like the self's, is a transcendent identity, which in all her phases we see her meaning to be. Thus Royalist and Roundhead "are folded in a single party." [11] A nation, by meaning to be itself, intends reality as a whole. The Tudor rose and the visionary roses in the garden at Burnt Norton are versions of the rose which, as Mary's flower, symbolizes the Incarnation. The crown, the symbol which the defeated Royalists left us, is a version of the divine power which, through purgation, "the crowned knot of fire," manifests God's love.[12] The movement of real time is shown, then, not in terms of national or personal success but in the development of consciousness. Time has passed; the England of 1940 is different from that of 1640, because the latter time includes the former in a wider conspectus. This widening is true progress, an enrichment of the potentialities of understanding, a movement toward the true conspectus, God's consciousness. Even though every person and every culture may have to learn the same lesson over again, this circling does not deny historical progress. For the person and the culture are real; at one time they were not and now they have come to be.

It is natural, then, that in "Little Gidding" the theme of suffering as purgation concludes in a public catastrophe which is, at the same time, an intensely personal one. The Nazi bomber is the Paraclete, while "The refining fire/ Where you must move in measure, like a dancer," alone can save the poet, whose art is of little use except to show him that as an effort "To purify the language of the tribe," it was a fainter version of the purgatorial experi-

10. Ibid., p. 140.
11. Ibid., p. 143.
12. Ibid., p. 145.

ence.[13] "History is now and England," because, through the losses time inflicts, the immanence of the real is manifest.[14] The poet finds the reality of his own life in the same way, at the same time. His knowledge costs him "everything"; the price is the same as that which England is paying. The price is the painful realization that one's losses are real, one's sins irrevocable. As Royce so vehemently argued, nothing can cancel the fact of past failures, since the past is really past. It is only through the meaningfulness of sin, as of misfortune, that it can be accepted as a fact. And its meaning is the reality which, as failure, it refers to. Reality is redemptive because it makes failure a means of revelation, thus giving it a place and a purpose. The poet must realize the bitter truth that he did not enter the gate to the garden of perfect love, that the voices are those of children he did not have and who will never be born. But only the love such failure indicates can give him the power to do so, just as England can only survive her present misfortunes by the power of that which her history always intended.

The intending is manifest in "Little Gidding" as the place of England's traditional faith. We are to feel that Little Gidding is more fully a place than the other three symbolic locations, and that there the poet is more vividly present and more completely himself. East Coker is historic only in that it is typical—a representative English village of the seventeenth century—but Little Gidding manifests an actual moment in England's past. The destruction of the religious house is an event within and a symbol of the Civil War, rather than a calamity in the course of nature—such as the fire which destroyed Burnt Norton. That the community there was disbanded by the Puritans and refounded at a later time is symbolic of the hope that England's faith may restore her and that in the cycle of history we will find that "Time the destroyer is time the preserver."

Yet Eliot's fundamental meaning is far broader than these: he

13. Ibid., pp. 141–42.
14. Ibid., p. 145.

means, I believe, that the wrong, "what has been," and the right, "what might have been," "Point to one end, which is always present." [15] This is the thought with which "Burnt Norton" begins. In realizing its application to the process by which a nation's identity is created, the poet discovers his own selfhood and the meaning of his past. Self and nation meet in Little Gidding, as the real place, "the ground of our beseeching," in a world made real in that it is both created and judged by God's presence. [16] In the winter landscape the "unimaginable/ Zero summer" is implied, and the refining flames of purgation glow as pentecostal fire in the snow on the hedgerow. [17] Considered simply as nature, the place makes the same reference as the self and the nation.

To be present in this place is to be fully oneself, to find one's location by discovering that here "the intersection of the timeless moment/ Is England and nowhere. Never and always." [18] But at best, the discovery is partial—an intuition, not a complete experience. As Thoreau expressed it, "That man who does not believe that each day contains an earlier, more sacred, and auroral hour than he has yet profaned, has despaired of life, and is pursuing a descending and darkening way." [19] For mankind reality must always transcend experience and stand off as the end of time, as a future—"*When* . . . the fire and the rose are one." [20] It is a true future in being the experience man develops toward.

To insist, as I have, on the action or forward movement of the *Quartets* may seem puzzling, because the state of consciousness which I have described the poet as gradually achieving seems to be present in every phase of the work. Still, this should not surprise us, since it is the major premise of Eliot's argument that the lower experience anticipates and contains the germinal elements

15. Ibid., p. 117.
16. Ibid., p. 143.
17. Ibid., p. 138.
18. Ibid., p. 139.
19. *Walden*, chap. 2, p. 61.
20. *Complete Poems and Plays*, p. 145.

of the higher one. The movement he traces is that of making explicit what was formerly implicit, converting intuition into understanding, and feeling into belief. Nor does the work's circularity contradict its progression. The poem, like time, must circle in order to advance, because the real is eternal and new experience is development in that it is a better view of the same reality which, in the old, was less fully known.

Perhaps the greatest achievement of the *Four Quartets* is of a stylistic kind. We find here a language at once varied and consistent. Its spare—even severely simplified—quality has often been noted. But it is worth observing, too, how wide a range of tones the dominant one contains, how many kinds of speech are made appropriate to the primarily didactic manner. As the speaker is now Eliot in his public role as poet, so the *Quartets,* viewed as a whole, are an address to his audience. Their musical guise is quite in line with this explanatory intent: the bard is expected to explain himself in song, and that the song of the author of *The Waste Land* will be at least as complicated as chamber music seems reasonable enough. What is remarkable is Eliot's ability to make music of a language so flat, as if he were able to create the sound of the violin from the clapping of wood blocks:

> What might have been is an abstraction
> Remaining a perpetual possibility
> Only in a world of speculation.[21]

That these plangent abstractions are made to yield up so fine a vibration is the result of Eliot's awareness that even in the language of scholarship words intend more than their neat conceptual referents and awaken echoes the more beautiful for their faintness; that "possibility," for instance, has a ring we do not usually hear. We have seen that Eliot's faith enabled him to reconcile communal experience and his own. It follows that a poem on this subject should be written discursively in the public language as direct explanation, and yet that the poet, without de-

21. Ibid., p. 117.

426

Still another voice is that of Tennysonian ruminations:

> . . . Had they deceived us
> Or deceived themselves, the quiet-voiced elders,
> Bequeathing us merely a receipt for deceit?
> The serenity only a deliberate hebetude,
> The wisdom only the knowledge of dead secrets
> Useless in the darkness into which they peered
> Or from which they turned their eyes.[26]

And in the lyrics several other voices show us the self, as poet, in a variety of roles. We find Tennyson's lyric manner:

> And hollyhocks that aim too high
> Red into grey and tumble down
> Late roses filled with early snow? [27]

And that of the Cavalier poets:

> Time and the bell have buried the day,
> The black cloud carries the sun away.[28]

Sometimes the voice seems to be that of Herbert:

> Who then devised the torment? Love.
> Love is the unfamiliar Name
> Behind the hands that wove
> The intolerable shirt of flame.[29]

At other times we catch the tone of early Romantic lyricism, Blake's, perhaps, or Shelley's:

> We move above the moving tree
> In light upon the figured leaf
> And hear upon the sodden floor
> Below, the boarhound and the boar.[30]

26. Ibid., p. 125.
27. Ibid., p. 124.
28. Ibid., p. 121.
29. Ibid., p. 144.
30. Ibid., p. 119.

priving this language of its public character, should develop within it the sound of a very personal speech.

This personal note is found not only in the obvious place, in such a line as "It seems, as one becomes older," or "I sometimes wonder if that is what Krishna meant—." [22] Such lines merely instance the public language in its colloquial form, and Eliot the conversationalist is but another of his public roles, only in degree less public than the seer intoning Delphic enigmas:

> In order to possess what you do not possess
> You must go by the way of dispossession. [23]

Between the two roles there is a third, the bard, the Whitman of the twentieth-century cosmopolis:

> The captains, merchant bankers, eminent men of letters,
> The generous patrons of art, the statemen and the
>   rulers,
> Distinguished civil servants, chairmen of many committees,
> Industrial lords and petty contractors, all go
>   into the dark. [24]

Or, to instance Whitman's rough grasp of the reader's elbow:

> Fare forward, travellers! not escaping from the past
> Into different lives, or into any future;
> You are not the same people who left that station
> Or who will arrive at any terminus,
> While the narrowing rails slide together behind you;
> And on the deck of the drumming liner
> Watching the furrow that widens behind you,
> You shall not think "the past is finished"
> Or "the future is before us." [25]

22. Ibid., pp. 132, 133.
23. Ibid., p. 127.
24. Ibid., p. 126.
25. Ibid., p. 134.

If Eliot's lyricism has many voices, his didactic passages are also uttered in different ways. At times the manner is that of the sermon:

> There are three conditions which often look alike
> Yet differ completely, flourish in the same hedgerow:
> Attachment to self and to things and to persons,
>   detachment
> From self and from things and from persons; and, growing
>   between them, indifference.[31]

There is, too, a scholarly tone, sometimes that of technical writing:

> Time present and time past
> Are both perhaps present in time future,
> And time future contained in time past.[32]

Or we hear it in a donnish aside:

> That was a way of putting it—not very satisfactory:
> A periphrastic study in a worn-out poetical fashion,
> Leaving one still with the intolerable wrestle
> With words and meanings.[33]

Or it appears as the manner of classroom explanation:

> . . . We appreciate this better
> In the agony of others, nearly experienced,
> Involving ourselves, than in our own.
> For our own past is covered by the currents of action,
> But the torment of others remains an experience
> Unqualified, unworn by subsequent attrition.[34]

But the voices merge and shift. For example, though the opening lines of "Burnt Norton" suggest a technical academic style,

31. Ibid., p. 142.
32. Ibid., p. 117.
33. Ibid., p. 125.
34. Ibid., p. 133.

the incantatory rhythm of this passage gives it also the tone of in-spired utterance. Each style defines a role or kind of selfhood, and by making the styles *continuous*, so that in any one others seem implicit, Eliot uses language to enact the integration of personal-ity. The multiple voices of *The Waste Land*, voices of others, overheard or consciously parodied from the literature of past cul-tures, are here united in a single speech, just as the various char-acters become aspects of one person. Eliot, like Whitman, con-ceives the ego as a congeries of persons, because in living, it enters into various relations. Each role has its appropriate mode of discourse and so defines the self in its own special way. But to the extent that consciousness is ordered, these selves become one, just as the spheres of action are seen to be versions of one world. In the *Quartets*, as in "Song of Myself," the self is seen most vividly in the process of moving from one to another of its roles—is seen as an activity.

What one finds in the style of the *Quartets* is a rapid modula-tion of the poet's voice, as it passes through a series of distinct but related modes of speech. The conclusion of "East Coker" well illustrates the method. There is, on the one hand, a marked collo-quial informality—"Home is where one starts from," and later, "Old men ought to be explorers"—and on the other, the grave and sonorous manner of the seer—". . . not the lifetime of one man only/ But of old stones that cannot be deciphered." [35] In its transition between these points, the style passes through various other modes. The manner of Ecclesiastes turns to that of Roman-tic love poetry, and then, a line later, issues into satiric qualifica-tion:

> There is a time for the evening under starlight,
> A time for the evening under lamplight
> (The evening with the photograph album.) [36]

35. Ibid., p. 129.
36. Ibid.

430

Soon after, the bard in his singing robes is heard intoning: "we must be still and still moving/ Into another intensity." The grand public manner then fades to a reflective Tennysonian lyricism: "The wave cry, the wind cry, the vast waters." And at last the prophetic voice is reasserted: "In my end is my beginning." [37]

The language levels are continuous because they all intend reality and exist as ways of describing it. As words, they point toward the Word. They form, then, a hierarchy, in which the higher fulfills and completes what the lower meant. Eliot can appear as himself in the *Quartets,* because he now enjoys a higher consciousness than that of the personae in his earlier poems and perhaps that which the flesh and blood poet of 1910–23 could feel justified in claiming. It is not, of course, a state of beatitude but a state of faith. He would show us that faith makes the self and the world of ordinary experience real, and in terms of style this involves, and is dramatized by, showing how our communal languages are made true by their reference to the Word.

In the hierarchy of linguistic modes the penultimate mode is a kind of ritual incantation in which a few key terms revolve to unwind their varied but related meanings. We have encountered it already in *Ash Wednesday:*

> If the unheard, unspoken
> Word is unspoken, unheard;
> Still is the unspoken word, the Word unheard,
> The Word without a word, the Word within
> The world and for the world.[38]

The *Quartets* often return to this manner:

> There is no end of it, the voiceless wailing,
> No end to the withering of withered flowers,
> To the movement of pain that is painless and
>   motionless,

37. Ibid.
38. Ibid., p. 65.

> To the drift of the sea and the drifting wreckage,
> The bone's prayer to Death its God. Only the
>   hardly, barely prayable
> Prayer of the one Annunciation.[39]

In *Ash Wednesday*, this style represents the most authoritative language, and at the end of that poem the speaker's sense of reconciliation is manifest by his ability to make this language his own: "Teach us to care and not to care." In the *Quartets*, however, the ritualistic manner is superseded by another and higher language, and has but a secondary place. Before explaining the change and the reasons behind it, I wish to emphasize the crucial function of the repetitive style. Its purpose, as in *Ash Wednesday*, is to dramatize the power of language to unite diverse experienced moments into a single lifetime. When at the end of "Little Gidding" Eliot repeats the bird song of "Burnt Norton": "Quick now, here, now always," the wider significance which the words now reveal to us illustrates his definition of the end of experience as a return to and realization of the beginning.[40] Yet the change in meaning depends upon the use of identical words; otherwise the end would simply be different, and the self a different person. By persisting, the words reveal the same intention throughout the self's successive phases and thus, on the level of language, prove his identity.

The repetitive style symbolizes language's approach to the Eternal Word. It is only an approach, of course, and this style would lack its authority were it not that Eliot has taken care to make his other kinds of speech seem fainter versions of it. What matters most is the continuity between styles—for example, the way such a line as "For us, there is only the trying. The rest is not our business" points toward the seer's exhortation, "Fare for-

---

39. Ibid., p. 132. "New Hampshire," one of the short landscape poems written in 1933, seems to be an important experiment in the repetitive style, and its blending of the imagery of bird song and children's voices shows that it is intimately related to "Burnt Norton," written in 1934–35.

40. Ibid., pp. 122, 145.

ward." [41] For the continuity indicates the direction—the move-ment—of all languages toward the Word, which is their total meaning, the reality all mean to express. The nearer the ap-proach, the fewer the words and the more inclusive their signifi-cance.

Looking back upon his past literary career, Eliot is reminded by his ghostly master that its purpose, in Mallarmé's phrase, had been "To purify the dialect of the tribe." [42] The refining of lan-guage to an ultimate spareness is a means of making style enact the soul's approach to the anticipated enlightenment: "A condi-tion of complete simplicity." [43] At the end it is clear that both are aspects of the process by which man's varied experiences in time lead him toward unity with God.

> All manner of thing shall be well
> When the tongues of flame are in-folded
> Into the crowned knot of fire
> And the fire and the rose are one.[44]

But it is significant that in these concluding lines the repetitive style is abandoned. Though logically all words find their meaning in the Word, this unity, as Royce contended in criticizing Brad-ley's view of the Absolute, cannot be one which destroys all things by absorbing them into itself. If the oneness of reality were the ultimate meaning of language, then Eliot's whole treatment of language would only serve to define the end of history in Poe's manner, as a cosmic annihilation, where all languages, like all ob-jects, simply disappear. Eliot would use the repetitive style for a purpose quite different from Poe's: to show not only the unity which gives languages meaning, but the continual and limitless creativity of God. Though all words mean the Word, God's pres-ence in the world through the Incarnation makes the diverse lan-

41. Ibid., pp. 128, 134.
42. Ibid., p. 141.
43. Ibid., p. 145.
44. Ibid.

guages, like the myriad selves and things of the world, real. Thus
there is for Eliot a language higher than the incantatory, the language exemplified by the words of Dame Julian of Norwich. "All
manner of thing shall be well" is a specimen of actual, rather than
ideal, speech, uttered by a particular individual at a specific point
in history. By echoing Dame Julian's words, Eliot means to show
that within history there have been occasions, as within physical
space there have been places such as Little Gidding, where the
Word has been made audible through words. The highest language is a human language in the same sense that God is a
human being, and the ultimate symbols—crown, fire, rose—are
objects in the world of human experience. Eliot must pass beyond
the repetitive style to show its validity. A word, like an image,
thought, or event, can only recur because there is ever more time,
a Creation endlessly renewed. Though languages tend toward, but
never reach, the Word as their total meaning, like planets circling
their sun, still the end "is always present" and its presence is
manifest by their movement toward it.

I have said that *Four Quartets* is a profoundly communal work
in that its primary object is to make valid the language of society
—not just for poetry, though that also is involved. It would be
wrong to think the enterprise merely a technical, artistic one. It is
rather an investigation of the way—or at least one way—in which
the truth of the communal language can be established. It involves the use of what we may call the language of faith. For this
Eliot's later poetry has often been found objectionable, on the
ground that he has rather too facilely overcome the problems of
experience and art by forcing dogmatic formulas upon them. If
the language of faith is dismissed, however, the questions it is
supposed to conceal or talk away still remain. For the real problem in finding an adequate language is that of reconciling the
community's diverse tongues. A culture so excessively specialized
as ours seems to have no communal language but, rather, a whole
series of special languages, each defining a distinct sphere of
thought within which the communal mind operates. If the tradi-

tional religious terms seem irrelevant, it is not because they are in themselves meaningless, but because the language of faith has come to seem just one among many, each autonomous and all seemingly irrelevant to one another.

How are these spheres, these tight little worlds to be related? The worlds of economics, law, art, history, and physics do not seem to add up to a communal world, or, when one considers the self, the worlds it must operate in—that of the citizen, the poet, the editor, the stockholder, the churchman, the husband—appear as diverse planes rather than a single field of action. The problem posed by the author of "The American Scholar," the problem of bringing man into unity as a self, is Eliot's central concern. Unless the diverse spheres of experience can be integrated, the self will remain a congeries of personae and the community a dogfight between autonomous systems, however complacently common sense may go on. Eliot believed the needed unity was to be found in language, in the necessary relations between modes of discourse. For as he had learned from Royce, the diverse worlds are worlds of discourse. And following Royce he concluded that their unity exists in their function; that all our special languages are interpretations of the one real world we always have to hypothesize. Because of this common function, the languages are continuous as well as discrete. They flow into each other, because each, by intending reality as a whole, transcends its own limits. It assumes a larger world, of which its subject is but one aspect.

Now these languages vary with respect to what they mean to be: some are narrowly technical; others aim to give a wide and comprehensive statement. And of the latter the language of faith, whether Christian or otherwise, by nature claims the highest function. It means to include all the rest by summarizing their essential meaning and rendering the fullest account. The validity of this language is not, then, to be tested simply by making a direct reference from it to experience, since experience is not simply "there," but varies according to our assumed sphere of discourse. The validity of the language of faith is shown rather by its rele-

vance to other languages, its ability to fulfill its claims of summarizing and completing what they imply. And we must judge
according to the occasion. It is always a question of whether in
this particular utterance the language of faith is meaningful. Eliot
would establish its authority by showing the way it fulfills and
integrates the other communal tongues. He considers it "true" in
just this sense and degree. Clearly, it is true for him not when considered by itself but in its relations to the other spheres of discourse which make up the self's world, just as God is known to
the self by his presence in the world as the Incarnate Word. And
Eliot's readers, who habitually concede that in some contexts—
the Bible, Dante, or Milton, to cite some obvious examples—the
language of faith is validly used, ought to adopt a like tolerance
here, judging the dogma Eliot's poems contain according to its
consistency with the kind of experience the poems record. This
we may call a religious experience, if we will or must, but having
given it a name, we must still consider what sort of experience it
really is.[45]

Not only do the *Quartets* bring together a very wide range of
common secular experiences, but they bring them into relation
with each other by a linguistic theory rather than a theological
dogma. Eliot works from a fact which seems significant and irre-
futable: that diverse languages coexist. If this fact be granted,
one can also grant the reasonableness of Eliot's conclusions: that
the coexistence of these languages indicates their participation in
a single system; that they are phases in a hierarchy of function or
intent, and that however imperfect the language of traditional
faith in fact is, it points to the logical necessity of the kind of discourse it aims to be. Since to Eliot life will make sense only to the

45. "The question whether a poet is a mystic is not, for literary criticism, a
question at all. The question is, how far are the poetry and the mysticism one
thing? Poetry is mystical when it intends to convey, and succeeds in conveying,
to the reader (at the same time that it is real poetry) the statement of a perfectly
definite experience which we call the mystical experience" ("The Silurst," a
review of Edmund Blunden's *On the Poems of Henry Vaughn, Dial*, 33 [Sept.
1927], 259).

extent that man possesses such a language, he regards the experience of the *Quartets* as no more real than the self's highest language will allow. Those who are put off by Eliot's religion unconsciously agree with the pharisaical among churchgoers, for they, too, adopt the heretical opinion that the faith is a set of lucid propositions and the God of the faithful fully known. Their objection is not really to Eliot's idea of reality but to his calling this reality "God." They have in this a confidence about the meaningfulness of words which Eliot is innocent of. He supposes that all languages are approximations, imperfect versions of reality, so that words are proved true only pragmatically, by their power to order experience. His is the least dogmatic and the most skeptical of religious poetry. To judge it fairly, one must ask not whether in the abstract the Nicene Creed is a true statement, but whether the experiences Eliot depicts hang together as credibly consistent.

This question soon brings us to that of Eliot's limitations—the kinds of experiences he leaves out. For a poem's self-consistency must appear to us, as readers, and it will do so only if it can draw a circle wide enough to include our major concerns. For most thoughtful readers Eliot's circle has seemed almost too wide. It is hard to name an aspect of modern life which his poetry does not touch, and we praise him, therefore, for his sense of *his* time. But I suspect that it is more generally his sense of time that matters. He has been able to write a poetry so variously relevant and inclusive because he saw from the first that within the problem of time nearly all our other problems meet—that the experience to which we appeal in validating thought is always a view organized temporally into past and future with reference to our viewpoint, the present, of immediate empirical sense data. Thus diverse fields of discourse could be related as different kinds of time experience, each based on its own special calendar, but all intending a conspectus of the whole. And within any field the variations of experience could be ordered in the same way. Poems, religions, societies reflect and comment upon each other by their common tending toward a view of reality as a total history. It is not that Eliot has in fact acknowledged every aspect of contemporary experience—how could he?—but that his way of viewing allows him to move at will among an indefinitely wide variety of concerns, so that one finds it hard to imagine any he might not have included in his poetry, had he wished to.

Eliot's sense of time has provided the basis for a valid and, to the contemporary reader, endlessly interesting way of writing poetry, because it has defined a credible and pertinent mode of experience. As I began by arguing, this mode of experience is a version of that which has proved the most propitious throughout American literature, and the kind of poetry through which he expresses it is, in its essential features, very like that of the best American poetry before his time. It is a poetry of realization. That in *Ash Wednesday* and the *Quartets* Eliot was able to depict progression or a developing action shows no lessening of his allegiance to the methods of the static poem. For the progression through time is effected by a markedly circular movement. It is perhaps the most grandiose manifestation of Eliot's wit to have ended by writing the poem of action by the method of the poetry of realization, a reconciling, it may be, of the European and American literary modes, as of Whitman with Dante and of an American childhood with a European maturity. So elaborate and difficult was the maneuvering which this undertaking required that it would be rash to conclude that Eliot has naturalized the poem of action in America. The *Quartets* show, rather, the resistance to it of the American habit of mind and how committed the American poet is to a literary form whose function it is to empty and reconstitute the single moment, discovering once again that "Eternity is Now." For Eliot the spiral ascent through a hierarchy of moments was made credible by the faith that the last and highest moment is the present which experience now always means to be.

I do not intend to conclude that the poem of action is more desirable than the static poem, or that American literature ought to

advance toward the mastery of it. It may not, as Eliot's very limited kind of action suggests, be a congenial form. My point is the
simpler one, that the way a poem develops—by realizing, by pro-
gressing, or in whatever manner—must depend upon beliefs
which have their source in the poet's assumptions about time.
Unless the poem's movement conforms to the poet's real mode of
experience, the form cannot embody the life it means to express,
and there will be a discrepancy between manner and meaning.
Further, there will not be the common ground upon which poet
and reader may meet, the community of tacit assumptions about
what one means by immediate experience, how one supposes
events in time are related, how one can know of past or future,
where we stand in history, and how the poem one is now attending
to may be said to exist. Literature must enlist belief; it must be
founded upon the credible; its fiction must be about the truth,
however obliquely. Writers in America will find that a great deal
of what they and the contemporary audience assume to be naturally, inevitably certain is really a set of habitual assumptions
learned from the conditioning effects of their culture. To recognize the presence of these assumptions in American literature in
the past is a means of recognizing one's own beliefs, if not as identical with those of earlier writers, at least as their collateral de-
scendents, bearing still certain hereditary traits, and bringing
with them the fatality of specific kinds of artistic success and
failure.

Faith in the advantage—the necessity—of the fresh start is the
most obvious trait of the American literary tradition, and a trait
which summarizes most of the others by the form it gives to the
writer's view of his art. Not only does the American poem end by
completing the moment, so that the self is pictured at the thresh-
old of an entirely new experience: "The past and present wilt—I
have fill'd them, emptied them,/ And proceed to fill my next fold
of the future"; and not only does the protagonist in American
fiction depart, at the end, like Huckleberry Finn, on a new journey, but the American writer pictures himself as an explorer whose

art is neither more nor less than the discovery of a new form, a new word, an original fiction. However, the fresh start is by now an old and honored fiction. To "make it new," utter the new word, and find the new art form is not likely to be done by blundering with raffish independence down the road to the same old answers, which are new answers only to the uninformed. To see that the fresh start assumes a very traditional view of experience—an isolated present whose meaning is to be found by discovering a direct relation to the eternal—and to know what has been done with this traditional view by American writers in the past would seem the essential condition for making of this fresh start a truly new beginning. Going on instinct will no longer do; for we see that it is not instinct, after all, but culturally conditioned habit—the least promising road toward a fresh start. Unable and justifiably unwilling to reject the culture of his nation's past, the American writer of today had best aim at such freedom as may be won by transcending it—by elevating habit into convention so that it can be knowingly employed.

Of this really fresh start—this most arduous but most promising course—Eliot is the main model. Not that writers ought to imitate his particular techniques in poetry; these are perhaps already the methods of the past. Rather, they should aim at his kind of thoughtfulness, his concern for what in a philosophic sense can now be thought credible, and his effort to make of that the basis of literary form. The quest for literal belief is the writer's primary function, and in American literature the most successful works have turned out to be those in which the questioning is the most lucid, rigorous, and unremitting. It is a literature of exploration and discovery, a literature, then, of doubt, which at its best ends, in the novel or poem, by displaying a land beyond the frontier, where new experiences await and new questions will arise. The new experiences and new questions are not to be separated; experience, in American literature, is essentially the process of answering a question. This is quite natural in a culture which began with the frontiersman suddenly stranded in an unsettled—uninterpreted—wilderness, and with the man of faith set down amid his own responses to discover their significance with respect to his immortal soul. From an early time, Americans acquired the habit of asking what the right questions are. Surely one of them is the question of what we take the present to be. For the present is the evidence from which we reason, and much depends upon how we define it.

Index

Absolute, 114, 222, 223, 359 n., 362-66 passim, 372, 379, 384-87 passim, 391, 397, 398, 414, 420, 433

Absolute Sovereignty, 36, 37, 95, 97, 101, 113

Action, literary, 18, 19, 46, 51, 52, 60, 61, 66, 76, 84, 94, 95, 140, 148, 167-69, 171, 173-76, 178, 179, 182-83, 189, 254-57 passim, 260, 261, 283, 288, 291, 292, 342, 345, 367, 387, 388, 396-98, 400, 402, 405-08, 411, 413, 425, 438, 439

Adamic myth, 16

Aeneid, 341

Aeschylus, 85, 377-79 passim

Affective fallacy, 24-25

Agamemnon, 377-79 passim

"Almanack for the Year of Our Lord 1648, An," 48

America, 20, 27, 32, 33, 36, 39, 41, 43, 59, 75, 87, 88, 140, 146, 185, 280, 286, 321, 339, 438

American literature, 1-2, 4, 10, 17, 19, 23, 25-31, 33-36, 39, 40, 43-46, 59, 60, 65-70, 73, 83, 85-86, 117, 154-55, 165-66, 168, 170, 283, 289, 342-44, 438-40; characters in, 1-2; writer(s) (general), 4, 19, 25-26, 36, 39-40, 46, 73, 86, 165; poetry, 10, 83, 283, 342-43, 438-39; idea of, 25; nationality and, 26-28; Puritan influence on, 29-31, 33, 35-36, 39-40, 43-46, 59-60, 65-70, 83, 85-86; symbolism in, 43-46; renaissance of, 44, 45; fiction, 59, 60, 155, 166, 168, 170, 439; novelist(s) (general), 60,

156; poet(s) (general), 86, 283, 438

American mind, 26, 29-33, 44, 88, 338, 438; defined, 26; Puritan influence on, 29-30, 44; geographic influence on, 31-32; foreign influences on, 31-33

American Philosophical Society, 89

American Renaissance, 44, 45

American Revolution, 33, 88, 146, 158

Analogy, 40-43, 47-50, 53

Anglicanism, 38

Anglo-Catholicism, 385

Antinomianism, 34, 38

Apuleius, 261-62

Aristotelian action, 288

Arnold, Matthew: "The Forsaken Merman," 350

Arrangement on the page, 11, 20-21

Austen, Jane, 183

Autobiography, 108, 141

Barth, Karl, *Church Dogmatics: A Selection,* 90 n.

Baudelaire, Charles, 242-43, 244, 246, 257, 378; *Baudelaire on Poe: Critical Papers,* 242 n., 257 n.; "Edgar Allan Poe: His Life and Works," 242 n.

Bergson, Henri, 351, 374

Berkeley, George, Bishop, 93

Bible, 436; references to specific books of, 55, 82, 166, 192, 254, 399, 430; Interpreter's Bible, 82 n.; *see also* Gospel; Scripture

Blake, William, 428

Blunden, Edmund: *On the Poems of Henry Vaughn,* 436 n.